Modern Southeast Asia Series
Stephen F. Maxner, General Editor

Also in the Series

FRAGGING

Why U.S. Soldiers Assaulted
Their Officers in Vietnam

George Lepre

Texas Tech University Press

This book is typeset in Berkeley Oldstyle Book. The paper used in this book meets the minimum requirements of ANSI/NISO Z39.48–1992 (R1997). ∞

Library of Congress Cataloging-in-Publication Data

Lepre, George.
    Fragging : why U.S. soldiers assaulted their officers in Vietnam / George Lepre.
      p. cm.
    Includes bibliographical references and index.
    Summary: "Examines the over 500 instances of 'fragging'—the use of fragmentation hand grenades by enlisted men to murder their own officers—that occurred during the Vietnam War. Uses archival evidence and veterans' testimonies to offer the issue's first comprehensive treatment"—Provided by publisher.
    ISBN 978-0-89672-715-1 (hardcover : alk. paper)   1. United States. Army—Officers—Violence against—History—20th century.   2. Vietnam War, 1961–1975—Psychological aspects.   3. Psychology, Military.   4. Vietnam War, 1961–1975—Casualties. I. Title.
    DS559.8.P7L47 2011
    959.704'38—dc22

                                                   2010036127

Printed in the United States of America
11 12 13 14 15 16 17 18 19 / 9 8 7 6 5 4 3 2 1

Texas Tech University Press
Box 41037
Lubbock, Texas 79409–1037 USA
800.832.4042
ttup@ttu.edu
www.ttupress.org

For PFC Bernard "Buddy" Seiden, USMC
(1922–1942)

Semper Fidelis

Contents

Illustrations

(following page 152)

Acknowledgments

The Lepre Family

Philip W. Logan

David W. Schill

Matt and Paul Reinert

Marine Corps University, Gray Research Center

Corporal Benjamen Turner, USMC

Naval Council of Personnel Boards (Capt. S. E. Jackson, USMC)

U.S. National Archives II, Modern Military Branch

CID Agents Association (Robert F. Coucoules)

Vietnam Veterans Against the War, Inc. (John A. Lindquist)

Mobile Riverine Force Association (9th ID) (Courtney Frobenius and John Sperry)

Americal Division Veterans Association (Les Hines, John "Dutch" De Groot, and Gary L. Noller)

25th Infantry Division Association (Butch Sincock)

101st Airborne Division Association Vietnam Veterans (Ed Harris)

Society of the 173d Airborne Brigade (Walter B. Daniel and Craig E. Thompson)

196th Light Infantry Brigade Association (Joseph M. "Doc" Kralich and Tony May)

Vietnam Dog Handlers Association (Randy Kimler, Bert Hubbell, Frank J. Steinhebel)

1st Marine Division Association (Jim Rill)

9th Engineer Battalion Association (Ed Wages)

1st Battalion, 5th Marines Association (Bill James)

K Company, 5th Marines Association (Harvey Newton)

H Company, 7th Marines Association (Ralph Sirianni)
Philadelphia (Pennsylvania) Police Department
AMSUS (Dr. Melvin Lessing)
Fred E. Pollock

FRAGGING

Introduction

ALTHOUGH soldiers have attempted to maim or kill unpopular comrades since the earliest days of armed conflict, at no time did such incidents become so frequent as during the Vietnam War. It was during that conflict that the colloquial term "fragging," meaning the employment of fragmentation hand grenades to achieve this aim, was coined to denote the practice. Between 1965 and 1973, several hundred fragging incidents occurred within U.S. military units in Vietnam, resulting in dozens of American and Vietnamese deaths and hundreds of injuries. Equally disturbing is the fact that few of the guilty parties were ever identified and brought to justice for their crimes.

It is remarkable that with the flood of secondary literature that has emerged concerning the Vietnam War, no in-depth study of the fragging phenomenon has appeared to date. Most authors have chosen simply to depict a typical fragging incident as the case of some overly aggressive career officer being assaulted by a group of disillusioned conscripts who believed their lives to be needlessly or recklessly placed at risk on the battlefield. While some incidents did follow this basic story line, research reveals that a significant number of fraggings were actually motivated by racial tension and illegal drug use, while others involved individuals assaulting men of equal or even lesser rank. Surprisingly, most of the incidents occurred in rear area support units that rarely if ever saw combat. When compiling fragging statistics, military officials included only those cases that involved the employment of explosive devices, omitting those assaults in which firearms and other weapons were employed. I have chosen to only briefly consider the shooting cases in this study, this owing to their differing physical and sociological characteristics. While the majority of the homicides observed during the war did involve the use of firearms, these incidents tended to be spontaneous in nature and were usually the result of disputes between soldiers of nearly equal rank. Fraggings, on the other hand, involved a certain degree of premeditation and were directed primarily at the leadership corps.

Recent years have seen the lore of the U.S. war in Vietnam assume a life of its own. Many postwar memoirs and veteran interviews presented as oral history include significant amounts of GI embellishment, proving the axiom that war stories improve with age. The fragging phenomenon has not weathered this storm unscathed: an enlisted marine, for example, told an interviewer that he had seen "five or six" officers murdered during his Vietnam tour, though research reveals that no officers in his entire battalion died by any cause during the entire war. In his treatise *America in Vietnam*, professor Guenter Lewy wrote, "Soldiers while away hours and days of boredom by writing home accounts of adventures and outrages that never occurred in quite the exaggerated form portrayed." Unfortunately, some authors have never taken the time to investigate the more dubious claims. In this work, textual records were used to construct a basic framework, while interviews with veterans complement the paper. In this way I hope to provide both the military's "official line" on the topic as well as what one historian called the "hidden transcript"—the story that the official accounts sometimes do not tell.

The veterans I spoke with provided accounts of what is a decidedly controversial subject. Many of the men had never discussed their wartime service with anyone, let alone a historian; one former marine was typical when he wrote, "I've tried to forget about Vietnam for almost thirty years, and for the most part I have been successful. . . . You have awakened a lot of memories and emotions in me . . . but I wish to give you my impressions from that time and I need to get this shit out of my system, so like it or not you'll be hearing from me again." I attempted to reciprocate by sending them copies of the military records I had found and reuniting them with lost comrades. As a result of these efforts, former members of a marine rifle company were able to hold a reunion. Two ex-officers from an engineer battalion, reunited after nearly thirty years, have since undertaken a joint business venture.

The first chapter of this book provides an overview of how armies are affected by social change as well as a synopsis of the decline of U.S. armed forces in Vietnam. This is followed by a chronological history of the fragging phenomenon and its physical particulars. The fraggers themselves are examined in the third chapter, and the most common motives for the attacks are probed there in depth. Chapter 4 deals with the military's response to fragging, both in terms of apprehending the guilty as well as the workings of the military justice apparatus. Chapter 5 offers a comparative analysis of U.S. and Australian forces in Vietnam, and the fragging incidents that plagued them both. The analysis is intended to test the book's conceptual framework. A look at the legacy of fragging and a brief conclusion round out the text.

A number of postwar publications that discuss particular fragging incidents elected not to print the names of those killed and injured in the assaults, implicitly attaching a certain shame to being targeted by their own men. The omission of the victims' identities denies them a human face; it makes it too easy to simply dismiss them as "the brass." I opted to use their names, for if there is any shame involved with fragging, it lies with the perpetrators, not the victims.

George Lepre
June 2010

CHAPTER ONE

Vietnam and the Demoralization of the U.S. Armed Forces

O N the morning of 6 August 1999, Inmate Number 86698–132 was released from the Federal Correctional Institution in Yazoo City, Mississippi. Some thirty years before, this prisoner, then known as Private William E. Sutton, U.S. Army, murdered a young helicopter pilot in Vietnam. The life sentence he received at his court-martial had since been commuted to thirty years, and his term of confinement had now expired.[1] Sutton was one of the last Vietnam-era military inmates to leave prison and his release officially ended the story of the Vietnam War fragging phenomenon. But even as Sutton departed Yazoo City, Americans were left to ponder how he and others like him could have so contemptuously turned their weapons on their own comrades. Was this just another concomitant of the "bad war" the nation had waged in Southeast Asia? Or was it a result of the worldwide youth-oriented social currents that engendered rebellion and came to define the late 1960s? These were among the explanations that have been offered to account for a dilemma that had never been seen before in the U.S. military. "It couldn't happen anywhere but here in Vietnam," testified one frustrated soldier at a fragging court-martial,[2] and there is little doubt that many Americans would have eagerly accepted such a facile assessment.

Why *do* armies sometimes turn on themselves? Military forces are first and foremost social organizations. They are composed of men whose motivating values and behavior are mainly determined by the dominant values of their respective societies,[3] and since societies occasionally experience upheaval, it is all but inevitable that corresponding sentiments will find their way into the ranks. Although factors such as training, doctrine, and weaponry play prominent roles in determining whether armies are effective, the most important aspect relating to their performance is the morale of their soldiers.[4] This is what enables soldiers to endure hardship and accept the dangers of combat. Irrespective if they are raised by peasant, early industrial, or postindustrial societies, by Western-style democracies or totalitarian dictatorships, armies of every composition have experienced crises in morale brought on by various forms of social change. The process often occurs in this way: when individuals enter the armed forces, they agree to forfeit their private existence for life in a group environment in which they are made to take on a host of responsibilities and obligations. During wartime, these come to include the threat of physical injury or death.[5] In return for these sacrifices, soldiers expect to receive certain forms of remuneration. In modern armies, the rewards usually assume both material and symbolic forms. Among the former are pay, promotions in rank, and decorations. Prominent among the latter are the sharing of the collective results of their participation,[6] such as battlefield successes, the satisfaction of defending a state or cause whose goals they identify with, as well as the perception of positive recognition from the civil society they are serving. When soldiers come to doubt the efficacy of their cause or believe that their labors are not being adequately compensated, they will react by limiting their efforts toward the completion of their mission. Should these feelings reach critical stages, the result is often behavior that is commonly considered to be deviant, such as desertion, mutiny, or, in the case of Vietnam, "fragging."

In order to maintain internal stability, social organizations exercise the concept of social control. The process involves the employment of various mechanisms designed to regulate the group members' behavior while leading them toward achieving the organization's goals. Effective social control is best maintained when an organization possesses several important prerequisites. Its leadership should be inspired and experienced in both specialty areas and personnel management. Clear objectives must be established and standardized processes employed to attain them. The newest and least socialized members of the organization must be convinced of its legitimacy and purpose. When any of these controls breaks down, the group's effectiveness can be greatly affected.

In the military context, social control is known as the maintenance of good order and discipline. To be sure, this task is somewhat simplified in the armed forces when compared to civil society, as the ranks are rigidly stratified, uniformity is demanded, and regulations are severely enforced by the strictures of military justice. "When they occur together, as they often do in large bureaucratic systems," Robert V. Presthus wrote, "hierarchy, specialization, and authority produce a distinctive psychological climate. Members are expected to behave consistently and rationally according to the technical and professional criteria, and to defer to the authority of the organization's leaders."[7] Since soldiers possess varying levels of commitment to the service during even the best of times, military leaders argue that the rigorous form of social control exercised in the armed forces is necessary to ensure unit cohesion, thus enabling the troops to undertake their unique duties. This form of control is also based, one sociologist has observed, "on the conviction that, in the last analysis . . . the soldier does not want to fight: [he must] be induced to do so by forceful measures."[8] That the world's armies have been notoriously successful in their efforts to dominate their members is evidenced by the universal view of military life as a strict and regimented affair in which individual needs yield to those of the army and its mission.

During its early existence, the U.S. military maintained social control largely through authoritarian means. Its leadership corps wielded enormous power over the enlisted ranks and physical punishments were frequently administered to errant servicemen. Cases of men being bound, beaten, or even "picketed," which involved hanging men by their thumbs, were common occurrences. Flogging, though briefly prohibited in the army, was employed in both the army and navy well into the nineteenth century. The method of discipline preferred by one officer was to take hold of the miscreant by his ears and vigorously shake him. The punishment was known as "wolling," and its practitioner was none other than future president Zachary Taylor.[9] Military prisoners were often singled out for particularly harsh treatment, and charges of brutality were lodged against confinement personnel after virtually every major conflict in which the United States has been involved.[10] During the Philippine Insurrection, for example, a boisterous private

who had been sent to the guardhouse to await trial for disrespectful
conduct toward his commanding officer was subjected to the "water
cure," a torture in which water was forcibly poured into the victim's
face. Although the man eventually died after suffocating on the gag that
had been placed over his mouth, a court-martial swiftly acquitted the
officer who had ordered the punishment.[11] The draconian military justice apparatus, namely the army's Articles of War and the Articles for
the Government of the Navy, were widely feared. Both systems of justice were occasionally revised through the years but few of these
changes came in the nature of reform.[12]

The late nineteenth century saw the rise of standing mass armies in
Europe.[13] As the imperial empires began to view each other with increasing suspicion, the traditionally small forces of the past were greatly
expanded as conscription brought millions of new men into the ranks.
Social control in these behemoths was maintained through the same
appeals to nationalism and perceived external threats from rival pow-
ers that echoed within civil society. These sentiments became so strong
that by the time the First World War broke out in 1914, thousands of
men flocked to recruiting centers to enlist. The U.S. Army entered the
conflict later but it generally followed the European model: when the
declaration of war against Germany came in 1917, some one million
men were inducted into the ranks and a mass army was created. The
Second World War constituted a near repeat performance of this process, with the army swelling to a hitherto unknown strength of over
eight million.[14] The perceived postwar threat of Soviet expansion led to
the revival of conscription in the late 1940s and its retention for over
twenty years.

The abandonment of the small peacetime forces of the past in favor
of the large standing armies raised during the world wars and the first
decades of the Cold War resulted in major changes in the U.S. military's traditional methods of social control. The larger armies included
significant numbers of conscripts, many of whom under other circumstances would never have entered military service. This new "egalitari-
anism" within the forces tended to generate increased legislative, press,
and even intellectual scrutiny upon military personnel policies.[15] In addition, technology came to play a greater role in the military establish-

ment while its membership attained higher educational levels.[16] As a result, the internal mechanisms used to keep soldiers in line began to more closely resemble those of civil organizations. Specifically, the military leadership began to rely on persuasion rather than coercion to maintain order; it was hoped that discipline could be based more on logic and reasoning rather than fear of rank or indiscriminate behavior.[17] Policy makers turned to social science research to increase efficiency and reduce the potential for personnel turmoil, while an overhaul of the military justice apparatus, the first in many years, resulted in a new court-martial system that in some respects reflected its civilian counterpart.

The relatively smooth transition from the type of harsh discipline that had tamed the old frontier army to that found in the modern military of the 1960s owed much to the efforts of the experienced officer and NCO corps. In addition to keeping rein over their charges, leaders served to counter the influx of those societal factors that might have borne an adverse effect upon the ranks. Accordingly, the military services continued to function effectively through major wars, massive demobilizations, red scares, economic depression, racial integration, and all of the other social turbulence that affected American society during the first half of the twentieth century. In other words, organizational change did take place within the services through time, but it usually did so at a slow, measured cadence of the leadership's own choosing. In the late 1960s, however, this began to change, and civil society began to play a larger role in calling the tune.

The United States in Vietnam

Several observers have written that the army the United States sent to South Vietnam in 1965 was the finest the nation ever fielded.[18] Led by veteran officers who had served in World War II and Korea, and manned by the best-educated youth ever to wear U.S. military uniforms, the military brimmed with confidence as President Lyndon B. Johnson sent it off to war. Its early performance in the field was indeed commendable, this reflected by the series of quick victories it won against its communist adversary. During Operation Starlite, in their first major engagement, the marines crushed the 1st Viet Cong Regiment.[19] Operation Hump saw the army's 173d Airborne Brigade dislodge well-armed communist troops from their positions northeast of Bien Hoa. Elements of the 1st Infantry Division achieved similar success in their baptism of fire against the enemy at Bau Bang. In what became known as the Battle of the Ia Drang Valley, the newly arrived 1st Cavalry Division sustained heavy casualties but succeeded in blocking the North Vietnamese Army's advance into the Central Highlands.[20]

In addition to these battlefield triumphs, further evidence of the "best army" thesis can be found in the area of troop discipline. Crime of any variety was rare during the initial American buildup in Southeast Asia; to the military police, such trivialities as traffic summonses and curfew violations were the order of the day. At the end of 1965, the army's court-martial rate in Vietnam was a low 2.03 per thousand men, while its worldwide rate was 3.55 per thousand.[21] Illegal drug use, which later became a critical morale issue, was all but insignificant during this period. In fact, army law enforcement officials were more concerned about the opiate problem among GIs stationed in South Korea than they were about drugs in Vietnam.[22] Race relations between black and white soldiers were harmonious, assaults against superiors unknown.

But in spite of its early successes, the U.S. military eventually bogged down in Vietnam. After losing their initial engagements against the Americans, the communists began to concentrate their troops in remote, unpopulated areas, luring U.S. forces away from pacification efforts and into inconclusive battles that would inflict casualties while eroding America's will to fight.[23] Although this change in strategy eventually proved to be successful, the GIs nevertheless continued to perform ably. Despite seeing heavy action, one brigade saw many of its noncommissioned officers volunteer "to remain [in Vietnam] for extended tours, and in many cases others, upon returning to the United States, asked to return to Vietnam to rejoin their unit. Although the brigade had been in Vietnam for two years, morale was still high."[24] Court-martial rates remained low through 1966 and dipped even lower in 1967.[25]

It was not until 1968 that a number of problem areas emerged. After successfully turning back the enemy's Tet Offensive, the U.S. military in Vietnam began to show signs of deterioration, and by the end of the year, morale and discipline had gone from points of pride to significant areas of concern. The reasons for this decline have long been debated; I will argue that it was caused by a unique combination of political, institutional, and social factors. Constituting the political factors were the nature of limited war and the unpopularity of the prolonged U.S. withdrawal from Southeast Asia. The institutional factors refer to the hurried wartime expansion of the armed forces and several controversial military personnel policies. These institutional changes in turn enabled a number of social factors that emanated in civil society to find their way into the services and wreak havoc within the ranks. But irrespective of the causes, the result was twofold: the troops could no longer be convinced of the war's viability and the harried leadership corps lost its ability to maintain a high level of social control in their units.

Limited wars such as that waged by the United States in Southeast Asia do not threaten the belligerent's immediate survival and therefore tend to receive less than total motivational support from its society as a whole.[26] One might say that the United States never really went to war in Vietnam, only its armed forces did, and the lack of any "war effort" at home diminished the conflict's significance. After repeated claims that victory was in sight, the beginning of 1968 saw the American public shocked by television images of the U.S. Embassy compound in Saigon under attack, military leaders requesting additional troops, and talk of diplomatic negotiations to end the fighting. By midyear, popular opinion had swung decisively against the war. For the first time, a majority of Americans believed that the U.S. war aim—to thwart the communist insurgency in South Vietnam—was no longer worth fighting for. This sentiment was intensified by the elimination of deferments from military service for graduate students, which further fueled the antiwar movement. The war's growing unpopularity at home eventually served to undermine morale among the troops in the field.

The attrition strategy employed by the U.S. military in Vietnam has received a considerable amount of criticism. Traditionally, America has waged war by bringing its superior firepower and massive logistics to bear on its enemies and obliterating them. This approach worked well against conventional armies and indeed it was successful in halting the "losing trend" in South Vietnam in 1965. But the military leadership's insistence on employing big-unit, "search and destroy" tactics eventually proved to be a liability. The Vietnam War was first and foremost an insurgency in which control of the local population was critical. Instead of focusing on security in the inhabited areas, however, the Americans attempted to fight a conventional war against North Vietnamese Army units and the Viet Cong. Large-scale operations, the generals believed, would allow for the maximum use of firepower and helicopter mobility to eliminate the enemy's main forces, thus starving local guerrilla units of reinforcements and supplies and making them easy prey for subsequent pacification efforts. Progress in this war without fronts was difficult to measure as it was virtually devoid of tangible symbols of success, so senior leaders came to rely on statistics, most notably "body counts," to gauge progress. Their goal was to reach what was called the "crossover point," the stage at which the enemy, having sustained so many casualties that they could no longer procure enough replacements, would relent in their effort to take over South Vietnam. As it turned out, American forces succeeded in winning the battles but not the war, as the communists were always able to replenish their losses. Attempts were made to "win" the villages, but these efforts generally enjoyed little high-level support as they did not reflect the military's preferred concept of operations, and failed to bring the desired short-term results. In any case, the idea of winning the "hearts and minds" of the Vietnamese was lost on many of our young servicemen, and, in light of the uneven performance of the South Vietnamese armed forces, frustration began to spread.

The managers of the conflict, both political leaders and the officer corps, also came under fire for a number of ill-considered personnel policies that were employed during the war. Critical among these was the individual rotation system. Instead of shifting units in and out of the war zone, which would have maintained unit integrity and strengthened primary group cohesion, soldiers were sent to Vietnam individually and assigned to existing organizations as replacements. There was also the decision to limit the tour of duty in Vietnam to one year (thirteen months in the case of the marines until 1969).[27] While its proponents argued that the one-year tour "gave a man a goal" and was "good for morale,"[28] its practice led to the existence of units composed of relative strangers due to the almost constant turnover of personnel. Researchers found that during the Second World War, the primary motivator among the troops was to "end the task," or win the war,[29] but the one-year tour in Vietnam created a view among the troops that "my war ends when I go home, whether it's won or not." In an effort to produce as many combat-experienced officers as possible, the army mandated that company- and field-grade officers in Vietnam were to spend only six months in command positions. This served not only to raise the ire of their enlisted subordinates, who were required to serve a full year in the field, but it also removed many men from their posts just as they were finding their feet as leaders. As the army's official history of the war has frankly admitted, "This 'revolving door policy,' which guaranteed the rapid rotation of officers in combat commands, was later criticized as representing careerism at its worst. It destroyed any prospect for continuity of command, it hurt field morale among the enlisted ranks, and it ultimately lessened the effectiveness of U.S. forces."[30] In their consideration of the six-month command tour, two military authors wondered if the army was more interested in training officers than in winning the war.[31]

The army and Marine Corps also experienced considerable difficulty in obtaining quality personnel. When large-scale deployments to Vietnam began, the services were greatly expanded in order to meet the immediate threat while maintaining the nation's global defense commitments. Active army strength increased from 969,066 men in 1965 to over 1.5 million in 1968. During this same period, the Marine Corps saw its active rolls jump from 190,213 to 309,771.[32] To fill the ranks, entrance and training standards were relaxed, draft calls were greatly increased, and the federal government's "Project 100,000" manpower program brought thousands of low-aptitude men into the military who normally would not have been inducted at all. Yet in spite of these measures, the services still struggled to maintain their authorized personnel strengths. To beef up units in Vietnam, major commands in the United States and Europe were inexorably stripped of manpower, often rendering them unrecognizable from their bulky prewar countenances. One general complained that the Seventh Army in West Germany "ceased to be a field army and became a large training and replacement depot for Vietnam" as more and more of its soldiers were levied to Southeast Asia.[33] In the case of the newly formed 5th Marine Division at Camp Pendleton, entire elements were detached and sent off to the war zone; during 1967 and 1968, two of its three infantry regiments, half of its artillery, and a tank company all left California to join marine units already fighting in Vietnam.[34]

The personnel situation was particularly serious at the leadership level, for the protracted conflict succeeded in decimating the ranks of junior officers and career NCOs. By 1971, those small-unit leaders who had not become casualties or left the service were often made to serve second or even third tours of duty in Southeast Asia.[35] These shortages could have been at least partially alleviated by activating trained cadres from the reserves and National Guard but President Johnson decided against this for political reasons. Instead, the services resorted to stop-gap measures to maintain strength within the leadership corps. The Marine Corps temporarily commissioned over four thousand warrant officers and staff NCOs to occupy officer billets while standard commissioning programs produced replacements, but recruiting efforts consistently fell short of reaching the assigned quotas of suitable men.[36] The army expanded class sizes at the military academy and its officer candidate schools. To alleviate its shortage of junior noncommissioned officers, a program was established in which privates who excelled in basic training were sent to special leadership courses and received accelerated promotions to NCO rank. Dubbed "shake-and-bakes" or "instant NCOs" by their peers, some of these young men possessed the requisite maturity required to fill the slots and responded well to these challenges while others clearly did not. Consequently, unit discipline and the overall prestige of the leadership corps suffered considerably.[37]

In addition to the debates over strategy and personnel policy, the military's integrity was called into question when a series of well-publicized scandals rocked the services. In what became known in the press as the "Green Beret Case," six members of the U.S. Army Special Forces were charged with executing a South Vietnamese national believed to be a double agent. This was followed by the club scandal, in which senior army officers and NCOs, including two generals and the sergeant major of the army, were accused of financial "irregularities" in the administration of the army club system in Europe and Vietnam.[38] After the story of the My Lai massacre and its subsequent cover-up surfaced a few months later, it remained a news staple for several years as the resulting courts-martial meandered through the military judicial system. Next came the revelation that army intelligence organs in the United States had illegally gathered information on private citizens and groups "with no connection to the Department of Defense except their reputed opposition to it."[39] A number of other episodes of somewhat lesser magnitude also came to light, including illegal border incursions by U.S. troops into Laos and Cambodia, allegations of abuses committed by American and South Vietnamese forces involved with the controversial Phoenix Program, and public revelations made by veterans and a handful of field-grade officers accusing the military in Vietnam of everything from incompetence to murder. Although the veracity of several of these accusations has since been challenged by historians, at the time they caused the armed services considerable embarrassment and resulted in a loss of standing in the eyes of the populace, particularly among younger Americans.[40]

Richard M. Nixon won the 1968 presidential election after promising to end U.S. military involvement in South Vietnam. He stipulated, however, that peace was to be secured with honor, meaning that America would not simply abandon its global Cold War commitments to the specter of world communism. Accordingly, "Vietnamization," as the U.S. withdrawal was known, was scheduled to take place not over a period of weeks or months but several years. To the troops in Vietnam, who were somehow supposed to ignore these developments and continue fighting as if nothing had happened, world appearances meant little. The sluggishness of the pullout and the belief that the U.S. military was no longer fighting to win led them to question their sacrifices, shattering any illusion of Clausewitz's ideal of an army as an unreflective institutional machine.[41] A general feeling emerged that a kind of organizational hypocrisy had taken over the war. On one hand, the men read press reports of Nixon administration officials conducting negotiations with the North Vietnamese to end the fighting, yet in many respects their day-to-day duties remained unchanged. While some units departed Vietnam for good, others continued to mount combat operations and sustain casualties. This caused the troops to blame the military leadership for the creation of what has been called a "counterfeit universe" in Vietnam: as political leaders spoke of withdrawal from Southeast Asia, the generals acted as if it were still 1966.[42]

Convinced that the time for aggressive battlefield tactics and rigid discipline had come and gone, many servicemen began to display a new lackadaisical attitude toward their duties. "Mission accomplishment," Lieutenant General William J. McCaffrey admitted, "has undergone degradation in some units, primarily in terms of lowered quality of performance."[43] In the combat arms, this meant increased sloppiness during tactical operations. During the 1970 Cambodia incursion, for example, a young company commander in the 4th Infantry Division decided to leave his unit's perimeter to search a suspicious-looking area, neglecting to bring a radio along. He and several of his men were pinned down by enemy fire and eventually killed because other friendly elements were unable to contact them and provide assistance.[44] A few days later, an element of the 101st Airborne Division conducted a "mad minute" firing exercise near Fire Base Bastogne, forgetting that an American listening post was stationed in the area. The devastating fire killed a sergeant and an enlisted man who were manning the position.[45] In an effort to lighten its load as it returned from the field, a marine infantry company decided to fire off some of its remaining mortar rounds. Unfortunately, several of the rounds were fired at an extremely high trajectory and landed within the company perimeter, killing four marines and an enemy prisoner.[46] Misdirected fire, accidental discharges, the careless handling of ordnance, and other mistakes came to cause nearly as many U.S. casualties during the Vietnamization period as did the enemy.[47]

In rear areas, American troops often performed poorly when conducting base security. As early as 1968, a North Vietnamese officer boasted, "All the U.S. defensive positions are very easy to get through. I can say that I have never encountered a tough one in my experience. . . . I just don't think you have a defensive barrier that is effective against us."[48] Between 1969 and 1970, communist sappers raided installations within the 4th Infantry Division's area of operations on five separate occasions and escaped without suffering a single casualty. In one attack, they destroyed nineteen helicopters and killed one GI. In another raid, they destroyed seven aircraft, damaged eight others, and killed two more Americans.[49] During a June 1970 assault on a petroleum storage site at Qui Nhon, two U.S. sentries were so terrified as a sapper detachment charged toward their perimeter that they simply played dead, allowing the enemy to enter the base and destroy the headquarters building along with 450,000 gallons of fuel. Seven Americans were killed and over a dozen more were wounded. Enemy losses: two.[50] The raiders revisited Qui Nhon the following year, attacking the Hill 131 signal site and escaping without loss, this owing to the fact that the hill's defenders most likely did not fire a single shot at them.[51] The result was the same at Cam Ranh Bay when communist troops snuck into a U.S. base and destroyed 1.5 million gallons of jet fuel.[52] The best known of these disasters was the raid on Fire Support Base Mary Ann in March 1971. After an intense mortar barrage, a group of sappers surged into the base and hurled satchel charges into the American bunkers, killing thirty-one GIs and destroying a field howitzer. U.S. commanders eventually resorted to employing Nung mercenaries and highly capable South Korean units to guard the large support centers at Cam Ranh, Qui Nhon, and Tuy Hoa.[53]

Troop discipline also suffered. "Discipline within the command as a whole has eroded to a serious but not critical degree," a senior officer in Vietnam wrote.[54] The decay was due in part to various social phenomena, including what one scholar called the "growing permissiveness in American society and an increase in social pathology."[55] The nation suffered from a crisis in authority that permeated all spheres of American life. Youth were drawn to activism and began to question long-standing societal paradigms. Illegal drug use became popular among young people, crime rose dramatically, and inner cities, long seething with social and racial discontent, exploded in revolt. America's military was in many ways a microcosm of society as a whole, and as these forces became prevalent among the civilian populace, so too did the zeitgeist affect the armed services. As one general remarked, "The average [serviceman] arriving in Vietnam in 1971 was probably only thirteen, fourteen, or sixteen years old when [the war] began back in 1965. So he grew up in a different environment than his predecessor did five or six years [before], and he brought many of the attitudes of that environment into the [service] with him."[56] Hence military leaders, like their counterparts in civil society, were forced to confront drug abuse, racial strife, and an authority crisis described by one veteran as "a clear rift that developed between the majority of the enlisted men and some junior officers on one side, and the command structure on the other."[57] Although the armed forces had successfully avoided the woes that affected civil society during previous social upheavals, Vietnam placed such great strains upon the military's junior leadership corps that the services were no longer capable of maintaining the high standard of discipline that existed during the war's early years. "What changed in the late 1960s," professor Ronald H. Spector observed, "was that the [military's] mechanisms for socializing and disciplining these elements had broken down."[58]

It should be noted, however, that not all servicemen in Vietnam responded to the withdrawal in a negative manner. "The typical reaction could go one of two ways," remarked one officer. "Either, 'I've only got a few more weeks or months to earn all my medals, so I can be a hero,' or the opposite: 'I'm not going to be the last one [killed].'" This dichotomy, along with the problems cited above, led to the rise of a bizarre dilemma within the ranks: the fact that frightening numbers of troops were attempting to kill fellow servicemen in the combat zone. Originally referred to as "doing a job" in GI slang, the exact origin of the term "fragging" in regard to this crime is unknown, although it was certainly in common use by early 1969 and has defined these incidents ever since.[59] The army officially defined the term "fragging" as "a slang expression originally referring to the use of a fragmentation grenade (or) other varied explosive devices, in other than combat-related action, by one person against another with a view toward: (1) killing or doing bodily harm to the victim(s), (2) intimidation of the victim(s).[60] The Marine Corps adopted a similar definition: "a deliberate, covert assault, by throwing or setting off a grenade or other explosive device, or the preparation and emplacement of such as device as a booby trap, with the intention of harming or intimidating another (individual)."[61]

Senior military leaders were faced with a hitherto unknown problem: how to stop their men from murdering one another.

CHAPTER TWO

The Fragging Phenomenon

A S was stated in the introduction, incidents of what has come to be known as fragging have occurred since the advent of armed warfare. Even history's most renowned fighting forces, from Napoleon's Grand Armée to Hitler's vaunted Wehrmacht, did not prove immune to this phenomenon. Indeed, such cases were not unknown in American military circles. Captain Adam Bettin of the 4th Pennsylvania Regiment was shot dead by a mutinous enlisted man during the Revolutionary War.[1] Braxton Bragg, who became one of the most famous commanders of the Confederacy, nearly fell victim to a bomb planted under his bed by a disgruntled subordinate.[2] At least four Union Army enlisted men were tried for murdering officers during the Civil War.[3] Major Frank J. Martinez was killed by a shaped charge detonated by one of his men in Korea.[4] In the interest of identifying an ideal type, however, it should be noted that at no time were such incidents considered routine, and commanders did not feel it necessary to implement special measures to prevent them. In a 1907 report regarding *United States v. Taylor*, a court-martial involving the murder of an army lieutenant, the judge advocate general wrote, "Offenses of the character disclosed in the charges and specifications in this case are fortunately rare in the military service."[5] When asked about fragging by a congressional subcommittee, the noted (and later controversial) American military historian S. L. A. Marshall testified, "In my experience, which goes back to World War I, and up through World War II, and then through Korea . . . I have never run into it."[6]

During the initial American buildup in South Vietnam, violence directed at fellow servicemen occurred at the same low rate observed during the nation's prior conflicts. The army did not keep statistics regarding fragging incidents during the war's early years, but its first case

is believed to have occurred in 1966. During the early morning hours
of 10 January, a fragmentation grenade was thrown into the orderly
room of C Company, 2/503d Infantry, 173d Airborne Brigade, injuring
Sergeant Coleman Jackson, Jr., who was billeted inside. Jackson told
investigators of a dispute he had had with another NCO shortly before
the attack, but there was not enough evidence for an arrest.[7] Marine
Corps records are similarly incomplete in this regard, but its first attack
may have taken place on the night of 3 December 1966 in the 1st 8-inch
Howitzer Battery. Fragmentation grenades were thrown at the battery
executive officer's quarters, the staff NCO club, an NCO billet, and the
mess hall. When it was learned that Private Stephen J. Dolan had made
the comment, "I'd like to throw a grenade at some of the lifers" and
confessed to a friend that he had committed the crime, he was taken
into custody. Dolan was subsequently convicted and sentenced to two
years' confinement but the verdict was overturned on appeal. The
charges against him were subsequently dropped when a rehearing was
determined to be "impracticable."[8] Almost a year later, the Marine
Corps sustained its first fragging fatality of the war when someone detonated an explosive device beneath First Sergeant William R. Hunt's
cot in the K Company, 5th Marines rear area. Hunt's bunkmate, Staff
Sergeant George C. Wallace, was suspected of committing the murder,
but investigators were unable to find sufficient evidence to charge him
and the case officially remains unsolved.[9]

Two critical events took place in 1968 that provided pivotal impetus
to what was to become the fragging phenomenon. The first was the
prospect of negotiations aimed at ending the war. On 31 March, President Johnson made a televised address to the nation in which he proposed a partial halt to the bombing of North Vietnam in order to lure
the communists to the conference table. Even more promising was
presidential candidate Richard M. Nixon's intimation that he would
end the war and withdraw U.S. military forces from South Vietnam.
Following his inauguration in January 1969, Nixon sent the new secretary of defense, Melvin R. Laird, to Vietnam to meet with senior military commanders and work out the particulars. "Vietnamization," as
the policy became known, called for a gradual withdrawal of U.S.
troops and the assumption of their duties by beefed-up South Vietnam-

ese forces. Although the first U.S. units left Vietnam that July, others remained in place for months or even years, as the Vietnamese struggled to take their places. From the time of Nixon's promise to end the war and his subsequent election victory, however, American servicemen began to see the fighting as all but over. Withdrawal, they believed, was imminent, and since the military was not mounting an all-out effort to win, they felt little inclination to exert themselves. This sentiment only increased as Vietnamization dragged into the 1970s, and when commanders made decisions that seemed to contrary to this trend, violence was the frequent result.

The second event was the 4 April assassination of prominent civil rights leader Martin Luther King, Jr. As several U.S. cities erupted in flames, senior military leaders feared that the violence might spread to Southeast Asia. General William C. Westmoreland, the MACV commander, "expressed concern that militant groups might attempt to spread the disorders now occurring in the continental United States to Vietnam." His deputy, General Creighton W. Abrams, was slightly more circumspect. "While I have no basis for feeling as I do," he wrote, "There is in my opinion a possibility that the racial unrest now exhibiting itself in our country could in some way infect our own men."[10] Prior to King's death, racial problems among U.S. troops in Vietnam were "for all practical purposes insignificant,"[11] but in the nine days following his murder, six command-level Serious Incident Reports involving racial violence were submitted in the army alone. These outbreaks included roving bands of black troops attacking lone whites after dark and brawls between small groups of soldiers divided along racial lines. In one incident, a black soldier was beaten by other blacks angered by the fact that he had been seen in an enlisted club drinking with a white friend.[12]

After hearing of Reverend King's murder, Privates First Class Robert E. Thompson and Robert B. Bell of B Company, 25th Supply and Transportation Battalion, 25th Infantry Division, refused to perform guard duty at Dau Tieng. When it was learned that their commander, First Lieutenant Donald G. Crawford, planned to initiate disciplinary action against the pair, racial tensions flared. As an officer inspected the bunker line on the evening of 5 April, he was informed of loud noise emanating from a normally unmanned structure on the base perimeter. He made his way to the area and discovered several black soldiers drinking beer, playing loud music, and "talking with racial overtones." He was able to disperse the group and notified Lieutenant Crawford of the incident. Crawford was also told of a similar gathering that had taken place in the enlisted men's club, and as he conferred with another officer on the matter, two explosions shook the unit orderly room. The lieutenant and several of his men proceeded to search the area and when one of them turned up an unexploded hand grenade, military police were summoned to the scene. A second search of the perimeter for additional ordnance was interrupted by yet another grenade explosion that injured Lieutenant Crawford, three military policemen, and six enlisted men from the 25th S&T.

Alarmed by these unprecedented acts of violence, the battalion headquarters dispatched Captain James W. Grisham to the unit as part of an official inquiry. On the evening of 7 April, a grenade exploded near the B Company orderly room. When Grisham ventured outside to investigate, a second grenade detonated in a nearby parking area, inflicting a minor wound to his leg. With this second attack in three days, it became clear to the leadership that they had a problem on their hands. "[There] appears to be a pattern forming at the 25th S&T," one official wrote.[13] Fortunately the battalion's woes ended there, though investigators were unable to make apprehensions in either case. Racial violence among U.S. troops in Vietnam received national attention several months later when the press covered the riot that erupted at the army's Long Binh stockade. On the night of 29 August, angry black inmates attacked custodial personnel and seized temporary control of prison facilities. They then began to randomly assault white prisoners, killing one and injuring several others in the process. Most of the violence ended within a few hours but a hardcore group of militants held out for over a month before finally surrendering to authorities.[14]

Morale clearly began to wane in Vietnam in 1968, and it was during that year that fraggings ceased to be abnormal occurrences. During that year, five soldiers were killed and over thirty others were injured in over forty fraggings counted within the army alone.[15] After returning to Washington and assuming the duties of army chief of staff, General

Westmoreland was informed of the assaults. "The first report of such conduct [fragging] was in 1968," he recalled. "[It was] related to a mostly black army transportation corps unit."[16] These assaults were a mere prelude of what was to come, and the weapon used in nearly all of the cases was the same—the fragmentation hand grenade.

The Weapon of Choice: The Hand Grenade

One aspect of the incidents that remained fairly constant throughout the war was the weapon most preferred by the perpetrators, the M26 fragmentation hand grenade. There were several reasons for this, the most notable being the lack of evidence it left behind. "The anonymous nature of use of a grenade whether by use of a triggering device (such as a trip wire) or thrown during hours of darkness provides the individual with an excellent weapon," one commander admitted. "The grenade or other explosive device is far more difficult to trace to the individual than for example the noise from an M-16 and the resultant effect of having to conceal the weapon."[17] Another officer wrote, "There are no fingerprints on a hand grenade."[18] Fragmentation grenades, or "frags" as the grunts often called them, also afforded potential killers breathing space while committing their crimes, for they were not required to face their targets during the assaults. The following case, which occurred in the 229th Supply and Service Company in 1970, is typical in this regard: "[At] about 2200 hours [Private Gary W. Creek] was observed standing across the street from Lieutenant Brown's quarters, which was a distance from his own. When asked his purpose, he replied that he was looking for beer. Approximately fifteen minutes later a solid object hit the roof of the quarters occupied by Lieutenants Brown and Ferguson, followed shortly by an explosion outside. Investigation disclosed a hole in the ground near the quarter's wall, with new fragment holes in surrounding walls and objects."[19]

While most grenades were simply lobbed at their targets as in the above-cited case, others were employed in more ingenious ways. The method of choice in the 170th Aviation Company involved the preparation of a time-delayed booby trap. When Staff Sergeant Roy L. Beard decided to kill fellow NCO Dannan R. Keays in 1970, he secured a grenade's spoon with masking tape and removed its pull ring. He then submerged the device in a small can filled with gasoline, hoping that the fuel would soon erode the tape's adhesive, releasing the spoon and causing the striker to detonate the grenade. Beard placed the contraption outside his intended victim's quarters but Keays was spared when the grenade tipped over, causing its spoon to lodge against the side of the can and thus preventing its detonation. The apparatus was discovered two days later, its engineer soon after. Beard was court-martialed and sent to prison for his ingenuity.[20] Military records reveal several other instances of fraggers using this particular method but it usually proved to be unreliable, as the devices either malfunctioned or were discovered before the grenades could explode.[21] More successful was a soldier who affixed a grenade to the front tire of a jeep with a pull wire secured to both the grenade's pin and the wheel well. When Captain Lester W. Gray and two soldiers of D Troop, 17th Cavalry, boarded the vehicle and began driving, the wheel's rotation forced the pin from the grenade. The ensuing explosion injured all of the vehicle's occupants.[22]

In addition to the fragmentation grenade, the M18A1 Claymore anti-personnel mine was another weapon sometimes employed by fraggers. The Claymore was a small, rectangular affair that could be detonated by a handheld firing device or trip wire. When it exploded, its effect was devastating: the mine sprayed hundreds of steel fragments into a sixty-degree, approximately fifty-meter-wide kill zone. Few survived run-ins with Claymores, and the fact that the weapon was employed in the U.S. arsenal for over forty years attests to its effectiveness. A homicide involving the use of this weapon occurred in the 1st Aviation Brigade in 1969. After receiving nonjudicial punishment for marijuana possession, Private William E. Sutton decided to kill his company commander and first sergeant. The intoxicated private set up Claymores beside their billets, well aware that the explosions would easily penetrate the outer walls of the structures and strike his victims. The first device did not so much as scratch the company commander but killed helicopter pilot Richard M. Arann, who was asleep in the building. Sutton later confessed to another soldier that he had triggered the first Claymore and started to run. "When [he] heard the warrant officer scream [he] almost stopped in his tracks. Then [he] proceeded to detonate the second one." The other mine also missed its intended target but sent shrapnel ripping into Sergeant Major Grant J. McBee, nearly killing him. Private Sutton was apprehended and sentenced to life imprisonment.[23]

Several fragging incidents involved use of the M14 incendiary grenade. Known to the troops as "Willy Pete," a reference to the white phosphorus allotrope it contained, the grenade became an inferno when detonated. Fortunately no deaths were recorded in cases involving this weapon.

Aside from grenades and mines, fraggers occasionally employed plastic explosives, dynamite, and even hand flares in their attacks. An incident observed in the 26th Engineer Battalion involved the use of a block of C4 explosive studded with metal spikes. One man threw a Molotov cocktail. Perhaps the most violent case of all, however, occurred when Private First Class Michael S. Crampton of the 43d Signal Battalion decided to kill Captain Ronald C. Edwards by firing a LAW anti-tank rocket at his tent. Edwards survived the attack and Crampton was rewarded with a ten-year prison sentence.[24]

U.S. troops in Vietnam were also supplied with a variety of nonlethal ordnance that was sometimes employed to harass or warn "friendly" targets. Smoke grenades, which were commonly available, were used this way, as were CS gas grenades, which released an irritating agent that could briefly incapacitate those exposed to it. The military's decision to use CS gas in Vietnam proved to be controversial and resulted in worldwide condemnation,[25] though this hardly deterred the fraggers. In fact, it has even been suggested in Vietnam War literature that these nonlethal grenades were employed as part of a macabre three-step fragging "cycle." When an individual was targeted for fragging, he might first have a smoke grenade rolled under his bunk as a warning. If his offending conduct persisted, a CS grenade would be similarly employed. Should this too prove unsuccessful in changing him, a fragmentation grenade was used to complete the cycle. However, I have found no cases in which this entire three-step process was used against any particular individual or group.

Firearms

There has been some debate in Vietnam literature as to what actually constituted a fragging incident. While the term "fragging" originally referred to the use of fragmentation grenades, some have stretched the definition to include all assaults on fellow servicemen, including those in which firearms were employed. When compiling its statistical data concerning fragging incidents, however, the army tallied only those incidents that fit its own definition of the term, cases that actually involved the use of explosive devices such as grenades and mines. Accordingly, attacks in which firearms or other weapons were used were not counted. Although this was strictly an administrative decision, it did not stop some pundits from crying cover-up. One academic claimed that the Pentagon "tried to minimize those few reports they did receive by counting only grenade-caused casualties, literal 'fraggings,' rather than including attacks on superiors by all means, including the use of rifles and machine guns, and the sabotage of helicopters."[26] First of all, the army's fragging statistics were compiled not by career-minded officials in Washington or Saigon but by the army's Criminal Investigation Division and the USARV provost marshal's office, both of which investigated criminal offenses irrespective of their circumstances. Secondly, "fragging" and "attacks on superiors" were not always one and the same, for rank was not an indubitable motive in the attacks. Most of the fraggers' grenades were indeed aimed at the leadership corps but there were also a fair share of cases in which junior enlisted men and Vietnamese nationals were targeted, and these incidents were included in the fragging statistics. Conversely, virtually all of the homicides involving firearms were cases of enlisted troops killing men of relatively equal rank.[27] In fact, of the several hundred Vietnam murder cases in which firearms were used, fewer than ten of the victims were officers. It is true, however, that the determined motives for some of the shootings, particularly racial tension and illegal drug use, were analogous to those of the fragging phenomenon, as were the handful that involved violence directed toward superiors. Of the latter, the case of Marine Corporal Charles Eason is typical.

When Corporal Eason voluntarily extended his tour of duty in Vietnam for the third time, he was awarded a thirty-day leave in the United States. Eason apparently had no desire to go home, and after what he claimed were two unsuccessful attempts to have his orders amended, chose to simply remain in the Da Nang area, where he visited friends and even went on patrol with various marine units. Shortly after returning to his own outfit, however, he was informed by Lieutenant Earl K. Ziegler that charges were being filed against him for disobeying orders. This angered Eason, who believed that his leave destination was irrelevant, and the officer's attempts to explain the matter to him were unsuccessful. As the two men discussed the situation, a clerk appeared and requested the lieutenant's presence in the unit mailroom.

"Is it about mail?" asked Eason. "Do I have any mail?"

"It's kind of funny you ask about mail now," scoffed Ziegler. "You came back from leave from Da Nang. You went down to supply and got your gear and you went back out to your position. Why didn't you check your mail then? If you have any mail we'll get it to you."

Eason then asked Ziegler if he could leave, because he "couldn't think straight." An eyewitness described what happened next:

Lieutenant Ziegler was looking in the mailbags . . . when Corporal Eason walked behind the counter with an M-16 rifle in his hand. [Eason] told one of the clerks to get out of the way. Lieutenant Ziegler turned around [and faced] the corporal. Eason said, "Funny, huh?" Lieutenant Ziegler threw his hands up and said "No" at which time Eason shot him with an automatic burst [and] followed him down with his weapon on automatic. He did not appear excited or mad; he had a sort of "You-get-what-you-deserve" look on his face.

"I murdered the lieutenant," uttered Eason. Sergeant David R. Green quickly collared Eason and relieved him of his rifle. He then escorted the killer from the building and forced him to the ground. "He shouldn't have fucked with me," the corporal declared. As Green began to bind him, Eason turned to him and said, "You don't have to tie me up, Sergeant Green. I'm not going to kill anybody else."

Corporal Eason was tried and convicted of premeditated murder and sentenced to fifty years' imprisonment. He was able to win a new trial on appeal, was found guilty of the reduced charge of voluntary manslaughter, and was released in May 1974 after serving only five years in confinement.[28] In December 1977, he was found dead inside his Pittsburgh home, having succumbed to carbon monoxide fumes accidentally inhaled from a space heater.

With the exception of incidents that are alleged to have occurred on the battlefield (which will be examined later), nearly all shootings occurred either during or immediately following disputes or altercations, and involved little attempt to avoid detection. In this respect, the shooters differed from the "stealthy" fraggers, so I did not include them when constructing my profile in Chapter 3 of the "typical" fragger.

"Fodding"

Not all servicemen in Vietnam enjoyed easy access to ordnance, so fragging inevitably took on other forms. "Fodding" (from "foreign object damage") in this context refers to the intentional sabotage of aircraft in aviation units. Specifically, the perpetrator would employ a foreign object to intentionally damage an aircraft in such a way that would cause it to malfunction during flight. The resulting crash would presumably destroy all evidence of the crime, particularly in the case of carrier-based aircraft.

One report of "fodding" appeared in antiwar activist Mark Lane's book *Conversations with Americans*, which contains transcripts of interviews he conducted with thirty-two Vietnam-era veterans. One of the men he spoke with, navy deserter Steve Woods, claimed to have served as an aircraft mechanic aboard the carrier USS *Oriskany* for nine months in the Gulf of Tonkin and alleged that some of the ship's aircraft losses were not the result of enemy action. "I don't know if I should even mention this," Woods confided, "but some of the pilots are real wise guys, real nasty." Those aviators who vocalized their dissatisfaction with their mechanics, he said, might receive a vicious surprise after take-off.

"Sometimes . . . one of us will tape a screwdriver in the intake. Then the plane is catapulted off, and then when he races his engine the whole thing explodes in the air." "Have you seen that done?" asked Lane. "Yes," Woods replied, "three or four times."[29] Upon closer scrutiny, however, it becomes clear that Woods's account is somewhat flawed. Casualty records and aircraft accident reports reveal that of the thousands of sorties launched off "Mighty O" from 1965 to the time Lane's book was released in 1970, only three aviators were lost in nonhostile crashes that occurred during takeoff or en route to the assigned target. One crash occurred during the ship's first Vietnam cruise in 1965, another on the second cruise in 1966, and the third in late 1967. Of these losses, the accident reports confirm that none involved an aircraft or its engine(s) exploding in mid-air.[30] Remarkably, one of the incidents was captured on film in a series of high-speed photographs and these clearly show that no in-air explosion took place. Another of the reports includes after-crash photographs of the aircraft and reveals that the cause of the accident had nothing to do with the plane's engines. Furthermore, the ship's muster rolls and monthly updates indicate that Woods was not on the ship when any of these crashes occurred.[31]

Although Woods's story is obviously problematic, a small number of confirmed "fodding" incidents did take place in Vietnam. What is difficult to determine, however, is whether the saboteurs were Americans or Vietnamese. One case occurred in October 1969, when a maintenance officer in the 101st Aviation Battalion at Camp Eagle found a grenade that had been placed into the fuel cell of a UH-1H helicopter. The grenade's pin had been pulled and its spoon secured with masking tape, but while the fuel caused the tape to loosen, the grenade failed to explode. During a March 1970 flight from Phu Hiep to An Khe, a helicopter pilot of the 238th Aviation Company was forced to make an emergency landing after experiencing engine trouble. When the aircraft was inspected, it was discovered that glass and paper had been inserted into its engine outlets. During a routine check of a U-21 aircraft at Sanford Airfield in Long Binh in June 1970, an alert mechanic found that a quart of oil had been poured into the plane's exhaust stack, which would have caused engine failure at an indefinite time after takeoff.[32] Several months later, someone wrapped sixteen rounds of 7.62 ammunition around a smoke grenade, pulled the grenade's pin, and placed the device inside the engine inlet area of an aircraft assigned to the 117th Aviation Company.[33] Subsequent investigations of these cases yielded no suspects.

Authorities seem to have been more successful in identifying the perpetrators of "fodding" incidents that occurred outside Vietnam. After being "harassed" by a petty officer, Airman George E. Martinson placed a penny and a nail inside the engine intakes of two naval aircraft at Cecil Field, Florida. The objects were discovered before any damage was done, and Martinson, who confessed to the act, was charged with "willfully and intentionally placing foreign objects in two jet aircraft engines valued at $800,000." Psychiatrists who subsequently examined the accused found him to possess a severe passive-dependent personality. They did not believe that Martinson intended to hurt anyone in particular let alone destroy the aircraft; rather, they determined that the airman's poor judgment and lack of insight, paired with suppressed rage, led him to act out against a symbol of the navy's authority, which he believed had persecuted him without cause. Despite their pleas for leniency, Martinson was found guilty and sentenced to a bad-conduct discharge and six months of confinement.[34] In October 1971, a maintenance supervisor in the army's 55th Aviation Company discovered that someone had inserted pieces of paper into the fuel tank and fuel pump of a Mohawk OVI Bravo at K-16 Airfield in South Korea. One of the company's enlisted men was identified as a possible suspect in the case, but authorities were unable to obtain enough evidence to charge him.[35]

Fraggings were rare in the navy and air force. From what documentation was available, I was only able to confirm a handful of incidents. There are a number reasons for this. In the case of the navy, relatively few sailors were stationed on shore in Vietnam when fragging became commonplace (by early 1971 there were only 16,500 blue jackets in country). With regard to the air force, several factors are believed to be responsible. The typical airman tended to be older than his army or Marine Corps counterpart. Nearly all were high school graduates and many possessed college backgrounds. Air force personnel often lived in less austere conditions than soldiers and marines, both physically and in terms of discipline, and many performed jobs deemed to be of "high caliber," while mundane chores were frequently relegated to local Vietnamese. The fact that fewer airmen enjoyed easy access to ordnance also played a role.[36]

Of the incidents within these services that did occur in Vietnam, none resulted in death. On 3 July 1969, a grenade was detonated at Binh Thuy Naval Base, injuring an enlisted man. A sailor was spotted running from the scene of the explosion and apprehended but the subsequent investigation failed to win a conviction.[37] In October 1970, Seaman Apprentice Fredie Montanez threw a concussion grenade at a fellow enlisted sailor while aboard a naval vessel moored at the Nha Be Logistic Support Base. Despite the intervention of a congressman on his behalf, Montanez was subsequently convicted of aggravated assault and served nearly two years in the brig.[38] The bloodiest incident to occur in the air force took place in December 1971 when a grenade was thrown into an officer billet of the 366 Munitions Maintenance Squadron at Da Nang Airfield. The explosion injured five of the squadron's ten assigned officers, including the squadron commander, as well as two civilian technicians who had been involved in testing a new munition.[39]

Environmental Characteristics

When reviewing military records regarding fragging, it becomes obvious that many of the attacks shared common elements. One feature of the cases that remained constant was the time of day, or, better, of night in which most of the incidents took place. Darkness obviously afforded fraggers added security against detection, both in terms of being identified by witnesses and in the low level of activity on military installations during that period. Another aspect found to be fairly consistent was location where the assaults took place. Most fraggings occurred in noncombat support units. Of the nearly one hundred grenade cases acknowledged by the army in 1969, fewer than one-third occurred in infantry units. Most were observed in such support outfits as the 64th Finance Section, the 647th Quartermaster Company, and the 27th Surgical Hospital, though one should consider the large number of support personnel as compared to those serving in the combat arms (the ratio was approximately 10:1) when making such an analysis. Nevertheless, the fact that most of the incidents occurred in support units allays the popular legend found in postwar literature that fraggers primarily targeted leaders who needlessly or recklessly risked their men's lives in combat, as does the fact that fragging incidents increased dramatically at a time when the American war was winding down and U.S. battle deaths were rapidly decreasing.

Why did REMFs ("rear-echelon motherfuckers"), as support personnel were derisively known, commit more fraggings than the combat troops? REMFs may not have faced the same physical dangers that the grunts did, but they were still in Vietnam. They were just as far away from home, it was hot, they too received "Dear John" letters, and with the war winding down they were made to endure what had become an almost garrison-type situation with its accompanying spit and polish. To make matters worse, the perceived harassment from superiors associated with garrison duty was not accompanied by the usual off-duty benefits or comforts of garrison life found in the United States.[40] A visiting congressional panel found that "the soldier in Vietnam has little or no way of dealing with his frustration in any constructive fashion. Most towns are off-limits and those that are not are limited in what they have to offer. The primary activity when they are permitted off the post is drinking in local bars and meeting with local women, most of whom are prostitutes.[41] It was also in the rear that two of the contributing factors to the fragging phenomenon—drug use and racial militancy—were usually found. As one marine mused, "Racial confrontations [in the rear] were becoming so common by 1969 that it was common to joke, 'I'm going back out to the bush where it's safe!'"[42] Esprit de corps waned in rear areas, while boredom, paired with the military's traditional fetish for mindless busywork, played a key role in leading young soldiers into mischief.

In his classic *Reveries on the Art of War*, Maurice de Saxe wrote, "The transition from fatigue to rest enervates [soldiers]. They compare one state with another, and idleness, that predominate passion of mankind, gains ascendancy over them. They then murmur at every trifling inconvenience."[43] The case of Private Gilberto Hernandez is an interesting example in this regard. After arriving in Vietnam in 1968, Hernandez served for nearly eleven months in the field as a machine gunner with the 101st Airborne Division. Despite being wounded and seeing "a lot of men killed," he was "aggressive, showed initiative, and was a good infantryman," his platoon sergeant later testified. It was not until he was posted to a secure rear-area unit to complete the final weeks of his Vietnam tour that his problems began. It was there that he came into conflict with Sergeant First Class Richard L. Atkins, Sr., a headquarters company mess sergeant. Nicknamed "Hardcore" by his unloving subordinates, Atkins had already been the victim of two CS grenade fraggings when Hernandez detonated a Claymore mine outside his living quarters. At trial, it was revealed that Hernandez had two prior special court-martial convictions involving disputes with his superiors, yet neither case had anything to do with the unit's combat mission.[44]

All of the fragging incidents cited in this study occurred in garrison or garrison-type environments. While inspecting defensive positions on Hill 190 near Da Nang, twenty-year-old Sergeant Richard Lee Tate of I Company, 1st Marines, found Lance Corporal Gary A. Hendrix asleep on guard duty. Tate collared the sleeping sentry and berated him, saying, "If I were a V.C., you would be dead!" Later that evening, Hendrix approached the old French bunker in which Tate and two other NCOs were sleeping, and dropped a fragmentation grenade through the gun port. The grenade landed between Tate's legs and exploded, killing him and injuring the others. Hendrix was convicted of premeditated murder.[45] It is interesting to note that in this instance, it was the perpetrator who had been "risking men's lives" and not the victim, contrary to the postwar fragging stereotype.

It is certainly possible, however, that instances of fragging did occur on the battlefield during combat operations. The lore of modern warfare is replete with tales of soldiers shooting unpopular officers in the back, and Vietnam is certainly no exception in this regard, but a look at casualty records suggests that these incidents, if any, were exceedingly rare. For example, from the time that the first Marine Corps ground units arrived in Vietnam in March 1965 to their departure in mid-1971, a total of 224 marine officers died of gunshot wounds sustained in battle. During that six-year period, the Corps took part in some of the hardest fighting in its history against an enemy whose tenacity was proverbial. Moreover, a number of these officers were witnessed committing acts of

heroism at the time of their deaths and were awarded posthumous decorations, including several Medals of Honor. While the possibility that
officers were murdered in the field certainly cannot be denied, even a
cursory look at casualty statistics rules out any preponderance of incidents. Vague references to such behavior flood Vietnam War literature;
what is lacking is precise information regarding particular cases.[46] Sans
the honest admissions of ex-servicemen, such incidents are impossible
to confirm, and these fatalities, if any, were invariably recorded as ordi-
nary battle casualties. How many men died this way? We will never
know.

It is at this point that a falsehood regarding alleged battlefield homicides, one that has made the rounds of Vietnam literature since the
early 1970s, will be laid to rest. In the above-mentioned book *Conversations with Americans*, marine "James D. Nell" of the 9th Engineers
claimed to have witnessed the murders of "five or six" officers during
combat operations in Vietnam. "I've seen it in the field," Nell said.
"Sometimes they get on your nerves too much."[47] Thorough investigation of this story revealed it to be completely unfounded. Unit personnel rosters and a 1996 Marine Corps investigation conducted at my
request confirm that Nell served in Vietnam with C Company, 9th Engineer Battalion, but in regard to the murders, they tell quite a different
story.[48] The truth is that not one commissioned leatherneck died in
Nell's entire battalion of *any* cause, hostile or otherwise, during his tour
of duty or, for that matter, the entire Vietnam War. The casualty information provided by the personnel rosters is further confirmed by the
unit's monthly command chronologies as well as data assembled by the
battalion's veterans association.[49] Of the "killings" themselves, Nell
maintained, "Generally everybody, almost, just about the entire company . . . would know it was going to happen. They would just wait
until he [the officer] was in the right position." Interviews were conducted with ten former C Company enlisted men who served with Nell,
and without my showing them the documentation I had accumulated,
all of them called him a liar.[50] I was even able to contact every commissioned officer assigned to C Company during Nell's time in Vietnam—
they were all alive and kicking nearly thirty years later.[51] In fact, the

only fatality that did take place in the company during Nell's tour occurred when a distraught enlisted man shot himself after receiving a
"Dear John" letter.[52]

Similarly problematic was an implication of a battlefield homicide
made by Lieutenant Colonel Anthony B. Herbert in his 1973 memoir
Soldier, a book that one reviewer called "a kaleidoscope of truth, half-
truth, and fabrication."[53] Herbert, an ex-battalion commander in the
173d Airborne Brigade, wrote of a young platoon leader who was allegedly murdered by his drugged-up troops in the field, but an exhaustive
investigation conducted by army authorities revealed that the shooting
was nothing more than a tragic accident. On 8 September 1968, the officer in question, Second Lieutenant Robert T. Elliott, III, of B Company,
2/503d Infantry, was ordered to emplace a squad-sized night ambush
near a suspected Viet Cong infiltration route in Quang Ngai Province.
Shortly after Elliott and his men departed their base camp, however,
things began to go wrong. According to several of his NCOs, Elliott,
who had only been in Vietnam for three weeks, was a poor map reader
and quickly became lost, leading his men in circles through the jungle
for over an hour while twice passing the planned ambush site. The lieutenant eventually selected a second location and divided his soldiers
into three groups, directing that two of the groups set up listening posts
along a well-traveled path, while the third group was to remain with
him in the command post. The men found these last-minute instructions confusing, and, critically, it appears that Elliott did not reveal the
exact position his command element would occupy to the troops manning the two listening posts. In any case, the men understood that once
the ambush position was in place, no one was supposed to move.

Several hours passed. Shortly after midnight, Private First Class José
M. Rosa-Contreras, who was monitoring radio traffic at the command
post, "moved off to the left of the position . . . to urinate." His movements
were noticed by the soldiers in one of the listening posts, who, in the
belief that they had spotted an enemy soldier, called Lieutenant Elliott
on the radio Rosa-Contreras was supposed to be monitoring to alert him
of their "discovery." Receiving no response, they radioed company headquarters. Testifying during an official probe, Rosa-Contreras admitted:

When I got back to the radio I heard the outpost on my right talking to company headquarters. I listened and heard him report seeing a gook, a Vietnamese, moving around. The moon was very bright and there wasn't any heavy brush in the area so I stood up to spot the gook. I couldn't see anything and got down again. Then I heard the outpost tell company headquarters that the gook had stood up and squatted down again. Headquarters told the outpost that if the gook didn't move again the outpost should fire on him. I decided that I had better awaken Lieutenant Elliott. I shook the guy sleeping next to me and told him to hold the radio. Then I crawled around two or three guys and shook Lieutenant Elliot. Just as I raised up from waking him I heard the first shot fired and I jumped into a small ditch. While I was still getting into the ditch heavy small arms fire came into our position and M-79 rounds began falling around us. I looked for Lieutenant Elliott and saw him hunched over and I pulled him toward me. I could tell he had been hit.

An M16 round fired from the listening post had struck Elliott in the abdomen. A sergeant's screams of "Cease fire!" halted the fusillade but the men's efforts to save their lieutenant were unsuccessful. "Elliott was in a state of shock, saying 'Please don't let me die,'" a squad leader wrote. "We attempted mouth-to-mouth resuscitation but [he] did not come out of the shock. He then became stiff and died shortly after the medics arrived on the scene."[54] An incredulous Rosa-Contreras rebuked his comrades for shooting in the first place. "I just got up to take a piss and you guys fired me up!" he exclaimed. Although Lieutenant Elliott was undoubtedly killed by his own men's guns, and drugs were indeed used by some in the unit (Rosa-Contreras was court-martialed for smoking marijuana several months after the incident), any intimation that foul play was involved in the officer's death is groundless. Diligent readers of *Soldier* will note that two differing accounts of the incident are provided in the text: it is first described as the case of a lieutenant who mistakenly ordered his own men to open fire on him; the second reference contains the murder claim. The latter version quotes Sergeant First Class Lucien T. Brewer as saying that Elliott "was still alive [after being shot], but they finished him off before the dust-off [medical evacuation helicopter] came in."[55] This is false, as a postmortem examination of the lieutenant's remains revealed that he sustained a single gunshot wound to the abdomen and no other injuries.[56] Moreover, Brewer was not present when the incident occurred and later denied making the statement.[57] In any case, the army's investigation, which was conducted in 1971, failed to substantiate Colonel Herbert's claim; why he persisted in including it in his memoir is unknown.

Bounties

A popular legend of the Vietnam War depicts vengeful enlisted men pooling their money and placing prices, bounties, on the heads of unpopular officers and NCOs. One source cites troops in the Mekong Delta, a likely reference to the army's 9th Infantry Division, engaging in this practice.[58] One officer so targeted was Captain Robin B. Heath. While conducting an inspection of his unit perimeter one evening in 1969, Heath found one of his soldiers painting what turned out to be signs offering a reward for his demise. "I was at 'Tiger's Lair' in Kien Hoa Province for about three months," he said.

> When I first came to [the 3d Battalion, 47th Infantry], I performed four Article 32 investigations for general courts-martial. Some of these were racial: in fact, they were all black soldiers. They [involved] field refusals. You just can't turn your guns on the people you work with because you think you go to the field too much.
>
> I took the [B] Company over the day [after some] men had been killed. It's kind of weird when you come into a unit and you're the newbie and you don't know anybody and all of this stuff happens.
>
> We had a lot of incidents of guys rubbing insect repellent into their wounds and mosquito bites and festering them up so they wouldn't have to go to the field. The first sergeant and I took care of that. We knew what their tricks were, so my company kept about twice the combat strength of the other companies. . . . I was the new guy on the block and they didn't tell me how the game was played, that you screw off and don't keep that many. There are a lot of games played in war.
>
> The biggest thing that people were afraid of [was] that if you were a

company commander and you didn't mind standing and fighting, they'd be afraid that you'd take them down in the jungle and you'd have to stay there and fight all night. If those troops thought that they [were] going to [the] jungle overnight, they'd do anything they could to keep from going because Charlie [came] in close on those banana dikes.

My first sergeant came to me one day and indicated that he was thinking of moving out of [our] hooch. I didn't know what was going on but I guess he had heard some rumors [that] I was going to get shot. Then on one evening a little later as I was checking the perimeter, I found a guy painting some signs. He was painting "dead or alive" on it or something, from what I gather, and there was a reward. I don't know how much money it was. I think it was a black fellow from 2d Platoon and I said, "You're up kind of late, aren't you?" and he said, "Yeah, kinda late." And that was about it; I just passed on through, I never even stopped to read them. They were about me as I found out, for me "dead or alive." I didn't know that I was doing that bad.

I transferred out of the battalion the day after or two days after they wrote the sign[s] up on me. The colonel thought it was best if they moved me out. I hadn't been there that long. I didn't think that I had that many people mad at me. After I left, I found out that I had a Viet Cong bounty on me as well as a troop bounty. You don't know, one day you might be popular, the next day you might be shot.[59]

The most infamous bounty ever posted involved a high-ranking officer who allegedly made the hit list: Lieutenant Colonel Weldon F. Honeycutt, a battalion commander in the 101st Airborne Division. In his efforts to seize enemy-occupied Hill 937, Colonel Honeycutt ordered an aggressive frontal assault that was ultimately successful but resulted in heavy casualties. The perilous terrain feature quickly acquired the soubriquet "Hamburger Hill" and earned Honeycutt the scorn of the antiwar press. *GI Says*, which was supposedly one of the many "underground" GI newspapers that appeared during the Vietnam era,[60] is said to have offered a $10,000 bounty for the colonel's murder. Although a number of authors have fancifully claimed that attempts were indeed made against Honeycutt's life,[61] military records fail to substantiate this,[62] and Honeycutt himself denied the charge:

I did hear of the newspaper called *GI Says* but never saw or read same. To my certain knowledge there were never any attempts made against me. To be sure, all anyone had to do was follow me around in the jungle or in the fire base night or day as I never used bodyguards or any other means of protection other than my pistol and AR-15 carbine.[63]

No one will ever know how widespread bounties were, but there is evidence that they predated Vietnamization. During the probe of a March 1967 fragging in the 3d 155mm Gun Battery, investigators learned that Lance Corporal William R. Thomas had offered Private Terry L. Kanekeberg $100 to "get rid of the people in charge of the battery." When confronted by authorities, however, Thomas swore that he had "meant nothing" by it and that his offer was only a "sick joke."[64] Lieutenant Colonel Robert L. Drudik, commander of the 1st Battalion, 7th Cavalry, in February 1970, described the problem in his unit: "Right now, the A Company commander, acting first sergeant, and one platoon sergeant have learned informally that 'contracts' are out to get them."[65] In the case outlined below, a confidential informant was able to provide authorities with the details concerning the pooling of a troop bounty.

The 2d Battalion, 8th Cavalry, was one of the last American ground units stationed in South Vietnam. By the beginning of 1972, its morale was at low ebb, as drugs, racial militancy, and indiscipline became endemic among its enlisted ranks. Commanders serving in the battalion's line units showed little patience in dealing with troublemakers, and found the Headquarters Company, which occupied the battalion rear area at Bien Hoa, to be a convenient dumping ground for their undesirable soldiers. It wasn't long before Headquarters Company became what the battalion commander called a "troubled unit."

Captain Samuel S. Vitucci, a twenty-four-year-old West Point graduate, was assigned command of Headquarters Company in mid-February. His battalion commander actually felt it necessary to caution him of the unit's condition before he took the job, warning that the company "had a drug problem and several black power advocates" within its ranks. Vitucci was well aware of the company's woes; he had already taken part in a number of shakedown inspections, and reported several of the troops for using drugs even before assuming command. He recalled:

Small plastic vials, used by our hardcore drug users who were using heroin, litter[ed] the company area. There was a great deal of drug paraphernalia throughout the barracks area. The troops had created partitions out of the bays. They decorated their areas with black lights, posters, beads, rugs, incense, and I smelled marijuana on several occasions. The black power movement was in evidence as well. It was not uncommon to see these individuals use black power salutes and make use of racist language to taunt other blacks and whites who were good soldiers.

I saw it as my job to clean this company up. When I took command I conduct[ed] frequent inspections in the billet areas and [began] to change the culture of the organization. There were no more black lights, no more separate living areas, no more burning of incense. I also began the process of getting the drug users to detox or getting them chaptered [administratively discharged] out of the army.[66]

These actions certainly had a pronounced effect on the company's posture, but as was the case so many times before in Vietnam, its malcontents chose to use violence to deal with their superior. Sometime in late February, Specialists Four Joseph B. Ancrum, Ronald D. Baker, Oliver M. Dean, Robert Murphy, and Henry W. Parker, Privates First Class Harold E. Collins, Maurice V. Gallagher, Horace Hogans, Jr., and Glen A. Poe, and Private Edward Tattnall gathered in a military barbershop to discuss the crackdown and its architect. All of the men had had run-ins with Vitucci since his arrival in the unit and several of them were slated for administrative discharges. The CID was investigating Ancrum for the rape of a Vietnamese woman and Gallagher had just beaten a murder charge in West Germany.[67] Vitucci continued:

I remember taking Dean's acting jack [acting sergeant's] stripes away from him for refusing a lawful order. I also removed him from the E-5 [promotion] list because of his belligerent attitude. I had enough paperwork on all but three of the ten [for administrative discharges] before I had commanded the unit for forty days. Unfortunately, I didn't have enough on Ancrum and Dean [who] were the most vocal and were the ringleaders. They were too slick. I know that Poe, Collins, and Tattnall had all been sent to the detox center in Long Binh and returned to the company and immediately began heavy use of dope again. One day I walked in on Poe as he was shooting heroin into his arm.[68]

The men collected a bounty payable "to an unidentified person to murder Vitucci."[69] The pool increased until it reached the sum of $500, which in spite of a recent military pay raise constituted well over a month's wages for a junior enlisted man. The plot was foiled, however, when an enlisted soldier loyal to the command structure overheard the conspirators and informed a senior NCO of the scheme. The battalion commander, who was in the field at the time, sent a helicopter to the rear area to whisk Vitucci away from any potential danger while military policemen hauled the alleged plotters to the stockade.[70] Charges were quickly preferred against the group but Vitucci dropped them when he learned that the informant "was afraid for his life and did not want to testify."[71] Instead, the pending administrative discharges were speedily processed and the others were transferred back to the United States, as Vitucci recalled, with "all the counseling and performance reports and an explanation of what happened preced[ing] them to their gaining units."[72]

Although military records and veteran statements confirm that bounties were in fact pooled in Vietnam, determining whether they played any real role in motivating enlisted men to assault their superiors is another matter. When asked about bounties by a military psychiatrist, only one of a group of twenty-eight convicted fraggers at the Leavenworth stockade said that there had been a bounty placed on his victim, and added that it had "played no part in his final action."[73] A number of the offenders profiled here pleaded guilty at their courts-martial and admitted to committing their offenses, yet none of them cited bounties as a motivating factor. In fact, their court-martial transcripts do not mention them at all. Bounties, it seems, were most often an extension of the loose talk offered by frustrated enlisted men as a way of releasing tension. The fraggers, I will argue in Chapter 3, were not stimulated to act by any financial motive; they committed their offenses because they genuinely felt that they had been wronged by their victims and were now "evening the score."

The Wrong Man

Perhaps the most tragic aspect of the fragging phenomenon was that the perpetrators often neglected to isolate their intended targets when they struck, and as a result, innocent bystanders were inevitably killed and injured in the attacks. One particularly heartrending case occurred in D Battery, 11th Marines, at Liberty Bridge (Phu Lac 6) in February 1969. Although no one has ever been convicted of this crime and hence the murderer's true target officially remains unknown, witness testimony paints a convincing picture of two men who happened to be in the wrong place at the wrong time.

Court-martial transcripts reveal that when First Lieutenant Francis A. Mauro, Jr., assumed command of D Battery, he found it to possess "poor morale, [and a] poor state of place." His efforts to reestablish order did not earn him much popularity among the militant elements of the battery's enlisted ranks and it wasn't long before talk of murder was in the air. While drinking whiskey with a friend on the evening of 27 February, Private First Class Walter Chambers, Jr., boldly announced, "I'm going to do a job on the C.O. tonight." Chambers, it was said, had made similar statements on several other occasions, once to the effect that he would perform the deed "before [his scheduled] rotation back to the States." At about 2340 hours, he and a companion, Private First Class Kenneth Williams, left the motor pool tent in which they had been boozing and made their way toward the battery's small arms bunker. While under way, Chambers repeated his intention to yet another marine who simply laughed, not taking him seriously. Williams later told investigators that he then saw Chambers enter the bunker and remove a grenade, but subsequently retracted this statement in court, claiming that he had been scared into making the declaration during initial questioning. In any case, Williams then fled the scene because he "didn't want to be there." Another witness observed Chambers approach Mauro's bunker.[74]

As fate would have it, the lieutenant was nowhere near his quarters that evening. Assigned to fire direction watch, Mauro had opted to sleep elsewhere in order to accommodate a newly arrived NCO, Haywood W. Ballance, who was slated to assume duty as the battery's new first sergeant. Also in the billet that night was Ballance's predecessor, First Sergeant Warren R. Furse. A career marine with over sixteen years of service, Furse was scheduled to return to the United States and his wife and children in a matter of days. Tragically, this was not to be, for shortly before midnight, the muffled explosion of a hand grenade rocked the bunker. Ballance staggered out, bleeding from the mouth, shoulder, and chest. Many of the battery's men assumed that an enemy mortar attack was in progress, and a full alert was sounded in the cantonment. Several marines raced toward the stricken Ballance and carried him to the battalion aid station.

"Where's the first sergeant?" they cried.

"In the quarters," gurgled Ballance.

Inside the bunker, Sergeant Furse lay dying, having sustained massive shrapnel wounds to his chest and abdomen. Frantic attempts to save his life were unsuccessful. Ballance was evacuated to Guam for medical treatment and eventually recovered from his injuries. Marine authorities immediately launched an investigation of the incident, and it wasn't long before their attention turned to Chambers. He was taken into custody and charged with Furse's murder.

Chambers's court-martial was convened over a two-day period in May 1969. Senior leadership was eager for a conviction and the 1st Division's most seasoned trial counsel, Captain Edward F. Kelly, was selected to prosecute the case. Sergeant Ballance returned to Vietnam to offer his testimony and Private First Class Williams was summoned from Camp Lejeune, North Carolina, where he had since transferred. Nevertheless, the government's efforts were unsuccessful, as its key witness, Private Williams, elected to change his story, and Chambers was acquitted of all charges. "Succinctly," Captain Kelly recalled, "I didn't have a case without Williams. [He] told a different story than the account related to the investigating officer at the Article 32 [pretrial] hearing. It was clear to me from the time I first met Williams that he was an acquaintance of

Chambers if not a friend."[75] Efforts were made after the trial to prosecute Williams for perjury but these too went nowhere. As for Lieutenant Mauro's misgivings about his unit, any doubts about their capabilities were dispelled shortly after the murder, when D Battery successfully repulsed a battalion-strength enemy raid on its positions. The marines gunned down over seventy-five of the attackers and suffered only sixteen fatalities, and navy corpsman David R. Ray was posthumously awarded the Medal of Honor for his heroic actions during the battle.[76]

It is simply impossible for any researcher to identify the intended target in every Vietnam fragging case, but it is clear that instances of men being maimed or killed by ordnance intended for others were commonplace. Corporal Thomas W. Fowler was an instructor at the 1st Marine Division's Land Mine Warfare School and was "intimately familiar with the use of high explosives." After he and another instructor quarreled over a fan, Fowler constructed a large bomb and detonated it outside of the man's quarters. The explosion destroyed most of the building but missed its intended target and killed Lance Corporal Roger L. Jones, who was uninvolved in the dispute. "I got the wrong one," Fowler was heard to say.[77] On 20 October 1971, a soldier assigned to the army's Vung Chua Signal Site sought to eliminate Captain Terry A. De Sande with a Claymore mine but killed Captain Richard J. Privitar by mistake.[78] In fact, of all the army officers who are known to have died in fragging incidents during the Vietnam War, only one was the intended target of the assault.[79]

During 1969, the year in which U.S. strength in Vietnam peaked at 543,400 troops, the frequency of grenade attacks increased dramatically. The army reported ninety-six actual assaults during that year, with another thirty cited as "possible." Thirty-two American and five Vietnamese deaths were recorded in these incidents, but a closer look at these figures reveals that not all of the victims were actually murdered. Of the American fatalities, two men were eventually found to have been victims of hostile action, three died during an apparent attempt to assault a military policeman, six had used grenades to commit suicide, and several others died in cases that were later found to have been accidental in nature, bringing the actual number of intentional homicide victims owing to fragging to eleven. Over thirty incidents are known to have taken place in the Marine Corps that year, resulting in nine deaths. Although the army's figures dwarfed those of previous years, one historian has suggested that the statistics are too low, and research reveals him to be correct.

In his book *The Spoils of War*, sociologist Charles J. Levy cited the twenty grenade incidents observed in the 3d Marine Division's tactical area during first eight months of 1969 and argued, "The Third Division contained four per cent of the American force in Vietnam at that time. By projecting, the . . . twenty cases become . . . over five hundred cases during the first eight months of 1969."[80] This implies that the army's figures are inaccurate, which they indeed are. In theory, whenever "a significant incident, crime, accident, wrongdoing or mismanagement which involve[d] [U.S. Army] personnel, property or equipment" occurred in Vietnam, regulations dictated that a Serious Incident Report, or S.I.R., be completed and submitted to USARV. The crimes included "murder, voluntary or involuntary manslaughter, assault with intent to commit murder or manslaughter, aggravated assaults, and unlawful or unauthorized discharge of firearms when injury occurs or unfavorable publicity can be expected."[81] When preparing its fragging statistics, the army simply tallied those S.I.R.s that involved the unauthorized detonations of explosive devices and grouped them into three categories:

"Actual assaults": incidents involving explosives in which the intent to kill, to do bodily harm, or to intimidate was the determined motive.

"Possible assaults": incidents involving explosives in which the intent to kill, to do bodily harm, or to intimidate was determined to be a possible motive.

"Non-fragging incidents": incidents involving explosives in which the intent to kill, to do bodily harm, or to intimidate was determined not to be a motive.

In 1969, there were 238 such reports, and upon review, ninety-six were categorized as actual assaults, thirty as possible assaults, and the rest as non-fragging incidents.[82] However, these reports were not always completed, and a review of military police desk blotters bears this out. For example, logs maintained by the 25th MP Battalion in 1969 detail the following grenade incidents, none of which is included in the army's official figures:

13 January: At 0005 hours, person(s) unknown discharged two grenades. Staff Sergeant Harold R. Pruitt of B Company, 725th Maintenance Battalion suffered a minor shrapnel wound of the right upper arm.

23 March: At 2030 hours, Master Sergeant Maurice A. Wilson, 25th Administration Company, notified this office that person(s) unknown had tied an incendiary grenade to his bedpost.

5 April: At approximately 0445 hours, person(s) unknown exploded what is believed to be a fragmentation grenade. Investigation revealed that the grenade exploded between the sand bag wall and the building in which Sergeant First Class Fred Powell, 341st Assault Helicopter Detachment, was sleeping. Powell received minor lacerations of the head.

13 April: At approximately 0045 hours, a grenade exploded between the commanding officer's quarters and the battalion staff officers' quarters of HQ & Company A, 725th Maintenance Battalion.

6 June: At approximately 0005 hours, person(s) unknown discharged a star cluster into the first sergeant's hooch, 372d Radio Relay Company, Cu Chi Base Camp.

19 June: At approximately 2300 hours, person(s) unknown threw an M26 fragmentation hand grenade toward First Lieutenant Hughes C. McClees (25th Supply & Transportation Battalion) who was standing outside his billets at Camp Ranier.

31 July: Between 2230 hours 30 July and 0330 hours, person(s) unknown armed and aimed an anti-personnel mine at First Lieutenant Frederick G. Irtz's quarters (HHC, 25th Aviation Battalion).

28 August: At approximately 2115 hours, a hand grenade was thrown at NCO Hooch #2, Company E, 725th Maintenance Battalion.

13 November: At 2230 hours, person(s) unknown threw a gas grenade into the NCO hooch, HHC Commandant.

22 December: At approximately 2255 hours, Staff Sergeant Paco B. Cook found an M67 fragmentation grenade under the pillow on his bunk (HHC, 1st Battalion, 5th Infantry).[83]

Desk blotters generated by the 1st Infantry and 101st Airborne divisions also reveal significant inconsistencies with the official figures.[84] An army press release admitted, "Fragging statistic[s] represent reported incidents" (emphasis in original).[85] Unfortunately, many Vietnam-era desk blotters did not survive the war, so a complete survey is impossible. But even if the documentation were available, it would still not tell the entire story. An official inquiry conducted in the 1st Cavalry Division revealed that of the six fragging incidents that occurred in the 1st Battalion, 7th Cavalry, in 1969, only four were logged in the military police desk blotter,[86] and of these only one found its way into the army's fragging statistics.[87] There were even a handful of cases in which S.I.R.s were completed but the incidents were not included in the official figures, this probably due to clerical oversight.

Fraggings continued to increase in frequency as the war dragged on. In spite of the fact that U.S. troop strength sank below the 350,000 mark, 1970 saw the number of grenade incidents in the army double those of the previous year. Two hundred nine actual assaults were tallied, including six on 21 April alone, and sixty-two others were listed as possible assaults.[88] Twenty-seven Americans and eight Vietnamese died, although only seventeen of the GIs were victims of intentional homicide.[89] Four soldiers managed to frag and kill themselves during apparent attempts to assault others. In one such case, a simmering racial dispute at Camp Enari led Specialist Four James E. Cooley of the 4th Infantry Division to frag a unit laundry room in which several white soldiers were sleeping. As he was attempting to force the grenade into the building, it exploded in his face, killing him instantly.[90] As had been the case during 1969, most of the 1970 incidents occurred in support units that did not frequent the battlefield; a murder was even recorded in the 38th Base Post Office at Long Binh.[91] Fragging was also on the rise in the Marine Corps, where nearly fifty incidents occurred within the 1st Division alone. In all, four leathernecks lost their lives.[92] Fragging in the 1st Division was so serious that the assistant division commander felt it necessary during orientation briefings to warn newly arriving officers of the threat.[93]

Fragging and the News Media

Although stories of individual fragging incidents accompanied return-ing servicemen to the United States, the topic received scant attention from the press until late 1969. It was then that a recently discharged marine, Sergeant Robert J. Parkinson, contacted a hometown California newspaper and related an account of an attempt made against his life in Vietnam.[94] His story resulted in "the receipt of numerous inquiries" by Marine Corps authorities, including one from U.S. Representative Barry Goldwater, Jr.[95] Parkinson later reiterated his story while testifying be-fore a Senate subcommittee hearing on drug abuse, telling legislators how his efforts to curb marijuana use in his supply unit made him "a very much hated man by [his] troops" and the target of an attempted fragging.[96] The Judge Advocate Division of the Marine Corps subse-quently investigated Parkinson's statements, and its resulting "point paper" corroborated nearly all of his testimony. Efforts at prosecuting Parkinson's assailant were less successful.[97]

Sergeant Parkinson's revelations were only the beginning. A partic-ularly bloody grenade incident in a marine maintenance battalion in February 1970 was the subject of two *New York Times* articles,[98] and the definition and practice of fragging were mentioned that October in an issue of *Life*.[99] By the end of 1970, journalists could see that the attacks were no longer isolated occurrences, and this prompted an Associated Press inquiry to army officials in Saigon. In response, the USARV In-formation Office prepared a statement on the subject that outlined par-ticular aspects of the plague and offered analysis of the incidents themselves. It revealed that the army had been keeping statistics on fragging since July 1970, that few injuries had been recorded but that even fewer apprehensions had been made, and that fraggings in Viet-nam were averaging about twenty per month.[100] Queries from UPI and CBS soon followed.

The first journalism to reveal the full extent of the fragging phenomenon was an Associated Press article published in newspapers na-
tionwide on 7 and 8 January 1971. Running under such dramatic titles
as "Tense GIs Carry Vendettas to Explosive, Fatal End" and "GI Bomb
Attacks on Officers Increase," the piece told the story of a senior NCO
who narrowly avoided injury when his men tried to kill him with a
five-pound bomb.[101] *Newsweek* raised the subject again a few days later,
and an editorial titled "Fragging and Bragging" appeared in the *Chicago
Sun-Times* on the twelfth. Reporters also heard of fragging as they covered the Vietnam Veterans Against the War, an organization formed by
ex-servicemen who had turned against the conflict, when it convened
its Winter Soldier Investigation in Detroit in late January. The event assumed the form of moderated hearings in which veterans provided testimony regarding their experiences in Vietnam. While most of their
accounts centered on alleged abuses committed against Vietnamese nationals, several grenade cases were mentioned. The now famous article
"The Collapse of the Armed Forces" by retired Marine Colonel Robert
D. Heinl, Jr., which appeared in *Armed Forces Journal* several months
later, was particularly damning and caught the eye of more than a few
military leaders, primarily because of its author's impressive service
background. The piece has since been cited by numerous antiwar writers as "proof" that the Vietnam-era military nearly disintegrated.

By the time the first fragging articles began appearing in U.S. newspapers, relations between the military services and the media had significantly deteriorated. What became known as the "credibility gap,"
the rift that emerged between the official information disseminated by
the Department of Defense on one side and the reporters' own observations and sources on the other, dated back to the early 1960s. Many
journalists believed that the military's information offices were providing them with a falsified picture of the war that did not reflect the real-
ities they saw in the field. Military leaders, on the other hand, charged
that certain journalists' personal opposition to the war was finding its
way into their reporting, leading them to concentrate on the bad news
"to the exclusion of all other events which might present a balanced
picture" of the conflict. As they saw it, the fraggers, drug users, and
racial militants grabbed headlines while those soldiers who quietly did

their jobs and stayed out of trouble were ignored. "The media may well create the monster rather than describe it," one general argued.[102] Accordingly, their responses to press queries regarding morale and discipline were often grudging.[103] This was no better illustrated than when army officials learned that CBS reporter Morley Safer planned to visit South Vietnam in early 1971 to do a story on Vietnamization. Ever since his controversial report regarding the marine assault on Cam Ne in 1965, senior officials had had their suspicions about the Canadian-born Safer; one complained that the journalist possessed "a strong anti-military bias."[104] On the eve of his visit, a memorandum was circulated warning that Safer was coming and "was planning a feature on 'fragging' incidents among American G.I.s." When the press learned of the memo and began reporting on it, MACV sheepishly took "corrective action" in the matter by reemphasizing its commitment to good relations with the press and apologizing to CBS.[105]

The first in-depth journalistic analysis of fragging was written by reporter Eugene Linden, who journeyed to Vietnam and visited several army units plagued by the assaults. Linden spoke with army lawyers and counselors on the subject and even interviewed convicted fragger Vance D. Thompson, whose court-martial had just ended.[106] The reporter published his findings in a January 1972 *Saturday Review* cover story that "generated extensive national interest." His insights were so esteemed in official circles that the article was circulated among the USARV command group, and an investigator from the House Internal Security Committee sought him out for an interview during a probe of alleged subversion of the armed forces.[107]

Much of the period journalism involving fragging followed the same basic line. Reporters usually began their pieces with definitions of the term "fragging" or graphic accounts of particular incidents. These were followed by army statistics concerning the frequency of the incidents and command reaction to them. Many of the articles then pointed to fragging and other disciplinary problems plaguing the services and concluded with predictions of an even gloomier future for the military in Vietnam. Overall, however, the mainstream press coverage provided by the major news outlets was generally accurate; indeed, the fragging phenomenon was certainly *news*, as it was unprecedented in the history of American arms, produced a considerable number of casualties, and posed a significant command concern.[108] The correspondents used military sources almost exclusively when preparing their articles and could usually find officials willing to provide them with commentary on the subject.

The early months of 1971 saw the fragging phenomenon reach its crescendo. It peaked in March, when twenty-six actual and nine possible assaults were counted.[109] News of fragging had been widely reported in the United States by this time and the military was well aware of the problem, but March was so bad that even the brass outside Vietnam complained.[110] It was at this time that one particularly gruesome incident was brought to the attention of an influential legislator at home. This story, which stretched from the steamy jungles of Vietnam to rural Montana and eventually on to the halls of Congress, is deserving of closer scrutiny.

Enter Senator Mike Mansfield

During the early morning hours of 15 March 1971, a disgruntled soldier of the 1st Cavalry Division lobbed a fragmentation grenade into an officer billet at Bien Hoa Army Base. Lieutenants Thomas A. Dellwo and Richard E. Harlan were killed in the explosion and a third officer was injured. Dellwo's distraught parents were so incensed by their son's death that they informed their senator of the incident, and it just so happened that this legislator was Senate Majority Leader Mike Mansfield, one of Washington's most influential power brokers and a stern opponent of American involvement in Vietnam.

Michael Joseph "Mike" Mansfield dedicated most of his adult life to government service. Born in 1903, he left his Montana home at age fourteen to join the navy during the First World War. He went on to serve in both the army and the Marine Corps in what was surely one of the most unusual military careers in American history (he enlisted in every branch of the service that existed at that time). After returning home, Mansfield studied history at the University of Montana and eventually secured a teaching position there, focusing his attention on Far East studies. Elected to Congress in 1942 and to the Senate a decade later, he became known for his low-key, bipartisan approach to foreign affairs. Initially a fervent supporter of Ngo Dinh Diem and his fledgling Republic of Vietnam, Mansfield gradually came to oppose U.S. involvement in Southeast Asia, and by the early 1960s he numbered among the war's first congressional foes. While continuing to publicly support Presidents Kennedy and Johnson and their Vietnam policies, he privately engaged in myriad attempts aimed at preventing the conflict's escalation. Though it was Kennedy who had appointed Mansfield majority leader and Johnson who served as a mentor to him during their years in the Senate, both presidents consistently rejected his views on the war; Johnson disparagingly referred to one of the many memoranda on the subject that he received from the Montanan as "milquetoast."[111] Mansfield supported President Nixon's plan for Vietnamization in 1969 but eventually soured on the idea and broke with Nixon after the controversial April 1970 invasion of Cambodia. The senator then engaged in frequent public criticism of the administration's policies in the region and leveled threats of congressional budget cuts in order to end the war.[112]

On 20 April 1971, Mansfield and fellow Montanan Lee Metcalf opened the Senate's daily business with harrowing accounts of Lieutenant Dellwo's death and revealed recently tabulated army fragging statistics. "What failure of order within our armed forces, may I ask first of all," a shaken Mansfield said, "has produced the kind of atmosphere that resulted last year alone in 209 'fraggings'? Even more important: What has caused this rather widespread and total disregard for human life and limb among our American soldiers? And what can be done about it?" He also took the opportunity to reiterate his desire for an end to the war and the draft while eulogizing his fallen constituent:

> In every respect, this young Montanan had every right and every reason to live. Like many other young men today, he volunteered for service in Southeast Asia to carry on a war, not of his making or choice, but prosecuted pursuant to policies formed and implemented here in Washington.
>
> Right now, my thoughts and deepest sympathy go out to a young widow and to a family back in Montana. Nothing can rectify their loss,

or the nation's. How inadequate is it to say we hope his assassin is apprehended, convicted, and receives just punishment for this craven act of violence? I have great faith in the system of military justice, but justice is very little compensation to the loved ones he leaves behind.

I received a copy of a letter which [Mrs. Dellwo's] son had written to her. It is a most eloquent letter but I shall not read it to the Senate because I consider it confidential. Her closing sentence contains the expression "May God have mercy." I can think of no better explanation at this time; nor one more appropriate to this entire matter.

Senator Metcalf followed:

This young Montanan, this soldier, was one of my nominees for West Point. He was anxious to serve his country. He was president of his church group and finished high school as president of the student body. When he was sent to West Point, he again attained popularity among his classmates. . . . He graduated from the Military Academy near the top of his class, served on the honor committee, and completed ranger training. . . . He was a talented musician, a boy who, had he been allowed to return to Montana, would have achieved an eminent career and would have been an outstanding citizen of this country.

Yet, in a senseless and insane moment, he was killed by a haphazard and random demonstration of an enlisted man who threw a hand grenade into an officers' barracks. I am certain, from going over the record and over his attainments and his achievements as an officer, that the hand grenade was not directed at this young man. It was just an insane and senseless gesture on the part of some young enlisted man who resented the activities of the officers who were in his command. This young Montanan was an outstanding officer, one of the finest officers of his grade and rank in the army.

The death of this boy is attributable to all of us. This insane and senseless action of one soldier in Vietnam is just a part of an insane and senseless war that should be brought to an end immediately. It is a cancer that is growing in the heart of America, and activities such as fraggings are only symptoms of what is going to continue if we do not get out of our involvement in Southeast Asia.

My heart goes out to the parents and to the wife of this very talented and able young man. We in the United States have lost the abilities of a fine, patriotic boy, but we are losing more than that in continuing this crazy action in Vietnam. We are losing the confidence of the American people. We are going to have a continuation of the involvement of these symptoms of senseless activity because we are perpetuating and continuing a senseless war.

So all I can say to the family of this fine boy is that they have my heartfelt sympathy. He died just as surely for his country had he died in a helicopter crash or receiving gunfire from the Viet Cong.

I say to my colleagues in the Senate: Let this be the beginning of the end of our involvement in Southeast Asia so that these things will not occur again.

Republican Charles Mathias of Maryland added:

I take these few moments to express my very deep, personal sympathy to the family of this young officer who has died so tragically, and also to the families of all the other servicemen who have died in similar incidents in Vietnam—all too many of them.

Mr. President, I would suggest that today the distinguished majority leader has, in a sense, made history because, for the first time to my knowledge, he has surfaced the word "fragging" on the Senate floor.

In every war a new vocabulary springs up. They are often words that are happy, words that are fun. I remember during World War II that "qidunk" became the word for ice cream and "gizmo" became the universal word for any kind of new gadget we did not quite understand. But in all the lexicon of war there has never been a more tragic word than "fragging." It implies total failure of discipline and the depression of morale, the complete sense of frustration and confusion, and the loss of goals and hope itself. I join the distinguished majority leader in his resolve and determination to see this evil, and all other evils that blight the spirit of man that have sprung from the miasmic swamps and bogs of Vietnam, be terminated with an end to this tragic war.

Senator Mansfield's closing remarks on the subject were as poignant as those ever spoken by any legislator:

> So many things have arisen out of Vietnam that bode ill for the American people and have from the beginning—"fragging," corruption, drugs, disease, casualties—now well beyond the 350,000 mark; not to mention the loss of treasure, which could be better spent in facing up to the problems of our people at home.
>
> An ill-starred adventure if there has ever been one—a most tragic and mistaken war. So many good, young men losing their lives, lives which could have been a credit to their nation for years and decades to come, lives which we can ill-afford to lose, and capabilities and careers which would have done much to map out the future of this country and help it to continue to be the great nation it should be and will be—God willing—with the passage of time.[113]

Despite their moving words, the lawmakers could do little but continue to urge that the ongoing U.S. withdrawal from Vietnam be completed as quickly as possible. As for the Dellwo case, twenty-two-year-old Private Billy Dean Smith was swiftly apprehended and charged with murdering the two young officers. Just as Senator Metcalf hypothesized, the authorities determined that Dellwo and Harlan were not the killer's intended victims; the actual targets, they believed, were the battery commander, Captain Randall L. Rigby, who had recommended Smith for an administrative discharge, and the battery first sergeant.[114] It was the fragger's apparent unfamiliarity with the officers' sleeping arrangements that cost the lieutenants their lives.

Due to the severity of the charges and Senator Mansfield's interest in the case, journalists from across the United States and even Europe covered Smith's court-martial.[115] Members of the antiwar movement also got involved and did what they could to assist in his defense. After the trial venue was moved from Vietnam to Fort Ord, California, sympathizers formed the Billy Dean Smith Defense Committee and several notable antiwar personalities made public appearances for him, including black activist Angela Davis and members of the Vietnam Veterans

Against the War.[116] Prominent Los Angeles attorney Luke McKissack volunteered pro bono legal representation. When the defense found itself short of funds, Hollywood actor Burt Lancaster came forward and donated $3,000.[117] Unsurprisingly, Smith's supporters proved to be anything but shy when it came to discussing their cause with the press; among other things, they accused the army of racism and rank privilege in its handling of the case. They pointed to the fact that while Private Smith, who was black, spent his pretrial confinement in a cramped prison cell, First Lieutenant William L. Calley, Jr., a white officer who had been convicted of murder in the My Lai case, received special permission from President Nixon to live in his private officer quarters both before his trial and after his conviction, pending appellate review.[118]

Smith's trial finally convened in September 1972. Prosecutors were determined to seek the death penalty in the case, arguing for its inclusion even after the Supreme Court's recent *Furman v. Georgia* decision, but the military judge rejected this possibility. The government's case against Smith was entirely circumstantial: it centered on several witnesses who claimed to have heard the accused threaten Captain Rigby and the first sergeant, and later say that he "didn't mean to kill the two lieutenants," as well as a grenade pin that was found in his pocket shortly after the incident occurred. Tool marks scratched into the pin, the army alleged, matched those found on the grenade's safety lever, which had survived the explosion and was found at the crime scene. The defense countered that a number of the prosecution's witnesses were unreliable and that CID agents had limited their investigation to Smith while ignoring other potential suspects. The grenade pin, McKissack argued, had been planted on his client by investigators. For a time, the trial was dominated by the testimony of dueling tool mark experts, each offering differing opinions on whether or not the pin could be proven to be that of the grenade used to kill the two officers.

The trial dragged on for weeks before finally concluding in mid-November. In the end, Smith was acquitted of the two murders. Even his conviction of the relatively minor charge of assaulting a military policeman was subsequently overturned on appeal. He was immediately released from the Fort Ord stockade, having spent nearly two years in pretrial confinement.[119] Following his discharge, Smith returned to his native Los Angeles, where he was arrested a number of times over the years and earned separate convictions in 1996 and 2004 that would hardly have surprised the army; the charge both times: assault with a deadly weapon.

The early months of 1971 saw the Marine Corps preparing to leave Vietnam. By the end of June, the marines were gone, having turned over their tactical responsibilities to the army and South Vietnamese troops. Five fraggings are known to have occurred in marine units in 1971, resulting in at least one injury.[120] One of these assaults took place in the 1st Division within a week of its departure in mid-April.

Although army strength in Vietnam dropped to fewer than 200,000 men by year's end, an unprecedented 222 actual assaults took place in 1971, while an additional 111 were listed as possible assaults. Seven Americans and five Vietnamese were killed in these incidents, although only four of the Americans, three officers and an enlisted man, were victims of intentional homicide. This low number of fatalities suggests a sort of change in the nature of the phenomenon. One general reported that "even though the numbers [of fraggings] have gone up, the actual number of deaths and injuries [has] gone down in proportion. There is a pattern that would indicate to me many are more in terms of intimidation."[121] Military police blotters reveal incidents of GIs leaving ordnance in or near the living areas of their adversaries with affixed written threats exhorting them to change their behavior. One such note, found attached to a Claymore mine, read, "There is more where this came from. Keep your shit up lifer and find out."[122] Staff Sergeant Dick T. Price of the 37th Signal Battalion found a trip flare on his bunk inscribed with the words, "Price, the next one won't be so simple." Another sergeant discovered one signed, "From Black America. [You're] shorter than you think."[123]

Despite the significant decrease in fatalities, however, fragging continued to plague the army in Vietnam. During 1972, twenty-eight actual assaults and thirty-one possible assaults were noted. Three deaths were counted, two GIs and one Vietnamese, but investigation revealed only one of the Americans to be a victim of an intentional homicide.

This was First Sergeant Johnny C. Martin of F Troop, 4th Cavalry, who was murdered with a Claymore mine on 11 May. Private Claude B. Johnson was sentenced to life imprisonment for the crime, but after serving five years in confinement, he won a new trial on appeal and eventually saw the murder charged dismissed, as several prosecution witnesses were no longer available to testify. He was immediately released from the Leavenworth stockade and admitted to a Veterans Administration hospital to continue psychiatric treatment he had been receiving in prison.[124]

Nearly all of the 1972 grenade incidents took place during the first half of the year. Indeed, the fragging statistics from January through May looked little different from those of the previous three years. With the departure of the last remaining large ground combat units, however, the incidents finally came to an end. There were no actual assaults observed during June or July and only one occurred in August. No figures are available for September and October, but while November is known to have sustained one actual assault, December boasted no incidents at all.[125]

The last recorded fragging incident that occurred in Vietnam took place on 5 February 1973 at Camp Holloway, when Specialist Four Roger R. Crout and Private First Class Carl K. Fraine of the 57th Aviation Company detonated a fragmentation grenade near a billet where two of the unit's cooks were sleeping. Both victims sustained minor injuries and investigators quickly arrested the malefactors. Crout and Fraine admitted the act but denied any malicious intent, claiming that they "threw the grenade in the air just to see it explode, without intending to injure anyone or to destroy any property." The authorities chose to believe them, for charges against Fraine were dropped when it was learned that he had attempted to talk Crout out of tossing the grenade, and Crout, who was convicted by special court-martial, was only fined $400.[126]

When Specialist Crout's court-martial adjourned in mid-February, America's involvement in Vietnam had all but ended. The last U.S. troops departed in March in accordance with the Paris peace accords and the South Vietnamese were left to go it alone. The ARVN toed the line at first but Hanoi's 1975 spring offensive ultimately proved to be too much for them. Communist forces rolled into Saigon and overcame the last South Vietnamese resistance on 30 April. The Second Indochina War was over.

Conclusion

During the war's early years, what became known as fragging was practically unknown in the U.S. military. Those few incidents that did occur were exceptional events so rare that they did not warrant command-level preventative action. By late 1968, however, the situation had changed, and fraggings began to take place in alarming numbers. Even as units rotated home and casualties decreased, the number of incidents continued to rise. This was due to the troops' increasing frustration that they were still in Vietnam so long after the withdrawal began. Fragging peaked in March 1971, exactly three years after President Johnson made his television address in which he spoke of "peace in Vietnam." In fact, many of the 1971 fraggers were still in high school when LBJ spoke these words, and some of the young enlisted men who were in Vietnam during the final months of the U.S. involvement were barely teenagers at the time.

Another remarkable aspect of the fragging phenomenon was that as Vietnamization wore on and incidents increased in frequency, the number of fragging deaths actually decreased. In 1971, for example, the number of actual assaults surpassed those of the previous two years, yet the number of fatalities fell to less than half of their respective 1969 and 1970 numbers. The theory that more of the later incidents were meant to intimidate rather than to kill seems to be the best explanation for this incongruity. The fact that so many of the earlier cases resulted in deaths or injuries was enough to convince leaders that the fraggers meant business, and this in turn further encouraged those enlisted men who were at odds with their superiors to use the threat of fragging as a bargaining chip to renegotiate the power structure within their units. Some even found that they could make their points with nonlethal smoke or chemical grenades. Tragically, those who persisted in using fragmentation grenades or deadly Claymore mines to do the job often missed their intended targets and struck innocent bystanders with their ordnance. Of the four 1971 fragging fatalities, three of the victims were believed to have been uninvolved in the disputes that led to the assaults, while insufficient information was available for investigators to make a judgment regarding the circumstances of the fourth.[127]

Although fragging incidents began to occur in significant numbers during the last half of 1968, it was not until early 1971 that the news media began reporting at length on the problem. The coverage may have seemed sensational to some but the articles that appeared generally had the facts right and described a personnel issue that was of significant concern and to which there was no end in sight. The military was surely loath to see its morale and discipline problems made public, particularly by the news media it had come to distrust. Blame for such issues as drug abuse and racial tension could be easily laid upon civil society as a whole, as it too was grappling with these problems, but no convenient explanations were forthcoming in the case of the fragging phenomenon. The Nixon administration was probably even less desirous of media scrutiny in this area, for international attention on the army's woes could only harm the U.S. negotiating position as peace talks with the North Vietnamese were conducted in Paris. But the fraggers were undeterred by these developments and continued to ply their deadly trade.

Of the several hundred fragging incidents that occurred in Vietnam, the 1971 double murder of Lieutenants Dellwo and Harlan attracted the most attention. Its gruesome nature, Senator Mansfield's public interest in the case, activist support for defendant Billy Dean Smith, and the subsequent court-martial all contributed to its notoriety. The case possessed pointed reminders of what went wrong in Vietnam: the unpopular draft, drug use, the racial aspect, and the authority crisis. The judge's decision to grant a rare venue change resulted in a stateside trial that served to illuminate the rift that Vietnam created in American society. As Smith's young supporters voiced criticisms of everything military to the press, the rest of the nation could only look on in horror at what the war had done to its armed forces.

CHAPTER THREE

Motives for Madness

W HAT caused the fragging phenomenon? Why did it occur in Vietnam and not during America's other wars? The answers lie in the changes that took place within what sociologist Charles C. Moskos, Jr., called the "enlisted culture" of the U.S. military.[1] These changes were reflections of both the armed forces and the civil society from which they emerged, as well as the particular conditions and attitudes prevalent in Vietnam during the later years of the war.

To begin with, "enlisted culture" is a reference to the primary group dynamic that is generated by the enlisted personnel within every unit in the military. It encompasses their backgrounds and societal influences as well as their interaction with each other, their military superiors, and their environment. Officers and career NCOs are normally excluded from this circle, as its membership is limited to those bonded by a common vantage point of shared organizational status and experience. In the U.S. military, the group is traditionally composed of males in their late teens or early twenties from working-class families, although the induction of large numbers of older draftees from other social strata during major wars has served to alter its composition. The enlisted culture is in a perpetual state of flux as its membership constantly changes. Veteran troops, who usually serve as the group's opinion leaders, leave the unit and are replaced by new men who bring with them the latest societal influences and opinions. In time, they too are internalized and incorporated into the group. Environmental changes at the policy level (such as escalation or de-escalation in the case of Vietnam) and the local level (transfers of certain superiors, changes in a unit's immediate mission or location, etc.) also weigh heavily in influencing the enlisted culture.

While the individual soldier maintains personal consciousness, the influence of the enlisted culture upon the soldier's social personality is significant. Each seeks to be accepted by peers and this desire helps to shape the soldier's attitudes and actions. Indeed, research on fighting men from World War II through Vietnam indicates that one of the primary influences and motivators is the peer group.[2] Several congressmen who toured U.S. military installations in Vietnam found that "peer group pressure 'to be one of the boys' was strong. The young man, seeking to establish his own identity, looks to join a group in which he will get approval and support."[3]

To most first-term enlistees and draftees, military service has proven to be unpopular. Traditionally, at least four of every five servicemen choose to leave the forces upon completion of their first enlistments. The reasons for their departures vary, though studies have found that the two strongest factors are the monotony of military life and resentment of the sweeping authority afforded to their superiors. While these factors have always generated cynicism within the ranks, the general sense of mission usually overrides them, and the military has been able to exercise sufficient social control among its junior members to allow the services to operate effectively. This was true during the world wars, Korea, and the Cold War as it progressed into the 1960s.

As we have seen, however, several factors combined to drastically change the Vietnam-era enlisted culture. Chronic personnel shortages forced the military to increase draft calls to fill the ranks. Changes in the Selective Service System in the spring of 1968 eliminated many of the deferments that students had used to avoid induction, and thus many post-Tet conscripts possessed college or even postgraduate degrees. These men tended to dislike military service as well as the war in Vietnam, and their often outspoken disapproval of both adversely affected the enlisted culture. Sociologist Kurt Lang wrote:

> Open criticism of the war [was] more concentrated among the educated. This same characteristic makes them less prone to commit a disciplinary offense. Nevertheless, their presence in large numbers can serve as a catalyst for the delinquency of others, who depend on firm authority to keep their own dispositions in check. Some such phenomenon was observed with the influx [of a large number of draftees] during the Korean War. Not only were these men better educated but they

were also more negative toward the military than were regular army personnel. Units with large numbers of draftees had higher delinquency rates than units where the number was small, yet it was the regulars and not the draftees who committed most of the offenses. The inference is that derogatory attitudes toward the army, openly expressed by many, changed the atmosphere sufficiently to trigger delinquency by others who were previously well-behaved.[4]

In addition to changes in the draft, there was another personnel decision that served to change the enlisted culture. In 1964, the President's Task Force on Manpower Conservation published a study it had conducted of the nation's male draft-age population. The task force found that 35 percent of the men it studied would likely be rejected for induction into the armed forces owing to their failure to meet the military's physical, mental, or moral standards. Indeed, the services rejected thousands of applicants each year on the grounds that they had failed to score in the top three categories of the Armed Forces Qualification Test (AFQT). Secretary of Defense Robert S. McNamara believed that some of these men could perform adequate service if given the chance while gaining valuable job training and experience. In 1966, he instituted Project 100,000, which revised military entrance standards. It called on the armed forces to annually induct 100,000 volunteers and draftees who had scored in the fourth category of the AFQT and would previously have been disqualified for service. From the time the program was launched on 1 October 1966 until its conclusion on 30 June 1971, Project 100,000 brought some 341,127 men into the military under its auspices.[5]

Although the Defense Department monitored the men's progress and found that most of them performed satisfactorily, the uniformed services detested Project 100,000.[6] At a time when technology was playing an increasingly greater role in military affairs, the forced induction of low-aptitude men into the ranks could hardly have been viewed in a favorable light. Though initial fears that the services would be compelled to turn away more-qualified applicants in order to meet their mandated accession quotas proved to be unfounded,[7] a significant minority of the "Category IV" personnel simply failed to make the grade. Statistics submitted by the army to a congressional subcommittee

indicated that Project 100,000 soldiers were convicted by court-martial
at a rate of over twice that of other troops.[8] A local study conducted at
the Qui Nhon Support Command found that its low-aptitude personnel "seemed to have lower stress tolerance and a relative lack of the
usual mechanisms for coping with stress." These men were referred for
psychiatric evaluation ten times as frequently as their higher-scoring
peers and nearly twice as many were considered for administrative discharges.[9] These shortcomings would have been tolerable at a time when
the military was not subjected to the great internal and external stresses
it faced during the Vietnam era, but during the 1969–1972 time frame,
Project 100,000 had the effect, as one officer put it, of tossing water on
a drowning man.[10]

As Vietnamization began, the war lost its sense of purpose in the
eyes of young enlisted men. At the same time, the strains that the long
conflict placed on the military's officer and NCO corps enabled societal
problems such as racial tension, illegal drug use, and the authority crisis to take on more prominent positions within the ranks. Without any
common purpose to unite them, relations between the leadership corps
and the enlisted ranks deteriorated, and a clear fracture divided the
troops into two camps. On one side stood the enlisted men, who had
grown up in a changing America and took a more questioning view of
both the war and the imbalance of power found within the military
hierarchy. The other group consisted of the command structure, which
consisted of men who for the most part belonged to an older generation
and had served for several years or more. Although many career soldiers eventually became pessimistic about the conduct of the war, they
still saw duty in Vietnam as *the army*, where institutional standards and
values were to be upheld and orders obeyed. This generated considerable resentment among the enlisted men, who felt that by serving in
Vietnam at all during the withdrawal was sacrifice enough. When the
enforcement of "unnecessary" or "stateside"-type regulations was determined to be overzealous, their usual griping about superiors escalated
to threats of physical violence. As one psychiatrist concluded, "The
prevalence and openness with which the assault of superiors was discussed by the troops provided an atmosphere that approached positive
sanction for such actions."[11]

It was within this hostile environment that emotionally unbalanced or immature individuals began acting out what more stable men resolved with loose talk. In his article "Fragging and Other Withdrawal Symptoms," Eugene Linden described a fragging incident in which "murder was not in [Private First Class Thompson's] heart, it was in the air. [He] is a passive man, easily impressed by the impulses of others."[12] After examining a fragger on trial for murder, a psychiatrist testified, "Depending on which way the wind was blowing was the way that [the accused] went."[13] A military defense counsel who represented another suspect described his client as a "follower" who was "of small stature, quiet and soft-spoken, and not assert[ive] in any manner."[14] A well-documented fragging in the 1st Marine Aircraft Wing that supports this thesis is the case of Private First Class Israel "Tony" Barrios.

On 21 June 1969, Master Gunnery Sergeant Fred L. Schaper became embroiled in a dispute with Private Ronnie E. Jiminez in a unit mess hall. Schaper, the mess sergeant, placed Jiminez on report and later testified at his court-martial, which resulted in the private's conviction and sentence to a brief stint in the brig. As he prepared to leave his unit, Jiminez confided his anger to his friend Tony Barrios, as a witness later testified:

> I was in the hooch when Jiminez, Barrios, and one or two other persons entered. . . . All of them appeared to be "high" on something. They began talking about an incident [in which] Jiminez had been thrown out of the mess hall by . . . the mess sergeant. Jiminez was saying that he hated that man and wanted to "get rid of him," and Barrios was repeating the words "Yeah, man" in response. Jiminez then walked over to his wall [locker] and took a fragmentation grenade from the top shelf. He then walked over toward Barrios, waving the grenade in his hand and saying, "Tony, I want you to do that man a job, I want you to blow him away." Barrios replied, "Yeah, man," and reached out and accepted the grenade from Jiminez.

On the evening of 1 July, a fragmentation grenade detonated between the mess hall and Sergeant Schaper's living quarters. No casualties were reported but authorities were unable to identify any suspects.

The case went unsolved for months until investigators finally located a marine who had overheard the original conspiracy. Barrios, who by this time had completed his tour of duty and returned to the United States, was hauled back to Vietnam to face trial. During his court-martial, he expressed remorse for his actions, conceding that he threw the grenade out of "a sense of false loyalty" to Jiminez. Recognizing the nature of the offense, the court convicted him not of attempted murder but of the reduced charge of assault with a dangerous weapon and sentenced him to a bad-conduct discharge, forfeitures of pay, and two years' hard labor. He was released in April 1971 after serving nearly nineteen months in confinement.[15]

The Barrios case involved an impressionable young man who acted not out of malice but manipulation. Though he had been disciplined for minor infractions in the past, Barrios would probably have completed his enlistment without fanfare had he not sought acceptance from a group of malcontented drug users whose violent tendencies set the stage for the crime that followed. The court-martial transcript tells the story: his friend Jiminez quarreled with the mess sergeant, conceived the idea for the fragging, and even supplied the grenade, yet it was Barrios who committed the crime. The situation must have posed something of a moral dilemma for him; he surely realized that the act was wrong, but his friend had handed him the grenade and told him what to do with it. One can almost hear him rationalizing, *I have to do it otherwise they'll think I'm chicken.* In the end, Jiminez's more dominant personality narrowly prevailed. The result was the halfhearted fragging in which the grenade was thrown from a considerable distance toward the sergeant's quarters and exploded harmlessly nearby. Ultimately, the only casualty in the affair was Barrios, who received a punitive discharge and spent almost two years in prison.

The Perpetrators

Fortunately for historians, the surviving documentary record of the Vietnam-era fragging phenomenon is considerable. Research in the holdings of various archives yields rich source material ranging from personnel records to criminal investigation files and court-martial transcripts.

But can textual records be used to construct a functional historical-sociological profile of the perpetrators? It could be argued that a racial militant serving in a frontline infantry company bore little resemblance to a drug user assigned to a support unit in a relatively secure rear area. Was an offender who threw his grenade in 1968 comparable to someone who committed a similar crime in 1972? The fact that some fraggers were apprehended while others were not further serves to cloud the picture; one military psychiatrist believed that this aspect "probably represents an important variable."[16]

In this study, I was able to identify fifty-four soldiers and seventeen marines, seventy-one men in all, who were convicted by military courts-martial of assaults with explosive devices against fellow servicemen in Vietnam. Offenders who employed nonlethal smoke or chemical ordnance were omitted from the survey, as such cases did not constitute serious attempts to kill or maim. Those who targeted Vietnamese nationals were also excluded. In order to test the data obtained from the textual documentation, I balanced it with the findings of Dr. Thomas C. Bond's clinical study, conducted at the Leavenworth stockade in 1972, of twenty-eight convicted fraggers. Finally, a rudimentary form of control was attained through comparisons with statistical data gleaned from a random sample of 470 army enlisted men who served in Vietnam in 1971, the year fragging reached its peak.[17] Although each individual fragging incident possessed its own unique set of personalities and environmental characteristics, I was able to assemble sufficient information to make some general observations about the perpetrators.

One of the most consistent similarities among the offenders was their youth. With an overall average age of twenty, a tabulation of the convicted fraggers' individual ages at the time they committed their offenses appears in Table 1 (page 68).

How do these numbers compare with the U.S. military in Vietnam as a whole? Data gleaned from the control sample of 470 army enlisted men reveals that 85 percent of them were twenty-three years of age or below when they arrived in Southeast Asia. As a group, the convicted fraggers were younger still, as some 92 percent of them had yet to reach their twenty-fourth birthdays at the time they committed their offenses, which in most cases was at least several months into their Vietnam

Table 1

Age	Number of Offenders
18	6
19	18
20	23
21	11
22	6
23	2
24	0
25	2
26	1
27	1
28	1

tours. Youthful immaturity traditionally plays a significant role in breaches of military discipline and these percentages help to explain both the presence of so many young men among the fraggers as well as the high overall court-martial rates observed during the Vietnamization period.[18]

The racial/ethnic composition of the convicted fraggers was at considerable variance with that of the control sample. Of the seventy-one men in this study, 56 percent were white, 36 percent were black, and 8 percent were Hispanic. The men in the control sample break down much differently, as 80 percent of them were white, 13 percent were black, 5 percent were Hispanic, 1 percent were Asian, and another 1 percent described themselves as "other."[19] This suggests that white servicemen were underrepresented among the fragging group, blacks overrepresented, and Hispanics relatively constant. Interestingly, the racial composition of the men in Bond's study was somewhat different, as there were only four blacks among his cohort of twenty-eight army fraggers.[20] This discrepancy can be attributed to two factors: first, a considerable number of minority offenders were observed among the marines included in this study, and, second, there is the time variable. When Bond conducted his study in mid-1972, many fraggers had already been released from confinement or transferred to the federal prison system. Nearly all of the soldiers convicted of fragging in 1971 and early 1972 were Caucasian and this provided a demographic different from those of earlier years when fewer Caucasians were convicted of the offense.

Most of the convicted fraggers were the products of broken homes. Their family histories were often so disturbing that the troubling details were offered in mitigation when the men faced military justice. One man's alcoholic father had beaten him and his mother until the couple divorced. The father then remarried but soon murdered his new wife, a crime for which he was sent to prison. For the traumatized son, leaving school and joining the army were means of escape.[21] Another man had been periodically shuttled between his divorced parents, his sister, a girlfriend's family, and a Canadian farm. He had then been returned to his physically abusive father, who had undergone years of psychiatric treatment subsequent to his combat service in the Second World War.[22] A third was the youngest of seven children in a home that was "marked by extensive conflict." His mother was an alcoholic who had attempted suicide several times and had once attacked her husband with a butcher knife. His parents eventually divorced and his father soon died.[23] One soldier's parents had divorced when he was three, after which he had been adopted by his grandparents. At age fourteen, he had been sent to live with a relative in Alaska, then to Utah, and eventually back to his adopted parents in Florida, where he enlisted in the army at age seventeen, having completed only ten years of formal schooling.[24] The records also reveal that at least forty-nine of the convicted fraggers, over two-thirds of the men in this survey, were high school dropouts. This does not compare favorably with the men in the control sample, 67 percent of whom graduated from high school.[25] Some had married but most were separated or divorced by the time they committed their offenses.

Historical studies of military offenders indicate that they were often in trouble with civil authorities before entering the armed forces. One such study of World War II general prisoners found that 58.6 percent of them "were known to have had at least one civil arrest for either a felony or a misdemeanor."[26] Of the fraggers profiled by Bond, the percentage was nearly identical: 57 percent admitted to prior civil arrests.[27] Servicemen of every era are familiar with the lore of borderline individuals being recruited into the armed forces by the civil justice system, and a number of the fraggers seem to have entered the military under these circumstances.[28] Based on available data, however, the civil offenses in question seem to be of a relatively minor, nonviolent nature. Of the men surveyed here, one man had been arrested for car theft,[29] another was a gang member who had been convicted of burglary,[30] and a third had been arrested for drug involvement.[31] Two of these individuals had been referred to authorities by their parents for ungovernability before joining the army. The fact that the men had only minor brushes with the law prior to their fragging convictions intimates that their violent behavior was controlled by an external element, namely Vietnam. After examining a fragger awaiting trial for murder, a psychiatrist wrote:

> The patient stated that he feels guilty only if he is caught doing something. Therefore, the major control of his behavior comes from without, that is society, not from within the patient himself. In an environment like the United States, this patient is generally able to control his behavior. This is evidenced by the fact that in civilian life he has had only minimal contact with the law. However, in an environment such as Vietnam, where combat is the order of the day, this particular patient cannot as effectively utilize the traditional controls of society against violence, and thus becomes much more dangerous.[32]

The "combat" atmosphere described in this case applies to the infantryman the psychiatrist examined, but what of the men serving in support units who never engaged the enemy yet committed similar crimes? Here again we must consider the changes in the enlisted culture that occurred during the later years of the war, for they appeared in units throughout the military irrespective of their assigned missions.

The military records I studied offer some data on the men's intelligence, specifically the scores they achieved on the Armed Forces Qualification Test. On the general technical (GT) section of the exam, which was the rough equivalent of the civilian IQ test, available scores on the surveyed fraggers reveal an average earned mark of 95, denoting "average" intelligence. Deviation in the scores is rather wide; they range from a low mark of 65 up to a lofty 143, which is higher than the scores attained by most servicemen, myself included. About one in six of the men placed in the Category IV range, which suggests (but does not definitively indicate) Project 100,000 affiliation. Unfortunately, the documentation used here does not specifically state if the men partook in the program. When Project 100,000 was first initiated, the army issued special service numbers to its "New Standards" men that identified them as participants in the program, but since the army discontinued the use of service numbers in mid-1969, identification is difficult, as many of the fraggers in this cohort entered the service after that time.

According to the military's *Manual for Courts-Martial*, all accused were presumed "initially to be sane and to have been sane at the time of the alleged offense." Those defendants whose mental states were in question received psychiatric evaluations from medical personnel. Shortly after his apprehension for murder and aggravated assault, Lance Corporal Gilberto Garcia attempted to jump out of a helicopter while en route to the Da Nang brig. Upon examination by a psychiatrist, he was found to be "dangerously psychotic."[33] No legal judgment was ever made in the case, however, as Garcia hanged himself while in pretrial confinement.[34] Ironically, had Garcia been judged unfit to stand trial, no disciplinary action would have been administered at all. In a 1969 case, Specialist Four Leon Carter of the 4th Infantry Division walked up to his company commander, First Lieutenant Ronald L. Kielpikowski, and killed him with his M16 rifle. Carter was subsequently declared "not responsible for his actions" and simply discharged from the army.[35]

A remarkable fragging case involving the issue of the perpetrator's mental state occurred in the 1st Marine Division in February 1969. Claiming that an unknown voice had taken control of his mind, Lance Corporal John W. Thomas tossed two grenades into a tent where several marines were sleeping. In the ensuing blast, Corporal Brian L. Wells was killed and another man was injured. Although defense counsel raised the issue of Thomas's sanity at his court-martial, a different motive for the killing also came to light:

Q. (Defense Counsel). Corporal Thomas, I direct your attention to
the early morning of 15 February. Would you explain to the court
what happened on that morning?

A. I was on my radio watch . . . and I was just watching the scope
trying to—I don't know, I was thinking about home; that's mostly
what I was thinking about. And a voice came in the back of my
head and told me to go over and pick up a grenade and kill Wells.
I walked over, I grabbed the grenade and I walked to the front of
the tent. I pulled the pin and I stood there with the grenade in my
right hand. I don't know, it just told me to kill Wells and my hand
started shaking. All of a sudden I popped out of it and I looked at
myself and I didn't know what to think. I thought it was kind of a
joke or something, I don't know. It just seemed real strange to me.
I put the pin back in the grenade and I put it back in the box, then
I walked back to the radar section. About a half hour later the
same voice came back and told me to go and pick up two
grenades. I went there; it told me to go directly to the tent, pull
the pins, and throw them in the tent. It was just growing stronger,
I can't explain it, it just kept getting louder and louder until I just
lobbed them in. And the minute that they came out of my hands I
realized what happened and I made a step into the door trying to
figure out where they went. I knew they were going to explode so
I turned around and made two or three steps and they blew up. I
ran back inside.

Q. How long has this voice been with you?

A. I can't remember how far back, sir.

Q. There's nothing you can do to prevent from happening what this
voice tells you what to do? It's supposed to happen?

A. No, sir. It just pops right out.

Q. During this period of time when this voice was talking to you, was
there any thought in your mind as to owing Corporal Wells any
money?

A. No, sir. The only thought in my mind was just that voice repeating
over and over, "Kill Wells."

Q. Was it your contention to kill Wells in order to get out of paying
him the $800.00 [that you owed him]?

A. No, sir. I believe it isn't.

Q. Going back to the discussion of the card game, you did in fact lose a great deal of money, is that correct?

A. Yes, sir.

Q. (Trial Counsel). Did you know that Wells was inside the tent?

A. Yes, sir.

Q. Did the voice tell you [how to commit the crime]?

A. It told me to pick up two grenades, sir.

Q. How did the voice know that two grenades were available?

A. I don't know, sir.

Q. Didn't you in fact pick up one grenade the first time?

A. Yes, sir.

Q. Why did you defy the voice the first time?

A. I don't know, sir. I popped out of it.

Q. Well, did the voice say, "Forget that last order?"

A. No sir, it didn't.

Q. But the voice never told you not to throw the grenade?

A. I'm not a zombie, sir. The voice takes control of me. I'm me but I'm really not.

Q. When was the last time you were in communication with your voice?

A. [During] the leave just before I come over to the 'Nam, sir. It was just about two months or something like this.

Q. What did the voice tell you to do at that time?

A. Go outside for a walk. I was watching some TV program that I was interested in and it just said, "Go outside for a walk."

Q. So, it's a kind of thing, you're sitting watching [a] TV program and, "Self, I think I'll go out for a while." So, you get up and go out?

A. It don't say that, sir. It's like a command. It tells me to, it don't ask me to.

Q. Has the voice ever told you to kill anyone before?

A. No, sir. This is the first time.

Thomas's story further unraveled when a witness testified that shortly before the murder he overheard Thomas say that if Wells were to be killed, then he, Thomas, would not have repay him the debt.

Unfortunately, no one took the statement seriously. The court eventually concluded that Thomas was able to distinguish right from wrong. "He knew that the grenades were going to explode," one court member reasoned. "[He] did not suffer from any psychosis." Thomas was convicted of premeditated murder and aggravated assault, and was sentenced to life imprisonment at hard labor. He was able to win a new trial on appeal but was reconvicted and was not released until 1978.[36]

Although the men who were tried and convicted of fraggings were found to be legally sane, a certain number of them did suffer from various personality disorders. The Marine Corps believed that such instability played a significant role in fragging offenses. "Frequently," read their profile, "the act is preceded by evidence of increasing personality disorders, either psychopathic or emotionally unstable in nature."[37] Dr. Bond found most of the convicted fraggers in his study to possess passive-aggressive personalities; they tended to shy from direct confrontations with figures they perceived as powerful and saw the hand grenade as an equalizer.[38] An American Division psychiatrist who examined David K. Locklin found: "The accused does not exhibit any psychotic disorder and does not exhibit any overwhelming neurotic tendencies. What he does exhibit is a character and behavior disorder of the anti-social or sociopathic type. . . . These are the types of people that comprise most juvenile delinquents, most criminals, and they are often said not to have a conscience. They are not very concerned with consequences and maintain a sort of day-to-day existence."[39]

Similar characteristics, especially the perceived lack of conscience, came to light as investigators interviewed Lance Corporal Gary A. Hendrix a few hours after he murdered a sergeant:

> Investigator: Why did you do this to Sergeant Tate? Did you dislike him?
> Hendrix: I dislike all lifers, including Gunnery Sergeant Gray,
>   Sergeant Tate, and Sergeant Smith.
> Investigator: Was this a spur of the moment thing?
> Hendrix: No, I've been thinking about it since I got here.
> Investigator: Did you mean to put the grenade outside the bunker to
>   scare the people inside?
> Hendrix: No, I meant to push it inside the bunker.

Investigator: Are you sorry that you killed Sergeant Tate?

Hendrix: No. I wanted to get all of them.

A military psychiatrist diagnosed him as an "immature personality with a marginal respect for social values."[40] Roger L. Aubert had been an "emotionally disturbed" child who was formally diagnosed as possessing a "character and personality disorder." Medication was prescribed but he was "continually in trouble." While growing up, he had difficulties with his teachers and was repeatedly expelled from school. After joining the army, he received eight nonjudicial punishments in less than two years.[41] Michael S. Crampton had been committed to a psychiatric center at age ten, as he "had extreme difficulty getting along with people, even children his own age."[42]

Owing to the frustrations and failures they experienced before entering the military and while in the service, the fraggers were often given to displacing their anger onto those occupying positions of authority, and tended to feel morally justified in performing their acts. As the Vietnam enlisted culture often provided an atmosphere that seemed to approve of such actions, they did not view fragging as murder. Eugene Linden observed that one of the men he profiled in his fragging article did not consider himself a criminal. "The magnitude of what he attempted still escapes him. [He] could not believe that he had committed a crime."[43] In another case, "expert testimony at trial indicated that the accused [Specialist Finch] lacked judgment, possibly to such a degree as to negate the ability to understand the consequences and implications of his act in throwing a grenade into the building wherein Platoon Sergeant Charles W. Ganus was sleeping."[44] Following his attempt to kill two sergeants with a homemade bomb studded with metal spikes, Private First Class William J. Schott wrote an angry letter to his commanding officer: "For some deep inset [sic] reason you feel that you want to destroy me. You want to put me in prison for four or even more than four years. . . . Just what kind of man do you think you are and would feel like after you did something like that? Why do you want to put this on my back?" Schott was sentenced to five years in confinement.[45]

Although the Vietnam War ultimately became deeply unpopular in American society, one would not draw such a conclusion from the fraggers' records. Most of the men profiled in this study volunteered for military service; in the case of the Marine Corps, nearly all of the convicted fraggers had enlisted. I reviewed the files to see if any of their enlistments were draft-motivated and found only three cases.[46] When compared with the control group, of which only 54 percent volunteered for service, this aspect is indeed remarkable.[47] Once in the military, several of the men specifically requested duty in Vietnam.[48] However, these decisions were probably made for personal reasons rather than any sense of patriotism. Dr. Bond believed that the fraggers he interviewed "viewed enlisting in the army either as a way of escaping from problems at home that they were unable to resolve or an attempt to prove their masculinity and independence."[49] Those who volunteered for the elite marines or army airborne units endeavored to become "part of something mighty, glorious, and indestructible" while impressing hometown contemporaries.[50] When military life failed to provide them with the sense of fulfillment they were looking for, they lashed out at the authority figures they perceived to be responsible for their predicaments.[51] One man admitted that the reason he enlisted in the Marine Corps was to "go to Vietnam and kill some gooks." Soon after his arrival in the war zone, however, he became "very dissatisfied" in the unit he was assigned to. As it turned out, the only person he ever managed to kill was an American sergeant, one of "a bunch of lifers who fucked over everyone all the time."[52] Another man came to Vietnam "expecting a fantastic experience, but the only job he had was that of a truck driver."[53]

The fraggers usually wore the lowest enlisted ranks, although three sergeants were also convicted of committing these crimes. The men in this study break down as shown in Table 2 on page 77.

The military documents from which these figures were extracted also reveal that one of reasons why these men held such low ranks was because at least forty-eight of them had had brushes with the military justice system before committing their fragging offenses. All of the twenty-four men serving in grades E-1 and E-2 had been reduced in rank owing to previous disciplinary action. Private Lamont Spears, for example, had received two nonjudicial punishments prior to an attempt to kill his company commander. While in pretrial confinement at the

Table 2

Rank	Number of Offenders
Private E-1	14
Private E-2 (USA)/Private First Class (USMC)	10
Private First Class (USA)/Lance Corporal (USMC)	23
Specialist Four (USA)	14
Corporal	2
Specialist Five (USA)	5
Sergeant	1
Staff Sergeant	2

Long Binh stockade, he was involved in a race riot that resulted in the severe beatings of several prisoners.[54] In fact, so many of the offenders performed poorly in their jobs and were prone to violence that a Marine Corps officer came to believe that alert commanders could sometimes foresee such incidents. "Investigations of acts of violence subsequent to their commission," he wrote, "reveal that in a large number of cases the behavior of the perpetrator prior to the crime made his ultimate action at least partially predictable. In most cases, he had been a marginal or submarginal marine, often with a record of offenses verging upon crimes of violence."[55]

The records also reveal each man's military occupational specialty, or MOS. These were the jobs the men were trained for during their first months in the service. The seventy-one convicted fraggers were schooled as shown in Table 3 (see page 78).

These data, while informative, should be viewed with caution. A number of men who were trained in their various specialties in the United States were assigned to very different duties after arriving in Southeast Asia. For example, one soldier who was trained as an infantryman was sent to Vietnam and assigned to an artillery battery as a cannoneer. Later, he was transferred to another battery in which he served as a Hawk Missile crewman.[56] A marine who was trained as an artilleryman suddenly became a supply specialist after reaching his new unit.[57] A marine grunt who arrived in Vietnam in 1970 was assigned to an aviation squadron and worked as a security guard at an

Table 3

Specialty	Offenders
infantrymen	15
armor crewmen	2
artillerymen	5
engineers	7
communications specialists	8
air defense artillerymen	2
aviation maintenance workers	11
motor vehicle operators	5
vehicle mechanics	6
supply specialists	4
food service specialists	4
personnel specialists	1
medical specialists	1

airfield.[58] Another man who was schooled as a mechanic was instead assigned to work as a cook.[59] After undergoing weeks of training as a pioneer, a soldier arrived in Vietnam only to become a truck driver.[60] But in spite of these alternate duty assignments, the data still provide us with a reasonably accurate environmental reflection of the fragging phenomenon. We have seen that most grenade incidents occurred in rear-area support units rather than frontline infantry outfits that engaged the enemy. Of the seventy-one convicted fraggers surveyed here, only fifteen were infantrymen and several of these were not assigned to infantry units when they committed their offenses.

A closer look at those fraggers who did serve in combat units reveals that in many cases their performances on the battlefield were undistinguished to say the least. Reginald F. Smith's fire team leader wrote, "Smith had been a coward from the time he first joined the company. He was scared to death to stand watch by himself even when we knew that things were safe or quiet."[61] A sergeant who served with Vance D. Thompson called his performance "a little below average" relative to the other members of his unit.[62] Accordingly, decorations for battlefield heroism were few among the surveyed men. Military records reveal that two of them were awarded the Army Commendation Medal with Combat "V." Thomas J. Benoit received his for "diving into a submerged personnel carrier and retrieving valuable equipment."[63] Gilberto Hernandez was awarded his in recognition of his heroic actions during a fierce 1969 firefight. After his machine gun malfunctioned, an unarmed Hernandez left his forward position to secure a replacement. Dodging enemy fire, he managed to obtain another weapon and additional ammunition. He then returned to his post and applied withering suppressive fire on the enemy, forcing them to withdraw.[64] The combat record of Alan G. Cornett, Jr., was exceptional by any standard and will be discussed below.

"We have [fragging] suspects that we know are drug users," said Brigadier General Elmer R. Ochs, commander of the 173d Airborne Brigade.[65] Of four fraggings that occurred in the 1st Brigade, 5th Infantry Division during the first eight months of 1970, searches of the suspects' living quarters uncovered varying amounts of marijuana and other drugs in all four cases.[66] A number of the fraggers had begun using drugs long before entering the military and continued to do so while in the service. David K. Locklin had abused drugs from the age of "about fifteen or sixteen. After coming into the army, his drug use increased considerably. In Germany he was using hashish, LSD, and speed. Before [murdering Captain Schneider, he] was smoking a lot of [marijuana]. He was consuming about one bottle of Obesitol a day."[67] Reginald F. Smith had used "marijuana, cocaine, opium, and various pills" since the age of fourteen and a search of his personal items conducted by military police following his arrest revealed over four hundred marijuana cigarettes.[68] "When we weren't on night patrol, we smoked grass pretty regular," admitted Gary A. Hendrix.[69] A witness at Private Sammy Wynn's court-martial testified that the accused "had taken some opium, smoked several pipe bowls of marijuana, and seemed exceptionally high" on the night he committed his crime.[70] Another man was convicted of possessing morphine, and two fraggers from the 26th Engineer Battalion confessed to extensive use of heroin, one claiming that he "had been using it for a couple of years" and "didn't remember much of what happened" on the night of the incident because of his habit. He endured withdrawal in the stockade.[71]

The records used to conduct this study reveal that eighteen of the surveyed men admitted to using drugs, with marijuana being the substance of choice. However, these sources do not provide sufficient data to form a complete picture. In many courts-martial, the accused pleaded guilty or accepted plea bargains and were not compelled to admit their drug use. While conducting his fragging study, Dr. Bond asked his subjects directly whether or not they used drugs, and found that 89 percent of them had at least experimented with illegal substances prior to their offenses.[72] This figure is considerably larger than the 69 percent of the control sample who had smoked marijuana,[73] and dwarfs the number of users found in a 1970 military drug study, which concluded that about 38 percent of its cohort had used drugs in Vietnam.[74] It also suggests that the convicted fraggers were in many ways similar to the military's portrait of what they viewed as a typical drug user: "Age: 19–22, rank E-4 or below, unmarried, less than a high school graduate, either draftee or non-career oriented enlistee, equally from field or support units on first overseas tour."[75] Although this description could fit thousands of men who did not abuse drugs or run afoul of military discipline in Vietnam, a pattern emerged among those who did. As one general said, "I don't know how many good marines might use drugs, but we do know that there is a very high correlation between the bad marines, the submarginal marines, and the drug users."[76] Another officer noted, "The chances are about as good that a high percentage of stockade candidates have tried marijuana as are the chances that the patients in an orthopedic ward have bone problems."[77] The military's sociological profile of the habitual drug user is similar to the fraggers: "These persons are generally from broken homes, have a lower education (are high school dropouts), have insufficient personalities to deal with their fears and stress (passive-aggressive personalities, immature, situational adjustment problems, low self-esteem, lack of long-term ambitions, etc.), and are likely to become involved in other behavioral problems within the military society."[78]

"During our visit to Southeast Asia," concluded one congressional panel, "we interviewed many people involved with chronic drug abuse, and without exception they had some 'hassle' or axe to grind with the military establishment."[79]

Many fraggers were actually under the influence of alcohol or drugs (or both) while carrying out their assaults, the substances serving to further impair their judgment and ease shaky nerves. Dr. Bond tells us that 87.5 percent of his subjects admitted to being intoxicated at the time of their offenses.[80] A military psychologist who examined Gary A. Hendrix testified: "[Hendrix] stated to me that [on the] night [of the murder] he had smoked at least five marijuana cigarettes and I can't help but think that given the suggestible nature of this man, this had a significant contribution to his being able to act out in that way. It may have released some of the control that he might have had and made possible for him to act in this fashion. I think the major reason why he did this isn't specifically because of marijuana but I think marijuana may have been just enough to cloud his thinking ability and make his already limited capacity to reason certainly not intact and perform an act which he thought very little of the consequences."[81]

Odd Men Out

While most of the offenders profiled in this study shared such like-nesses as age, rank, and substandard military performance, a small number of them served creditably and were not disciplinary problems prior to their fragging offenses. Among the exceptions was Specialist Four Thomas J. Benoit, who used a fragmentation grenade to kill a friend after a drunken argument. During Benoit's trial, his company commander and first sergeant testified that he had a clean record and was "a key man in the company."[82] Specialist Four John R. Lilly had completed one tour of duty in Vietnam as a mechanic and was awarded the Bronze Star (for merit, not valor). He was serving a second, apparently involuntary, tour in Southeast Asia when he threw a white phosphorus grenade at an officer.[83] Specialist Four Norman R. Shirley had been awarded the Army Commendation Medal, was recommended to attend a leadership course, and was next in line to become an NCO within his unit. At his court-martial, Shirley's former platoon leader declared that in spite of the seriousness of the offense, he "would have no objections to having the accused back under his command."[84] But it was twenty-eight-year-old Staff Sergeant Alan G. Cornett, Jr., who truly broke the mold of the "typical" fragger. A good soldier who had never been in trouble with either civil or military authorities, Cornett had finished high school and two years of college before enlisting in the army in 1965. He volunteered for the Special Forces and served multiple tours in Vietnam, receiving the Bronze Star with Combat "V," the Vietnamese Cross of Gallantry, the Combat Medic Badge, and a recommendation for the Silver Star.

In 1972, Sergeant Cornett was assigned to an advisory team that supported the South Vietnamese army. He soon came into conflict with his unit's executive officer, Lieutenant Colonel Donald F. Bongers, who disapproved of the sergeant's Vietnamese wife. Bongers proceeded to make Cornett's life miserable, forbidding him from leaving the team's compound on weekends or bringing his wife on post. At one point, he even took to observing Cornett's movements with binoculars. Cornett asked several superiors for assistance, including a colonel who served as the team's senior advisor, but was unable to resolve the matter. Believing that no one would help him, he took to drinking heavily. On the afternoon of 30 November, Colonel Bongers was seated in the team's radio room when Cornett tossed a grenade into the building. The colonel managed to jump clear of the blast and escape injury. After Cornett was taken into custody and charged with attempted murder, his distraught wife attempted suicide.

Fortunately for Cornett, several officers and senior NCOs appeared at his court-martial and testified to his good character as well as Colonel Bongers's harassment. Among them was a captain who stated that Colonel Bongers was "a very well-meaning individual but his handling of personnel leaves something to be desired. . . . I feel the accused was treated unfairly." Another captain said, "LTC Bongers seems to be more careful of how the accused spent his time than how other individuals did." A sergeant admitted, "LTC Bongers means well, but hurts people by concentrating on little things which generates hostility." Obviously impressed, the court sentenced Cornett to only one year of confinement. No punitive discharge was awarded, thus allowing him to remain in the military, and after his release, Cornett went on to serve for seventeen more years, retiring in 1989 with the rank of master sergeant.[85] In 2000, he published a memoir detailing his Vietnam experiences, and, to his credit, included an accurate account of the incident.

In its efforts to maintain required personnel strengths in Vietnam and elsewhere around the world, the armed forces were forced to accept many men who under other circumstances would have been found to be unsuitable for military service. With this in mind, it would be easy to dismiss the fraggers as yet another unwelcome burden brought upon the services by the war in Southeast Asia. While surviving documentation regarding the grenade throwers does indicate that most of them were mediocre soldiers at best, the presence of outliers like Sergeant Cornett among their ranks challenges any sweeping judgments regarding their performance. Perhaps the closest one can come to making an analysis in this regard would be to say that more often than not the fraggers were indeed substandard, but that a handful of them did perform reasonably well at their jobs and their crimes constituted aberrant behavior. Irrespective of their duty performance and varied individual situations, the fraggers' intended targets were often the same: their superiors.

The War against the Brass

The most significant aspect of the fragging phenomenon was the fact that the majority of the assaults were perpetrated by enlisted men against those occupying leadership positions. After reviewing Serious Incident Reports of 126 actual and possible fraggings that occurred in 1969, army officials determined that seventy of the incidents (56 percent) appeared to have been directed against officers or NCOs (or both), seventeen (13 percent) targeted enlisted men, seven were aimed at Vietnamese nationals (6 percent), and thirty-one (24 percent) were cases in which the intended victim could not be determined. Statistics for 1970 are similar.[86] Of forty-seven incidents that occurred in the 1st Marine Division in 1970, sixteen of the intended victims were identified and all of them were officers or NCOs.[87]

Leaders were usually the targets of the fraggers' grenades because the most significant conflict within the modern armed forces derives from superior-subordinate antagonisms.[88] Despite the fact that many

Vietnam-era officers shared their men's working-class origins and that the privileges of rank in the U.S. military were not as pronounced as those prevalent in other armies, the enlisted men were still products of a democratic society and often resented the authority granted to leaders because it paralleled class distinctions.[89] This sentiment was exacerbated by the differences in the training received by each. In his book *The Grunts*, former marine infantry officer Charles R. Anderson persuasively argues:

> The . . . immediate and telling differences between small unit leaders and troops had their origin in the training given each. Junior officers and NCOs in training are constantly urged to "take care of their men," to "think of the troops first." But troops and leaders settled on different definitions of this concept. To the latter it meant keeping each man functional in a combat sense. To the troops, however, taking care of them meant sparing no effort to soften the adversities with which combat presented them. The platoon sergeant and the lieutenant were somehow supposed to make the tour in combat go as easy as possible. In pursuing their own understanding of the take care concept, small unit leaders issued a constant stream of orders that seemed to the troops to make even less tolerable the adversities of life in the bush.[90]

When new leaders completed their training courses and were assigned to field units, the military employed such controls as inspections and evaluation reports to ensure greater investment in the larger organization—the army—than in their subordinates.[91]

As U.S. forces began to withdraw from Southeast Asia, many junior enlisted men became hostile toward those officers and NCOs who persisted in vigorous conduct of their missions. "They would kill you in a minute if you wanted to do the job right," lamented company commander Robin B. Heath. "Before long, I had a price on my head."[92] Leaders who wanted to fight were perceived as "ticket punchers" who sought to advance to the next rank at their men's expense. In infantry units, Anderson noted, the enlisted men feared that "they would get stuck with a lieutenant or platoon sergeant who would want to carry out all kinds of crazy John Wayne tactics, who would use their lives in an effort to win the war single-handedly, win the big medal, and get his picture in the hometown paper."[93]

The opposing views of officers and their men regarding "crazy John Wayne tactics" are clearly discernable when studying their reactions to a tactical innovation developed during a 1969 combat operation. Normally, when U.S. infantry units encountered fortified communist positions such as bunkers, they would fall back and allow mortar or artillery fire to "soften" the target before assaulting it. One company commander found this procedure to be ineffective, as it provided the enemy with an opportunity to withdraw and avoid casualties. He believed that the best tactic was to assault without supporting fires, and instead use the heavy weapons to strike targets *behind* the enemy positions, thereby cutting off their potential escape routes. Senior leadership loved the idea, as it allowed their units to close with the enemy and inflict maximum casualties upon them,[94] but to many of the junior enlisted men who were ordered to conduct the assaults, this amounted to suicide.[95] The company commander's argument that such measures ultimately saved American lives in the long term by killing more of the enemy meant nothing to the troops; by 1969, their only long-term objective in Vietnam was to safely complete their tours and return home.

The rift that developed within the ranks is further illustrated in a questionnaire that was administered to members of the Army Concept Team in Vietnam (ACTIV), which among other things was employed in research-and-development functions in the war zone. ACTIV officers and enlisted men were asked eight questions relevant to the fragging phenomenon. While the two groups agreed on some of the environmental factors that led to indiscipline, the responses reveal a divergence of opinion regarding responsibility and possible avenues of corrective action:

1. What do you believe is the reason for these activities (fraggings)?
Officer responses:
   a. Permissiveness
   b. Not enough activity during [Vietnamization]
   c. Lack of communication between leaders and subordinates
   d. Lack of discipline
   e. Rapid promotions; no experience to handle situations

Enlisted responses:
    a. Attitude toward officers
    b. Harassment
    c. Lack of leadership
    d. Too much time on hands
    e. Officers and NCOs act too superior
    f. Lack of discipline
    g. Lack of communication between ranks

2. What type of individual performs these activities?

Officer responses:
    a. Insecure individuals
    b. One who has experienced a history of frustration
    c. Drug addict
    d. Black power advocate, way to obtain equal opportunity

Enlisted responses:
    a. Individual at possible breaking point
    b. Psychologically abnormal
    c. React against authority
    d. Insecure or unbalanced individual

3. What type of individual is the victim of these activities?

Officer responses:
    a. Persons who are in authority
    b. Individual who fails to provide positive leadership
    c. Mostly officers and NCOs

Enlisted responses:
    a. Officers and NCOs
    b. Anyone in a leadership position
    c. Officer or NCO who thinks "They know it all"
    d. Individual who wants himself to look good at all costs
    e. Leader who lacks communications with men

4. What actions are required to prevent these activities?

Officer responses:
  a. Discipline and troop information program
  b. Improve communication between the grades
  c. Need vast improvement in the selection of leaders
  d. Eliminate [from the service] ring-leaders, break up unlawful assemblies
  e. Stop permissive approach [to discipline]

Enlisted responses:
  a. Understanding between superiors and subordinates; communication
  b. Stop harassment
  c. Better control of explosives
  d. Fairness and honesty at all times
  e. Allow enlisted men more initiative

5. In the event that these activities occur, what actions should be taken to locate and punish the guilty?

Officer responses:
  a. Punish individuals; don't suspend sentence
  b. Offer award for information on who was involved
  c. Interrogation by professional law enforcement officers
  d. Take closer look at amnesty program

Enlisted responses:
  a. Punish as required
  b. Try to find problem—interviews
  c. CID investigation
  d. Tighter control of explosives

6. Are these activities part of a larger problem? If yes, what is this problem?

Officer responses:
  a. Moral decay in society
  b. Drug problem

    c. Permissiveness

    d. U.S. Army not trying to win war; individuals sitting back waiting for DEROS [return to United States]

    e. Junior officers and NCOs lack experience

Enlisted responses:

    a. Breakdown in communications

    b. Poor leadership—all the way up the chain of command

    c. Officers and NCOs don't respect lower enlisted men

    d. Political and economic problems in US and RVN

    e. Lack of discipline

7. Do you have any *personal knowledge* of any of these activities? If yes, give appropriate details.

Officer responses:

    a. When I was in [unit redacted in survey], four CS grenades were thrown into the [officer quarters] . . . and in the MP building. . . . There was a general dissatisfaction with the methods that the MPs used [these were not explained] and with an officer who resided in the BOQ. Apparently it was a warning.

    b. Our unit first sergeant was fragged in his hooch. He was, I believe, wrong in his handling of the men and they hated him. He was more interested in police calls and haircuts than fighting the war. He never talked to the men and had a very haughty attitude.

    c. The [unit redacted in survey] had an incident while I was there. Their approach to a fragging was instant reorganization of suspected troublemakers. They handled threats by replying to the threatmaker, "I'm sorry you said that, I'll have to give that information at your court-martial if you carry out that threat." The potential fragger is now isolated and can't carry out his threat without fear of severe punishment. This approach seems to put the fragger on the defensive, which he abhors. He must feel that he is in the driver's seat.

    d. In the unit next to us the problems built over a long period of time until the enlisted men of the unit began to act almost together with "fragging" considered the only end. It was avoided by getting a new first sergeant and commanding officer who could communicate with the enlisted men.

Enlisted responses:

None

8. Do you have any other comments or recommendations?

Officer responses:

    a. Soldiers don't trust superiors

    b. Junior officers leave a lot to be desired

    c. Rapid promotions

    d. Emphasis should be placed on respect rather than authority

    e. Lack of discipline

    f. Less permissiveness on drugs; "Amnesty program"

Enlisted responses:

    a. Too much segregation between officers, NCOs, and lower enlisted men

    b. Discipline—must start at the top

    c. Adapt to needs of enlisted men

    d. Unnecessary hardships and harassment[96]

The scenario of an aggressive career officer being assaulted by disillusioned subordinates has become what many students of the Vietnam War see as the quintessential fragging incident, and the following case, in which the Marine Corps suffered its sole officer fatality attributed to fragging during the war, follows this line.

Reginald Floyd Smith was the seventh of ten children born to a ghetto family on Chicago's West Side. Claiming a lack of interest in academics, he left school and enlisted in the Marine Corps in February 1968. With the Tet Offensive in full swing, his duty assignments could hardly have come as a surprise: boot camp, infantry training, Vietnam. Initially, Smith probably seemed little different from the many thousands of men who were entering the ranks at the time; he managed to earn average ratings for conduct and proficiency while in training, and his personnel file reveals no evidence of any disciplinary infractions during his first few months in the service. In Vietnam, he was assigned to K Company of the 9th Marines, but after several bloody months in the jungle, he was determined to avoid any further combat service. During Operation Dewey Canyon, he intentionally broke his left hand and was medivacked from the battlefield.[97] He then falsified a sick-bay record in an attempt to remain on light duty, and later absented himself from his unit for over a week. When his superiors finally caught up with him, Smith received "office hours," marine jargon for nonjudicial punishment under Article 15 of the Uniform Code of Military Justice. The sentence: reduction in rank and a return trip to his outfit.[98] This hardly deterred the wily Smith, who promptly re-broke his hand and was again evacuated from the field. He eventually joined several other "wounded" marines who occupied the company rear area at Quang Tri Combat Base, including one who had broken his own finger and another who had injected saliva into his knee. The men whiled away their days smoking marijuana and avoiding the war.[99]

Smith's conduct did not please First Lieutenant Robert T. "Tim" Rohweller, K Company's commanding officer. A brawny poster-board marine of the old school, Rohweller had entered the Marine Corps in 1963 as an enlisted man and earned an impressive record of achievement. Assigned to the elite 3d Reconnaissance Battalion, he was first sent to Vietnam in 1965, where he took part in nearly one hundred long-range reconnaissance patrols, some of which operated over fifteen miles from friendly positions.[100] He was twice recommended for meritorious promotion and was awarded the Bronze Star with Combat "V" for heroism. Upon his return to the United States, Rohweller attended officer candidate school and finished in the top 1 percent of his class. He then requested a second tour in Vietnam and returned in 1968. His fitness reports were a blur of ceaseless adoration: "Inspires immediate confidence." "An aggressive, dynamic individual who leads by fine personal example. Unlimited growth potential." "The best lieutenant in the battalion."[101] As a company commander, Lieutenant Rohweller liked to be known as a "hard charger." He was fond of saying things like, "We're going to do this *the Old Corps way*."[102] But in many respects the

Marine Corps of the Vietnamization period was not the "old Corps" that Rohweller knew, and such sentiment failed to resonate among the enlisted ranks. One of his junior officers wrote:

> Tim Rohweller . . . was without question a proficient leader. He had more combat experience than any of the rest of us. When Tim arrived he worked us hard. . . . [He] was a strong person and a demanding leader. Because he was new and he was tightening us up a little bit, I cannot say that he was well liked by everybody, [but] he was respected, and in combat that is what matters.
>
> Tim was concerned about people in the rear who were not getting back as quickly as they should have been. He was insistent that we could not afford to have people lounging in the rear when we needed every available hand at the front.[103]

Lieutenant Rohweller eventually made his way to the rear area and confronted Smith and his companions, informing them that they would soon be returned to the battlefield. Late that evening, the gang was busy smoking marijuana and griping about the lieutenant when Smith announced his plan to frag him. "I'm gonna kill that motherfucker," Smith was heard to say. "Lieutenant Rohweller will never make it out of Vietnam alive."[104]

During the early hours of 21 April 1969, Smith tossed a grenade into the company office where Lieutenant Rohweller was sleeping. Although court martial testimony provides several differing accounts of the incident, Smith's version indicates that he was physically unable to commit the crime alone, this owing to the bulky cast set on his broken hand. He asked several friends to assist him but found no takers. He then approached Private First Class Bobby R. Greenwood:

> I just walked over and said, "Greenwood, I want you to hold the door for me while I throw this frag," and he said, "Okay." He got up and walked out and he was in front of me and I was behind him and he went over [to the company office] and opened the door. I hooked the pin of the frag on my thumb and I tried to pull it out, but it was quite a bit of pain because that was one of the spots where I broke my hand.

"Hurry up, Smitty!" urged Greenwood.

"I can't get the pin out!" Smith gasped.

"Pull harder!"

According to Smith, "There was a noise made [inside the company office]. I thought it was made by [Lieutenant Rohweller]. I thought he had woke up. I got the pin out and I just threw it in and turned around and ran back to the hut."[105]

First Sergeant Walter J. Mendon, Jr., later testified: "I was awakened by an explosion. One of my clerks came to my hooch and said, "Somebody fragged the skipper!" I went immediately to the company office and found it in a state of confusion. A hole was in the floor behind the head of Lieutenant Rohweller lying in the cot, perforations throughout the roof and office, and corpsmen attending to the lieutenant."[106]

Grievously wounded in the explosion, Rohweller was evacuated to the USS *Repose* for emergency medical treatment but died several hours later. Sergeant Mendon quickly assembled a company formation that Smith attended with the grenade's pull ring still wrapped around his finger. "They caught him red-handed," his military defense counsel recalled. "He was probably higher than a kite."[107] Damning evidence emerged when one of Smith's companions, Private First Class Earl H. "Hercules" Brooker, informed authorities of the original conspiracy after learning of the lieutenant's death.[108]

When questioned by authorities, Smith maintained that his act was motivated in part by Lieutenant Rohweller's actions in the field during Operation Dewey Canyon. He claimed that Rohweller had delayed the emplacement of a listening post until after dusk, which led to an enemy ambush and the subsequent death of Private First Class Michael J. "Frenchy" Frencl on 26 February 1969.[109] But when I discussed this subject with over a dozen former K Company members, both officers and enlisted men, the assertion that Rohweller was accountable for Frencl's death elicited choruses of "Smith is full of shit" from the ex-marines.[110] One of them, himself the author of a detailed study of Dewey Canyon, wrote:

Private Smith's version of Tim [Rohweller] being responsible for [Frencl] being killed is nothing but fabrication. First of all, listening posts were set up by platoon commanders, not the company commander. Secondly, Dewey Canyon was a fiercely fought operation and we took a lot of casualties. I was wounded about two weeks into the operation. If marines going out to set up a listening post were ambushed, I have a very difficult time understanding how that can be the company commander's "fault" given the nature of combat and our enemy. We were in triple canopy jungle and the enemy traveled in two- or three-man teams. They always knew where we were and any one of us was at all times in danger of being shot. . . . [Smith] was in the rear and had no intention of going back to the jungle, and [his] motivation for murder was that he did not want to go back.[111]

Typical of the enlisted men was Stephen G. Fairman:

Smith's comments are no more than a load of self-serving bullshit designed to minimize or mitigate his actions after being caught. I can recall no talk at the time of Frencl's death of the company commander bearing any culpability for the events of that night. The first memory I have of this is after Smith did his deed. Sending out a listening post at or after dark was not the criminally incompetent act Smith makes it out to be. Rather, it was the norm. Listening posts and ambushes were invariably sent out during "stand-to," so Smith's contention that this was an abnormal event precipitated by an incompetent commander simply doesn't wash. . . . Everyone was fully aware we were facing a very competent enemy who always had home-field advantage.

Grousing and sniping inevitably took place anytime something untoward happened. There was an ever-present coterie of individuals who blamed all their problems on everyone in a position of authority. To them, if resupply didn't bring mail, it was because the first sergeant was too incompetent to put it on the helicopter. If [one] platoon went on patrol while the rest of the company stayed on perimeter duty, it was because [the platoon commander] volunteered for it. If someone was killed or wounded, it was because Lieutenant Rohweller was too gung-ho.

Lieutenant Rohweller was universally disliked by all and sundry. This is not to imply that he was in any way incompetent, but rather a comment on his management style. If he had been a commander on Tarawa, or Iwo Jima, or at the Chosin Reservoir, he very probably would have been perceived as exactly the right kind of officer for that time and place. In Vietnam in 1969, no one wanted to be the last man killed on the last day of the war. Lieutenant Rohweller was viewed as being more aggressive than he had to be in prosecuting a war we knew we weren't going to win. To be fair, I'm sure he was simply carrying out orders he was receiving from battalion or even division. Unfortunately, Lieutenant Rohweller was *there*. He was a highly visible officer giving orders that generated a great deal of animosity among teenage marines who just wanted to go home. He was a lightning rod for all the resentment that couldn't be vented on the battalion or division officers who *weren't* there.[112]

Adam W. Mackow added: "Smith was full of B.S. regarding listening post procedure. Most of the time during Dewey Canyon the listening posts moved out at dusk or after to prevent the enemy from observing them moving into their night position. At the time of Frencl's death, the blame was placed on the NVA. We had not heard any word that the listening post's timing was bad. This was a major infiltration route and the NVA was everywhere."[113]

Interestingly, Smith was asked to explain his motive by a host of psychiatrists while in confinement in the 1970s and not once during these interviews did he mention Private Frencl's death. Instead, he revealed that "undue harassment" and "continual run-ins" with the lieutenant led him to perform the wanton deed. He also cited "finding the war to be disappointing," "not being happy in the Marine Corps in the war," and a "dispute about pay records" between himself and the company administrative chief, who Smith identified as "a very close friend of (Rohweller's)," a dispute that he said had occurred on the night of the murder.[114]

Smith's parents arranged for prominent Chicago attorney and future Illinois Senate president Cecil A. Partee to represent their son at his court-martial, and a pretrial agreement was reached in which Smith pleaded guilty to avoid a possible death sentence. He was sentenced to life imprisonment, although this was commuted to forty years by the convening authority in accordance with the plea bargain.[115] Greenwood and another of Smith's companions, Private First Class David Napier, also faced courts-martial for their alleged complicity in the murder, but both were acquitted of all charges. Greenwood's verdict came in spite of the fact that he had admitted to a navy psychiatrist that he had played a role in the murder; because he had not been advised of his constitutional rights prior to the examination, his confession was ruled inadmissible at trial.[116]

Less than a year after Lieutenant Rohweller's death, Quang Tri Combat Base was the scene of yet another fragging incident motivated by an officer's alleged battlefield aggressiveness. By early 1970, the 3d Marine Division had departed Vietnam and had been replaced by U.S. Army units, among them C Company, 1/77th Armor.[117] A number of C Company's tankers accused their commanding officer, Captain Thomas Murphy, of "playing war games in the field." This was a reference to the officer's habit of conducting training exercises during periods in which the fighting waned, a practice that they claimed "left the company exposed all the time." After a night of drinking in which he allegedly consumed "eight to ten beers or more," Specialist Five Ralph J. Elliot set up two stolen Claymore mines outside Murphy's quarters in such a way "that the blasts from each Claymore would cross each other." The drunken Elliot was only able to detonate one of the mines, but the force of the blast was such that it blew a large hole in the wall of the captain's room and inflicted shrapnel wounds to his legs, back, and abdomen. Elliot later claimed that he "just intended to harm Captain Murphy enough so that he wouldn't come back to the company" and in this he was successful, but he also found himself in the stockade charged with aggravated assault. During his court-martial, the issue of Captain's Murphy's "war games" was raised. One enlisted witness testified:

> Witness: The old man [the company commander] wanted to play too many war games everybody thought.
>
> [Trial Counsel]: Like what?
>
> Witness: I mean like go to the field and try to do what John Wayne does.
>
> [Trial Counsel]: Was this training exercises?

Witness: Well, sir, that's what he meant it to be, but it wasn't to us.

[Military Judge]: What was it to you?

Witness: It could have been your life, sir.

[Military Judge]: In other words, he was unnecessarily risking the
    lives of the troops as far as they were concerned?

Witness: Yes, sir.

Yet when a lieutenant was questioned concerning this practice, he disagreed, saying, "I don't think the unit commander treated it lightly as a 'war game.' You can see where it's needed. . . . We may go through a week of practicing infantry." Here again we see evidence that supports Charles Anderson's thesis that the different training given to officers and their subordinates resulted in different views of how the war was to be fought. As for Elliot, he was convicted and sentenced to twenty-five years of confinement at hard labor. He was paroled in June 1975.[118]

Leaders perceived to be tactically incompetent on the battlefield are also alleged to have fallen prey to fraggers. Such incidents probably involved infantry units, as they performed most of the war's fighting and dying. Although 1969 saw the ground-pounders comprise about 10 percent of the army's strength in Vietnam, they sustained most of the casualties incurred during that year, and as a result, some may have targeted leaders believed to be inept or cowardly.[119] One should be careful when associating this motive with particular fragging incidents, however, for a number of men who were apprehended and stood trial for these crimes attempted to portray their victims as ineffective in order to justify their behavior, as in the Rohweller murder cited above. In a similar case, Private Larry Lee Hart confessed that he had booby-trapped the door of a troop billet for a "thrill." When asked about his victim, Hart replied, "I just knew him by sight. I've only been in the company three days." A year later, while bragging to a fellow prisoner in the stockade, Hart, who had been in Vietnam for less than a week when he committed his crime and had never seen combat, assumed the role of the hard-bitten veteran. He referred to his victim, nineteen-year-old Private First Class Merrill V. Beasley, Jr., as a "coward" who "was responsible for several people in the platoon being injured."[120] In reality, Hart's outfit, A Battery, 1/8th Artillery of the 25th Infantry Division, had not engaged in ground combat against the enemy during his brief time in the unit. The same is true of Beasley, who had only been in Vietnam for a short time prior to his death.[121]

Postwar scholarship has accused the leadership corps of yet another sin that led to fragging, though the case is far from airtight in this regard. In their 1978 book *Crisis in Command*, retired military officers Paul L. Savage and Richard A. Gabriel rejected the "sick society" argument that had been offered as an explanation for the myriad problems that plagued the army during Vietnamization, and offered a sort of Weberian substitute in its place. The real reason for the army's decline, they argued, could be laid squarely at the feet of the officer corps, which they believed had discarded the traditional gladiatorial techniques of military leadership (charismatic) in favor of the managerial style found in the modern business corporation (bureaucratic). Officers were now focused on building their careers rather than maintaining effective units, and their disregard for their subordinates' welfare is what led to fragging. "In Vietnam," Savage and Gabriel wrote, "too often the troops perceived their officers as unwilling to assume the burdens of combat they themselves carried and reacted in a most violent manner—they tried to kill them."[122] While *Crisis in Command* earned considerable praise for its attack on careerism—a problem the army halfheartedly admitted did exist—the assertion that it was a motive for fraggings is somewhat flawed, as most of the incidents occurred in rear area support units that did not engage in ground combat operations. How could the "burdens of combat" motive be applied to fragging when the majority of offenders and victims never faced the enemy? Moreover, those grenade cases that did take place in infantry units often involved the targeting of just the type of leaders that the authors claimed the military was lacking: hard-nosed commanders who had served multiple tours in the war zone.[123]

What was judged to be either overzealous or inept leadership was not the only motive that led troops to attack their superiors. A review of court-martial transcripts and other documents regarding fragging reveals that the perceived harassment of subordinates was the primary reason for most grenade assaults. To an officer or NCO who identified with the military's professional ethos and organizational goals, what might have been seen as necessary toward the completion of his unit's mission or the maintenance of discipline may have been viewed by a junior enlisted man, who did not necessarily share these sentiments, as harassment. If the channels of communication were closed between leaders and their subordinates, as they so often were during the Vietnam era, the possibility of settling disagreements without the threat of violence was eliminated. This was the case when Specialist Four Norman R. Shirley of the 101st Airborne Division fragged Platoon Sergeant Charles L. Nowling in July 1969. Although commanders viewed Nowling's leadership style as "tough but fair," Shirley saw the matter differently. He believed that the sergeant "made work for the platoon" and "was a cause of aggravation" to his troops. Another man testified that Shirley "had been pushed to his limit by [Nowling's] harassment."[124]

The alleged harassment of subordinates also played a role in fraggings that were unrelated to the military mission. Overseas tours often strain military marriages, and in a wartime environment like Vietnam, where grief or depression could only be expressed in a destructive manner, the receipt of "Dear John" letters led a number of frantic young husbands to act irrationally.[125] Three of the surveyed fraggers were attempting to obtain emergency leaves from their units to sort out their personal affairs when they came into conflict with superiors they believed were giving them the "run around." After learning that his wife was living with another man and had given birth to this man's child, one soldier became angry because "he had been unable to obtain emergency leave. He decided to throw a grenade in hopes that this would shock his superiors enough to give him leave."[126] Another GI received a letter from his wife that was addressed to him but contained a letter she had written to a friend. The letter spoke of how she loved another man and had posed nude for him. He too threw his grenade while awaiting leave.[127]

Military life certainly strained Specialist Five John W. Wheat's marriage. The nineteen-year-old Wheat had tied the knot with a local girl while home on leave from West Germany in April 1969, but financial problems precluded his new bride from accompanying him when he returned to Europe. Just when he succeeded in making arrangements to send for her, he was shipped to Vietnam. His wife wrote him regularly at first but the mail soon slackened, and he received his "Dear John" letter shortly before their first anniversary. As a chaplain and the Red Cross attempted to arrange a home leave, Wheat obtained tranquilizers from his unit's dispensary to calm his nerves. Unfortunately, he took overdoses of the pills and began sleeping during duty hours, leading his superiors to threaten him with disciplinary action. Wheat became particularly angry with Staff Sergeant William H. Marley, an NCO with whom he had been friendly in the past but who was now cracking down on him. Although his leave was eventually approved, Wheat continued to nurse the grudge against his former friend and decided to eliminate him. On the day before he was to depart Vietnam, Wheat, who fancied himself as an ordnance expert, booby-trapped the interior of his unit's ammunition bunker. Sergeant Marley was to have visited the structure on the following morning but for some reason did not. Instead, Captain John C. Seel entered the bunker and was killed in the ensuing explosion. By the time the grenade detonated, Wheat was already on his way home but CID agents caught up with him at Honolulu International Airport and dragged him back to Vietnam to face a court-martial. When he was told that his grenade had killed the wrong man, Wheat "began to cry . . . he broke up." He was convicted of murder and sentenced to twenty years of confinement, but was paroled in 1979.[128]

Enlisted men's resentment of their superiors eventually became so intense in some circles that leaders were sometimes attacked for the most trivial of actions. Private First Class George M. Ercolin of the 173d Airborne fragged First Lieutenant John R. Hamilton after the officer forced him to have his hair cut.[129] One court-martial concerned a fragging over cigarettes:

Staff Sergeant Neiswander was in his billet when the accused [Private David W. Bost] came to the bunker and asked for some cigarettes. Neiswander gave the accused two packs of cigarettes. The accused appeared mad because he was given only two packs.

"You're only going to give me two fucking packs of cigarettes when you've got all those goddamn sundry packs?" asked Bost.

"You can get more packs tomorrow morning," replied the sergeant.
After the accused [departed], Neiswander . . . heard a thud, looked
up, and saw a figure running away. . . . He then saw a man who ducked
down just before the explosion. This was, at the most, thirty seconds
after giving Bost the cigarettes.

When he heard the blast, Sergeant Gerald L. Harden believed that
an enemy mortar barrage had begun, and took cover. As he looked
around, he saw smoke pouring from what had been Neiswander's bunker and made his way to the heavily damaged structure. He found
Neiswander nearly buried alive in the debris. "Bost fragged me!" Neiswander cried. "Oh my God, my legs, Jerry, help me!" Harden quickly
cleared the rubble and was able to free his injured friend. Bost was apprehended and sentenced to eight years of confinement. He was released in 1974 but was later rearrested on a parole violation and did not
leave prison until 1979.[130]

Racial Tension

Although President Harry S. Truman officially laid the Jim Crow army
to rest in 1948, the Vietnam era saw an unprecedented upswing of racial enmity between blacks and whites in the armed services.[131] What
caused this increased tension? The black soldier of the late 1960s was
much different than his predecessor who fought in America's earlier
wars. Racial pride imbued by the civil rights movement transformed
him into a man in search not only of equality but an appropriate societal position in which he could maintain his own ethnic identity. "We
weren't living in no power vacuum in Vietnam," black marine Clarence
J. Fitch explained. "There was a certain growing black consciousness
that was happening in the States, and also over there in Vietnam. . . . It
was a whole atmosphere." There was also the persona of Martin Luther
King, Jr.

Fitch continued: "I think people really listened to Martin Luther
King. He talked about how blacks were dying at a greater rate, and he
was the first person we really ever heard say that, even though it was
something we knew. You just looked around you and said, 'Well, they're

just using us as cannon fodder.' A lot of blacks fought valiantly at points, but a lot of them didn't see the sense of dying in this war. There were people that would go so far as to hurt themselves enough to get out of going to the bush. I seen people shoot themselves in the arm or the foot or the legs to get one of those stateside wounds. I seen people fake injuries. We knew we was dying at a higher rate, so we felt very much justified not to add to this fucking figure."[132]

There has been much debate among historians concerning the veracity of King's assertion that blacks were being killed in disproportionate numbers in Vietnam. At the time he made the statement in February 1967, he was indeed correct,[133] and his remark was in any case widely believed by black servicemen, particularly those who were at odds with the "establishment."

Black soldiers complained of racism within the ranks of the armed forces. Of the one thousand investigations conducted by the USARV Inspector General's Office during the first nine months of 1970, sixty-one involved alleged racial prejudice. Among the points of contention were the "Afro" hairstyle, the lack of products preferred by black personnel in post exchanges and clubs, harassment from military police, the use of racial epithets, display of the Confederate battle flag, and alleged preferential treatment afforded to white troops regarding promotions, duty assignments, and the military legal system. While the investigations revealed fifty-three of the claims to be unfounded, and many of the accusers (62.3 percent) were individuals who issued their complaints in the hope of avoiding various types of unfavorable personnel action, the military acknowledged that a certain degree of prejudice did exist. The following examples, gleaned from a Marine Corps bulletin, are representative of the valid claims:

A first sergeant heard loud music in the living quarters of his battalion rear. He entered one hooch and found a group of seven Negro marines listening to a tape recorder. He ordered the tape recorder turned off and the marines to disperse, saying, "I don't want any of you gents planning any riot tonight." In the second hooch, two removed from the first, he found a group of Caucasian marines also listening to a tape recorder as loud as the first. He merely ordered the group either to turn down the tape recorder or turn it off; he did not disperse the group nor cast aspersions upon the marines' intentions.

Another first sergeant was awaiting service at the bar of a staff NCO club. The bartender was talking to a Negro staff NCO. The first sergeant called the bartender down to his position, then asked if he could be served or whether the bartender was "going to talk to that nigger all night," a remark that should not have been made at all but which was also overheard by another Negro staff NCO.[134]

Through perceived injustices, both real and imagined, young black enlisted men tended to maintain close relations with each other, resulting in the emergence of a primary group consciousness and further amplification of their grievances.[135] When such a manifestation occurs, one officer wrote, "the experience of one member quickly becomes the experience of his buddies." This voluntary segregation fostered alienation and distrust between black and white servicemen, and small groups of radicals began to accept violence as an acceptable means for resolving disputes. As the Black Power movement began to emerge in America, racial militancy found its way into the ranks of the armed services, and the Vietnam era saw numerous acts of racially motivated violence, including beatings and even murders, take place on U.S. military installations around the globe.

Race played an important though not central role in the fragging phenomenon. We have seen that two of the earliest Vietnam fragging incidents were motivated by tension stemming from Reverend King's assassination in April 1968. Establishing race as a motive in other cases, however, is more difficult. Though the races of the perpetrators and their intended victims were known in many grenade cases, this data does not provide any indication of whether the assaults were racially motivated. Many fraggers targeted victims of the same color while others who attacked men of different races or ethnicities did so for reasons unrelated to race. Military statistics provide us with some assistance in the matter but are not definitive. For example, the army studied 126 actual and possible assaults that occurred within its ranks in 1969 and concluded that twelve of the incidents (9.5 percent) appeared to involve "possible racial motives," twenty-eight incidents (22.2 percent) gave no indication of racial motives, and eighty-six incidents (just over 68 percent) failed to provide sufficient information for analysis. Of 271 fraggings counted in 1970, sixteen (5.9 percent) appeared to involve possible racial motives, 36 (13.3 percent) indicated no racial motives, and 219 (just under 81 percent) failed to provide sufficient information for analysis.[136] A Marine Corps study of racial incidents that occurred between October 1968 and June 1969 lumped grenade incidents together with firearm discharges, thus making precise analysis impossible, though at least one case is known to have involved a grenade.[137] Of nearly fifty incidents that occurred in the 1st Division in 1970, three were "definitely racially related."[138] In fact, racial hatred in the Marine Corps was the cause of the bloodiest fragging incident observed during the entire war.

On the evening of 5 February 1970, four black marines of Force Logistic Command's maintenance battalion decided to kill some "beasts"—white marines. While a music group performed at the unit's club, two grenades were tossed onto the crowded patio floor. The first failed to explode, as its user failed to remove the protective tape that secured its spoon. The second killed Corporal Ronald D. Pate and injured sixty-two others. In his study of Marine Corps justice during the war, Lieutenant Colonel Gary D. Solis described the incident:

> Corporal Ronald E. Gales admitted breaking into an ammunition storage locker, assisted by Lance Corporals (Joseph L.) Jones and James B. Addison. They stole twelve M26 fragmentation hand grenades. . . . The three were then joined by Lance Corporal Andrew M. Harris, Jr.
>
> In the early evening darkness, Gales, Harris, Jones, and Addison walked to the enlisted club. Jones entered to warn blacks inside to leave, but because of the crowd, reached only a few. Those he did reach left without question. According to Gales, when Jones rejoined the other three outside the club, Harris exclaimed, "I'm going to fire a whole bunch of these beasts up!" and lobbed a grenade over the fence. When it failed to detonate, again according to Gales, Harris tossed the second grenade over the fence. Blacks and whites alike were wounded in the explosion that followed.

The post reaction force went on alert immediately after the explosion, believing that an enemy attack was in progress, but when the first grenade was found in the debris, it became obvious that the attack was an inside job. The four men were eventually apprehended but subsequent courts-martial acquitted them of all charges, despite the fact that the government granted Gales immunity from prosecution in return for his testimony.[139] Racial tension within the battalion remained so tense that less than a week after this incident, yet another fragging took place. After becoming involved in a dispute with one of his superiors, Private Ronald L. McDonald flung a grenade into a hut occupied by several white NCOs. One of the victims, Gunnery Sergeant Fred C. Johnson, recalled both the tension and the ensuing attack:

> We had trouble with the blacks in the company. I was the company gunnery sergeant, [and] I had a lot of run-ins with them. You'd go down to the hut if you wanted one for office hours or something and they'd all get around you. Sometimes I'd have to take a chaser down there with me with a shotgun to get somebody and bring them up for office hours; [I] almost had to pull them out of the rack.
>
> [Gunnery Sergeant Franklin J. Salamone] was [McDonald's] supervisor. McDonald was on marijuana and all that, wouldn't want to work, and one thing led to another. It was just a beef between the two of them.
>
> I guess it was about nine o'clock at night. I'd turned in. Ronald McDonald the clown. He threw [the grenade] in the wrong end of the hut. And he threw it in and I heard it rolling on the floor and it must have woke me up—halfway woke me up—and I turned over. . . . [When it exploded], I thought that a mortar round had come in there and I turned back over to see a hole in the floor. I was the only one that got hurt. [Salamone] got a scratch. They whisked me off to the hospital; I just wanted to put a band-aid on it.[140]

McDonald was quickly apprehended, and in this instance justice was swift and severe: he was convicted and sentenced to eighty years of imprisonment. Upon review, however, the sentence was reduced to twenty-five and later to ten years. He was released in February 1979.[141]

The incidents observed in Force Logistic Command reveal two different patterns observed in racially motivated fraggings. The Pate murder involved one segregated group attacking another. Such cases often occurred after fistfights or similar confrontations, and were usually very bloody. During an outdoor floor show staged at Long Binh's Camp Frenzell-Jones in September 1969, approximately twenty-five to thirty black soldiers were involved in a disturbance and were ordered to disperse by a senior NCO. Shortly afterward, two grenades were thrown into the audience, fatally wounding Sergeant Timothy A. Cook of the 199th Light Infantry Brigade, and injuring fifteen others.[142] In another incident, a grenade hurled into a racial brawl at Tuy Hoa Army Airfield in January 1971 wounded twenty-nine soldiers.[143] A few months later, a member of the BBU (Black Brothers United) was accused of detonating a white phosphorus grenade in the enlisted mess at Cam Ranh Bay, an explosion that injured thirty-one.[144] After a black soldier was arrested at Tuy Hoa in August 1971 and charged with aggravated assault, approximately forty-five black troops gathered around the provost marshal's office and demanded his release. When the man was returned to the custody of his unit for transfer to the stockade, several nights of fraggings and arson ensued.[145]

The second pattern, as described in the McDonald case, involved a superior-subordinate relationship in which the enlisted man claimed racially motivated harassment. At Dong Ha Combat Base in July 1970, such an incident occurred after Staff Sergeant Clarence D. Hodges of the 3d Squadron, 5th Cavalry allegedly called one of his subordinates, Private Bruce Perry, "boy." Perry reacted by placing a Claymore mine next to Hodges's quarters and detonating it, in his words, "to scare him." As it turned out, Hodges was severely injured. Perry later confessed:

> During the evening of 24 July, I took about seven BTs [Binoctal tablets] and this made me high. That same night Hodges called me a boy I got a Claymore mine off one of the tracks [vehicles]. After I was high on the BTs I started thinking about Staff Sergeant Hodges and the more I thought about it the madder I got. So just before midnight, I set the Claymore up on the sand bags outside Hodges' hooch. I connected a

wire that was about seventy-five meters from the Claymore. I ran wire to the area between the shower room and the bunker. I then hooked the charger handle up to this end of the wire and then I pushed the charger handle causing the Claymore to explode. I then disconnected the charger handle and threw it up under the bunker. I ran around to the front of the dayroom and looked inside and saw several people sitting inside. I asked if anybody had got hurt and someone told me that Hodges was hurt. I then ran back down to my hooch and went to bed.

Perry was court-martialed and sentenced to ten years of hard labor.[146]

Although most of the racially motivated fraggings I found involved black servicemen attacking whites, I did find a few cases perpetrated by white troops against their black counterparts. The early months of 1971 saw elements of the 5/46th Infantry erupt in racial violence. A number of fights took place between E Company blacks and several whites of the attached sniper element. On the night of 2 March, a movie was shown in the company area during which threats were exchanged. Later that evening, white private Kenneth W. Chaky was "still a bit 'riled up'" when a group of armed blacks passed his tent. He and a friend then noticed a lone GI wandering in the darkness nearby. Chaky testified: "I saw [a soldier] walking down the road and I said, 'If this guy is black, I'm going to frag him.'" As the solitary figure passed, Chaky saw that the soldier was indeed black, and tossed a hand grenade at him. His target, Specialist Four Sperlin T. Dancy, heard the grenade drop and immediately dove to cover. Fortunately, he was uninjured in the explosion. Dancy observed Chaky and his companion fleeing the scene and was able to identify them to the military police.[147]

Racially motivated violence in Vietnam eventually became so widespread that it evolved from surreptitious fragging-type offenses to open hostility. Such sentiment was actively encouraged by radicals at home, who exhorted blacks in Vietnam to commit violent acts against the predominantly white command structure. In his article "To My Black Brothers in Vietnam," Black Panther Eldridge Cleaver wrote, "You need to start killing the racist pigs who are over there with you giving you orders. Kill General Abrams and his staff, all his officers. Sabotage supplies and equipment, or turn them over to the Vietnamese people."[148] The following homicide further explicates the tension that existed between the races during the later years of the war.

Camp Radcliff was a large U.S. base located in Kontum Province, the site of some of the war's fiercest battles. By 1971, much of the local fighting involved not the Viet Cong but blacks and whites of C Troop, 1/10th Cavalry, a unit that had won fame in the previous century as an all-black "Buffalo" regiment on the North American plains. Shortly after assuming command of C Troop in early January, twenty-three-year-old Captain William F. Reichert found himself in the center of a power struggle between the unit's leadership and five Black Power advocates. On one occasion, several of the latter refused to work; when confronted by First Sergeant James M. Emerich, they physically attacked him. The incident was reported through legal channels but because Emerich had "instigated" the dispute, no charges were filed. According to an official query, Reichert had informed his squadron commander, Lieutenant Colonel John Mason, about the gang and its activities on three separate occasions but "no action was taken to relieve the problem of racial tensions in the unit." Well aware of the danger they faced from the group, both Reichert and Emerich prepared sealed letters to be opened by authorities in the event of their deaths. Reichert's letter read:

> I have reason to believe the following individuals, all black power advocates forming a [clique] within C Troop, 1/10 Cav., might cause me bodily harm due to my efforts to turn them into soldiers in the U.S. Army. Frag grenades have been found in SP4 Taylor's clothing:
>
> PFC Mc Kinney, Carl
>
> PFC Moore, Alex
>
> PFC Moyler, James P.
>
> SP4 Taylor, Larry
>
> SP4 Harvey, Ambus J.
>
> I consider any harm that comes to me as a result of actions by the above individuals a direct result of (1) the wholly inadequate U.S. Army legal system in USARV which is further amplified by (2) the political, play-it-safe attitude and actions of the squadron commander, LTC John Mason, who has failed to back his chain of command in dealing with

black power criminals. . . . Signed, William F. Reichert, CPT, Armor. Envelope to be opened . . . only if need arises.

It appears that some white soldiers took it upon themselves to aggravate the already tense situation. During the month of January 1971, C Troop's blacks alleged two smoke-grenade fraggings and said that an M16 round had whistled through their billets. Amazingly, a white lieutenant admitted that he knew who had thrown the grenades, but refused to identify the culprit to authorities. The blacks too had reported grievances to higher echelons, at least once directly to Colonel Mason, but believed that "only a small degree of trying was ever done to relieve the problems."

On the afternoon of 27 January, having learned that their platoon was to be sent to the field, Specialist Four Ambus J. Harvey and Private First Class James P. Moyler loaded their rifles and proceeded to the unit orderly room to see Captain Reichert. They first confronted Sergeant Emerich, who informed them that the commander was not there. Both men threatened Emerich in no uncertain terms: "The number one swine is never in when we want to see him, but that's okay. We are going to do you a job after we see him." The sergeant noticed that their weapons were loaded, a violation of unit policy, but made no move to defuse the situation, lest he be "attacked or shot for trying to do so," as he later said. "[I] could not take action against two men who were armed."

Emerich immediately left the building and made for the third platoon area, where he found Captain Reichert and informed him of the crisis. The two were returning to the orderly room when Moyler and Harvey appeared. Reichert approached Moyler.

"Are you going to the field?" the captain asked.

Moyler didn't answer.

"I'm giving you a direct order to pack your bags and go to the bush with your platoon!" barked Reichert.

"I'm tired of the blacks being fucked with!" replied Moyler, pointing his finger in the captain's face.

As Reichert attempted to push the private's hand away, Moyler raised his weapon and squeezed off a burst of automatic fire. Captain Reichert fell to the ground, dead. Although a black medic quickly relieved Moyler of his rifle, it hardly spelled the end of the almost surreal scene. When an NCO attempted to cover the slain officer with a poncho, he was prevented from doing so by Private First Class Michael Evans, who stood over Reichert's body and raised his clenched fists in a Black Power salute. "Don't cover the rabbit up!" shouted Evans. "All you rabbits take a good look. That is what we're going to do to all you rabbits!"

It was not until a helicopter landed nearby and Colonel Mason stepped out that the troops began to disperse. Before long, scores of military police, CID agents, and a military intelligence element descended upon the camp, taking Moyler into custody and interviewing potential witnesses. Remarkably, even the presence of numerous law enforcement officials could not put an end to the racial enmity. Despite a claim that there was "no white backlash" after the killing, one investigator witnessed four racial fistfights at the base on 30 January alone.[149]

At his court-martial, Moyler, who was charged with premeditated murder, claimed that the shooting was an accident. To the surprise of many, the court only convicted him of the lesser charge of unpremeditated murder and sentenced him to fifteen years of confinement. He was released in 1975 after serving only four years.[150] Not as fortunate was Colonel Mason. While the inspector general's report of the incident praised Mason for the "vigorous and appropriate action" he took after the murder, senior leadership had quite a different opinion of the matter. Lieutenant General William J. McCaffrey, the USARV deputy commanding general, believed that Mason should have been aware of the tense situation in C Troop before the shooting occurred, and taken steps to correct it. McCaffrey subsequently issued Mason a scathing letter of reprimand and recommended that the army revoke the Legion of Merit the colonel had been awarded for his service in Vietnam. In an obvious attempt to damage Mason's military career, McCaffrey even took the unusual step of contacting the chief of officer personnel operations in Washington and informing him of the matter. "I consider it important," McCaffrey wrote, "that in your personnel management actions regarding LTC Mason, you should be aware of my action."[151]

Incidents such as this were certainly not unique in Vietnam during this period. In another racially charged case, Specialist Four James E. Paul of the 25th Infantry Division opened fire on a group of white soldiers at a USO show, killing Sergeant Joe E. Raber and Private First Class Gary R. White and wounding ten others. He boasted of killing "rabbits" shortly before his arrest.[152] When two white majors of the 5th Infantry Division ordered some black soldiers to reduce the volume of their stereo set, the men defiantly turned the music up full blast. After one of the officers yanked out the plug, Specialist Four Alfred B. W. Flint pulled out a pistol and shot both of them. Major Michael F. Davis was struck in the head but was able to drag himself to a first-aid station. Major Robert Degen was not so lucky.[153] On the evening of 31 May 1970, Jerry L. Thompson of the 3d Squadron, 5th Cavalry, entered an enlisted men's club at Dong Ha and pointed his rifle at Staff Sergeant Russell Corley, the white club manager. Corley drew his .45 caliber pistol and shot Thompson five times, killing him. As Corley was being escorted from the club, an unknown person lobbed a hand grenade into the building, injuring Captain David J. Rogers.[154] After fatally shooting Fred C. Hendricks, Specialist Four Oliver R. Robinson of the 555th Maintenance Company stood over his victim's corpse and rendered a Black Power salute.[155] Melvin Smith, a self-proclaimed Black Muslim, shot First Sergeant Archie D. Carnell nine times, killing him instantly. He then attempted suicide but failed, and was court-martialed after recovering from his self-inflicted injuries.[156] By the end of the war, nearly every American division in Vietnam had sustained at least one racially motivated homicide, owing either to fragging or overt violence.

Perhaps the most bizarre racially charged case of all, however, occurred on 31 December 1970 in So Chin Village, which had been the scene of several violent clashes between black deserters and the military police. While conducting an investigation near a local brothel, two white CID agents, Warrant Officer Ralph R. Wiest and Specialist Four Leroy E. Halbert, Jr., were assailed by a group of black soldiers from the

542d Signal Company who recognized Wiest as CID. When one of the men shoved the barrel of his rifle into Wiest's chest and threatened to "blow his shit away," the veteran agent pulled out his pistol and shot him. A Wild West–style shootout ensued, and when the smoke cleared, Halbert and Private Larry J. Anderson were dead, and another soldier was wounded.[157]

Not all of the racial violence that occurred in Vietnam involved troops assaulting men of other colors. Militant blacks were sometimes critical of their more moderate peers, who they derisively referred to as "Oreos"—black on the outside and white on the inside.[158] This attitude was also encouraged by stateside radicals; in his above-cited article, Black Panther Eldridge Cleaver called for the elimination of "traitors," those blacks who did not support Black Panther policies.[159] As far as fragging is concerned, however, I was only able to find one case in which a black serviceman was targeted for alleged support of the command structure against militant elements. On 7 July 1971, a group of black soldiers from the 101st Airborne Division smashed chairs over the heads of two whites and threatened several others at a Camp Evans mess hall.[160] Vaughn M. Rooks, a black soldier who was friendly with the victims, reported the malefactors to authorities. Rooks feared retaliation and it was not long in coming. Less than a week later, he was about to enter his living quarters when he noticed a tripwire rigged in the doorway. Joseph M. Kralich, a seasoned medic and victim of the 7 July assault, disarmed the booby trap. He recalled:

It was early evening when [Rooks] was saying that his hooch was "boobytrap-wired to a hand grenade," so I went to investigate. The commanding officer, executive officer (who was useless), and the first sergeant were keeping everyone back from the man's hooch. After checking the doorway, steps, etc., I entered.

I had a flashlight I used to reflect light off the tripwire and search for any other wires or devices. This was not the first time I had handled ordnance and when the CID team arrived they seemed quite pleased that someone possessed a sense of calm. I outlined the situation: one fragmentation grenade with a straight pin [was secured] to a wire extended across the doorway into the room. The grenade itself was lying on its side in a two-quart can. The wire was taut and I reasoned that if this was a serious booby trap, the fuse could be set for instant detonation, but I doubted that these Camp Evans "REMFs" possessed the expertise to set such a device. We decided that the best option was to re-insert the grenade's pin and, if necessary, drop the grenade over the side of the well-fortified hooch. I cut the window screen so I could either jump out or toss the frag down. I picked up the grenade and the CID agent inserted the pin and bent back the tips.

There was a great deal of discussion [among the troops] as to if it was a "real" grenade and some direct implications that Rooks had set the device himself.

I was later called upon to testify about the fight at the mess hall. I guess I gave accurate testimony as three of the blacks were convicted.[161]

No one was ever convicted of the attempted fragging, however.

Drug Abuse

Illegal drug use among young Americans reached alarming proportions in the late 1960s, and the emergence of illegal drug use in military units in Vietnam reflected this societal change. During the U.S. buildup in Southeast Asia, drug abuse was rare. From 1 July 1965 to 1 July 1966, a period in which U.S. strength in Vietnam grew to about 270,000 men, only one hundred investigations involving possible drug activity were conducted, but this proved to be the calm before the storm. In September 1966, MACV informed the U.S. Embassy in Saigon of its finding that marijuana, opium, and morphine were readily available to troops in the Saigon area,[162] and the Long Binh–Bien Hoa and Da Nang areas were later found to be little different.[163] Press reports alleging widespread marijuana use by U.S. troops began to appear in the fall of 1967, and while military officials attempted to downplay such claims, by late 1968 they were forced to concede that the problem "had grown to considerable proportions."[164] Even more alarming was the appearance of high-potency heroin in early 1970. Addiction became a problem, drug-related deaths spiked, and more and more veterans were

Table 4

Year	Drug Apprehensions
1965	47
1966	344
1967	1,722
1968	4,352
1969	8,446
1970	11,058
1971	11,161

returning to the United States with drug habits.[165] Statistics generated by several investigating agencies disagreed regarding the exact percentage of drug users within the ranks, but the numbers of drug apprehensions made by law enforcement (see Table 4 above) were enough to dissuade even the most convinced of doubters that the military in Vietnam was in trouble. To place these figures into perspective, a look at the numbers provided for the last two years is in order. Despite the fact that troop withdrawals reduced U.S. strength in South Vietnam from 473,000 in January 1970 to just over 185,000 by the fourth quarter of 1971, the number of drug apprehensions remained virtually constant.[166] As the largest of the services, the army sustained the brunt of the drug problem but the navy and air force were not without their own drug woes.[167] The Marine Corps too was not immune; one senior commander admitted, "Every one of my battalions has investigations going on all the time."[168]

The prevalence of illegal drugs in Vietnam bore a significant effect on the fragging phenomenon. Most of the men convicted of fragging offenses used drugs, and authority figures attempting to stymie drug activity within their units were often the targets of their assaults. On the evening of 22 April 1971, Lieutenant Colonel Freddie C. Austin, a battalion commander in the 173d Airborne Brigade, noticed a small group of enlisted men who appeared to be smoking marijuana. After observing the men for several minutes, Austin and another officer approached the GIs and placed them under apprehension. A subsequent search revealed one of them to be in possession of the drug, and as the guilty party was taken to the military police station, the others were dispersed to their living areas. Colonel Austin returned to his office and was discussing the incident with several colleagues when a small object came flying through the front door. "Grenade!" screamed one of the officers, and they all hit the floor. Fortunately, the grenade was a dud and failed to explode. One of the smokers, Specialist Four Ignacio Garcia, Jr., was apprehended, and pleaded guilty to the charge of attempted murder.[169] When marijuana users in the 173d Assault Helicopter Company grew tired of their NCOs conducting drug searches, one of them decided to booby-trap a bunker with a grenade. After a snooping sergeant found the device hidden under a sandbag, an ordnance-disposal team led by Staff Sergeant Robert A. Whitted was summoned to disarm it. As his assistant lifted the sandbag, Whitted grabbed the grenade and turned to throw it into an empty bunker when it prematurely exploded, killing him instantly. Specialist Four Louis E. Holdgrafer admitted to placing a grenade on the bunker where Whitted was killed, and was to be tried for the sergeant's murder, but the case fell apart when it was discovered that the CID had apparently failed to advise Holdgrafer of his rights prior to questioning. Accordingly, the charges against him were dismissed.[170]

Fraggers also attacked military policemen and their adroit drug-sniffing dogs. The following case was observed in the marines' 1st MP Battalion: "At 2100 hours on [2] January 1971, Company A reported that an M-26 hand grenade was found with the pin pulled, wrapped in clothing on a marijuana dog handler's rack. The pin was replaced and the grenade confiscated. CID investigated the incident and conducted a shake down with negative results."[171] During 1969 and 1970, the army recorded eight fragging assaults against personnel of the 18th Military Police Brigade. In early 1971, a white phosphorus grenade was thrown at the CID agents' living quarters in Di An.[172]

Fragging and Antiwar Activism

Although it is evident that societal issues such as racial tension, drug use, and the authority crisis played prominent roles in the fragging phenomenon, finding a link between anti–Vietnam War activism and fragging is far more problematic. On its face, the rise of small, violent parapolitical groups within the youth culture of the late 1960s logically suggests that extremist elements might indeed have found their way into the armed forces and contributed toward the commission of these acts. In any case, the debate over this subject has raged since the early 1970s, with the analyses falling into two camps. On one side are the government and military sources, which tend to examine individual grenade cases in search of political motivations and, finding none, conclude that politics played no role. Some antiwar writers, on the other hand, favor a more conceptual approach, arguing that fragging and the GI "revolt" of that era were a part of a larger political struggle against immoral U.S. policies at home and abroad.

Military authorities were convinced that antiwar activism did not play a role in the fragging phenomenon. The subject was examined during a 1971 congressional probe called the "Investigation of Attempts to Subvert the U.S. Armed Forces," and no evidence of such sentiment was found.[173] Indeed, the fraggers' personnel records indicate that nearly all of them had volunteered for military service and several specifically requested duty in Vietnam. Dr. Bond found that the convicted fraggers he interviewed "generally seemed apolitical; most had enlisted in the service and supported the war effort. . . . Most of them were loners who were not given to participating in idealistic causes."[174] A similar study of Vietnam heroin users found that while the addicts frequently used "militant" rhetoric, this "did not reflect a 'radical-left' political ideology and did not represent a rejection of conventional values and living patterns."[175] Their use of such language suggests identification with the antiauthoritarian aspect of Vietnam-era youth culture. The fraggers were probably similar in this regard; they likely parroted the attitudes expressed by their more-sophisticated, better-educated peers, but when confronted with frustrating personal situations they were unable to handle, they acted out in their own clumsy, violent way.

Countering this argument are antiwar veterans, academics, and others who have produced a veritable mountain of literature and other media on the GI movement that emerged within the U.S. military during the late 1960s. The movement was composed of those servicemen who came to oppose the war in Vietnam. Many of these men had been gung-ho volunteers who marched off to fight America's enemies as their

fathers had done before them only to become disillusioned by the conflict. They challenged the war's legitimacy as well as the authority of
the military leadership, and sought to effect social change both within
the armed forces and in the society from which they had emerged.
These authors point to the unprecedented number of desertions, fraggings, combat refusals, and other acts of indiscipline observed during
the last years of the war, and cite Vietnam as their cause.

So who is right? Based on my own research, I found that both sides
could declare victory. Opposition to the war does not seem to have
played any *direct* role in individual fraggings, as it was never known to
be a stated motive in the attacks, thus strengthening the military thesis.
However, antiwar soldiers and sentiments did help to shape the Vietnam-
era enlisted culture, which in turn influenced the fraggers. This helps
to explain both the paucity of references to politics in military documentation and why the fragging phenomenon occurred in Vietnam and
not during the nation's earlier wars. From the material I assembled on
the men in this study, I found only two fragging cases in which possible antiwar or antigovernment utterances are mentioned. In *United
States v. Boyd*, a prosecution witness testified that Private First Class
Warren J. Boyd was discussing "politics" (no further explanation of this
term is provided) and "lifers" in his unit when he declared, "Something
has to be done." Minutes later, a grenade exploded in the company
commander's quarters. Boyd denied having committed the crime, in-
sisting that his remark about "something being done" referred to the
Vietnam situation and troop withdrawals rather than any intended action against members of his unit. This seems unlikely, however, as Boyd
had twice voluntarily extended his tour in Vietnam and had served
nearly two full years in country at the time of the offense. Moreover, he
was facing disciplinary action from the victim when the crime was
committed.[176]

More convincing is *United States v. Harris*, a case tried in the Americal Division. The accused, Private Ronald L. Harris, had nearly completed his tour in Vietnam when he was charged with lobbing a grenade
at the 26th Engineer Battalion's NCO club, slightly injuring an enlisted
man. Harris pleaded not guilty to the charges against him, and his record of trial contains no explanation of his actions, so his motivation is

not known. However, he did make a politically charged statement to the court that reflected the dissatisfaction felt by some black soldiers of the era:

> When I first arrived in Vietnam, I was originally in the communications section of 26th Engineers, but because I was a little tongue-tied on the radio, they sent me to a line platoon at LZ Ross. From there, I was sent seven miles further out into the field although I didn't know a damn thing about mines or any booby traps. I did what I was told and went next to LZ Baldy and then to LZ Hawk Hill. Hawk Hill was new then and I worked hard, sometimes two shifts, and finally I came back to Chu Lai and into commo again. I asked questions then, but I couldn't get any answers. I asked why there were so many brothers out in the field and why I couldn't buy Afro Sheen in the PX. Because I couldn't get answers I was obliged to stop being good and become a militant. . . . The army depreciates a man and it depreciates his life and it doesn't stand for a damn thing. If a democracy was good you wouldn't have to fight for any [in] Vietnam; people would be fighting to get it.[177]

Harris was found guilty and sentenced to a bad-conduct discharge, forfeitures of pay, and six months of confinement. During his post-trial interview with the division's staff judge advocate, Harris declared that he did not like the military and would not return to duty if offered the chance. While such a statement might seem unsurprising, court-martial records reveal that nearly all of the convicted fraggers sought exactly the opposite in the hope of avoiding prison time and punitive discharges. A few even wrote impassioned pleas to their respective convening authorities, begging for the chance to earn honorable separations from the service.[178]

I also found two instances in which soldiers who belonged to antiwar organizations were suspects in fragging cases, but research reveals the incidents to be decidedly nonpolitical. In one case, a member of Andy Stapp's American Servicemen's Union (ASU) became involved in a dispute with a sergeant over the burning of incense in a bunker shortly before the incident occurred.[179] The other instance is cited in David Cortright's book *Soldiers in Revolt*. Private First Class Richard

Wayne Buckingham, a member of Vietnam Veterans Against the War, was serving as a cook in the 538th Transportation Company in Long Binh when he and Specialist Four Richard O. Strain were accused of fragging First Sergeant Laguala A. Vega on 8 April 1971.[180] The two were briefly held in pretrial confinement in connection with the case but several other suspects also surfaced. One of latter was overheard saying that Vega and Sergeant First Class Jake W. Leake were going to be fragged because of their actions within the company, rather than for any political motive.[181] The government eventually withdrew its charge against Buckingham, who would have faced his second court-martial in the space of a year: in June 1970 he had been tried in West Germany on charges of rape and sodomy, and was acquitted.[182] Buckingham left the army in 1972 but couldn't stay out of trouble: only weeks after his discharge, he strangled a seven-year-old girl to death and was sentenced to life imprisonment. A judge released him in 1999 in the belief that he "would not pose an unacceptable risk" to society but Buckingham was quick to prove him wrong; in 2002, he was sentenced to serve several more years in his native Ohio for assaulting yet another female.[183]

The military's argument that antiwar activism played no direct role in fragging is further bolstered by the fact that all of the above-mentioned causes of the fragging phenomenon—drugs, racial tension, and the authority crisis—were present within American military units around the world and were not particular to Southeast Asia. Disgruntled servicemen attacked their superiors on military installations from Kansas to Korea during this period, and the motives for this violence were strikingly similar to those perpetrated in Vietnam. After being reprimanded for avoiding work details at Fort Riley, Specialist Five Ennis Thomas walked into Captain John M. Salzer's office carrying a .38 caliber pistol. "I'm back," said Thomas, as he raised his weapon and shot Salzer dead. In May 1970, black soldiers stationed in Hohenfels, West Germany, committed several acts of racially motivated violence, and Private First Class Alphonso L. Lewis injured ten white soldiers in a unit mess hall with a fragmentation grenade.[184] Several months later, two soldiers of the 535th Engineer Company at Schwetzingen placed a grenade booby trap into the gas tank of their company commander's vehicle.[185] On the morning of 6 May 1971, only hours before he was to be administratively discharged from the Marine Corps, Private Charles H. Henderson drove to a remote location at the Naval Ammunition Depot in Hawthorne, Nevada, and planted a bomb on a military truck. But as he was installing the device, it detonated prematurely, killing him and seriously injuring an accomplice.[186] Black militants at Camp Humphreys, South Korea, stole a case of fragmentation grenades from an ammunition bunker and detonated several of them at various locations on the base. One soldier and two Korean guards were injured, and a CH-47 helicopter was damaged. In the following days, grenades were detonated in a unit parking lot and near the living quarters of a senior NCO.[187] Mutinies and drug abuse also plagued American units outside of Vietnam. During the first eight months of 1970 alone nearly one thousand sailors and marines were admitted to naval hospitals in the United States with diagnoses related to drug use.[188]

The antiwar movement consisted of a broad-based group of individuals and organizations that were as varied as they were numerous. Its members certainly opposed the war in Vietnam but this does not necessarily mean that they endorsed violence. "We are sympathetic to the frustrations that lead to an act of 'fragging'," said an antiwar civilian attorney who represented active-duty servicemen in Vietnam, "although we can't condone throwing a live grenade at someone."[189] Several organizations did attempt to make contact with young enlisted men during the Vietnam era but these groups generally sought to build the GI movement and provide it with politicized consciousness rather than urge the troops to kill their commanders. Moreover, organizations such as the ASU are not known to have ever collectively planned or carried out any fragging incidents. More typical of ASU activities were well-publicized group actions such as its plan for a "GI International Strike" on 15 April 1970, which called for the troops to register inspector general complaints, boycott mess halls, partake in mass sick calls, etc.[190] Individual acts of violence such as fraggings were not part of the itinerary.

The support for fragging that *did* appear within the antiwar movement tended to come from its most strident circles. Remarks attributed to actress-turned-activist Jane Fonda gloated over the phenomenon:

The army is running scared. . . . The guys are made to turn their guns
in at night, but still any blatantly racist officer can expect a hand grenade might roll under his tent flap some night when he's turned in. . . .
No smart officer would send his men on a dangerous mission, ask them
to cut their hair or beards or stop smoking pot, because he would be
shot.[191]

While antiwar organizations are not known to have orchestrated or
carried out any fragging incidents, some radicals championed the alienation that emerged between the military leadership corps and the young
enlisted men, and were quick to equate this "class warfare" with their
own activism. They roared with approval when the men turned their
guns (and grenades) around on the brass and politicized the fragging
phenomenon to conform to their own agenda. Some of the "underground" GI newspapers they produced used shrill rhetoric that sanc-
tioned or even encouraged fragging. An article found in the ASU's
official organ, the *Bond*, went as far as voicing approval of the 1970
murder of Staff Sergeant Paul E. Reed of the 173d Airborne Brigade:

Another Lifer Dropped From Rolls

Since the Vietnam War began, over 45,000 of our GI brothers and half
a million Vietnamese people have been killed. We know that most of
the GIs who have died didn't want to have anything to do with this
rotten war, but they were forced to fight and forced to die.

However, some people go to Vietnam not because they are forced to
but for their own gains in rank, pay, and black market rackets. One of
these pig lifers, S.Sgt. Reed, of the 173rd Abn., thought that he could
get away with all this and fuck with the E[nlisted] M[en] as well. Along
with the other pigs in his unit, he constantly drove his men and put
them in a bind where they were fighting to stay alive—or [for] his glory
and for the profits of the moneymen who run this country.

It's always a pleasure to hear that one of these pigs has got his just
desserts [sic], and on Oct. 29th someone presented Reed with a real
lifer's reward—a hand grenade. Reed died two days later but his spirit
lives on as long as lifers are getting people killed.[192]

But even here not all of the journal's readers agreed. One ASU member penned an eloquent letter to the editor expressing his fear that the antiwar movement was "in danger of adopting a policy of violence." Nevertheless, the *Bond* was hardly the only GI newspaper to cheer for the fraggers. During his 1972 stateside trial for the murders of Lieutenants Dellwo and Harlan, Private Billy Dean Smith became a cause célèbre in the pages of several radical publications that slavishly praised him as a "valiant opponent [of] the most heinous war of genocide in modern times," a victim of a "government conspiracy," and a man forced "to fight another war of aggression for a government that has offered him only brutal racism and depression-ridden streets."[193] Fort McClellan's *Left Face* called fragging "an effective way to deal with 'lifer chickenshit'" and urged its readers to "Seize the time!" *Up From the Bottom*, a paper printed in California, ran a story concerning a 1971 antiwar demonstration in which a dozen Vietnam veterans from the San Diego Veterans Union assembled at San Diego State University to "remind everybody that the Vietnam War was still going on." Donning military uniforms and carrying toy M16 rifles, the men "patrolled" the campus, hunting for "Viet Cong," who had been recruited from the women's studies department. "The women," the piece read, "won all the battles and the vets (except for the sergeant and lieutenant who were fragged on the spot) defected to the Vietnamese."[194] There was even one antiwar paper that was titled *Fragging Action*, although it seems to have disappeared shortly after its premiere at Fort Dix, New Jersey.

It was presumably from Western publications that the North Vietnamese learned of the fragging phenomenon. In several of her radio messages aimed at U.S. troops in South Vietnam, communist broadcaster "Hanoi Hannah" spoke of enlisted men fragging "officers and non-com officers who insist on sending them out on combat missions." She even mentioned one particular grenade incident, the Billy Dean Smith case, which had received significant coverage in many news journals and antiwar sheets.

There was one grenade incident for which the perpetrators did have an incontrovertibly "idealistic" motive, though it did not involve antiwar activism. On the night of 5 November 1970, a group of fifty to sixty

black soldiers of the 1st Cavalry Division gathered in a vacant tent at
Fire Support Base Buttons "to find ways and means of doing something
to 'Whitey' to force him to pay attention to the blacks."[195] Private Garen
P. Thibodeaux called the meeting to order and declared, "This is the
time for us to get together and start hitting back at the white man like
he has been hitting us!" One man suggested fragging an enlisted club
frequented by white soldiers but this idea was quickly rejected, as many
of the men had white friends and did not want to injure anyone.[196] It
was eventually decided to "hit 'the man' in his pocket" by destroying
expensive equipment, so on the following evening, Specialist Four Jeffery J. Fryer and Private William H. Brown, Jr., obtained grenades and
used them to destroy two of their unit's helicopters.[197] The act was certainly successful in attracting command attention, but the perpetrators
were apprehended after an intense CID investigation.[198] When Fryer
admitted to procuring the grenades and Brown confessed to throwing
them, authorities moved quickly to remove the men from the ranks.
Fryer, Thibodeaux, and alleged conspirator Private Michael S. Vanderberg were administratively discharged within weeks of the incident;
Brown was convicted of willfully damaging the aircraft and sentenced
to nine months of confinement.[199]

The grenade incident at Buttons provides an interesting insight into
the "politics" of the fragging phenomenon. The black soldiers who carried out the attack at the helipad took a "big picture" view of their situation in Vietnam. Angry with the system they believed treated them
unfairly, they lashed out at impersonal symbols of that system. The
convicted fraggers, on the other hand, were unprepossessing of such
ideas. They too felt slighted, but their intellectual horizons extended
little further than the personal beefs they had with their superiors.
Rather than making political statements, they attempted to kill or injure the men they believed to be responsible for their misfortunes, in
many cases for the most trivial of reasons.

There were also grenade incidents that were simply the results of petty
feuds and drunken fistfights among servicemen. One man booby-
trapped the vehicle assigned to a soldier who had been bullying him.[200]

Another tossed a grenade at a man who had severely beaten a friend of his.[201] The very first fragging murder committed by an American during the war was the result of a card game (Tonk) gone bad. After a night of heavy drinking and several rounds of cards, an argument ensued between Specialist Four Marvin Baldwin and Private First Class Willie F. Robertson of the 20th Engineer Battalion. The two eventually came to blows, and when Baldwin emerged on the losing end, he obtained a grenade and sought to even the score. But as was the case in so many fragging homicides, the wrong man paid with his life. When the grenade detonated, it killed Private First Class Paul E. Nadeau, who was attempting to diffuse the situation, and injured several others.[202]

A singularly unusual fragging was the case of Staff Sergeant Frank Contreras, a veteran NCO who had fought in Korea. According to a military police desk blotter, Contreras caught two soldiers engaging in a homosexual act inside a troop tent in Dau Tieng. Incensed, he allegedly tossed a grenade into the tent, wounding one of the men in the head, arm, and side.[203] Contreras was apprehended by authorities but quickly released, presumably owing to a lack of evidence. Several weeks after the incident, Contreras was wounded in action and subsequently received the Silver Star for valor. He retired from the army in 1969 after twenty years of service.[204]

Fragging and South Vietnamese Nationals

More than a few of the fraggings that took place during the war involved South Vietnamese nationals. These incidents were often the results of contact between Americans and Vietnamese that was unrelated to the military mission; in fact, several were the contaminants of alcohol-related brawls that erupted in base camps or Vietnamese cities. In the great majority of these cases, GIs targeted Vietnamese, although cases were also observed in which South Vietnamese troops attacked Americans.

When the American buildup in Vietnam began, relations between U.S. military personnel and their Vietnamese hosts were generally cordial. Yet it was a South Vietnamese soldier who caused the first two American fragging deaths of the war. On the night of 14 July 1966,

ARVN private Huynh Van Tri tossed a grenade onto the patio of a bar frequented by U.S. servicemen in Vung Tau. Eleven Americans were injured, and Specialists Five David L. Cox and John L. Dodson eventually died of their wounds. When Vietnamese authorities arrested Tri several days later, he admitted his crime, claiming that several black GIs had beaten him several days earlier and that he had thrown the grenade in retaliation.[205]

As the war continued, relations between U.S. troops and local nationals considerably worsened.[206] Many young GIs came to possess thoroughly negative images of the Vietnamese. To them, the fact that they were needed in Vietnam at all intimated that the South Vietnamese armed forces were incompetent. Vietnamese culture was seen as primitive and unappealing. Viet Cong guerrillas usually dressed in civilian clothes and blended in with the civilian population, causing the Americans to view their hosts with suspicion, and racial biases led them to lump together all Vietnamese as "gooks." In rear areas, the Americans' interaction with local nationals was often limited to dealings with street peddlers and prostitutes, suggesting that the Vietnamese were out to exploit them.[207] Such sentiments were exacerbated by veteran troops who delighted in frightening newcomers with lurid tales that ranged from the somewhat plausible to the patently ridiculous, and the stories were told and retold until they became a kind of mythology.

For their own part, many Vietnamese resented the large American presence in their country. Staggering numbers of civilians were killed or made homeless by U.S. firepower.[208] Road accidents involving military vehicles and local nationals became commonplace and, during the late years of the war, often led to physical confrontations and protests.[209] Individual acts of cruelty, usually perpetrated by young, immature servicemen against Vietnamese noncombatants, became fixtures in military police desk blotters. The 1968 MACV Command History conceded that "recent untoward reaction by US Forces personnel to situations involving contact with Vietnamese citizens and their property show that some of our personnel either do not understand or are not concerned about the relationship between personal attitudes of US personnel and the goals which we are seeking to help this country attain."[210]

News of Vietnamization and the opinion that the Americans were aban-
doning South Vietnam to the communists further served to sour the
relationship.

As word spread of the pending U.S. withdrawal from Vietnam, acts
of violence became more frequent. On 30 March 1969, an ARVN soldier shot and killed Sergeant Chester H. Terry, Jr., of the 9th Infantry
Division, during a traffic dispute.[211] In June, South Vietnamese troops
of the 142nd Regional Force Company opened fire on a U.S. Marine
Corps CAP detachment, killing one marine and wounding another.[212]
Several weeks later, Lieutenant Colonel Nguyen Viet Can, commander
of the 11th Airborne Battalion, and two of his junior officers entered a
Saigon nightspot and confronted an American GI they found with an
attractive Vietnamese woman. Colonel Can shouted, "I've been in the
army for sixteen years and I'm tired of seeing Americans with Vietnamese girls!" When two American MPs arrived at the scene, the ARVNs
shot and killed them.[213] Several cases of fragging were also observed.
On 16 April 1970, Private Le Can Chuong of the 1st ARVN Armor
Regiment tossed a grenade into a movie theater occupied by fellow
Vietnamese and U.S. troops of the 31st Engineer Battalion, killing Specialist Five Edward L. Hubler, Jr., and injuring dozens of others.[214] In
another incident, six South Vietnamese soldiers attempted to frag an
American advisor who was attached to their unit. The NCO was un-
harmed in the attack, but his assailants were never identified.[215]

Conclusion

Pioneering sociologists studying combat units during the Second World
War established the concept of the primary group in the military context. It was the daily interaction between the men in these small groups,
the scientists reasoned, rather than patriotic sentiments, that motivated
soldiers to fight. When the dynamic within a particular group changed,
for better or for worse, so too did the men's effectiveness in the performance of their duties. During the late years of the Vietnam War, the
primary groups that comprised the U.S. military underwent this type
of change, and their performance was duly affected as a result. When
the usual organizational controls employed against undesired social

change failed, the armed forces experienced a crisis in morale and discipline that it had never before seen.

The accumulated data on the convicted fraggers suggests that they were more often than not troubled men who became further troubled by Vietnam. Most of them had left school and volunteered for military service at very young ages in order to escape from unresolved difficulties at home. They functioned well enough to be allowed into the service and complete their initial training, but once they arrived in Southeast Asia, problems surfaced. The men found that they had blundered into a war that was devoid of the glory they sought and for this they chose to hold their leaders responsible. Accordingly, commanders who demanded strict discipline or initiated unfavorable personnel action against them became targets.

Although there had been race riots in several U.S. cities during the initial U.S. buildup in Southeast Asia, relations between black and white troops in Vietnam remained harmonious until the assassination of Martin Luther King, Jr., in April 1968. Just as the voice of Black Power was beginning to drown out more moderate voices in the United States, news of King's death touched off the first manifestation of racial violence in Vietnam. Even then it began slowly, with a few nocturnal assaults and half-hearted grenade incidents that seemed to end as soon as they started. But the Long Binh Stockade riot in August of that year revealed that racial violence was now a part of life in the Vietnam-era U.S. military.

Drugs played a dual role in the fragging phenomenon. First, many fraggers used drugs, and, as Dr. Bond discovered, were intoxicated when they committed their offenses. This led to the conclusion that drug intoxication may have clouded the offenders' judgment enough to cause them to act out violently. Second, those leaders who cracked down on drug use in their units provided yet another motive for the attacks. When both of these factors are considered together, it might lead to the conclusion that drugs were perhaps the single most important aspect of fragging. It is only when one considers the historical chronology of the war that drug abuse can be placed in its proper setting. The U.S. military command admitted that drugs were freely available to the troops in Vietnam as early as 1966, yet it was not until the pivotal political and social events of 1968 that fragging incidents began to occur in large numbers. Therefore, drugs played an important, albeit secondary, role in the phenomenon.

The debate over antiwar activism and its role in fragging continues within Vietnam War literature. Military sources cite law enforcement data or Dr. Bond's clinical study and dismiss the fraggers as low-functioning, disturbed men whose aberrant behavior did not reflect the attitudes of the average soldier. While it is true that many of the convicted perpetrators have been shown to possess these characteristics, this position fails to explain why so many grenade incidents occurred in Vietnam and not during America's other conflicts. On the other hand, antiwar writers chronicling "GI resistance" tend to anoint fraggers, deserters, and other Vietnam-era offenders as revolutionaries by assuming that their motivations were political. This argument is also inadequate, for most studies of these men conclude that their actions had more to do with poor situational adjustments to military life than politics.[216] Furthermore, it does not explain why certain men performed these acts while the great majority of their peers did not. What is needed is a synthesis of the two positions that explains both why the fragging phenomenon occurred during the latter years of the Vietnam War and why these particular individuals were the ones who acted this way.

Once the crisis in morale and discipline emerged, the military had to face phenomena that in previous years it had managed to avoid. This was a dilemma that the services proved unable to overcome, as will be seen in the next chapter.

CHAPTER FOUR

The Military's Response

W HEN the U.S. military began its Vietnam buildup, its thinking was strongly influenced by the lessons it had learned during the Second World War and Korea. Senior leaders believed that morale and disciplinary problems could be solved the same way they had been dealt with in the past: through the exercise of effective leadership. In November 1965, the army published a new edition of its military leadership manual in which young officers and NCOs were told how leadership could overcome "the internal and external stresses [that] tend to cause a man to function ineffectively." These "stresses," the manual stated, included "rumor, fear, hunger, illness, enemy fire, anxiety, [and] fatigue."[1] Clearly the authors were referring to the experiences of previous conflicts, for the Vietnamization period introduced several new, unanticipated factors that were not considered, these ranging from the war's unpopularity to the social problems the troops brought with them when they entered the service. The leadership corps, which by this late stage of the war was stretched to the breaking point, was hard-pressed to meet these challenges. Nevertheless, the brass persisted in its traditional view that leadership could save the day. General Westmoreland, for one, was convinced that fragging was a "spin-off of unit discipline" and that the solution was to "hold leaders accountable."[2] Accountable or not, events proved that it would take more than leadership techniques to stop the fraggers.

The advent of the fragging phenomenon caught senior military leaders off guard. Although the army and Marine Corps both possessed well-organized law enforcement organizations, no command-level policies existed to combat the violence because the morale and discipline problems that emerged during Vietnamization had never been experienced on such a large scale. As a result, leaders at the brigade and division levels were forced to improvise appropriate anti-fragging measures through trial and error before command-level guidelines were instituted. Though grenade incidents began to occur in army and Marine Corps units at about the same time, the two services did not take uniform action to end the problem. Both took great pains to end the plague but fell short of finding a solution.

Fraggings began to occur in Marine Corps units in significant numbers during the early months of 1969. The 3d Marine Division was hit particularly hard, with three men killed and over a dozen injured within a ninety-day period.[3] The division commander, Major General William K. Jones, was a tough infantry officer who had won the Navy Cross at Saipan during World War II. Now faced with the dilemma of fragging, he decided on firm action to end the problem. On 4 July 1969, he issued an order that came to be known as Operation Freeze. The plan provided guidelines that were to be followed immediately after a fragging incident occurred in order to identify and apprehend the perpetrators, a task that had proven elusive. It called for military police and, if necessary, a stand-by reaction force to first seal off the area where the crime had taken place. Roll calls were then to be conducted and all missing personnel as well as those present who were not assigned to the unit were to be apprehended and interrogated. Junior NCOs and enlisted men were to be confined to their quarters, and all leaves and transfers postponed for the length of the investigation. The area was then to be thoroughly searched for evidence. Finally, the men themselves were to be questioned.[4] In an attempt to minimize peer influences, the order stipulated that interrogations were to be conducted individually; as Jones explained, the interrogators would "call in each marine and point out to him his responsibilities as a man, a marine, and a Christian." A senior officer described the procedure this way:

> We have a technique we call Operation Freeze, which means that if you have a crime of violence of this kind, everything in that unit stops. We put up a physical cordon around the area and everyone is regarded as a material witness until the investigation has been completed. [This] means nobody goes on R&R, no one rotates back to the States, no one even goes to the post exchange until the investigators are satisfied that they've wrung out every bit of information that's available.[5]

Though similar measures had been taken since the earliest fragging incidents, at no time had such a standardized procedure been instituted by a senior commander.

About a year after drafting his "Freeze" guidelines, General Jones assumed command of all Marine Corps forces in the Pacific. He soon learned that fragging was again on the rise in Vietnam. "They were having another rash of fragging in III MAF," he later told an interviewer. "I went out on a visit there [on 14–15 July 1970] and had a big session with all the division commanders and I told Keith [McCutcheon, commander of III Marine Amphibious Force] about my division order. And I said, 'Keith, you've got to stop this.' He agreed . . . of course. So I sent my order to him and he took it, and he wrote a III MAF order based on that order."[6] The result was Force Order 3120.4, which was distributed to all Marine Corps units in Vietnam. The order's success in apprehending perpetrators can best be measured by the case of the 1st Marine Division. "Of the forty-seven incidents in 1970," wrote assistant division commander Edwin H. Simmons, "twenty-two were solved, from which thirty-seven suspects/offenders were identified through investigation. However, markedly better results were obtained as the year progressed. During the first half of the year, ten of the twenty-six acts were solved (38%). During the following three-month period, five of ten were solved (50%), while during the last three months of the year, seven of eleven were solved (64%). Much of this progress may be attributed to the implementation . . . of 'Operation Freeze.'" Long-term data concerning the plan's effectiveness is unavailable, as it was not fully implemented until a time when the leathernecks were preparing to quit Vietnam, and, as General Simmons pointed out, "few, if any, such incidents will occur in the units standing down."[7]

The Marine Corps also opted to limit the amounts of ordnance issued to troops in rear areas, seeking to limit the fraggers' accessibility to the tools of their trade. These measures doubtlessly prevented such maladies as accidental discharges but they also bore a negative effect on enlisted morale. One marine told visiting Congressman William F. Nichols:

> We came over here to fight a war. Like, when I was on Hill 65, you
> can't fight a war with forty rounds [of ammunition] and two

magazines. They took all our rounds and stuff away from us and they said as long as you are in the rear you won't need this.

Mr. Nichols: Why did they restrict you to forty rounds?

Marine: People were fragging lieutenants, officers.[8]

What was perhaps the earliest anti-fragging effort mounted by the army was initiated not by a senior commander but by a recently discharged enlisted man. During 1969, the 1st Battalion, 7th Cavalry, sustained more than its share of the incidents—six within a nine-month span, resulting in a number of injuries. All of the attacks were aimed at the unit command structure: several grenades were thrown at NCO billets, while others detonated near the battalion's S-1 (personnel) office and company orderly rooms. One of the wounded men, Sergeant Stephen S. Canaday, was discharged from the army in January 1970. Shortly after his release, he penned a letter to his former division commander, Major General E. B. Roberts, voicing his concerns about the incidents. "I am a former 'Skytrooper,'" Canaday wrote, "[and] am writing out of concern for my fellow man and due to a serious situation which had not been handled properly nor corrected." He continued:

During the period that I served with [1/7th Cavalry], there were seven attempts of murder (I hardly see any other way to title it) within the battalion rear by means of grenade throwing. Not one of these cases were solved; several were not even investigated (unless you consider a CID report an investigation). One of these incidents . . . could very easily have had further investigation and proper action taken, had anyone taken an interest.

Many people within the battalion found out that Patrick Sprauer threw a grenade at the Headquarters Company orderly room on 7 September 1969 because he told several personnel within the Maintenance Section. This was reported to the sergeant major and a couple of officers. Yet nothing was done about it.

I feel that a few personnel were out to get First Sergeant [Tyson C. Gilland] and did soon after the 7 September incident. [They] realized that Sprauer and others had gotten away clean and therefore, they felt confident that they could get 1SG [Gilland] without much trouble. I feel that 1SG [Gilland] may not have been "fragged" if someone had taken an interest in the previous incidents. I also feel confident that these incidents will continue unless someone steps in and takes proper action. . . . General Roberts, I bid you to see that this action is taken.[9]

Upon receipt of Canaday's letter, the division's provost marshal, Lieutenant Colonel Ronald R. Rasmussen, began an in-depth inquiry concerning the ex-sergeant's allegations. Written statements were obtained from thirty-two of the battalion's soldiers and information was compiled on possible perpetrators, motives, and, not surprisingly, Canaday himself. What Rasmussen found was a unit little different from any other serving in Vietnam in 1970. The enlisted men reported a multitude of problems, from stress caused by an increased guard commitment to drug use and racial tension. Officers complained of the length of time required to confirm personal claims and process administrative discharges as well as the lack of pretrial confinement. It was also discovered that two of the fraggings had not even been reported to the military police. But contrary to Canaday's claims, Rasmussen learned that some measures had indeed been taken to remedy the problem: an interior guard had been posted and additional lighting had been installed in the battalion rear, a sign-in/sign-out roster was established for enlisted men and junior NCOs, and access was denied to company areas to all but unit personnel during late-night hours. Efforts were also made to expedite disciplinary action against lawbreakers, and greater emphasis was placed on early identification of command problems and proper counseling of soldiers.

Rasmussen concluded that fraggings were caused by the army's inheritance of larger societal problems. Contrary to the period's increasingly lenient mores, he recommended stricter unit discipline to restore order:

> If fraggings are to abate, an entire crackdown on lawlessness must start. This means that leaders who measure leadership by statistics must do so combined with liberal doses of sage wisdom. When the social ills of a strife-torn permissive society are foisted upon the army, we can well expect to have soldiers ending up in jail. The first step in solving the problem army-wide in Vietnam is to reverse the overall at-

titude concerning confinement. . . . Then, at every echelon, we must convince the soldier that a society will remain a good society as long as the law is upheld. Anything else will produce chaos. The third step is to retain commanders who are willing to punish the deserving swiftly and impartially. The positive impact of a hard-nosed commander is dramatic. Knowing that punishment is sure to come is one of the greatest deterrents available to prevent crime.

But not everyone agreed with this "get tough" approach. While the division's senior legal officer praised Rasmussen's report and agreed that a more suitable policy regarding confinement would be desirable, he did not believe that a crackdown on discipline would serve as a cure-all for the battalion's woes:

I don't see it as a panacea for all that ails us in the area of discipline. A carte blanche policy on confinement would only invite the weak commander to sweep all his problems under the rug. If there were no restrictions on confinement, there would be 100–200 division personnel in the stockade. . . . [There exists] a desire for simple solutions, Draconian measures for the most part. The problems are far too complex to admit of easy answers. A response of "put 'em in jail" to every challenge of authority will not work, it will only exacerbate the situation.

Many of the statements, particularly those [of] the officers, assume that all virtue is on one side. While no amount of harassment or poor leadership justifies "fragging," some of the statements from the E-4s and E-5s [the specialists, corporals, and sergeants] indicate that some of the problems may have been caused by the failure of the junior officers and NCOs to communicate with the enlisted men.

Additionally, this officer spoke of his own efforts at shortening the time necessary for trying courts-martial and his willingness to try "particularly troublesome" cases as soon as possible.[10] Nevertheless, complaints about the lack of pretrial confinement in Vietnam persisted,[11] as did 1/7's morale problems. Several months after Rasmussen submitted his report, racial strife racked the battalion's B Company, resulting in an attempt upon the company commander's life.[12]

The army's first command-level response to fragging came in September 1970. Lieutenant General McCaffrey, the USARV deputy commanding general, penned a letter to his field commanders outlining the problem of what he called "non-combat grenade and firearm incidents." During the first eight months of 1970, he wrote, there had been eighty-five of these assaults, many of which were aimed at officers and NCOs. McCaffrey thought that there were two major contributing factors that led to the incidents: first, that the enlisted men did not feel that their leaders had established an atmosphere conducive to the discussion of their problems; and, second, that there was a lack of security and accountability of grenades and firearms. He believed that communication was crucial in halting the attacks: "Unit leaders must know their men, so that enlisted personnel will routinely seek out their officers and NCOs for assistance when confronted with a problem. The officers and NCOs in turn must actively demonstrate their interest and sincere willingness to provide the necessary guidance and assistance. This has always been the privilege and the responsibility of an officer."

McCaffrey reminded field commanders that soldiers with psychological problems should be directed toward medical channels before they caused any harm. To limit the availability of lethal ordnance to troops in rear areas, he urged that strict control measures and accountability of weapons, ammunition, and grenades be maintained.[13]

As was the case with the marines, a number of army organizations in the field responded to fragging by adopting their own measures. On 1 September 1970, the American Division issued a reference letter on the subject. "There appears to be an increasing number of incidents involving the unauthorized detonation of explosive devices," the letter read. "Many of these incidents are commonly referred to as 'fragging' in which grenades are exploded in the vicinity of NCO and officer quarters." The letter established a procedure to be taken in case an incident occurred:

a. Notify military police.
b. Have an immediate muster of all troops in the area.
c. Cordon off the scene of the crime.
d. Insure that evidence is not disturbed until the arrival of the military police or criminal investigators.

In addition, an officer from the division's military police company was tasked with maintaining statistics on the incidents and running correlations "to determine which areas are the biggest offenders and saturate this area with patrols and find out where these unauthorized detonations are likely to occur."[14] In December 1970, Lieutenant General James W. Sutherland, Jr., whose XXIV Corps shared several of South Vietnam's northern provinces with the marines, obtained a copy of the latter's 3120.4 order and sent it to the Americal Division commander. The order, Sutherland wrote, "prescribe[s] certain policies and procedures in effect within III Marine Amphibious Force which merit our consideration. These are forwarded for your information and possible adaptation to programs of your command."[15] Inspired by the marine experience, the Americal assembled a large team of investigators and dispatched it to crime scenes to interrogate suspects. The MPs jokingly called the group the Super Heavy Interrogation Team, or S.H.I.T.[16] Colonel Verner N. Pike, the Americal's provost marshal in 1971, wrote: "The Division SOP required a unit in which a fragging occurred to notify the military police, who would show up in platoon strength. [They would] fall the unit out in formation and keep them under armed guard while the other M.P. elements searched the entire unit area for evidence or a missing soldier. . . . I remember one fragging incident in Chu Lai in the spring of 1971. Everyone in the unit was turned out of the hooches [and made to stand] in formation for hours until someone got tired and 'ratted' on the miscreant."[17]

The division also published a circular regulating the custody and control of weapons and explosive devices. It called for the consolidation of weapons in centrally located arms rooms and required commanders to conduct periodic inspections and monthly inventories of all weapons. In addition, a "Division Weapons and Ammunition Inspection Team" was to conduct quarterly checks of unit arms rooms. The division commander even went as far as removing grenades from rear area bunker lines and moving them into controlled areas, a move that generated considerable media attention.[18]

The 173d Airborne Brigade adopted its own measures to deal with fraggings. Its version, which was not unlike the Americal's, told unit commanders to:

(1) Cordon off the scene of the incident.

(2) Call an alert; keep alert in effect until arrival of CID investigators.

(3) Place any suspect under guard until cleared or placed in pre-trial confinement.

"Living quarters should not be searched until after the investigation team has completed its work," cautioned General Elmer R. Ochs, commander of the 173d. "Admissibility of the evidence may be jeopardized if the search is not executed properly. Secondly, untrained searchers will have no idea of what they are looking for and may unwittingly remove incriminating evidence."[19] The 173d also limited its men's access to ordnance. "Fragmentation grenades are not used for base camp defense. . . . Such use would require the express approval of the [brigade commander]."[20] A member of a visiting congressional subcommittee in Vietnam queried Ochs about this practice:

> Congressman Nichols: General, do you issue weapons to all your command?
>
> General Ochs: No, sir. People in the base camp area here do not carry weapons. They are available to them, but they are kept under lock and key readily available and not in a central location, but dispersed in this area—his area of work or area of billets. This has not always been the case. It has been a tightening up. As the war grinds down and we have very little contact [with the enemy] here and less need for the weapons, and as the [shooting and grenade] incidents begin to plague us, we tighten up.[21]

Circular 190–3 and the "Moratorium"

As journalists published their fragging stories during the first weeks of 1971, military leadership began to feel the heat. In the face of increasing press scrutiny and upcoming congressional hearings, Department of the Army officials in Washington sent a confidential cable to senior commanders in Vietnam in late January demanding answers. "[The] U.S. news media is giving considerable coverage to fragmentation grenade incidents in RVN," the cable read. "The following information is required: (a) a definition or meaning of the term fragging in Vietnam; (b) detailed statistical data, including categorization of the types of incidents, such as against officers or NCOs, unit vs. unit, racial, etc.; (c) actions commanders are taking to reduce or control fragging incidents; (d) assessment of the threat posed by these incidents; and (e) any other information which will assist DA in addressing the subject."[22] On 5 February, General McCaffrey broached the subject at a USARV staff conference and asked for suggestions on how to combat the problem. Accordingly, a "brainstorm session" was conducted between representatives of the three relevant branches of the USARV bureaucracy: the provost marshal's office, which was responsible for law enforcement, the staff judge advocate office, which handled legal matters, and the office of the deputy chief of staff for personnel and administration, which dealt with personnel procedures and troop morale.

The meeting produced three preventative measures that were combined to form a prospective USARV order. The first measure involved limiting troop access to explosive devices. To this end, a radical step was suggested: a command-wide recall of all fragmentation grenades in USARV. In conjunction with the recall, a moratorium on the issuance of grenades would be declared while unit leaders conducted thorough searches of troop areas for hidden ordnance. Once an inventory was made, grenades would then be distributed only to units that engaged in close combat with the enemy. Each soldier would have to sign a hand receipt upon issuance and would face disciplinary action if he could not account for their loss or expenditure. Any man found carrying an unauthorized grenade was to be charged with possession of a dangerous weapon. Officers were to conduct daily inventories of grenade stocks as well as frequent shakedown inspections of their men's billets for weapons and other contraband.[23]

The second suggested measure dealt with education and training. Representatives from the personnel and administration office had long believed that new soldiers did not understand the "destructive potential" of explosive devices. "I believe that fragging is a fad, and the individual does not actually realize the damage one of these grenades can do," one official said. "We have sent word back to [the United States] that a grenade demonstration, possibly against a plywood figure of a man, should be presented to soldiers before they arrive in Vietnam. The destructiveness of a fragmentation grenade would be readily apparent. I believe this would reduce the level of incidents significantly."[24] The USARV planners even envisioned a one-time class for all soldiers in Vietnam demonstrating the lethality of grenades. "The idea," they said, "was to make it clear that the grenade is not a 'firecracker' to be used to frighten or terrorize, but that it is a highly dangerous weapon whose effects can kill indiscriminately."

The third measure was the "islands of defense" concept. Barbed-wire obstacles were to be installed to separate unit areas, motor parks, and supply yards, while armed guards would staff "gates" within the enclosed areas and limit access to troop areas. "Such control would make it more difficult for the would-be grenade thrower to operate and tend to reduce the number of possible suspects [to those located within the enclosure] in the actual event," the planners wrote.[25]

After the conference adjourned, a number of other USARV staff offices were asked to submit ideas about how to curb fragging. Though most responded with little more than the usual demands for a crackdown on discipline, a number of particularly innovative proposals were subsequently added to the measures proposed at the conference. One suggested an informal form of social control: use of the military's press organs to change the fragger's image among the troops:

> Expose the perpetrator for exactly what he is—a coward. As long as the perpetrator does not regard himself as a coward, his self-respect remains intact. Once he is exposed to himself and the small number of his peers with whom he has credibility, any illusions they may harbor are shattered and all concerned are less able to rationalize the cowardly act into a noble one.
>
> The troop leader can discredit the potential "fragger" if he anticipates the problem and addresses it from this point of view. We [USARV] can help by publicizing this philosophy through our communications media. The potential "fragger" who repeatedly hears himself described by AFVN and [Stars and Stripes] as a despicable coward . . . is much less likely to identify with this image.[26]

Another suggestion was that court-martial proceedings in fragging cases be "convened in the minimum allowable time under the law and the results of trial[s] be widely publicized."[27] But the planners also learned that there was no shortage of dissent regarding their prospective measures. Many believed that the grenade recall was logistically impractical and that the weekly inventories of weapons stocks were too much of an administrative burden. Opposition was also voiced to the grenade lethality demonstration, which instead of its intended purpose of educating the troops could propagate the fragging idea and lead to an increase in incidents. The islands of defense concept, it was argued, would mean increased guard commitments for the enlisted ranks and intensification of their unrest while serving notice of the command's uneasiness regarding fragging.[28]

In spite of these doubts, a draft version of the prospective order was prepared and distributed at a USARV commanders conference on 21 April.[29] Each senior officer was asked to provide comments on the draft, and while some proved reticent in responding, others had plenty to say on the subject.[30] General Ochs objected to the draft's use of the slang term "fragging":

> "Fraggings" should be called for what they are—murder or attempted murder. The term "fragging" implies an irresponsible, permissive act. More accurately, these occurrences describe furtive, cowardly attempts to murder, maim, or intimidate and, for the most part, are planned to minimize chance of detection/apprehension.[31]

Ochs was not alone is his distaste for the "f" word. Several other commanders made similar recommendations,[32] and MACV responded by outlawing official use of the term:

6 May 71
From: COMUSMACV
To: VMAC
Subject: Use of the Term "Fragging"
1. A slang term which has recently come into widespread use in this command is the verb to frag (alternate forms: fragged and fragging). These

terms are commonly used in reference to the murder or attempted murder of one American by another, usually through the use of explosives.

2. A casual slang term is clearly inappropriate when used in reference to premeditated murder, attempted murder, or aggravated assault. The felony appears less serious than when called by its proper name. "Fragging" apparently does not carry the same stigma that murder does.

3. Use of the words frag, fragged, and fragging in official correspondence and reports will cease immediately. Criminal acts will henceforth be described in the appropriate legal terminology.[33]

The final version of the anti-fragging directive, which was titled "Reduction of Shooting and Grenade Incidents" and released as USARV Circular 190–3, was drafted on 15 May. It called for something unprecedented in the annals of warfare: for seven days, the U.S. Army would stop issuing hand grenades to nearly all of its soldiers in Vietnam. During that period, shakedown inspections were to be conducted within all USARV units and inventories made of ordnance stocks. In addition, a near carbon copy of the marines' Force Order 3120.4 was appended to the circular to assist commanders in apprehending suspects, and the USARV staff judge advocate and information offices were ordered to publicize convictions in fragging cases. Once this was completed, effective leadership and improved physical control of ordnance were prescribed to prevent further incidents.

Originally planned to begin on 1 June 1971, the grenade moratorium was postponed for two weeks and did not start until the fifteenth. Most of the inspections seem to have taken place without incident, although some of the officers conducting the searches quickly found that they had their hands full. As one group was shaking down an infantry unit's area, it was gassed with a CS grenade.[34] After the commander of the 585th Engineer Detachment secured his men's weapons in the unit arms room, he found a grenade on his desk with an attached note that read, "Captain Seymour, give us our weapons or else."[35] As usual, the army chose to look at the bright side; according to a transcript of a USARV commanders' conference held in early July, the plan had succeeded in achieving some of its goals. "No commands requested any exemption from the inventory moratorium," beamed the briefing offi-

Table 5

Month (1971)	Actual Assaults	Possible Assaults
July	21	9
August	24	4
September	17	16

cer. "The inventory introduced a windfall of benefits besides improving the control of munitions and [explosive] devices. A considerable amount of contraband was found, to include knives, machetes, razors, hatchets, bayonets, assorted types of ammunition, smoke grenades, etc."[36] But in spite of its best efforts, the army did not succeed in stopping the fragging phenomenon. Eighteen incidents occurred during June, including several *during* the moratorium. In the following months, the number of fraggings actually increased, as shown in Table 5 above.[37]

In a letter to MACV Commander Creighton W. Abrams, General McCaffrey admitted that "an analysis of the September statistics reveals that . . . grenade incidents remain unfavorably high."[38] Equally disappointing was the fact that there was no increase in the number of perpetrators apprehended. Of those fragging cases that occurred in the six months after the moratorium (July–December 1971), only three convictions were obtained.[39] One reason for the poor results was the fact that the soldiers were still able to obtain explosives. "It was easy for troops to get arms, ammunition, and grenades," wrote one officer who served in the 1st Cavalry Division after the moratorium. "[They] made contact with local villagers and other units. There was a large black market in many of the villages where they could get almost anything."[40] Moreover, some units just did not comply with 190–3's exhortations to secure their ordnance. The Claymore mine used in an October 1971 homicide was removed from an unlocked Conex container.[41] The Claymore believed to have been used in a 1972 murder was simply dragged off the base perimeter.[42] No one noticed that the mines were missing until it was too late.

The army sought to avoid what it called "undue publicity" regarding its new anti-fragging measures but it was not long before word reached

the press.[43] Reporter Ted Duvall of CBS News asked USARV for a copy
of Circular 190–3 but was refused. He was eventually permitted to submit a list of questions regarding the circular to which army officials
prepared terse, carefully worded responses."[44] Surviving documentation from this episode reveals both the army's sensitivity on the fragging issue and its inherent distrust of the press. After this guarded
response was provided to mainstream CBS, one officer, fearing that
radical journalists might pick up the story, warned, "While these answers don't seem too controversial in themselves, other media could
take a different tack with the story and we would be required to provide them equal information."[45]

It was not until the bulk of U.S. military forces had quit Southeast
Asia that the army conducted a command-level analysis of fragging
incidents. During a visit to South Vietnam in January 1972, General
Westmoreland met with USARV staff members and discussed the fragging problem at length. Westmoreland directed that "an in-depth study
of 'fraggings' be made to determine contributive factors."[46] USARV officials held several meetings on the subject in early February and discussed how such a study could be conducted. One recommendation
called for an "in house" project to be carried out by personnel already
in Vietnam, another proposed bringing in behavioral scientists from
the United States, while a third suggested a combination of the two.
The idea of the study group conducting an "on scene" evaluation of an
incident immediately after its occurrence was also considered but
judged to be impracticable as so few of the crimes were solved, and due
to the ongoing troop withdrawals from South Vietnam. To save time
and resources, the "in house" study was selected, though its proponents conceded its limited behavioral science and analysis capabilities.

The project turned out to be a disappointment. The only source
materials available to the study group were Serious Incident Reports
and CID reports of investigation obtained from the provost marshal's
office, and since these documents were more often descriptive than
analytical, they lacked the psychological data necessary for the type of
study Westmoreland had envisioned. As a result, the group was able to
assemble little more than a chronological list of the crimes along with
such details as the time of day and locations where they occurred, the

type of explosives used, the races of the perpetrators and victims, etc. "It seems to me that this action is a loser," wrote the USARV chief of staff upon his review of the study. "[I] recommend we quietly drop this."[47] Accordingly, General McCaffrey sentenced the project to a slow administrative death and did not forward the results to Washington. But when Pentagon officials began making inquiries on the subject several months later, a small bureaucratic war ensued. As General Westmoreland had retired from active duty by this time, his acting successor, General Bruce Palmer, Jr., finally allowed USARV to shelve the project. "We wore them down," mused one of McCaffrey's officers.[48] Ironically, just as the USARV bureaucrats were throwing in the towel, Dr. Bond was busy at the Leavenworth stockade conducting interviews with nearly thirty convicted fraggers for his own study.

In addition to remedies to prevent fraggings, military leaders sought to curb their motivating factors. In the case of racial strife, the army conducted an assessment of the matter in 1969 and instituted measures to deal with identified problem areas.[49] The following year, MACV issued a directive instructing commanders to ensure equal opportunity in their units, maintain open channels of communications with their men, and, in an effort to co-opt potential militancy, establish human relations councils to prevent racial crises from developing. By October 1971, 725 of these groups were meeting in South Vietnam, and special workshops were organized to ameliorate the continuing problem of personnel turnover. The councils were joined by battalion awareness teams and the Afro-American Cultural Association, a group formed at Tan Son Nhut Air Force Base that sought to bridge the communications gap between commanders and their men.[50] The Marine Corps fell back on its "Green Marine" policy, which proclaimed that marines were not black or white, but "green."[51] This concept proved to be ineffective because it discounted the significance of the men's pre-service attitudes and experiences. Army Lieutenant Colonel James S. White, a black officer whose insights on race were highly esteemed, noted:

The army has a race problem because our country has a race problem. Our soldiers enter the service as products of that society and continue, in this age of instant television communications and over-efficient press, to live as members of that society even while on active duty. They are not naïve on the subject of race. Our soldiers have been made aware of it in many ways and have built up a variety of attitudes long before they ever put on a uniform. A Negro in a uniform does not cease being a Negro and become a soldier instead. He becomes a Negro soldier.[52]

In September 1969, several weeks after a particularly bloody racial attack at Camp Lejeune, North Carolina, in which a white corporal was beaten to death,[53] Marine Corps Commandant Leonard F. Chapman, Jr., issued a directive known as ALMAR 65 (To All Marines Bulletin #65), which called on officers and enlisted men alike to put an end to the strife. Although the order officially frowned upon racially conscious Black Power salutes and symbols, blacks were allowed to sport Afro haircuts and perform racially oriented customs—like the handshake called "dapping"—while off-duty. An Equal Opportunities Branch was formed, while an effort was undertaken to alleviate the underrepresentation of blacks among the officer ranks of the Marine Corps.[54]

The army viewed illegal drug abuse as the most serious of its morale-related problems during the Vietnam era. As Vietnamese drug laws were not well defined, MACV pressed Saigon for assistance in curbing the flow of drugs while utilizing troop education to prevent usage.[55] Senior leadership claimed that "all commanders and troops were educated as to the dangers to health and criminal penalties involved in the use of marijuana" but the message apparently did not reach everyone, as Courtney L. Frobenius, who served as a platoon leader in the 9th Infantry Division in 1968–1969, remembered:

> As I didn't use drugs, I didn't know what they were. I had never had any classes in officer candidate school about them. I didn't have a clue so I assumed my unit was drug-free! At least that was my assumption until one day when we were in the field [and] the lead squad was taking its time searching some hooches. I radioed up and asked what the problem was and [received a peculiar answer]. So I walked up to the squad and saw a sight I will always remember: there was Gonzales, a strapping six-footer, holding a plastic bag in one hand and using his M-16 as a shield with the other while this 80-year-old, four-foot-tall

Vietnamese woman was beating him with her cane. I could plainly see that he had something of hers so I told him to give it back. It was a bag of marijuana! This old woman smoked marijuana. It was from this day on that I began to notice the strange aromas where the troops bunked, and my men's red, glassy eyes.[56]

The army's early efforts against marijuana were unsuccessful owing to the failure of the Vietnamese government to limit the drug's availability as well as the fairly common attitude among young enlisted men of the harmlessness of recreational marijuana use. This opinion, as the brass was quick to point out, was one that servicemen often brought with them into the armed services from civilian life. Undaunted, MACV took to using helicopters to locate marijuana fields in the Mekong Delta and utilizing marijuana-detecting dogs, which had been employed by the U.S. Customs Service with considerable success.[57]

Once heroin use among U.S. troops in Vietnam became a problem, the military's antidrug efforts intensified. In August 1970, MACV formed the Drug Abuse Task Force. Chaired by an official from the Justice Department's Bureau of Narcotics and Dangerous Drugs, the group included military members as well as civilian representatives of the U.S. Embassy, the customs service, and USAID. After several months of study, a new program was initiated that "provided for education, investigation, enforcement, and rehabilitation." Among the initiatives was a new education program, special "drug abuse suppression councils" to assist unit commanders, joint U.S.-Vietnamese law enforcement bodies to further coordinate their efforts, several administrative measures, and, perhaps most controversially, an amnesty and rehabilitation program designed to aid those men seeking to end their drug dependence.[58] The establishment of drug rehabilitation centers on military bases in Vietnam, such as Camp Holloway's Highland House, the Crossroads Center at Long Binh, and the 173d Airborne Brigade's Sky House at LZ English, generated considerable attention among legislators at home as well as journalists looking to publish stories on the subject.[59] Seventeen such centers were in operation army-wide by mid-1971, and over four thousand soldiers were treated during the first three months of the year.[60]

In June 1971, persistent drug use in both Vietnam and among youth

in the United States led President Nixon to order his "drug counterof-
fensive." The military responded with a massive drug user identification program in which mandatory urinalysis testing was to be performed
on all servicemen in Vietnam. Experimenters and users were sent to
in-country treatment centers while addicts were medically evacuated to
military hospitals or Veterans Administration facilities in the United
States. In September, the first drug education field teams, consisting of
military instructors, Vietnamese representatives, and civilian ex-ad-
dicts from the National Council for the Prevention of Drug Abuse, began canvassing South Vietnam. The teams presented informal talks to
small groups of personnel, and these were found to be unusually effective in alerting the troops to the dangers of drug use.[61] Renewed attempts were made to obtain the cooperation of local authorities, and
while some Vietnamese proved to be responsive to the effort, others
were reluctant to cooperate, in some cases because they were involved
in the traffic themselves. "It [is] not contested by our briefers in Southeast Asia," a group of visiting congressmen found, "that local nationals
holding public office in Vietnam are involved in illicit drug traffic. We
are told that this is one of the most discouraging aspects of drug suppression efforts in the country. The same is true in Thailand."[62]

For their part, the Marine Corps enacted its own education program
to inform its men of the dangers of drug abuse, and made half-hearted
attempts to rehabilitate drug users. It steadfastly refused to enact amnesty programs like those of the army until ordered to do so by the
Department of Defense, and for the most part simply drummed its
junkies out of the service.[63] In any case, with the period's societal mores
and the easy availability of illegal drugs in Southeast Asia, the military
was simply unable to end the problem.[64] "The only effective drug suppression for U.S. personnel in Vietnam," Congress concluded, "will
come with the withdrawal of our troops from that country."[65] The best
summary of this sad story is provided in a statement given by a legal
officer who once confronted a marine who appeared to be under the
influence of drugs:

"Just between you and me, have you had a little pot today?" asked the
officer.

"Sir," the man replied, "Just between you and me, I've had a little pot *every* day."[66]

As we have seen, the Marine Corps was firm in its belief that many of the fraggers were mentally unstable when they committed their crimes. One general encouraged company-grade officers to take preventive action in any case where a man's unusual behavior suggested that he might do something desperate:

> We would much rather prevent these fraggings before they occur than catch the offender *after* they occur. [T]here are a surprising number of cases *after* it happens, that we learn things like, "Oh, yes, we were worried about Bill, he'd been acting funny," or "So and so said he was going to frag the gunny," or the corporal or sergeant says, "Well, I put the man on report to the platoon leader but he didn't do anything about it." Or they say, "We were watching him." Well, you can't watch a person like this.
>
> What [is] your responsibility? Simply be alert to the potential offender, and never take lightly a report from one of your NCOs that he has a problem, or a problem marine. If one of our corporals or sergeants turns in a marine and says, "I've got a guy who is a drug user," or "I've got a guy who says he's gonna frag the gunny," or "I've got a guy who seems like he's going off his rocker," you do something about it. Now that doesn't mean that the corporal or the sergeant will always be right; they'll make mistakes and there'll be personality conflicts. But you still have to do something about it. Maybe all that needs to be done is to have that marine suspect transferred elsewhere in the company or elsewhere in the battalion without any prejudice whatsoever just to get the two of them apart—maybe that's all that needs to be done. But something needs to be done, or if you don't do it, you're (1) inviting a tragedy, or (2) you have nullified the value of one NCO. Because if you don't back him up, he'll train in and secure. And we've got numbers of NCOs in this division who've done exactly that, who say, "Screw it! I did my job and they didn't back me up. I'm just gonna go along with the crowd from here on in."[67]

As the services realized that their efforts to combat these problems were meeting with only partial success, they resorted to the use of administrative discharges to purge the ranks of substandard personnel. In early 1970, Marine Corps Commandant Chapman ordered all of his commanders to "clean house" through the administrative separation of their ineffective marines. In an official Marine Corps history of the war, the 1st Marine Division is cited as an example of the order's effect. Whereas only 121 administrative discharges had been issued within the division during all of 1969, over 800 were processed in 1970.[68] In the case of the army, statistics regarding their "duds" are equally telling. During fiscal year 1969, a total of 7,865 general discharges were issued army-wide. This figure jumped to 11,262 the following year and climbed even higher in 1971. Undesirable discharges more than doubled between 1969 and 1970 and reached nearly 16,000 in 1971.[69]

The Military's In-House Detectives

In their efforts to identify and apprehend fraggers, the military detective agencies, the army's Criminal Investigation Division (CID)[70] and the Naval Investigative Service/Marine Corps CID, were employed to investigate fragging cases and bring the malefactors to justice. It proved to be a difficult task. To begin with, the sleuths were often at a loss to determine if an incident involved fragging at all. Retired army CID agent Robert F. Coucoules offers these accounts to prove the point:

> I recall that while working out of Long Binh CID Detachment, I was assigned an investigation concerning the fragging of [Sergeant First Class John W. Baker, Jr.], a combat unit mess sergeant. I remember that I was flown to a small firebase to conduct the investigation, [and that] it was commanded by General George S. Patton's son.
>
> My investigation disclosed that someone [had] lodged a frag grenade, with the pin pulled, in a wooden door leading into a tent where the unit first sergeant and the mess sergeant were living. . . . It seems that the mess sergeant was the first to leave the tent and when he opened the door, the grenade apparently fell to the ground in front of

him. He leaned over, possibly to pick it up or see what it was. This was determined by the pattern of shrapnel in the front of his body and the pattern left on the sandbag wall immediately behind him. The investigation failed to identify the person who planted the grenade. However, a small Vietnamese youth who had access to the compound as a "houseboy" was observed leaving the area during the night. He was never seen again.

Another case I investigated involved three U.S. soldiers [Privates George Hoskins, Jr., Grafton L. Perry, and Cortez A. Randolph] who were killed by a grenade in a [stolen] 2 1/2 ton military vehicle along the Main Supply Route near Long Binh. It seems that the vehicle was speeding and a military policeman pulled it over to the side of the road. While standing next to the driver's door, an explosion occurred in the cab, injuring the MP and killing two of the soldiers, the third dying later at the hospital. Upon inspecting the scene inside the cab, it appears that after pulling over, one of the soldiers pulled the pin from the grenade, possibly with the intention of throwing it at the MP. It looks as if he dropped it on the floor near the feet of the soldier sitting in the middle of the cab and it exploded at that location. I went to the hospital and attempted to talk to the wounded soldier who initially survived the blast but he died in my presence without speaking. Since we could not prove intent on the part of any of the three soldiers, their deaths were determined to be accidental.

[One] experience I had with a grenade involved myself. One day I drove a jeep to Saigon on business. When I returned to Long Binh, someone noticed a grenade on the top of the jeep's canvas top. We called the EOD people who disarmed it. The pin had been pulled but because of a defect the grenade had not gone off.[71]

Did these incidents constitute fraggings? Accidents? Enemy action? Such were the questions that military investigators were left to ponder. "These cases were very difficult to solve as the victim [often] died," Coucoules continued. "The physical evidence linking anyone with the crime was usually destroyed. Normally, the only option we had was to find someone other than the enemy who wanted the victim dead."[72] After investigating an attempted fragging in the 173d Airborne and coming up empty, Agent John Fay wrote, "The investigation essentially died because the only thing we had was an indication that the subject didn't like the intended victim. The suspect is reported to have said that the sergeant 'was always walking in [his] shit,' i.e. that he was always finding fault with him."[73] Compounding the problem was the large number of cases in which soldiers and marines were killed while playing with grenades and other ordnance.[74] Even off-duty pranks could cause casualties. "Some of them we know are just plain horseplay rather than deliberate attempts to murder," said General Bruce Palmer, Jr.[75] Despite their non-felonious nature, administrative error led some of these cases to be included in the army's statistics.

There were several other problems unique to Vietnam that hampered investigators' efforts to solve the crimes. Fraggers' grenades were often mistaken for enemy mortar rounds, so crime scenes were often compromised in the ensuing chaos.[76] In one extreme case, the leaders of an engineer company believed an explosion that occurred in their compound to be "the result of an enemy attack." It was not until the following day that they realized their mistake and reported the incident to the military police.[77] Genuine hostile action did sometimes play a role: in one instance, a witness was killed in action shortly after the incident occurred.[78] In another case, a fragging suspect in the American Division was himself fragged and killed—by the Viet Cong, who tossed a grenade into the truck in which he was riding.[79] Another suspect who was awaiting trial for murder was among the casualties when the communists mortared the Da Nang brig in September 1969. He was evacuated for medical treatment in Japan, where he promptly deserted.[80] Tropical weather could be a factor: in a 1970 murder case, a heavy rainstorm washed away muddy footprints believed to be those of the killer.[81] The one-year tour of duty also played a role, as witnesses and even some victims were frequently rotating out of the country and had to be recalled, thus delaying legal proceedings.

Investigators found it difficult to obtain information from enlisted men owing to what General William K. Jones called "the typical teenage no-squeal syndrome": young servicemen were often reluctant to turn in their peers.[82] "I'd say that the troops were not eager to provide info," agreed Agent Fay.[83] This was due in part to the primary group cohesiveness fostered by military service, particularly in units engaged in combat. The individual soldier, as one sociologist wrote, comes to depend on his primary group and "his spontaneous loyalties are to its immediate members whom he sees daily and with whom he develops a high degree of intimacy."[84] For an enlisted man to come forward and inform on a fellow soldier or marine is exceptional. To do so during the Vietnamization period, when communication between the enlisted ranks and the command structure was strained to say the least, was truly a tall order. The tension that existed between the "lifers" and the young, one-term enlistees was what led, in part, to the fragging phenomenon in the first place.

Another problem was fear of the military justice system. Removed as they were from the command level, junior enlisted men tended to ascribe unlimited authority to their leaders and dreaded any collective disciplinary action that might ensue. One veteran described the mood in his company after an officer was murdered: "The initial feeling was one of enormous trepidation. Upon learning of Lieutenant Rohweller's death, no one knew what would happen next. Would the entire company be hauled in for questioning? Would the company be split up, [with] everyone transferred hither and yon? Would we get a new group of officers who would land on us like a 900-lb. gorilla?"[85]

This led to inaction and the urge not to get involved in the investigations. Once the military police or CID appeared in the cantonment and began exerting pressure on the enlisted men, many of the latter simply wanted the entire incident to somehow just go away as painlessly as possible, solved or unsolved. The following account is remarkable in its candor, and reinforces this point. William Marrow was a member of H Company, 7th Marine, on the night of 8–9 May 1969 when he witnessed the murder of Staff Sergeant Paul J. Seymore. Despite the fact that Marrow liked and respected Seymore, he did not offer the authorities any information:

I am the only witness to the fragging of that hooch that night. . . . I was sitting outside my unit's hooch on some sandbags smoking a joint [when] out of the corner of my eye I detected movement off to my right. I determined it to be two figures moving down behind the latrine. I couldn't determine if they were marines or Cong (all types of people move around at night in the rear area, you can't just shoot at everything that moves). Then they threw something towards the lifers' hooch. BOOM! BOOM! Two loud explosions. I saw in the light of the explosions that the two "sappers" were headed back over the hill behind the latrine where they came from.

We all felt sorry for the death of Sergeant Seymore. He would talk to us like we were his sons. If you had a problem you could go to him and talk to him or get good advice. He was like a buffer between us and the lifers and we all missed him when he died. The CO was real afraid because the rumor was that he was the actual target but they missed him and hit Seymore instead.

Why didn't I . . . tell someone about what I saw and heard? For what? I've seen it a hundred times over the past year or so. It's a war going on, people die or get hurt all over the place. Report what? Two Viet Cong sappers came and went? We are inside a perimeter [performing] security, whenever something happens inside of your defenses, you are on full alert in those holes. . . . It ain't my job to report shit, I'm going home in ten days![86]

The case was never solved.

In some instances, reluctance among enlisted men to aid authorities was also caused by the fear of retaliation by the guilty parties. The situation was aggravated by the fact that suspected offenders awaiting courts-martial were often not confined, this due to military guidelines and the lack of facilities available for pretrial confinement.[87] In *United States v. Boyd*, a government witness testified that when CID agents first interviewed him, he denied having any information regarding the case, owing to his fear of being fragged himself.[88] Threats of such action were actually made against a prosecution witness by Private First Class Roger L. Aubert. After being accused of tossing a grenade into a latrine where an NCO was relieving himself, Aubert swore, "If I am charged with this, I will frag all the witnesses that testify against me. I hope I get a general court-martial, because when I get back to the States, I am going to get a civilian lawyer and beat it, and I'm going to come back and kill every son-of-a-bitch that testified." Authorities learned of the

Incidents of American servicemen murdering their superiors were not unique to the Vietnam era. In 1906, William Taylor of the 24th Infantry Regiment shot and killed his company commander, First Lieutenant Robert B. Calvert (left), in the Philippines. Justice was swift in the case: Taylor was court-martialed and executed for his crime. (Courtesy of the United States Military Academy Library)

JUN 5 1907

THE WHITE HOUSE,

June 5 , 1907.

In the foregoing case of Private William Taylor, Company M, 24th Infantry, the sentence is confirmed and will be duly carried into execution at such time and place as may be designated by the Commanding General, Department of the Visayas, Philippine Islands.

Theodore Roosevelt

President Theodore Roosevelt personally approved Taylor's death sentence. (Courtesy of the U.S. National Archives)

MINE, ANTIPERSONNEL: M18A1

MINE, ANTIPERSONNEL: M18A1

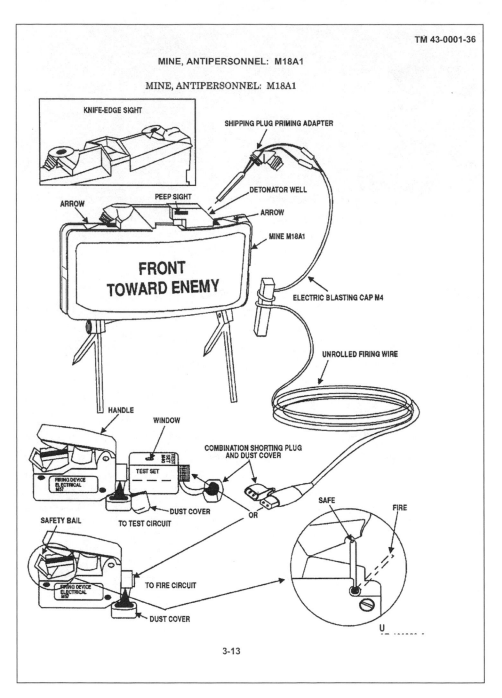

The M18A1 Claymore anti-personnel mine. (Courtesy of the Department of the Army)

The M26 fragmentation hand grenade. (Courtesy of the Department of the Army)

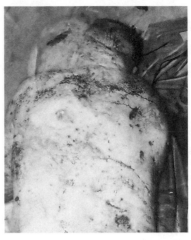

CID photograph of the torso of a fragging victim murdered with a Claymore mine. (Courtesy of the U.S. National Archives)

A number of fragging incidents involved the emplacement of booby traps. On the night of 5 December 1970, Private Robert B. Rutledge of the 1st Marine Division placed a grenade booby trap in the doorway of a billet occupied by Major William J. McCallum (right). Fortunately, the device was discovered in time to avert a tragedy. (Courtesy of the U.S. National Archives)

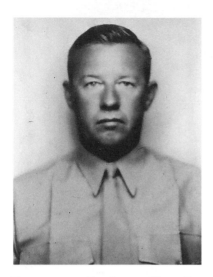

The wrong man: First Sergeant Warren R. Furse, USMC. "He was loved by all in the battery," one of his subordinates later wrote. "He was like a father to us." (Courtesy of Brian McGinty)

Marine Private Reginald F. Smith, shown here in a 1979 prison mug shot, fragged and killed First Lieutenant Robert T. Rohweller in 1969. Smith was himself murdered in prison in 1982. (Courtesy of the Federal Bureau of Prisons)

The wrong place. Many fragging victims were actually innocent bystanders caught in the wrong place at the wrong time. This is the bunker in which Marine First Sergeant Warren R. Furse died in 1969. The fragger's intended target, a lieutenant, was long gone when the grenade detonated. (Courtesy of the U.S. National Archives)

Senate Majority Leader Mike Mansfield brought fragging to America's attention after Lieutenant Dellwo's murder. (Courtesy of the Library of Congress)

Private Billy D. Smith is all smiles after his acquittal of murdering Lieutenants Dellwo and Harlan. (Reprinted with permission of the Associated Press)

First Lieutenant Thomas A. Dellwo was called "one of the finest officers of his grade and rank in the army" and his exceptional record speaks for itself. Yet in a moment of insanity, a fragger took his life. A West Point yearbook squib about Dellwo, shown here in his 1969 graduation photo, read: "Tom mastered West Point from the Cross Country Course to his math electives. He will always be remembered by those who knew him with the deepest admiration and respect." (Courtesy of the United States Military Academy Library)

Congressional Record

United States
of America

PROCEEDINGS AND DEBATES OF THE 92^d CONGRESS, FIRST SESSION

SENATE—Tuesday, April 20, 1971

The Senate met at 9:45 a.m. and was called to order by Hon. ROBERT C. BYRD, a Senator from the State of West Virginia.

The Reverend Samuel L. Gandy, dean, School of Religion, Howard University, Washington, D.C., offered the following prayer:

We gather this day, our Father, as citizens and statesmen who are believers in a free society, and who seek day in and day out within this historic Chamber to devote ourselves to the basic goals of democratic faith and function.

We gather afresh this day to further the living documents of a free society by sustaining within ourselves an honest and rigorous exercise of mind and spirit. We cherish the privilege which is ours to move always in the direction of justice and along the pathway of freedom, to the end that the endowment of human life, under Thee, shall hold priority in all our deliberations.

We beseech Thee, our Father, so to strengthen us that our courage shall transcend our faintheartedness; and that the inevitable debates on vital issues may be vigorous as we differ and far from folly to dicker.

May our institutions honor Thee by their clarion call to liberty and equality and the love of humanity, keeping us ever mindful of so glorious a heritage and ever loyal to so precious a promise: O, Thou, who art the Lord of life and the source of our strength. Amen.

DESIGNATION OF THE ACTING PRESIDENT PRO TEMPORE

The PRESIDING OFFICER. The clerk will please read a communication to the Senate from the President pro tempore (Mr. ELLENDER).

The legislative clerk read the following letter:

U.S. SENATE,
PRESIDENT PRO TEMPORE,
Washington, D.C., April 20, 1971.
To the Senate:

Being temporarily absent from the Senate, I appoint Hon. ROBERT C. BYRD, a Senator from the State of West Virginia, to perform the duties of the Chair during my absence.

ALLEN J. ELLENDER,
President pro tempore.

Mr. BYRD of West Virginia thereupon took the chair as Acting President pro tempore.

THE JOURNAL

Mr. MANSFIELD. Mr. President, I ask unanimous consent that the reading of

CXVII——684——Part 9

the Journal of the proceedings of Monday, April 19, 1971, be dispensed with.

The ACTING PRESIDENT pro tempore. Without objection, it is so ordered.

Mr. MANSFIELD. Mr. President, unless the acting minority leader has something to say, I should like to be recognized at an appropriate time.

The ACTING PRESIDENT pro tempore. Does the majority leader seek recognition under the standing order, or does the Senator from Montana wish to be recognized under the order of yesterday?

Mr. MANSFIELD. Under the order of yesterday.

The ACTING PRESIDENT pro tempore. The Chair thanks the Senator.

"FRAGGING" IN VIETNAM

Mr. MANSFIELD. Mr. President, 1 week ago yesterday, a young constituent of my distinguished colleague (Mr. METCALF) and myself, an Army first lieutenant, was to have ended his tour of duty in Vietnam. He was a West Point graduate, an honor student in high school, a National Merit Scholarship semifinalist, president of his student council and of his CYO chapter, and a three-sport letterman. He graduated from the Military Academy near the top of his class, served on the honor committee, and, following graduation, completed a course in Ranger training. In every respect, this young Montanan had every right and every reason to live. Like many other young men today, he volunteered for service in Southeast Asia to carry on a war, not of his making or choice, but prosecuted pursuant to policies formed and implemented here in Washington.

On March 15, just 4 weeks before his tour was to end, this young Montanan was killed. He was not a victim of combat. He was not a casualty of a helicopter crash or a jeep accident. In the early morning hours of March 15, the first lieutenant from Montana was "fragged" to death as he lay sleeping in his billet at Bien Hoa. He was murdered by a fellow serviceman, an American GI. "Fragging" so I have been advised by the Secretary of the Army, refers to the use of a fragmentation grenade in combat than a combat situation by one person against another to kill or do bodily harm. While I carry on my person at all times the death and casualty figures arising out of this tragic war, none reflect expressly the killing and maiming that are caused by "fragging"—by the act of one American serviceman, who, for whatever reason, unleashes a grenade

against a fellow American serviceman. It is a grim statistic of this war that I shall not lose sight of.

The questions that arise from such actions are profound, indeed. What failure of order within our Armed Forces, may I ask first of all, has produced the kind of atmosphere that resulted last year alone in 209 "fraggings"—murders of one GI by another with weapons that are supposed to be used only against the Vietnamese enemy? Even more important: What has caused this rather widespread and total disregard for human life and limb among our American soldiers? And what can be done about it? Surely, a soldier's access to weapons can be curtailed while he is not in a combat area. That such is necessary is an unfortunate side effect of this war. The Army has found this alternative necessary. It is being practiced now in Vietnam. But even confiscation of a soldier's weapons when not in combat does not reach the real problem. The atmosphere that drives an American GI to kill his fellow GI or superior is the real problem. I feel deeply, however, that the only solution is the total dissolution of our involvement in Indochina. "Fragging," I fear is just another outgrowth of this mistaken and tragic conflict.

Right now, my thoughts and deepest sympathy go out to a young widow and to a family back in Montana. Nothing can rectify their loss, or the Nation's. How inadequate it is to say we hope his assassin is apprehended, convicted, and receives just punishment for this craven act of violence. I have great faith in the system of military justice, but justice is very little compensation to the loved ones he leaves behind.

Mr. President, I am in receipt of a letter from the mother of this young Montanan in which she, in part, has the following to say:

> The reason for this letter is to ask your help in working for a volunteer army. Several weeks ago, he (her son) told me he did not think anyone should be forced to serve in our armed forces; and if what we read in the paper is true, I will have to agree with him.

I, too, agree with that sentiment. I think I should say that I am a cosponsor of the bill which seeks to create a volunteer army, based on the recommendations of the Gates Commission and the President. In that respect I have joined with Senator HATFIELD and other Senators, including the distinguished Senator from Arizona (Mr. GOLDWATER), to try to achieve this end.

I also received a copy of a letter which

10871

A display of racial unity by black soldiers in Vietnam, 15 January 1971. A number of fragging incidents were racially motivated. (Reprinted with permission of Corbis)

U.S. troops exchange heroin vials in Vietnam, July 1971. Drug-related fraggings were frequent during the war's latter years. (Reprinted with permission of Corbis)

Sergeant Diaz's quarters after the explosion. (Courtesy of Frank J. Steinhebel)

Sergeant First Class Rafael A. Diaz of the 101st Airborne Division was murdered in 1970 after cracking down on drug use in his unit. (Courtesy of Frank J. Steinhebel)

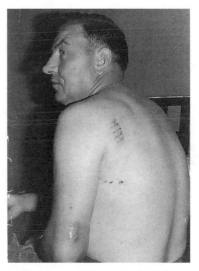

Marine Gunnery Sergeant Fred C. Johnson reveals his injuries after being fragged by Private McDonald in February 1970. (Courtesy of the U.S. Marine Corps)

The army's suspect in Diaz's murder: Private First Class Theodore Gibbs. (Courtesy of Frank J. Steinhebel)

Private David K. Locklin (at left with hat) shortly before he murdered Captain Scott E. Schneider (inset) with a grenade. (Courtesy of Tom Dever and Randy C. Dunham)

Fragging incidents involving American troops and South Vietnamese nationals became frequent during the war's latter years, and resulted in casualties on both sides. In 1971, Specialist Four Anthony M. Ambrosino was accused of killing a South Vietnamese soldier with an M79 grenade launcher but an army court-martial acquitted him of the charge. (Courtesy of the U.S. National Archives)

Australian units in Vietnam also had their share of fragging incidents. Lieutenant Robert T. Convery was one of two Australian officers who were murdered by their subordinates. Private Peter D. Allen was convicted of killing the lieutenant, and sentenced to life imprisonment. He was paroled in 1980. (Courtesy of the National Archives of Australia)

On the night of 20 October 1970, Australian Warrant Officer Neville L. Krause of 8 RAR entered his living quarters to find this grenade booby-trap awaiting him. Authorities later determined that the grenade was inert and surmised that it was intended as a warning. Several diggers who had been disciplined by Krause were questioned but the culprit was never found. (Courtesy of the National Archives of Australia)

The fraggers' worst enemy: Major General William K. Jones, USMC, architect of Operation Freeze. (Courtesy of U.S. Marine Corps University)

HEADQUARTERS
1st Marine Division (-) (Rein), FMF
FPO San Francisco, California 96602

DivO 5830.1
1/HSA/tim
13 Dec 1970

DIVISION ORDER 5830.1

From: Commanding General
To: Distribution List

Subj: Standing Operating Procedures for Prevention of Crimes
        of Violence

Ref: (a) ForO 3120.4
        (b) DivO P8000.I
        (c) DivO 8020.2

1. Purpose. The purpose of this Order is to establish procedures;
including coordinative actions, so as to reduce the incidence of
acts of violence within the 1st Marine Division (-) (Rein), FMF.

2. Cancellation. DivBul 5830 of 24Oct70

3. Background. Acts of violence, including such reprehensible
crimes as murder, rape, assault, and armed robbery, are abhorrent
in themselves and are particularly deleterious to the efficiency,
combat effectiveness, and morale of a military command. Especially heinous and despicable is the form of assault and attempted
murder known colloquially as "fragging." Recent Division actions,
including vigorous implementation of reference (a), have markedly
improved the investigation and solution of these crimes and the
bringing to justice of the perpetrators of these acts. However,
further emphasis must be placed upon the prevention of these acts
before they occur.

4. Information

    a. All camps, cantonments, combat bases and fire support bases
have designated commanders who have the responsibility to implement
the provisions of reference (a), colloquially known as "Operation
Freeze." Vigorous implementation of the provisions of reference (a)
and this Order should result not only in further improvement in the
apprehension of malefactors, but also should serve as a deterrent
to premeditated acts of violence.

    b. The weapons of war, conveniently at hand, provide a ready
means by which lethal acts of violence can be committed. For example, in almost every incident of "fragging" the instrument used

The first page of a Marine Corps anti-fragging order.
(Courtesy of U.S. National Archives)

HEADQUARTERS UNITED STATES ARMY VIETNAM
APO San Francisco 96375

CIRCULAR
NUMBER 190-3   15 May 1971

(Expires 15 May 1972)
Military Police
CONTROL OVER FIREARMS AND DANGEROUS WEAPONS

1. __PURPOSE__: To provide a procedure to improve control over firearms and dangerous weapons within this command to eliminate shooting and grenade incidents.

2. __GENERAL__: a. The number of shooting and grenade incidents occurring within RVN is unacceptable. The loss of life and injury resulting from intentional use of these weapons in attempts to intimidate, assault, and murder, as well as accidents, is a growing matter of concern. This circular is designed primarily to restrict the availability of firearms and dangerous weapons to those personnel who require them to accomplish their duties. In particular, a concerted command-wide effort must be made to eliminate the detonation of explosive devices by an individual with the intent of killing or doing bodily harm to the victim(s) or intimidating the victim(s).

b. An analysis of past incidents reveals that many of the young men involved did not feel that their leaders had established an atmosphere conducive to discussion of problems. The situation had created barriers to communication and had generated mistrust and disillusionment on the part of the younger men toward their officers and noncommissioned officers.

c. Positive leadership on the troop level will solve most, but not all, of the problems. Officers and noncommissioned officers must actively demonstrate their interest and sincere willingness to provide the necessary guidance and assistance. The control measures in para 3, below, are a partial solution. The resolution of this situation rests in positive unit leadership and supervision. This applies equally to combat service support, combat support, and combat units. Discipline, law and order remain a function of this command.

3. __POLICY__: The following will be effective 15 May 71:

a. Reports of incidents. All incidents involving the use of explosive devices, as defined at Appendix I, for suspected attempted intimidation, assault, or murder are reportable as Serious Incident Reports (SIR) in accordance with para 5, USARV Reg 190-47.

b. Command-wide inventory.

(1) A one time command-wide inventory of all weapons listed at Appendix I will be conducted on 15 Jun 71. A moratorium on issue of these items will be in effect from 15 Jun 71 to 22 Jun 71.

(2) On 15 Jun 71 all issues by ammunition logistical installations, except for validated Combat Essential (CE), Emergency Resupply (ER), and Tactical Emergency (TE) requirements, of DODIC's listed at Appendix I, will cease. This

FOR OFFICIAL USE ONLY

The first page of the army's anti-fragging order. (Courtesy of the U.S. National Archives)

CASE PROGRESS REPORT		CASE NO.

DATE	INVESTIGATOR	INVESTIGATOR ACTIVITY
2215 hours 9 JAN 71	O"NEAL	At 2215 hours on 9 JAN 1971 I was notified by the D/S that there had been an unauthorized detonation of a chemical device, in B CO , 123 AVN'S unit area. Preliminary investigation disclosed that on 9 JAN 71 at approximately 2150 hours ,person(S) unknow detonated a M7A3 CS Grenade near the northeast corner of building number 54, which is used as the NCO living area. Investigation who disclosed an informant who may be able to identify the subject in this case. The informant stated that he came out of buildingxxnumber one of the buildings in the company area, and ran into building number 51 to get a protective mask. While he was in building number 51 an individual name unknown came int to the building, and stated I think that I got them that time or words to that affect. An attempt was made to identify this individual at this time but met with negative results. This individual individual may possibly be identified later, oxxxxifxxxxfxxANxxi on the 10 11th of Jan 71. There were nine other personal in building number 51. They were identified as TATARO, LEIBLE, LEPPERT, WILSON, SHAWVER, MARTIN, LEWIS, HOLLAND, and STROMLEY. These personal stated that they had been in building number 51 all evening and had not seen anyone run into the building, and they knew nothing of the chemical device being detonated.
0100 hours 10 JAN 71	O'NEAL	Attempted to lift prints from the M7A3 grenade that was thrown in CO B. 123 AVN BN area. The prints that were lifted were not enough for comprising.
11 JAN 71 1400 hours	O'NEAL	LEPPERT, JAMES D was identified as the person who had made the statement the night that the grenade was thrown in CO B. LEPPERT was frink fi was called to the office at which time he was printed, and questioned about the statement that he had made on the night of 9 Jan 1971. LEPPERT stated that he had made the statement but he did not throw the grenade nor did he know who had thrown the grenade.
12 JAN 1971 1300 hours	O'NEAL	Closed out case.

A military policeman's report on a 1971 fragging incident. Although an informant provided information concerning the crime, and a partial fingerprint was lifted from the chemical grenade canister (inset), there was not enough evidence to make an arrest. The case was never solved. (Courtesy of U.S. National Archives)

Military investigators were able to identify suspects in many fragging cases, yet relatively few convictions were obtained. Specialist Four Roy D. Roberts was accused of throwing a grenade at an officer's tent but the army was unable to convict him. Several months later, he was charged with murdering a nine-year-old Vietnamese girl but was again acquitted. Private John J. Castro was one of three suspects in a 1971 racial fragging, but investigators failed to find enough evidence to support charges. Fellow accused Felix Troche-Perez was not so lucky: he was caught with over five pounds of marijuana and sent to the stockade. (Courtesy of the U.S. National Archives)

When military justice failed to stop the fraggers, one career soldier took matters into his own hands. First Sergeant Thomas J. "Top" Vernor, a veteran of three wars, shot and killed a young enlisted man who had injured two NCOs with a grenade in January 1970. (Courtesy of Dan Gilotti)

5. (C) DATE:PLACE OF ACQUISITION: 28 JULY 1971, DANANG

6. (U) EVAUATION:

7. (U) SOURCE: DET E, CID, 8TH MP GP, AND 37TH SIG BN, DANANG

8. (U) REPORT NUMBER: 1C1D/070/71

9. (U) DATE OF REPORT: 281700H 71

10. (U) NUMBER OF PAGES: 1

11. (U) REFERENCE: CI SPOT REPORT

12. (C) ORIGINATOR: TEAM 4, DANANG

13. (U) PREPARED BY: FERGUSON: BAN/TEAM 4

14. (U) APPROVING AUTHORITY: S-2, 1ST MI BN

15. (C) SUMMARY:

    A. (U) AMP REFERNCES: AMS SERIES L7014; SCALE 1/50,000; SHEET
        6641 III.

    B. (C) SYNOPSIS: THIS 525TH MI GROUP CI SPOT REPORT CONTAINS
INFORMATION CONCERNING THE EXPLOSION OF A FRAGMENTATION GRENADE NEAR
THE BOQ AT 37TH SIGNAL BATTALION, DANANG.

    C. (C) NARRATIVE: AT APPROXIMATELY 0110 HOURS ON 2P JULY 1971,
A FRAGMENTATION GRENADE WAS DETONATED BY UNKNOWN PERSONS NEAR A BOQ
AT 37TH SIGNAL BATTALION (37TH SIG), DANANG, RVN. CW2 DAVID ISOM, S-4
OFFICER AT 37TH SIG, HAD JUST RETIRED FOR THE EVENING WHEN HE HEARD
A PERSON OUTSIDE HIS WINDOW SAY: "WE GOT HIM." MOMENTS LATER A FRAG-

Fragging incidents involving possible racial or political motives attracted the attention of military intelligence. Spot reports (see above and following page) were prepared, and suspected radicals were added to the army's "dissident list." (Courtesy of the U.S. National Archives)

JOINT MESSAGEFORM

PAGE	DRAFTER OR RELEASER TIME	PRECEDENCE ACT	INFO	LMF	CLASS	CIC	FOR MESSAGE CENTER/COMMUNICATIONS CENTER ONLY
							DATE – TIME	MONTH	YR
1 OF 8	011700H	PP	PP		CC		021349Z DEC 70

BOOK NO

MESSAGE HANDLING INSTRUCTIONS

FROM: CGUSARV LBN RVN

TO: CINCUSARPAC

INFO: DA

CGCONARC

COMUSMACV

CGUSAINTC FT HOLABIRD MD

CONFIDENTIAL

AVHDO-SC

USARPAC FOR GPIN-SC; DA FOR ACSI-CIA: CONARC FOR DCSINTEL; MACV

FOR J22; USAINTC FOR ICDI

SUBJECT: Dissidents in the Army — Monthly Status Report, Period

Ending 30 Nov 70 (U)

A. Your GPIN-SC 210303Z May 69 (C), subj: Dissidence in

the Army (U)

B. My AVHGB-C, 300631Z Nov 69 (C), subj: Dissident Activity (U)

C. Your GPIN-SC, 260259 Feb 70 (C), subj: Dissidents in the

Army. (U)

D. My AVHGB-C, 051206Z Mar 70 (C), subj: Dissidents in the

Army (U)

DISTR:

DCSOPS; DCSP&A; DCSOPS, I&S (2); PM; SJA; AG; AG-R

DRAFTER TYPED NAMED, TITLE, OFFICE SYMBOL AND PHONE	SPECIAL INSTRUCTIONS
DON B. EDISON, MAJ, AVHDO-SC, 4294	
TYPED NAME, TITLE, OFFICE SYMBOL AND PHONE	
JOSEPH W. HEYRICK, COL, AVHDO-S, 5502	
SIGNATURE	

SECURITY CLASS CONFIDENTIAL

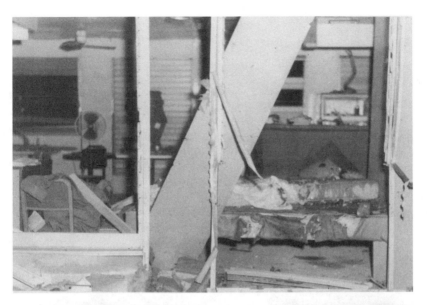

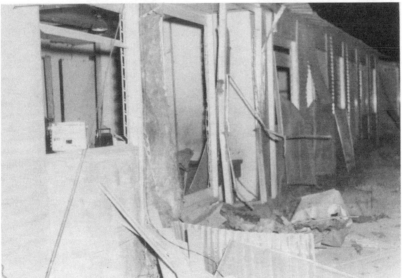

America's last Vietnam fragging fatality, First Sergeant Johnny C. Martin, died inside this shattered billet in Long Binh in May 1972. (Courtesy of the U.S. National Archives)

Sergeant Martin is immoralized on the Vietnam Veterans Memorial.
(Author's private collection.)

threats and simply added them to Aubert's charge sheet.[89] While awaiting trial for his unsuccessful attempt to frag a senior NCO, Private First
Class Israel "Tony" Barrios learned that Corporal Grover H. Smith was
one of the government's witnesses. Barrios confronted Smith and made
it clear to him that testifying could be hazardous to his health. "If I get
a life sentence," Barrios warned, "your life will end." The corporal was
unimpressed, and here, too, the threat returned to haunt the fragger.[90]
Nevertheless, it was not until the latter half of 1970 that the Marine
Corps drafted an order that formally called for the protection of infor-
mants. The effect of this measure was that "in one particular case four
persons thus protected gave information resulting in the conviction of
four . . . suspects."[91]

The fact that reticence existed among the enlisted ranks to report
fraggers, particularly in cases where officers or NCOs were attacked,
also raises the question of whether the incidents enjoyed popular support with the troops. Here again one must weigh the societal factors
that influenced the enlisted culture during the Vietnam era and fostered a kind of "us-against-them" mentality among the troops toward
their superiors. Charles Levy points to the extraordinarily low number
of arrests made in the 3d Marine Division as evidence that fragging
"had the wide support of enlisted men who were unwilling to assist the
investigations."[92] Although Levy unquestionably champions the fraggers in his book, several other sources do lend a degree of support to
this view. One is the record of a 1971 congressional subcommittee
hearing in which this exchange occurs:

> Rep. G. Elliot Hagan: There [are] two or three [fraggings] a month [in
> the] 173d Airborne Brigade.
>
> General Ochs: We have caught some suspects. . . . There are a
> number of people who tell their friends, but anyone in authority has
> never been able to catch them.
>
> Rep. John E. Hunt: In other words they have excellent security.[93]

One particularly revealing CID report regarding a 1972 fragging
case concluded: "[Perpetrators] of the incident are unknown. Investigation revealed that [Captain Lester W.] Gray is disliked by a majority of

personnel in the unit because of his strict policies on narcotics."[94] In fact, transcripts of many CID investigations and courts-martial contain testimony from young GIs that seems to support the incidents, but whether these statements indicate true solidarity with the fraggers or were simply loose talk made out of frustration is open to question. From *United States v. Crampton*: "Probably half the company at the time felt that the attempted 'fragging' incident might have a good effect."[95] From *United States v. Elliot*: "[The witness] heard the accused say that he'd 'like to blow [Captain Murphy] away' [but] he had also heard quite a few other people make the same statement at other times."[96] From *United States v. Fitzgerald*: "Everybody makes threats about the lifers all the time."[97] From *United States v. Hurley*: "People kept asking me when I was going to do it. The morning it happened, everybody came up to me smiling and thought I did it."[98] From CID Report of Investigation 70-CID958–43687: "Hey Sarge, aren't you glad that someone finally got rid of him?"[99] From *Unites States v. McCracken*: "Nobody in the company liked Major Jones."[100] From *United States v. Peterson*: "They were all saying something should be done to Lieutenant Cashman."[101] From *United States v. Shirley*: "When questioned by the military judge, Sergeant Wakeley stated that there were others in the unit who had hard feelings toward the victim."[102] From *United States v. Spears*: "Neither Private Dunn, PFC Jarman, nor PFC Archie considered the talk of 'fragging' to be serious, since such talk in the company had been commonplace."[103] From *United States v. Strate*: "All witnesses stated that conversations about 'gassing lifers' were common at Fire Support Base Katum."[104] From *United States v. Thompson*: "Almost everyone in the squadron had talked about killing Captain Young at one time or another."[105] While such testimony is certainly suggestive, veteran Joseph M. Kralich was on the mark in his assertion that "rumors and myths about fragging were told by a few 'anti-war' or 'anti-military' soldiers and then repeated and modified to fit the situation."[106]

Similarly, several of the men who did come forward and offer information to military authorities were motivated solely by self-interest. Some did so out of fear of incrimination, having participated in conspiracies or even the fraggings themselves.[107] In one case, a crafty CID agent duped a potential witness into believing that his fingerprints had been lifted from the spent launcher of a LAW anti-tank rocket that had been fired at an officer's billet. Fearing that he would be charged with the crime, the man immediately identified the perpetrator. He had denied any knowledge of the incident during several previous interrogations.[108] One man's motivation for coming forward appears to have been self-preservation: as marine investigators probed Lieutenant Rohweller's death, Lance Corporal Brooker was alleged to have said to an officer, "I'll tell you what happened if you keep me out of the field."[109]

It should be noted, however, that there were also grenade assaults in which the exact opposite was true. After the Dellwo-Harlan murder, the CID agent on the scene moved the suspected fragger away from the immediate area of apprehension, fearing that the man's life was in danger from other soldiers who were outraged by the attack.[110] Sergeant First Class Clyde J. Ball was killed at soon-to-be-infamous Fire Support Base Mary Ann in July 1970, and Americal Division member Gary L. Noller recalls: "Upon returning to Mary Ann, I [was] told of [Sergeant Ball] getting killed in a fragging incident. I heard the story from someone in the mortar platoon. [He] stated something to the effect that [Ball] did not deserve to die this way and a few of the guys wanted to find out who did it and even the score. I do not know if the guilty party was ever identified."[111]

He never was. Shortly after returning to his unit to await trial, accused fragger Bruce Perry was himself the target of a grenade attack and narrowly escaped injury.[112] After First Sergeant Warren R. Furse was murdered, the saddened men of his battery sent his widow so many flowers that the bouquets filled a two-and-a-half-ton truck. Ex-marines from far and wide continued to write and visit her for years after the war.[113] Upon his acquittal for Furse's murder, Walter Chambers, Jr., requested a transfer far away from his former comrades, writing, "I desired to be assigned to a geographic area where I would not come into contact with personnel with whom I had served in the 2nd Battalion, 11th Marines."[114] As CID agents probed the death of Staff Sergeant Paul E. Reed of the 173d Airborne, several junior enlisted men voiced their suspicions that Private First Class Frederick J. Osher had committed the crime, but since none of them could place Osher near Reed's quarters when the grenade detonated, no charges were filed.[115]

During the investigation of another homicide, a private came forward and revealed that shortly after the explosion had occurred, a fellow soldier had suddenly appeared and begun laughing, saying "Sergeant Lutz got it and I hope he dies."[116] An enlisted man who agreed to become an undercover informant in a 1970 case told authorities of Private First Class Theodore Gibbs's alleged boasts that he had "committed the perfect crime," which was believed to be a reference to the murder of Sergeant First Class Rafael A. Diaz.[117] It is perhaps fairest to say that some fragging incidents did enjoy a measure of acceptance among the more radical elements in Vietnam while others did not. This dichotomy is best illustrated in the following case, in which an alert soldier actually foiled a fragging in progress.

On the night of 14–15 March 1969, someone fragged First Sergeant Clarence J. Carden of Company L (Ranger), 75th Infantry, 101st Airborne Division. Although his billet sustained considerable damage, Carden emerged from the attack unscathed and stubbornly resolved to remain in the unit. His assailant proved equally determined and attempted a second assault less than three weeks later. But as the fragger approached Carden's quarters and released his grenade, he was spotted by Private First Class Neal E. Rooney, who was walking his interior guard post. Well aware of the danger to his sleeping sergeant, Rooney valiantly rushed forward and picked up the grenade, which had bounced off the structure's front door and rolled toward him, and tossed it into an unoccupied area where it exploded without causing any damage or injuries. He then gave chase to the fleeing assailant, firing four shots at the shadowy figure before losing him in the darkness.[118] Although the army was unable to obtain a prosecution in the case, it did recognize Rooney's heroism by awarding him the Soldier's Medal.[119]

During the latter years of the war, when crime levels skyrocketed despite massive troop withdrawals, agents were swamped with cases. "Due to the case load," Agent Fay wrote, "partnering was not really an option. If a case wasn't workable, you had no choice except to put it aside and concentrate on those that were."[120] Nevertheless, the CID often went to great lengths to solve even the most perplexing cases, particularly when a fatality was involved. Within hours of Captain Scott E. Schneider's murder at LZ Dottie, multiple investigators converged on the base and an arrest was eventually made.[121] In the following case, I have reproduced portions of the military police report to provide a picture of an investigation from start to finish.

At approximately 2150 hours on 9 January 1971, person(s) unknown detonated a chemical grenade near the senior NCO quarters of B Company, 123d Aviation Battalion. Unit NCOs emerged from the billet after the incident and searched the area, finding the spent grenade canister and its spoon. Unfortunately, they neglected to conduct a personnel muster that could have revealed a missing soldier, and did not notify military police for twenty-five critical minutes.

It wasn't until 2215 that military police investigator Donald P. O'Neal was informed of the crime. After arriving at the 123d perimeter, he began conducting interviews with B Company's enlisted men. During one of these sessions, a soldier revealed that after the grenade detonated, he had overheard an unidentified GI remark, "I sure got them good that time." An initial attempt at identifying the statement's author was unsuccessful, as was O'Neal's search for usable fingerprints on the grenade canister. The investigator persisted, however, and on the afternoon of 11 January, the man who had allegedly made the statement, door gunner James D. Leppert, was finally identified. Leppert denied any involvement in the incident, claiming that he had been in his quarters playing cards with several other soldiers when he heard the "familiar 'pop'" of a chemical grenade. After fingerprinting Leppert, O'Neal conducted the questioning:

Q: What time was it when you heard this familiar pop?
A: I don't remember what time it was.
Q: Were you, Tataro, and Martin the only persons in Hooch #51 when you heard the popping sound?
A: We were the only ones up at that time. . . .
Q: Did you throw the grenade on 9 January?
A: No.
Q: Do you know who threw the grenade on the night of 9 January in Company B?
A: No.
Q: Is there anyone you suspect of throwing the grenade?

A: No.

Q: Did you make a statement on the night of 9 January when the grenade was thrown that you got them good this time?

A: No.

Q: Did you make any statement after the grenade was thrown?

A: Yes, I made a statement to the fact that they got it good this time, or words to that effect.

Q: Were you glad that the grenade was thrown at the NCO hooch?

A: I don't have any feelings either way about it.

Q: How long have you been assigned to Company B, 123d Aviation Battalion?

A: I have been there since August 1969.

Q: Is this the first time a gas grenade has been thrown in the area?

A: No.

The absence of physical evidence or eyewitnesses and Leppert's denial forced O'Neal to close the case. It was never solved.[122]

The Role of Military Intelligence

In addition to the criminal investigators, the intelligence branch also played a role in the military's response to fragging. Senior leadership's fears that that political subversives might enter the ranks and attempt to destroy the armed services from within dated back to the time of the Russian Revolution. For example, several doughboys serving in the American Expeditionary Forces in Europe during and after the First World War faced courts-martial for making what were variously described as "disloyal remarks" or "seditious utterances" against the army, the president, or the nation.[123] A 1919 stockade riot at Fort Leavenworth was blamed on socialists and "Wobblies," the latter a reference to members of the Industrial Workers of the World, a radical labor union.[124] During the interwar period, communists were all but excluded from the service, especially after passage of the Hatch Act in 1939. But with the reintroduction of conscription the following year and America's subsequent entry into the Second World War, the government relented and permitted radicals to enlist. Even then the army remained skeptical, maintaining a watch list of potential subversives, and initially barring communists and other "politically disaffected" individuals from the officer corps and sensitive assignments. These measures were relaxed after U.S.-Soviet relations had warmed and the War Department was seeking to avoid offending the Russians, and it was only then that nearly one hundred of the most deserving men received commissions. With the advent of the Cold War, however, the military's antiradical strictures returned with a vengeance.[125]

During the Vietnam era, military intelligence exerted considerable effort in preventing possible attempts by antiwar groups, extremist political parties, and racial militants to infiltrate the armed forces. To keep potential dissidents out of Southeast Asia, new recruits and re-enlistees were made to complete questionnaires regarding past or current associations they might have had with any of over two hundred groups reported by the attorney general as "having significance in connection with the national security." The organizations in question bore many political stripes, ranging from the Socialist Workers Party to the Ku Klux Klan.[126] In cases where such ties were admitted, security investigations were to be conducted, these usually involving inquiries to the Federal Bureau of Investigation. These men were supposed to be barred from assignments in Vietnam but the system did not always work smoothly in this regard. One soldier, who had allegedly belonged to the Progressive Labor Party (PLP) and been expelled from Harvard University for his actions during campus protests, was about to be shipped to the war zone when he was "flagged," pending an investigation of his party membership and "numerous dissident-type activities." Before investigators had even completed their work, however, the man was sent to Vietnam anyway and remained there for several months until the army decided to return him to the United States.[127] Another soldier suspected of PLP membership was also flagged when he received orders for Vietnam, but here too the army didn't like what it saw and retained him at Fort Hood, Texas.[128] An infantryman who made no secret of his membership in the Young Socialist Alliance was due to be sent to Vietnam when the brass thought better of it and instead transferred him to a post where it was felt that he could do little damage: Fort Greely, Alaska.[129]

Radicals who did make it to Vietnam and were discovered quickly became the recipients of intense command attention. Background investigations were initiated while the men were reassigned to duties that kept them away from classified materials and, it was hoped, precluded them from engaging in political activity. A report from the 25th Infantry Division reveals the measures taken against one suspect: "DISCOM reported that Gary Franklin Lettman, E-5, alleged member of the Young Socialist Alliance (YSA), was under investigation. Lettman is now assigned to a position where he has no access to classified information. Investigation has not yet revealed any active attempts by Lettman to distribute dissident material in the unit or to recruit members for YSA. There has been no indication that Lettman's membership has aversely affected the unit's operational capability. Finalized investigation will be forwarded as soon as possible."[130]

In addition, USARV established a "dissident list" in 1969 that contained the names of soldiers believed to have ties to extremist groups as well as those known to have partaken in antiwar or antimilitary actions.[131] One man was placed on the list after it was learned that he had planned an abortive "Fast for Peace" at Pleiku for Thanksgiving 1969.[132] Several months later, it was noted that he had "distributed leaflets calling for a protest meeting against orders limiting the number of dogs to one per company-sized unit at Camp Radcliff." A soldier who had been arrested by local authorities during the 1970 civil disturbances at Isla Vista, California, was also listed.[133] Other men were added to the list owing to their involvement in the production of the myriad underground GI newspapers that emerged during the Vietnam era. One soldier was mistakenly listed when it was reported that he had posted an antiwar placard on his unit's bulletin board, but when it was learned that this information was incorrect, his name was removed. The list was kept current by monthly updates that announced new additions as well as those previously listed whose Vietnam tours had ended.

Army intelligence used the same approach in dealing with racial militancy. In February 1970, USARV produced a report titled "Efforts by Individuals and Militant Groups to Promote Racial Unrest in the Army," which told senior commanders to monitor possible extremist activity in their units "on a low-key basis and without publicity." After

Eldridge Cleaver's article urging black soldiers to kill General Abrams and his staff appeared in the 21 March 1970 edition of the *Black Panther*, senior officers were asked to furnish "any information regarding distribution of the paper, related activity, and the effect of these activities."[134] As was the case with the political dissidents, suspected racial extremists were to be assigned nonsensitive duties and monitored by their commanders. Private Howard M. Dean, Jr., was believed to have been involved in one or more acts of racial violence while stationed in Long Binh in 1970. It was decided to transfer him to the 25th Infantry Division at Cu Chi where he was placed under surveillance. The 25th soon grew tired of him as well, and he was administratively discharged from the army.[135]

Military intelligence elements were involved in analyzing a number of the acts of violence that took place during the Vietnamization period. Whenever a fragging or other incident occurred that possessed possible racial or political overtones, a team from one of the 525th Military Intelligence Group's six provisional battalions would visit the crime scene and conduct an investigation, usually in cooperation with CID elements and unit leadership. A "Counter Intelligence Spot Report" would then be submitted on the case, detailing whether politics or race were causal to the incident. Since most fraggings went unsolved, efforts at determining the perpetrator's motivations were usually unsuccessful, and the few surviving spot reports found in army records reveal little more than narrative summaries of the crimes.

Fraggers and Military Justice

Soldiers and marines charged with fragging offenses were tried under military law. The legal system employed by the armed services in Vietnam, the Uniform Code of Military Justice (UCMJ), had been instituted during the Truman administration. The system was something of a compromise; after sharp criticism of the administration of military justice during the Second World War, the UCMJ was designed to provide improved due process to the accused and eliminate command influence while retaining the tools commanders needed to maintain discipline. Its architects believed the system was "as applicable and as workable in time of war as in time of peace," and Vietnam certainly put this thesis to the test.[136]

Accused fraggers were usually charged with attempted murder or aggravated assault (UCMJ Articles 80 and 128, respectively). Those who succeeded in killing their victims answered to Article 118, premeditated murder. Communicating a threat, which fell under the (literally) catchall Article 134, was a familiar feature on men's charge sheets, as were conspiracy charges in cases involving multiple assailants. General courts-martial, which were reserved for the most serious military offenses, were normally convened in fragging cases. These courts were empowered to impose the severest of punishments, including death sentences.

The UCMJ worked well during the early years of the Vietnam War, when disciplinary infractions were few and military lawyers' caseloads were manageable. But with the sharp rise in crime during Vietnamization, military attorneys were inundated with cases. Major General George S. Prugh, judge advocate general of the U.S. Army, wrote: "With the rapid troop buildup, the military attorneys trying courts-martial in Vietnam labored under a staggering caseload. Time imposed unrelenting pressure on all who were involved with a case. Given the twelve-month tour of duty in Vietnam, it was an unusual case that did not involve at least a few key persons who were due to rotate back to the United States in a short time. . . . Under the best of conditions the preparation of a case for trial requires a formidable amount of work and a reasonable amount of time. In the Vietnam war zone, there were aggravations enough to frustrate the most placid attorney."[137]

Prugh offered the statistics in Table 6 (see page 163) as proof.

To lend a degree of context to these figures, the Americal Division will be cited here as an example. In 1970 alone, 5,567 courts-martial and nonjudicial punishments under Article 15 of the UCMJ were administered in the division. And just as the criminal investigators had learned, problems unique to Vietnam could make prosecutions difficult. Some courts-martial were not tried until several months after the alleged crime was committed, so witnesses often had to return to Vietnam after having completed their twelve-month tours and having rotated out of Southeast Asia. "Many witnesses are simply lost," admitted

Table 6

Year	General courts-martial tried	Special courts-martial tried	Summary courts-martial tried	Nonjudicial punishment administered
1968	302	6,798	2,119	59,178
1969	377	7,314	2,231	66,702
1970	300	4,964	597	64,534
1971	350	3,678	434	41,237
1972	113	774	187	3,283

one attorney. "We have not tried one major case where both prosecution and defense has not been hurting for witnesses."[138] The international date line was responsible for weakening a trial counsel's case in one court-martial when a witness summoned from the United States arrived in Vietnam to testify, only to find that the trial had already ended, as someone had forgotten that Vietnamese time is one day ahead of the Western Hemisphere. The accused was acquitted.[139] In another lost court-martial, two key prosecution witnesses admitted that they "had been addicted to heroin and were going through withdrawal" when the fragging occurred. One of them testified that he was "somewhat confused" about the incident because he was "coming down from heroin" and that his decision to testify came after he and a friend "drew straws from a hat."[140] Although these problems were thrust upon defense counsel as well as prosecutors, it was the latter who were tasked with obtaining the burden of proof in their cases. To further complicate matters, a number of accused fraggers secured the representation of seasoned civilian attorneys (these usually paid for by their families) who journeyed to Vietnam to provide their services,[141] as well as the Saigon-based Lawyers' Military Defense Committee (LMDC). Founded in 1970 by several antiwar attorneys, the LMDC volunteered pro bono legal representation to poor, mostly minority offenders.[142] And when all else failed, letters of complaint were frequently dispatched to home district legislators alleging myriad abuses.[143]

Defense counsel employed a number of different courtroom "tactics" in fragging cases. Since most fraggings were aimed at officers and NCOs, one of their primary concerns was command influence. In units

that sustained large numbers of grenade incidents, motions were sometimes made for changes of venue, the defense attorneys arguing that the
accused would be precluded from receiving fair treatment in these
"hostile" environments. During a fragging court-martial convened in
the Americal Division, the defense counsel (awkwardly) reasoned: "If a
situation is such in a command where there is sufficient prejudice and
hostility against an accused or a particular type of crime, there may be
a motion for a change . . . of venue. . . . The number of fragmentation
grenade incidents we have in this division and the basic problem involved in the feeling of this command is a matter of general discussion
in this command; that there are fragmentation [grenade] incidents, obviously since many of these incidents are directed towards officers,
which would also affect the court."[144]

Venue changes were rare during the Vietnam era, and indeed the
tactic failed in this instance.[145] Similar attempts in the fragging-plagued
1st and 3d Marine Divisions were also unsuccessful.[146] Yet a judge in
the 1st Cavalry Division approved such a motion in *United States v.
Smith* and the trial was moved from Vietnam to Fort Ord, California.[147]
Passage of the Military Justice Act of 1968 established an independent
trial judiciary within the armed forces and the new position of military
judge, which permitted defendants the option of being tried "judge
alone," the military equivalent of the civilian bench trial.[148] The accused
could now leave their legal fates in the hands of military judges rather
than court members, as the latter were usually officers or senior NCOs
who likely possessed strong opinions about offenses such as fragging.
A study of this procedure conducted by the U.S. Army Judiciary found
that during the last quarter of 1969 and the first quarter of 1970, over
80 percent of the accused tried by general and special court-martial
opted for courts without members.[149] Of the sixty-five surveyed fraggers who were tried after the act's implementation, at least forty-two, or
some 64 percent, are known to have made this request. On the other
hand, LMDC attorney Joseph Remcho opted for full courts in his cases
but attempted with unusual success to have junior enlisted men appointed as members. He charged that the services deliberately excluded
low-ranking servicemen from the selection process, thus guaranteeing
that courts would be composed exclusively of officers and NCOs. This

procedure, he argued, failed to provide his young enlisted clients with juries of their "peers."[150] During a court-martial involving a fragging in the army's 571st Ordnance Company, Remcho managed to have several junior enlisted men appointed to the court, including one who appeared in the courtroom wearing a large peace medallion. Not surprisingly, the defendants were acquitted.[151]

The penalties for fragging offenses were severe. The typical convicted fragger could expect to receive a bad-conduct or dishonorable discharge, forfeit all pay and allowances, and be reduced to the lowest enlisted grade. The periods of imposed confinement varied from case to case, ranging in length from three months to life. Nearly two-thirds of the men pleaded guilty at trial, often to reduced charges in order to receive lighter sentences. Those convicted of premeditated murder faced mandatory sentences of death or confinement at hard labor for life, although military prosecutors rarely sought capital punishment, as Marine Corps trial counsel W. Hays Parks explained:

> To the best of my recollection of my service from 1966 to 1969, there was little consideration given to trial of a case as a capital case. We knew a capital case had to be near perfect in order for a sentence to survive the appeals process, and most of us were pessimistic that such a sentence would ever be carried out; it had been such a long time since anyone had been executed in the naval service, and domestic [civilian] executions had declined if not ceased. However, that was of little assurance to some accused, and as a prosecutor I often would agree not to try a case as capital if the accused would plead guilty. It didn't always work, as defense counsel had a pretty good idea sense for what was possible or probable.[152]

Indeed, no death sentences were imposed upon the men in this study.

The convicted fraggers were transferred to military confinement facilities in the United States to serve their sentences. For soldiers, this usually meant the United States Disciplinary Barracks at Fort Leavenworth, Kansas, while Marine Corps prisoners were normally dispatched to the Naval Disciplinary Command at Portsmouth, New Hampshire.

Several of the murderers who received long sentences and were considered to be poor candidates for rehabilitation were subsequently transferred to civilian institutions within the federal prison system.[153]

Despite the severity of their sentences, few of the convicted fraggers
served more than a fraction of their adjudged terms of confinement.
This was due in part to decisions reached at the appellate level, both in
the services' own courts of review and the civilian-staffed Court of Military Appeals. A considerable number of convictions were overturned,
resulting in the dismissal of charges or orders for new trials. In his
analysis of this process, Lieutenant Colonel Gary D. Solis wrote, "The
rehearings were cases originally tried in the combat zone in which the
result had been set aside upon appellate review. Problems of proof inherent in retrying offenses long past, committed at scenes far away, often led to 'not guilty' findings."[154] In the 1977 rehearing of Private
Claude B. Johnson, for example, prosecutors at Fort Leavenworth were
unable to produce several key witnesses, including a friend of Johnson's who had been convicted of a lesser charge in connection with the
case and refused to testify without a grant of immunity, another ex-
soldier who declined to appear voluntarily and was not amenable to
service of process because he lived and worked in Saudi Arabia, and a
Vietnamese national who presumably lived in communist Vietnam, a
country with which the United States maintained neither diplomatic nor
commercial relations. As a result, the murder charge was dismissed.[155]

Appellate judges remedied minor procedural errors found to be
prejudicial to the accused by reassessing sentences. In some instances,
they even reduced the awarded terms of confinement whether such errors were present or not. "The appellant's threats against his superior
officer strike at the very heart of military discipline in a combat zone
and at a time when the incident rate of 'fragging' of superiors by subordinates is on the increase," wrote one jurist during an appeal of 1971's
United States v. Creek. "It takes little imagination to visualize the chaos
and utter breakdown in discipline that would ensue if superiors are
subjected to the continuing terror of assassination by subordinates who
do not believe that they are amenable to orders or otherwise resent authority." Yet in spite of this rhetoric, the court opted to shave a year off
Private Creek's three-year prison sentence, citing the conclusions of an

army psychiatrist who found that Creek "appears to have lived a very chaotic life" and opined that neither Creek nor the government would benefit from prolonged confinement.[156] After reviewing Thomas W. Fowler's court-martial and rejecting his appellate defense counsel's assignments of error, the Naval Court of Military Review affirmed his murder conviction but demurred on his life sentence. "We do not believe that society's interests would better be served by confining this young Marine for the rest of his life. Accordingly, only so much of the sentence as provides for confinement at hard labor for 25 years . . . is affirmed." The Naval Clemency and Parole Board further reduced Fowler's sentence and he was released after serving less than eight years in prison.[157]

One man who had exhausted the formal appeals process attempted to obtain redress through the use of several legal maneuvers. After two appellate courts affirmed his life sentence, Gary A. Hendrix filed an Article 138 "Complaint of Wrongs" to the Secretary of the Navy, alleging inadequacy of counsel and lack of jurisdiction of his court-martial. Among other things, Hendrix argued that he could not remember committing the murder and that his assigned military defense counsel and psychiatrists had "brainwashed" him into believing that he had. He also blamed his lawyer for failing to obtain a change of venue in the case. When this effort proved unsuccessful, he submitted a writ of habeas corpus to the Court of Military Appeals claiming the same errors. This too was denied, and Hendrix subsequently filed suit in the United States Court of Claims. Although this venue did not possess the requisite authority to restore him to duty, it could determine that his discharge had been illegally awarded and thus entitle him to back pay.[158] Accordingly, Hendrix requested that he be released from confinement, awarded an honorable discharge, and granted back pay and allowances owing to the allegedly unconstitutional deficiencies in his court-martial. The court was unmoved and ultimately dismissed the case.[159]

Good conduct time and paroles further reduced imposed penalties. As he passed sentence on fragger Ignacio Garcia, a military judge told the accused, "I'm sure with good behavior here in the future you will serve nothing like five years' time." The judge's words proved to be prophetic: the convening authority in the case reduced the sentence to four years in accordance with a pretrial agreement, and Garcia was released from confinement after serving less than eighteen months.[160] In fact, the men's behavior while in confinement had much to do with the amount of time they spent behind bars. The cases of murderers Thomas J. Benoit and William E. Sutton may serve as examples in this regard. Both were sentenced to life imprisonment for their crimes, but their post-trial conduct played significant roles in the amount of prison time they served. At Benoit's post-trial interview, the staff judge advocate described him as "courteous and responsive" and praised his appearance and bearing. While in the stockade, he acted as an orderly and expressed remorse for his actions. In announcing its sentence at the court-martial, all of the court members and even the military judge submitted individual petitions for clemency. He was paroled after serving less than four years.[161] Private Sutton also received clemency recommendations at his trial, but his behavior while in confinement was quite different than Benoit's. During one seven-month period, he was "involved in multiple incidents including failure to stand count, [being] out of place, [possessing] contraband, lying to a guard, [engaging in] homosexual abuse, attempting to procure homosexual acts, [making] homosexual threats, fail[ing] to stand by for an officer, communicating threats, and assault." He was subsequently transferred to the federal prison system and served the better part of thirty years behind bars.[162]

As discipline eroded in Vietnam during the early 1970s, debates over such issues as pretrial confinement, the legal definitions of what constituted "inspections" and "searches," and the length of time required to process cases led some officers and NCOs to lose faith in the military justice system.[163] "There is growing concern," wrote one senior officer, "that the UCMJ is becoming more of an antagonist than an ally in efforts to control discipline and has led to weakness in the chain of command." "A belief exists that some courts have become permissive of bad discipline and overzealous in protecting the individual at the expense of the collective needs of the military structure. In addition, long delays in accomplishing final action on disciplinary cases are destroying the deterrent value of prompt punishment."[164]

Since the war's end, a number of senior leaders have gone as far as condemning the Uniform Code of Military Justice in Vietnam.[165] In 1975, retired Generals Westmoreland and Prugh published a now-famous article in a prominent civilian law journal that criticized the UCMJ and recommended a number of changes. They concluded:

> The Uniform Code of Military Justice is not capable of performing its intended role in times of military stress. . . . It is presently too slow, too cumbersome, too uncertain, indecisive, and lacking in the power to reinforce accomplishment of the military mission, to deter misconduct, or even to rehabilitate.[166]

Transition to the All-Volunteer Force

As the U.S. military departed from Vietnam, it underwent a profound organizational change. Shortly before the 1968 presidential election, Republican Party candidate Richard M. Nixon had announced his intention to end the draft and form a new all-volunteer force. Once in office, he ordered the services to carry out the initiative. While young men across the nation who were dreading induction rejoiced at the news, the military viewed it with concern. With the exception of a brief period following the Second World War, the armed forces, and the army in particular, had depended on conscription as an essential source of personnel since President Franklin D. Roosevelt had signed the Selective Service and Training Act in 1940. By the late 1960s, the military's unpopularity among young Americans led many to believe that the services would be unable to find enough qualified recruits to fill the ranks. To be sure, many senior officers, including General Westmoreland, believed that military service was an obligation of citizenship and favored the draft's retention. Others feared that the formation of an all-volunteer force would result in the military becoming an employer of last resort in which the poor and minority groups would be greatly overrepresented.

In their efforts to attract new recruits, the services endeavored to make military life more amenable. Junior enlisted pay was increased and bonuses were offered to lure men into hard-to-fill positions in the combat arms. In what became known as the VOLAR, or the Volunteer Army program, commanders of selected installations in the United States and Europe were encouraged to experiment with new methods aimed at keeping their subordinates in the service. Facilities were upgraded and those duties that were seen as unnecessary nuisances, most notably kitchen police, were all but eliminated.[167] To the horror of the remaining old-timers from the days of the "brown boot army," such controls as off-post passes and bed checks were eliminated, and haircut regulations were relaxed.[168] These measures were controversial to say the least and led to charges that the military was becoming too soft with its men.[169] In response to the critics, those involved with creating the all-volunteer force argued that the new army they envisioned would be more professional than its conscripted predecessor. In truth, they also knew that the reforms they were implementing were of fundamental necessity: without them, the army's continued existence was in jeopardy.

Even with these new measures, the army struggled to meet its personnel quotas as the draft neared its end. Fearing the worst, Congress dramatically cut active army strength, reducing it to its lowest level since the dark days of the "New Look" policy in the late 1950s. To fill the remaining vacancies, recruiting command was greatly expanded and the first attempts at radio and television advertising were made. In addition, increasing numbers of women were accepted into the Women's Army Corps.[170] Despite these actions, the army's personnel shortage continued into the early 1980s. The war in Vietnam might have gone away, but its stigma remained.

Did Fragging Affect Low-Level Military Decision-Making?

One intriguing aspect of the fragging phenomenon is the question of whether fragging affected low-level military decision-making. Vietnam literature seems to believe that it did, although some authors differ on the level of its influence. Eugene Linden wrote, "Through intimidation and threats—verbal and written—and scare-stories, fragging is influential to the point that virtually all officers and NCOs have to take into account the possibility of fragging before giving an order to the men under them."[171] Joseph Remcho of the LMDC was more modest, saying, "Commanders are not operating under the assumption that there will be a plot to get them if they get tough with their men, but they are all particularly aware that 'fragging' exists."[172] Lieutenant Colonel Robert L. Drudik, who led the 1st Battalion, 7th Cavalry in 1970, wrote, "The weak officer or NCO will succumb to these threats, thus allowing the rabble to have its way. The tough commander or NCO may end up dead or maimed, as were Captain Carvolth and 1SG Gilland."[173]

It is true that fragging did intimidate at least some leaders in Vietnam, and its effect was most likely felt in regard to the enforcement of minor regulations unrelated to the combat mission, although these are often relaxed in such an environment in any case. When one general attempted to crack down on indiscipline within his command, USARV Chief of Staff Charles M. Gettys cautioned against pushing too hard:

> Your positive approach to enforcing the standards of appearance and discipline and order is commendable. Improved standards may reasonably be expected to result. However, I do have some reservations concerning the appropriateness of such an ambitious program conducted within such a short time frame. Your program, energetically implemented, may reasonably be expected to yield a backlash of complaints, Congressional inquiries, threats and use of explosive devices against the enforcers, and increased drug usage.[174]

After Captain Schneider was murdered in 1970, military policeman John "Dutch" De Groot observed, "My partner and I calmed things down and turned everything over to the CID agents. I remember a young second lieutenant who was very nervous and the only advice I could give him was 'Don't aggravate your troops.' When I look back on this I guess that it probably did not [encourage him to reenlist] in the army."[175] With regard to fragging and drug enforcement, an NCO in the 173d Airborne told a group of visiting congressmen, "It's hard to catch the guys and once you get him, then you've got to worry about your own self. . . . You have the problem of nailing them and if you can't nail them, then you've got the worry of sleeping at night."[176] Some leaders refused to submit to the "coercion" but prepared for the worst. "[I] used to sleep with my gas mask in Division HQ," Brigadier General Theodore C. Mataxis of the Americal Division admitted. "[The] disaffected and druggies would pop tear gas grenades upwind."[177] Testimony from *United States v. Rosine* is similar: "Captain Reams indicated that he did not sleep in his hooch on the evening of 25 October 1971, because he feared it would not be safe."[178] After First Sergeant Johnny C. Martin was murdered, his Vietnamese domestic testified:

> When the first sergeant was still alive, he seemed to be worried about his personal security. He usually said to me that he was straight and serious so he was hated by the GIs, mostly the soul brother GIs. He often advised me to lock up the door any time I departed the room, and to . . . not enter his room when he still slept in the morning; if he was startled in his sleep he would assault me as his hostile. And I usually saw him putting some sticks or [a] knife near his bed. One day before his death, he . . . moved his bed.[179]

A number of particularly daring officers actually forced the issue and faced down their would-be assailants. Lieutenant General Victor H. Krulak described the actions taken by his son, company commander and future Marine Corps commandant Charles C. Krulak, when he was threatened:

> My youngest son told me that shortly after he took over his company . . . that he was a little rough on the troops in terms of their day-to-day activity. A young Negro PFC observed to him that this wasn't the way to help in longevity. He said, not knowing any better, "I grabbed him by the shirt and hit him and said, 'You son-of-a-bitch, if you ever say anything like this to me or anybody else around here, I'll kill you.'"
>
> He said, "I didn't mean it, but the man collapsed and I did not send him back to . . . our rear echelon, which was the common thing to do to get him out of your hair. I kept him there and watched him and he was not only obedient, he was terrified."[180]

Since so many Vietnam fragging assaults were aimed at officers and NCOs, some have asked whether members of the leadership corps ever attempted to retaliate in kind against their subordinates. In his book *Flower of the Dragon: The Breakdown of the U.S. Army in Vietnam*, journalist Richard Boyle claimed to have proof that officers engaged in this practice, which he called "counterfragging." During a wartime interview with Brigadier General Theodore C. Mataxis, who had briefly served as the acting commander of the American Division, Boyle raised the question of possible retaliation by unit leaders. He later transcribed excerpts from the conversation in his book:

> Then sometime in 1969, Mataxis said, the lifers began their own fragging against the enlisted men. The officers, he explained, had lost faith in the Judge Advocate General's office and had decided to take matters into their own hands.
>
> "What could I tell them?" he asked, somewhat sadly.
>
> I had heard stories about counterfraggings before, but this was the first time I had confirmation from a U.S. general.[181]

Yet another reporter, William Shawcross of the *Sunday Times*, attributed similar statements to Mataxis.[182] When I asked the general about his remarks, he admitted to meeting with Boyle and "philosophizing about the war," but categorically denied confirming the practice of "counterfragging." He wrote, "You will note [that] he quotes me as saying 'sometime in 1969.' [From] 1968 to 1970, I was in Iran. I didn't arrive back in Vietnam until the summer of 1970! And in the time I was in the American I never even heard a hint of 'counterfragging'! I told him that . . . if an NCO had a close friend killed by fragging I could conceive of a 'revenge counterfragging.'"[183]

While it is evident that General Mataxis offered some loose commentary on the subject, there is little material evidence to support the existence of so-called counterfragging, either in the American Division or any other U.S. military organization in Vietnam. Of all the grenade assaults outlined in the military police desk blotters, Serious Incident Reports, CID studies, and other documentation I have assembled, no commissioned officer is listed as even a possible suspect in any grenade attack on a lower-ranking soldier. I have found a handful of instances in which junior NCOs were fragging *suspects,* but in only one case was a sergeant accused of targeting his subordinates. On the night of 13 March 1970, an explosion occurred inside a bunker manned by paratroopers of the 173d Airborne Brigade, killing teenaged enlisted men Douglas R. Roest, Allan Ruttiman, and Thomas Urquhart. Sergeant David W. Goings, a twenty-one-year-old "shake-and-bake" NCO from Ohio, reported that a communist rocket had struck the bunker, but other men in the unit had their doubts. An NCO and several enlisted men eventually came forward and told a chaplain of their suspicions that the explosion had been caused not by enemy action but by a Claymore mine detonated by Goings himself. On previous occasions, they claimed, Goings had referred to the victims as "potheads" whom he "had to get rid of," and he was seen near the bunker just before the explosion took place. Because the information was not regarded as privileged, the chaplain informed the battalion commander of the story and a CID investigation was initiated. For his own part, Goings denied that he had caused the explosion and a search of the area uncovered a fragment that he claimed was part of the enemy rocket. Investigators also located several Claymore mine detonators but these were found inside the bunker. Sufficient evidence was eventually assembled to refer the case to trial but a general court-martial acquitted Goings of all charges.[184]

Although counterfragging never really seems to have gotten off the ground, there was one case of "rough justice" administered by a senior NCO upon a suspected fragger shortly after a grenade incident occurred. Nineteen-year-old Private Eugene Hood of the 1st Cavalry Division was about to be administratively discharged from the army when he threw a grenade at an NCO billet, injuring three sergeants. Not satisfied with this result, he grabbed an M16 rifle and began menacing his victims, two of whom were now lying on stretchers awaiting medical evacuation. An alert soldier who happened upon the scene managed to disarm Hood by knocking the weapon out of his hands but the show was over when First Sergeant Thomas J. "Top" Vernor appeared. Never one to suffer indiscipline in the ranks, Vernor raised his own rifle and emptied half a magazine into Hood's chest, killing him instantly. The CID investigated the shooting and questioned several eyewitnesses, including Private Johnny C. Gordon, an acquaintance of Hood's. Gordon admitted that his friend had thrown the grenade but swore that Hood was unarmed when Vernor killed him. The CID agreed, concluding that the shooting was indeed unlawful. Ultimately, however, it was the unit commander's decision whether to believe Private Gordon, who was considered to be "below the standards of a soldier," or Top Vernor, who had fought in the Second World War, the Korean War, and served three tours in Vietnam while earning two Silver Stars, four Purple Hearts, and numerous other decorations. "The Commanding Officer exercised his prerogative and did not take action against Vernor," read the final report. Case closed.[185] A similar incident had occurred in the same division only weeks before when another first sergeant, angry over a fragging that had just occurred, hunted the assailant with a shotgun and fired a blast into a troop bunker. An officer assigned to investigate the incident recommended that the sergeant be reprimanded for his actions, but when it was learned that the NCO in question had been awarded the Medal of Honor during a previous tour of duty in Vietnam, it is doubtful that anyone volunteered for the job.[186]

Fragging and Tactical Operations

There were a handful of occasions when particularly bloody fragging incidents disrupted small unit leadership. On the evening of 20 October 1969, B Company, 4/23d Infantry, was preparing to depart on an airmobile mission when a hand grenade was thrown into an officer billet. Killed in the blast was the company's executive officer, twenty-year-old First Lieutenant John D. Revier. In addition, the company commander, Captain Frederick A. Drew, was injured, as were platoon leaders James Kent and John S. Parrott. Captain Drew remained on duty with the unit but was forced to borrow an officer from another company and appoint several sergeants as temporary platoon leaders until replacements could be obtained.[187] Investigators suspected Specialist Five Willie J. Reed of committing the crime, but were unable to accumulate sufficient evidence to obtain a conviction.[188] During the early morning hours of 28 November 1969, both the troop commander and first sergeant of HHC, 1/7th Cavalry, were severely injured by a grenade. Later *that same day*, a fragger nearly took out the entire leadership corps of the 178th Maintenance Company.

Similarly, there were a few instances in which grenade incidents directly affected combat operations. In the Revier murder, the Tay Ninh base camp was locked down for several days as CID agents conducted their investigation, thus delaying the planned airmobile operation. As agents arrived in Phu Bai to investigate the 1970 murder of Sergeant Rafael L. Diaz, the 101st Airborne Division's 47th Infantry Platoon (Scout Dog) was confined to its unit area for the duration of the probe. As a result, one former platoon member recalled, operations in the field were cancelled "for about a week" as the investigation ran its course. There was one incident, however, in which a unit's tactical commitment actually precluded the CID from conducting an investigation. On the night of 11 July 1969, a grenade was thrown into a tent at the Cua Viet R&R Center, killing Private First Class Ralphael S. Yokoi and injuring seven others. But because Yokoi's unit, B Company of the 4th Marines, was slated to begin Operation William's Glade on the following day, investigators were never called to the scene. Several weeks after the murder, an infantry officer conducted an informal administrative investigation of the incident and the case was closed without further action.[189]

During the latter years of the war, officers were sometimes forced to bargain for their men's consent before undertaking combat operations in the field. "Working it out" or "talking it out," the euphemisms by which this practice was known, referred to the give-and-take that occurred between leaders and their troops when the latter were reluctant to fight.[190] The fact that such incidents occurred at all suggests that leaders generally did not shirk from assigning potentially hazardous tasks to their units, and it was during one such refusal that a grenade incident was narrowly avoided in the 101st Airborne Division.

Following his disciplinary transfer to D Company, 2/506th Infantry, Private Robert E. Edwards quickly earned a reputation as a troublemaker. Within days of his arrival in the unit, he began urging fellow black soldiers to refuse field duty. Noting that he had only received a suspended court-martial sentence for doing so in his previous outfit, he exhorted others to follow his lead. On the evening of 4 October 1968, only hours before the company was scheduled to begin a combat operation, two men, Specialist Four Ernest Cooper and Private Charles Hatcher, agreed.

The unit's leadership was quick to learn of the pair's intentions. First Lieutenant Paul D. Amato, a new platoon leader, spoke to the men in an attempt to change their minds. Cooper, whose brother had been wounded in Vietnam a short time before, wasn't listening.

"I'm scared," Cooper said. "I don't want to go back to the field."
"I need you," the lieutenant cajoled. "I can't leave you in the rear."

Amato also discussed the problem with the company commander, Captain Charles E. Nation. Known as an able field commander and strict disciplinarian, Nation had little patience for dissent in his ranks. "This is nonsense," the captain scowled. "I don't want to hear anything about people not going to the field. *Tie them up and throw them on the helicopter.* Do you understand?"

"Yes, sir."

On the following morning, as the company prepared to depart, Cooper and Hatcher resolved to remain behind, despite warnings from several command figures. They approached their squad leader, Sergeant William G. Holland, and voiced their grievances.

"I'm too short," said Cooper, whose tour in Vietnam was nearing its end.

"I'm scared," said Hatcher.

The group was soon joined by Private Edwards, who just wasn't going.

Holland summarily dismissed Edwards and sent him off to his platoon. He then had Cooper and Hatcher gather their equipment while he secured their weapons. After the pair was ordered to join their unit, the men moved to a position near the company formation but did not fall in. Then Lieutenant Amato arrived.

"You're going to the field whether you like it or not," announced the lieutenant.

"I'll kill the first man who lays his hands on me!" warned Cooper.

"Sergeant Holland, get the rope."

Amato grounded the equipment he was carrying and ordered several other soldiers to do the same. "You're not going to hog-tie me!" cried Cooper. Other platoon members began urging the rebellious pair to obey the lieutenant. Although Cooper remained defiant, they had more luck with Hatcher, whom they soon persuaded to change his mind. It was then that Edwards, who had observed the incident from his platoon, broke ranks and burst into Amato's formation.

"When did the army start tying people up?" he demanded. "I'm not going to let you hog-tie my brothers and force them to go to the field."

"You're not in this platoon," snapped Amato. "Move out!"

By the time Sergeant Holland returned with the rope, the confrontation had degenerated into the type of trash talking for which servicemen are famous.

"I'll whip any man's ass that lays a hand on me or any one of them," said Edwards.

"Any man in my platoon can whip your ass," Amato retorted. "Even Sergeant Holland standing right here by you. Try him."

Holland dropped the rope and prepared to square off when Edwards stepped back and pulled a grenade from his pocket.

"You'll all go up with me if you try to tie us up!" threatened Edwards.

"Cowards!" screamed Amato. "You're a disgrace to the army!"

Shortly after Edwards produced the grenade, Major Freddie Boyd, the battalion executive officer, bravely approached the formation and ended the standoff, ordering that Edwards and Cooper be taken into custody. Edwards surrendered his grenade to a senior NCO without incident.

First Lieutenant William B. Franks, D Company's executive officer, was issued an M16 rifle and temporarily assigned to guard the prisoners. He noticed that Edwards was wearing his cap improperly and attempted to correct him.

"Fix your hat," ordered Franks.

"Why? I'm going to jail anyway," replied Edwards.

The lieutenant reached over and snatched the cap from Edwards's head. An enraged Edwards lunged at Franks and the two began struggling. The lieutenant attempted to shoot Edwards but could not as he had forgotten to charge his rifle. Edwards eventually wrestled the weapon away from Franks but was restrained by other soldiers. "I'll kill all you white bastards!" the private swore.

As Edwards and Cooper were being led away, Hatcher grew increasingly restless.

"Where are they taking them?" he asked.

"To jail," someone replied.

With that, Hatcher left the platoon and rejoined his friends.

The incident in Lieutenant Amato's platoon was witnessed by many of D Company's enlisted men, and as the troops began departing toward the helipad, two other black soldiers, Privates Clarence L. Jackson and Ledridge Taylor, Jr., decided to act. They left their platoon and proceeded to the unit orderly room where Cooper, Edwards, and Hatcher were being held. "You might as well guard us because we're [also] not going," they told the guards.

The prisoners were dispatched to Fire Support Base Bastogne, where they were confined in a Conex container. Cooper eventually changed his mind and returned to his company while the other four faced disciplinary action.[191] Private Edwards pleaded guilty to several assault charges and possession of nearly a pound of marijuana. He received a suspended six-month prison sentence before being administratively discharged from the army in January 1969.[192] Hatcher, Jackson, and Taylor received suspended sentences for their refusal to go to the field. When ordered to rejoin their unit, all three again refused and, like Edwards, were discharged in January 1969.[193]

Upon learning of the events of 5 October, the division commander, Major General Melvin Zais, ordered his inspector general's office to conduct an inquiry of the incident. When asked about the practice of binding disobedient subordinates, Captain Nation steadfastly defended his decision, arguing that the battalion commander, Lieutenant Colonel John C. Childs, had "talked to the company commanders and told us to do all we could to get these people in the field." He believed the procedure to be effective. "There are two people in the company now who were brought out to the field [in this manner] and now they are doing a fine job and we have had no further problems with them," he claimed. "There comes a time when they get scared and it takes a little urging to get them to go again." But the inspector general disagreed, recommending that letters of admonishment be issued to Childs and Nation for their roles in instituting the binding procedure and to

Lieutenant Franks for "goading Private Edwards" and "unnecessarily inflam[ing] an already tense situation." Zais concurred and administered the reprimands.[194]

Vietnam also saw singular instances of young, company-level officers refusing to carry out what they viewed as overly hazardous or unnecessary assignments on the battlefield. I found two such incidents that took place in the 101st Airborne Division in 1970, but in both cases the platoon leaders in question refused owing to concern for their men's safety and not out of fear of them. The unique small unit environment found in Vietnam often shaped interpersonal relations between junior officers and their men, as sociologist Roger W. Little wrote: "The platoon leader occupied the lowest position of all officers in the chain of command. As the degree of risk increased, the intensity and frequency of the platoon leader's interaction with enlisted men increased, and, correspondingly, significant interaction with status peers [other officers] decreased. The more he participated in their activities, the more he tended to share the sentiments of the men he commanded, and his willingness to use the sanctions available to him diminished correspondingly."[195]

One of these cases involved First Lieutenant John J. Haracivet of A Company, 1/502nd Infantry, who was ordered to emplace a night ambush position near Fire Support Base Birmingham. As his men prepared to leave the base, he thought better of it. "This is highly unorthodox," he told one of his sergeants, "but I am not going to send the 'hamburger' [ambush patrol] out." He then instructed his troops to send false radio messages to the command post indicating that they were outside the wire. The ruse was discovered, however, when the company commander made an unannounced late-night inspection of the perimeter and stumbled upon the troops who were supposed to be out manning the ambush. Charged with willful disobedience of a lawful order and misconduct before the enemy, Haracivet defended his decision not to send his men out, arguing, "It was quite dark and dangerous to move out in front of the bunker line at night." He was found guilty of the reduced charges of dereliction of duty and ordering his men to make a false report, and fined $800, but his conviction was subsequently overturned on appeal.[196]

Conclusion

The military's response to the fragging phenomenon can best be called uneven. At the division level and below, some leaders took initiative by limiting their men's access to weapons in rear areas and improvising effective countermeasures such as General Jones's Operation Freeze. At the command level, the Marine Corps response was almost singularly attributable to Jones, and it was not until the latter half of 1970 that the majority of Marine Corps units in Vietnam implemented his "Freeze" guidelines. The larger, more bureaucratic army responded more slowly. General McCaffrey's October 1970 letter to his commanders was a good, albeit late, start, but the 1971 grenade moratorium came only as a knee-jerk response to embarrassing press coverage at home. Even then the USARV staff took several months to draft the plan and implement it, while continued inattention to ordnance security at the unit level enabled at least two killers to obtain their weapons after the post-moratorium regulations were supposed to be in effect.

General McCaffrey cited the two-way breakdown in communication that emerged between the command structure and the enlisted ranks as a major contributor to acts of violence in Vietnam. In this he was correct, and the command structure endeavored to maintain channels intended to alleviate such problems. But the chaplains, inspectors general, and "open door" policies instituted by well-meaning commanders were often dismissed as being part of the military establishment. Rather than believing that they could confide in or reason with their superiors, those who engaged in fragging felt cornered by the chain of command and did not view reaching out to their leaders or some other arm of the military bureaucracy as a possible solution to their ills. Unable to control their impulses, they saw violence as the only way to voice their grievances.

Despite the efforts of CID personnel and military prosecutors, most of the Vietnam fraggers succeeded in evading justice. The limited amount of evidentiary material left behind at crime scenes made grenade cases notoriously difficult to solve, while the reluctance displayed by young enlisted men to assist investigators hampered efforts at identifying offenders. Military prosecutors faced their own difficulties in

fragging cases, these ranging from witness procurement to the seasoned civilian counsel sometimes secured by the accused. One can see
why so few of the perpetrators were identified and prosecuted.

The perceived shortcomings of the military justice system described
above led Generals Westmoreland and Prugh to blame the UCMJ for
failing to support commanders in their efforts to maintain discipline in
Vietnam. In many ways, however, the military's transition from the old
Articles of War, in which unit commanders possessed considerable authority to discipline their men, to the new "judicialized" UCMJ was all
but inevitable. Well-publicized criticisms of the court-martial process
voiced after the Second World War led to the establishment of a new
legal system that afforded the accused substantially increased due process. This trend continued into the 1960s in the form of several important high court decisions and additional reforms to the UCMJ. From an
organizational standpoint, the shift was also unsurprising: since the
armed services themselves were becoming increasingly bureaucratized,
it was only logical that the military justice system would also move in
this direction. Such maladies as fragging, racial violence, and rampant
drug abuse could hardly have been predicted by the services, as they
had never been encountered on such a large scale, and the immense
backlogs of cases that emerged within some commands led to long trial
delays, fewer convictions, and frustration on the part of unit commanders. To make matters worse, what was regarded as leniency administered by military courts, particularly during the appeals process,
virtually ensured that convicted fraggers served the lightest of sentences for their crimes. Traditional enlisted fears of the military justice
apparatus and the age-old legend of long prison terms spent "making
big rocks into little rocks" proved to be all but unfounded during the
Vietnam era.

Young enlisted offenders often shared their superiors' disdain for
the military justice system, although for inherently different reasons. In
spite of its improved safeguards, many young servicemen continued to
view the UCMJ as omnipotent and predisposed toward the whims of
the command structure. For all of the effort expended to create a system that at once "protect[ed] the rights of those subject to the code . . .
without impairing the performance of military functions,"[197] the result

was that military justice in Vietnam pleased virtually no one. Unit commanders and enlisted men alike became convinced that the system worked against them. Regarding racial cases, a battalion commander complained, "It is very apparent that the Negro soldier has 'whitey' on the run."[198] Meanwhile, army social scientists surveying angry minority inmates at the Long Binh stockade were told of how "military justice is a joke."[199]

The military's long-term approach to ending fragging and the other disciplinary problems that appeared during the Vietnam era lay with the formation of the all-volunteer force.[200] The institutional changes that were made within the services to achieve this aim were nothing short of revolutionary: instead of reverting to the old coercive methods of the past to restore discipline, military leaders pushed even further in the direction of persuasion to attract quality volunteers. Although some of these moves generated considerable resistance from career servicemen and eye rolling from veterans of older generations, the decision ultimately proved to be the right one. "A radical change has taken place in the values and norms of the younger generation," sociologist Jacques van Doorn observed, "most of which are very much at variance with the goals and life style of the traditional military."[201] In other words, whenever youth changes, the military must also change and move toward youth. How else could the armed services obtain suitable personnel if its values stood contrary to those of the young people it was trying to recruit? The changes that were made culminated in the professional all-volunteer force that emerged in the 1980s.

What effect did fragging have on officers and NCOs at the unit level? Surely it caused some to take such actions as changing their sleeping arrangements or arming themselves while in rear areas. But did this coercion have any effect on the orders they issued, as some observers have claimed? Reactions among the leadership corps varied from man to man. Some, like the nervous young lieutenant described by John De Groot, may have turned a blind eye to all but the most egregious breaches of discipline. Others, like future Marine commandant Krulak, fearlessly faced down any would-be assailants but sometimes found themselves on the receiving end of their subordinates' ordnance, as did First Sergeant Johnny C. Martin. It seems likely, however, that many of

those who felt that the threat of fragging was real in their units reacted
the way one old sergeant did:

> I lock my door when I go out, and I check for booby traps when I come
> in. I'm leery of getting in dark places. But I have never been a worrier,
> and I don't reckon I'll start now. I'm concerned about it, but I'm not
> worried.[202]

He spoke these words during a press interview not long after his men
tried to kill him with a homemade bomb.

CHAPTER FIVE

Fragging in the U.S. and Australian Forces: A Comparative Analysis

I N Chapter 1, I suggested a conceptual model to illustrate how armies sometimes experience crises in morale. In the proceeding narrative, a historical explanation was presented to show how a combination of political, institutional, and social factors led to such a dilemma within the U.S. military during the latter years of its Vietnam involvement. But can such an explanation be applied to cases outside the American experience? Have other armies endured crises of morale and discipline under similar circumstances?

Australian troops served alongside their U.S. allies in Vietnam since the early 1960s, first as advisors to the South Vietnamese army and later in a brigade-strength task force. After the Americans began their withdrawal from Southeast Asia, the Australians followed suit and removed their own units. Within the context of this study, two fundamental questions are raised. First, did the pullout affect morale in the Australian ranks? Second, did Australian troops resort to assaulting their superiors as the Americans did? I will examine these questions in the form of a comparative analysis of the two forces and their respective Vietnam experiences.

The many similarities between U.S. and Australian forces in Vietnam provide a unique opportunity for comparative analysis. Both were Western armies sent to fight a limited war on the Asian mainland in a form of "forward defense" against the perceived threat of international communism. They began their Vietnam involvement in advisory roles before deploying ground forces in 1965. After the Tet Offensive, popular sentiment in the two countries turned against the conflict, and sizable antiwar movements emerged on both sides of the Pacific. Both nations then undertook gradual withdrawals of their forces over a period of years.

Although Australian troops delighted in making favorable comparisons between themselves and the Americans,[1] they too experienced problems in the area of morale and discipline during the latter years of their Vietnam involvement. This is because many of the same factors that created such discord within the U.S. ranks were also present within Australia and its armed forces: a long, unpopular war that was ending with indecisive results, institutional strain upon the army, and the emergence of unchecked societal influences among the troops. Although physical manifestations of these effects were more difficult to discern in the much smaller Australian force, those that did appear were familiar enough: at least eleven fraggings are known to have occurred in Australian units in Vietnam, resulting in two officer deaths.

Australia in Vietnam

In 1964, President Johnson asked other nations of the South East Asia Treaty Organization (SEATO) to contribute toward the anticommunist effort in South Vietnam. Australia had in fact maintained a small advisory team in the country since the early 1960s, and when LBJ asked for more men, long-time Australian prime minister Sir Robert Menzies responded by assembling an infantry battalion group and sending it to Bien Hoa in May 1965. A year later, the group was expanded in size to become 1 Australian Task Force (1 ATF) and a base camp was established at Nui Dat. The task force consisted of two (later three) infantry battalions, an artillery regiment, an engineer squadron, a cavalry troop, an armored detachment, and a squadron of the elite Special Air Service. Logistical support was provided by a separate group stationed at Vung Tau.

When Australian ground forces initially deployed to South Vietnam, their combat readiness was, like that of their American counterparts, believed to be unmatched in their nation's history. The first unit to arrive was the 1st Battalion, Royal Australian Regiment (1 RAR). Composed exclusively of volunteers, it was said of the battalion that "no better trained or better equipped military force ha[d] ever left Australian shores."[2] In August 1966, Australian troops proved their mettle during the Battle of Long Tan, when a company from 6 RAR stood its ground against a numerically superior enemy force. Within twelve months, the Australians were able to wrest most of Phuoc Tuy Province from the communists. Senior U.S. commanders praised the task force's performance and even awarded a Presidential Unit Citation to the men of Long Tan. Meanwhile, polls taken at home indicated that most Australians supported the war: in May 1965, 52 percent of those queried declared themselves in favor of the Australian commitment, with 37 percent opposed and 11 percent undecided. The approval rating jumped to 61 percent in 1966 and 62 percent in 1967.[3]

The 1960s were, if nothing else, a period of transition for the Australian army. The challenges posed by such threats as Indonesia's policy of confrontation toward Malaysia and increasingly bellicose rhetoric from communist China and North Vietnam led Menzies's Liberal-Country coalition to introduce conscription in late 1964. In less than five years, the army ballooned from a prewar strength of about 22,500 to a whopping 40,000. This massive expansion and the length of the Vietnam commitment led to the appearance of institutional strains similar to those experienced by the American military. More and more younger men with less maturity and experience were promoted to leadership positions. By late 1967, this condition was discernable enough to warrant special attention; during a meeting of senior officers held in December, the 1 ATF commander "pointed to the number of disciplinary offenses and exhorted his officers and NCOs to supervise their troops more closely." In its appraisal of 1968's Operation Coburg, the official Australian history of the war complained:

A spate of accidental casualties occurred during the operation. Many involved instances of Australian soldiers firing upon other Australian troops. Major General MacDonald, COMAFV, concluded, after studying the reports of the incidents, that they were mostly due to a "combination of poor (or even lack of) orders, failure to observe such orders as these were, and 'trigger-happy' soldiers.

These incidents highlighted the "sheer lack of basic knowledge" of many junior NCOs and officers. "The army was paying the price," Mac-Donald concluded, "for its rapid expansion and transition."[4]

Although the U.S. and Australian armies shared a number of common organizational characteristics, there were also key differences between them. At the height of their Vietnam involvement, the Australians had about 8,500 men in South Vietnam, including over 1,000 sailors and airmen, whereas U.S. strength reached 543,400. There is also the matter of the forces' composition. Vietnam-era conscription ultimately proved to be unpopular in both the United States and Australia, but here too there were differences between the systems used in the two countries. With Australia's National Service scheme, a ballot system selected twenty-year-olds for two years of army service, including possible overseas duty. Great pains were taken to ensure that the procedure was fair, and deferments were liberally awarded. Of the 804,286 young men who registered, only 63,740 were called up, and of these less than one-third served in Vietnam.[5] In the United States, the war in general and the draft in particular were considerably more exacting. In April 1967, for example, it was found that the U.S. military personnel in Vietnam represented 2,350 troops per million of the total U.S. population of 200 million, whereas Australian personnel represented only 520 troops per million of Australia's population of 11.7 million.[6] There was also Project 100,000, which forced the U.S. military to accept thousands of substandard personnel it normally would have rejected. Australia never enacted any program to purposefully induct such men. In South Vietnam, most Australian troops were limited to the isolated forward base at Nui Dat or the rear area at Vung Tau, greatly easing military police duties. American forces, on the other hand, were spread out at hundreds of outposts throughout the country, making them far more difficult to control. As we have seen, much of the violence that erupted among U.S. troops in Vietnam was racially motivated. On the Australian side, the issue of whether to conscript Aboriginal males into the forces had been considered but never resolved,[7] and while some native men did volunteer, Australia sent what was for all intents and purposes a white army to Vietnam.

Illegal drug use, which became the most serious morale problem to affect U.S. forces in Vietnam, played a far less serious role in the Australian ranks. The task force's first scattered drug cases came to light in 1969 but the issue was blown out of all proportion by a news story that appeared early the following year.[8] After a newly discharged national serviceman was arrested with marijuana, his court testimony that a fellow soldier had smuggled a half pound of the drug out of Vietnam led the *Australian* to run a story under the headline "Diggers in Vietnam Using Marihuana, Court Told."[9] Military leaders were able to downplay the incident but resolved to keep any future drug cases out of the papers. Whenever the task force issued formal guidelines or informational papers on drug abuse, the texts usually opened with statements like "We do not at present have a drug problem in this force" but just as surely concluded with such calls for discretion as "I do not wish the paper to have a wide circulation. . . . We must be careful not to give the impression that we are in any way apprehensive," or "I do not wish that drugs be given prominence in discussion within 1 ATF." In any event, sporadic drug apprehensions continued to be made, these invariably involving marijuana. The Australian records reviewed for this study make no mention of their men using hard drugs such as heroin.[10]

While illegal drugs did not play any major role in leading Australian troops into trouble, the same cannot be said of alcohol. Excessive drinking has long been a part of the exaggerated masculinity exhibited by young men serving in Western armies but the level of abuse displayed by Australian soldiers provided their leaders with cause for alarm. The commander of Australian troops in Vietnam believed that "there is far more drunkenness in this Force, with all the problems that flow from it, than in any previous [Australian] force."[11] Virtually every act of violence committed by the Australians against their peers was saturated with booze. The murder of one officer stemmed from the decision to suspend a unit's beer ration. In another case, a drunken private celebrated Christmas by pumping bullets into a sergeants' mess. Two NCOs were killed and another was wounded.[12] Each of the three diggers convicted of assaults with explosive devices admitted to being heavily intoxicated when they committed their crimes.

The first fragging case known to have occurred in the Australian task force took place in late 1967 and involved the murder of an artillery officer. Lieutenant Robert G. Birse of 4 Field Regiment died from wounds he sustained after a grenade was rolled into his position at Fire Support Base Bravo. Authorities charged Gunner Leonard E. Newman with the murder, alleging that after alcohol had been banned within the battery's lines, Birse had threatened him with disciplinary action for drinking on duty. Newman, it was later learned, had told at least one other man of his intention to scare the lieutenant with a grenade. The battery commander later testified that Newman, a national serviceman, "had been showing signs of increasing mental instability and appeared to be 'cracking.'" It was believed that his anxiety was caused by his frustration "over delays with his request for leave to visit his wife and new baby in Australia." A court-martial found Newman guilty of manslaughter and sentenced him to five years' imprisonment but his conviction was later quashed on appeal and the charge dismissed.[13]

The Birse murder appears to have been an anomaly in the task force during this period, as no other incidents are recorded within its ranks for the next twelve months. In 1969, however, four cases occurred, all of them aimed at authority figures. The "us-against-them" nature of these cases mirrored those taking place in the U.S. ranks, with enlisted men taking an increasingly dim view of leaders who sought to maintain "excessive" standards. The first three incidents came more as warnings rather than actual attempts to kill; an investigator described them as "a way in which to express grievances." One occurred in 1 Troop, 1 Field Squadron, shortly after a junior NCO was replaced by veteran Staff Sergeant Brian J. Lamb, who did not care for the troop's state of discipline. Lamb wrote: "I found that discipline in the troop was sadly lacking. As a result of this I tightened up on the discipline by making the troop form up in three ranks when called on parade and insisted that every member would be dressed properly—boots clean, etc. . . . I made my intention clear to the troop and particularly to the NCOs that I was going to lift the standard of discipline in the troop. Up to the time of the incident I hadn't charged any person nor had I singled out any one individual. I was working on the troop as a whole."

The troop's sappers voiced their dissatisfaction with these measures by detonating an explosive charge in Lamb's living quarters. The sergeant was not present when the device exploded, and he avoided injury, but many of his personal belongings were destroyed.[14] Two similar cases took place in August: one in B Squadron, 3 Cavalry Regiment, where the determined motives were the men's anger over an order regarding dress for the evening meal, restrictions on use of the canteen, and a new policy regarding leave, and another in A Company, 6 RAR, where the points of contention included the men's dislike for their commander's perceived habit of forcing A Company to do more walking than the battalion's other companies while in the field, providing little free time between operations, restricting canteen hours, and employing strict disciplinary practices.[15]

The investigations of these incidents indicate that they enjoyed a measure of approval among the enlisted men. None of them was solved, this owing in at least part to the men's reluctance to assist investigators. In the 1 Field Squadron case "the motive appeared to be a dislike of SSgt Lamb. . . . The attitude taken by the majority of the troop members as to SSgt Lamb's tightening of discipline soon became apparent. Every member interviewed could account for his whereabouts at the time prior to the explosion and also have his claims corroborated by another member. Again, the majority of members stated that they hoped that the person responsible would not be caught and that they feel it may teach SSgt Lamb a lesson."[16]

When a member of the Special Investigation Branch questioned A Company, 6 RAR, regarding the grenade thrown at the commander's tent, he too encountered a "wall of silence" regarding the incident. He reported: "The majority of personnel state that they did not hear the explosion, but had to be woken up as the company sergeant major called 'stand-to.' Some members live only 87 feet from the point of the explosion. A large majority expressed the view that they were pleased that the incident had taken place." After reviewing the August cases, the commander of Australian forces in Vietnam suggested that company-grade leadership might have been partly responsible for the assaults. "As far as can be determined," he wrote, "the grounds for complaint on each occasion were petty and could easily have been resolved in a routine matter. Perhaps inexperienced man-management at junior leader level has been a contributing factor to these incidents."[17]

Far more ominous was the year's final incident, a murder that took place in 6 Platoon, B Company, 9 RAR. The unit had all but completed its one-year tour in Vietnam and was about to return to Australia when tragedy struck. The victim, Lieutenant Robert T. Convery, was a young officer from Victoria whose military career had gotten off to a rough start. In what was possibly the most adverse fitness report ever submitted, his battalion commander wrote, "With regard to his general incompetence, I have NO hesitation in stating that he is NOT up to the standard required of a platoon commander in a regular battalion. I request that he be removed from [this unit] immediately and reposted." But Convery's bearing and performance improved in the coming months, and when he was sent to Vietnam in late 1968, he began to mature into a good platoon commander. He was in any case well liked by his peers, who knew him as "a very cheerful, easy going fellow." As his unit prepared to depart Vietnam, Convery spoke eagerly of returning home and marrying his fiancée.[18]

Convery's killer, twenty-year-old Private Peter D. "Pedro" Allen, was a different story. The son of a World War II veteran, Allen had grown up in Tasmania in an environment that was alternately described as "stable and happy" or "fairly chaotic, . . . with a lot of violence between the father and the brothers within the family." Whatever the truth, Allen had barely reached his teens when he began to flounder. Though intelligent, he left school at fifteen and proceeded to drift from job to job, eventually finding work as a bricklayer. The only things he seemed to excel at were drinking and brawling, the latter earning him two juvenile assault convictions. He first attempted to enlist in the army in 1966 but was rejected and made to wait for two more years until he was finally allowed into the ranks. His service record reveals numerous minor disciplinary infractions, these ranging from public drunkenness and short unexcused absences to an assault on a Vietnamese taxi driver. Once in the field, however, Allen served as a forward scout, and by all accounts performed well during the few actual encounters he had with the enemy. Nevertheless, life in an infantry battalion did not suit him, for he submitted a written request for a transfer but was refused. He was then sent to Lieutenant Convery's platoon, where the two men quickly became enemies.[19]

During subsequent interviews with investigators and an army psychiatrist, Allen spoke at some length of his dislike for Lieutenant Convery. "I already knew him from 1 RAR," he said. "He didn't have a clue in the bush. [He was] always back, cringing like a dog, really." Allen conceded that the lieutenant was good at calling in artillery fire on enemy targets but claimed that Convery failed to accompany his men on sweeps and issued questionable orders. In garrison, the pair's relationship further worsened; Convery charged Allen with drinking in the lines and for refusing an order to attend a signal course, for which the private received twenty-eight days of field punishment. Furious, Allen resolved to get even.

On 22 November, 6 Platoon was spending one of its last days at Nui Dat, its men exchanging addresses and talking anxiously of their imminent departure for Australia. Private Allen spent a number of hours drinking in his unit's "boozer." After it closed, he and several friends gathered in a nearby troop tent where the party continued. Among other things, the men discussed their dislike of Sergeant Thomas H. Cross and how "it was a wonder he hasn't been zapped." One man even suggested that Cross should be "ambushed." At about midnight, Lieutenant Convery appeared and put an end to the festivities.

"Break up the party and put the lights out," he ordered.

The men did as they were told and switched off the lights. They then waited for the lieutenant to leave, and, once he was out of sight, lowered the tent's flaps, turned the lights back on, and resumed drinking. Convery later returned to the area and when he found that the party had recommenced, he sternly ordered the revelers to bed.

For Private Allen, who by this time had consumed some twenty beers, Convery's actions were too much to bear. As he later said, "The thought to kill Mr. Convery has been with me for some time and . . . the talk of ambushing the sergeant and the beers I'd had revived the thought and I carried it out."

Allen took a grenade from his field gear and moved to leave the tent. Before exiting, he paused briefly to ask Private Garry J. O'Reilly for a cigarette. As O'Reilly obliged, Allen whispered, "If you hear an explosion, say nothing." He then walked the short distance to Lieutenant Convery's quarters. He later wrote:

I then sneaked up to Mr. Convery's tent. When I got there, he had his light out but was talking to the new platoon commander from 8 RAR.

I heard him say he was going to charge us the next morning and was
going to make sure that Corporal Cunich would lose his stripes.

I sat down outside his tent and waited until they were both quiet. I
then went round to Mr. Convery's side of the tent. . . . I just pulled the
pin out, put the grenade on [his] bed and ducked down. . . . As soon as
it exploded I ran down to my tent.[20]

When the grenade detonated, the force was such that it tore the lieutenant's bunk to shreds. A jagged piece of shrapnel ripped a hole in the
tent's roof and blood-spattered pieces of bedding littered the floor. Convery was heard to moan for several moments but soon died. Mission
accomplished, a drunken Allen stumbled back to his quarters and went
to bed.

Within hours of the murder, Captain Peter A. Langman of the provost unit arrived from Vung Tau to conduct an investigation. After
speaking with unit commanders, he sealed off the B Company perimeter and ordered that all grenades be confiscated. He then moved to 6
Platoon's lines to view the crime scene and interview unit personnel.
Using the platoon roll book, he summoned each of 6 Platoon's diggers
individually and inquired as to his whereabouts when the murder occurred. Private Allen was among the first to be called but played dumb.
"I don't know anything that may assist you," he lied. "I went to bed
about 11:30. I went to sleep. . . . We went on parade about 1:30." But
conversations with others in the platoon told Langman otherwise. Private O'Reilly informed him of Allen's warning of an impending explosion just before the incident occurred and Lance Corporal Albert W.
Bennett reported that seconds after he heard the grenade detonate, an
out-of-breath Allen burst into the tent they shared and dove into bed.
After speaking with the remaining platoon members, Langman recalled
Private Allen.

"We have questioned everyone in 6 Platoon," the captain announced.
"There are a few things we have to clear up with several people, okay?"

"Yes," responded Allen.

"Would you mind going through the times that you went to bed
and heard about the explosion?" Langman asked.

Allen stuck to his story. "I got to bed about 11:30 and was woken about 1:30. That was the first I knew about it," he repeated.

Having heard the accounts given by O'Reilly and Bennett, Langman knew that Allen was lying. He decided to trap him.

"Are you sure about that? Could it have been later?"
"Only about ten or fifteen minutes," offered Allen.

Langman had his man. He wasted no time in dropping the bomb. "I have been told that you got to bed just after the explosion."

Allen was stunned. As he later admitted, "Someone said they saw me; [I] must have mucked up my story somewhere." Ten or fifteen seconds of awkward silence ensued. Then he folded.

"Alright, I did it," he said.
"Did what?" asked Langman.
"I killed Mr. Convery."
"How did you do that?"
"With a grenade."
"Where did you get the grenade?"
"From my webbing."

At this point, Langman halted the interview and informed Allen of his legal rights. After receiving a cigarette and a soft drink, Allen voluntarily wrote out a three-page confession and was placed under close arrest. Remarkably, he even agreed to perform a macabre reenactment of the murder for a military film crew. "It's okay, I don't mind," he was heard to say.

Allen's court-martial convened at Vung Tau in January 1970. The trial transcript reveals that considerable attention was devoted to the defendant's mental state, as several psychiatrists were brought in to examine him. For his own part, Allen freely admitted to committing the murder, saying:

The reason I killed Mr. Convery was because when I was in 1 RAR he was my platoon commander and he used to hold parties in the lines with the rest of his platoon. When I got to 9 RAR, he was again my platoon commander and in the first week I was there he charged me for drinking beer in the lines. Not long after this he was having a party in his own tent. After this he ordered me to do a signal course which I didn't want to do. He again charged me for disobeying a lawful command.

One of the doctors asked him about his feelings regarding the murder and if he felt he was justified in killing the lieutenant. "It never entered in my head that I was doing wrong," Allen explained. "I thought I was doing it for the good of the blokes." He was then asked if he would do it again.

"Now I wish I hadn't done it," he answered.

"Why?" the doctor queried.

"I would be home now," responded Allen. "It has caused me and everyone a lot of inconvenience."

Even the doctor must have winced after he asked Allen if he regretted killing Lieutenant Convery. "I've got no conscience about it," Allen replied.[21]

In spite of these incriminating admissions, Allen's assigned counsel, Lieutenant Colonel Barrie E. Egan, mounted a spirited defense. Ironically, this was not Egan's first grenade case: exactly two years before, it had been he who represented Gunner Newman at his court-martial. But the prosecution's evidence was overwhelming and the subsequent guilty verdict and life sentence were all but inevitable. Allen was returned to Australia, discharged from the army, and delivered to Tasmania's notorious Risdon Prison to serve his sentence. He was paroled in July 1980 after serving just over ten years.

Lieutenant Convery's murder bears a number of eerie similarities to those incidents that were occurring within the U.S. ranks at the same time. The demands of "forward defense" necessitated the army's massive expansion and led to the induction of persons who in previous years would not have been allowed into the service. Allen, who had been rejected when he first tried to enlist in 1966, was later accepted, as the army's strength nearly doubled and new men were desperately needed. His spotty disciplinary record in the service further reflects his poor situational adjustment and underscores the army's initial judgment about him.

Other parallels can be seen when examining the murder itself. Just as many of the American fraggers were influenced by the "loose talk" of their more mature peers, Allen conceded that his friends' boozy discussion of ambushing the sergeant played a role in his decision to kill Lieutenant Convery. It is interesting to note that while Allen was a volunteer, all but one of the men who partook in the conversation regarding Sergeant Cross on the night of the murder were national servicemen. The Australians found that their "Nashos," as the conscripts were popularly known, were "more mature, less rattled, less enthusiastic and more stolid than the general run of the mill regular recruit—who is younger, more sleepy, more 'aggressive,' . . . and more frequently drunk."[22] In other words, the draftees were able to resolve their anger with tough barracks talk. One man who was present described it this way: "I overheard a discussion about killing . . . Sergeant Cross. I didn't pay much attention to it because these conversations aren't rare at times." Allen, on the other hand, was unable to deal with frustration in this manner and carried his threat through. Intoxication, another hallmark of the U.S. incidents, was present here in the form of Allen's heavy drinking in the hours before he committed the murder. (He also admitted to smoking marijuana on several occasions in Vietnam but is not known to have used the drug on the night of the incident.) This case also possessed an institutional likeness that both armies rued: after Captain Langman succeeded in solving the case and the military prosecutor won a conviction in court, Allen served only ten years of his life sentence for committing one of the most heinous murders of the war. While many fraggers simply hurled their grenades at their targets from considerable distances, Allen actually walked up to Convery's tent and physically placed the grenade next to the sleeping lieutenant, all but ensuring his death. "I was hoping it would kill him," he later admitted.[23] His total lack of remorse for the murder is no better illustrated than in his reference to the crime as an "inconvenience" to himself and others.

In 1970, Australia began to scale down its Vietnam commitment. After the United States announced a new troop withdrawal, the Australians

decided to reduce the strength of their task force by not replacing 8
RAR when it completed its tour of duty that November. Two grenade
incidents are known to have occurred in Australian units that year; one
involved a drunken sapper in 1 Field Squadron who took it upon himself to rig an explosive charge and destroy his commanding officer's
toilet. When asked why he had done it, he responded the way so many
others had before him: "I don't know why I blew the toilet but there has
been a lot of talk in the squadron about seeing the [commanding
officer]'s toilet go up. I guess all the talk must have played on my mind
and that is probably why I did it."[24] The second incident involved a
booby-trap warning aimed at a warrant officer in the soon-to-be leaving Eighth Battalion. As was the case with the grenade warnings issued
the year before, no enlisted men offered information about the incident
and the investigation was closed without any arrests being made.[25] The
remainder of the task force was withdrawn in late 1971, during which
three more incidents occurred, none of which involved any fatalities.[26]

Conclusion

This comparison of U.S. and Australian forces in Vietnam suggests that
a particular combination of political, institutional, and social factors
may cause armies to suffer from crises in morale during limited wars.
However, researchers should be careful not to make broad generaliza-
tions based on this exploratory analysis. The two armies examined
here operated under nearly identical conditions in the same conflict, on
the same territory, and during the same time period. Careful research
and analysis of other armies during different eras is required before any
firm conclusions can be drawn. Such case studies can serve to further
develop, enhance, and reshape the type as necessary. Possible choices
include the Soviet army during the later years of its Afghan War or even
the Israeli Defense Forces during their occupation of Lebanon in the
1980s. It is hoped that these studies might eventually contribute toward
the construction of a typology of modern military demoralization.

Exactly how much demoralization occurred within Australian units
in Vietnam? If one were to compare the record of fragging incidents
that occurred in the Australian task force to a similar American list, it

would appear that the Australians fared rather well. But when one considers the size differential between the two forces, injurious U.S. personnel policies such as a more pervasive draft and Project 100,000, and the absence of racial tension within the nearly all-white Australian ranks, it becomes clear that from the time of all-volunteer 1 RAR's arrival in 1965 to Lieutenant Convery's murder in 9 RAR four years later, the Australian force in Vietnam underwent a marked institutional change. The strains of the war first appeared in the form of lowered performance and increasing numbers of accidents both in the field and in the rear. Once the word of negotiations and possible withdrawal spread, grenades began flying. In his examination of Australia's participation in the war, veteran and historian Robert A. Hall wrote, "The Australian Army in Vietnam [never] came even close to disintegration. . . . However, there were some nascent signs of discontent and disintegration. . . . It is probable that all major units of the Australian army operating in Vietnam experienced them." The documentary record supports this conclusion.

The records I reviewed indicate that at least eleven grenade incidents occurred in Australian units in Vietnam. As was true with the Americans, some of the Australian assaults were intended to kill their targets while others were attempts to intimidate. An exact number of cases cannot be determined, as at least one and perhaps more of them were never investigated. Robert A. Hall's history of 8 RAR includes the story of a grenade threat of which the company commander admitted that "no investigation was conducted. . . . 'There was no point in reporting it. There was no point of calling in the Military Police because you wouldn't have found anything.'"[27] The Australians did not take any command-wide action regarding fragging, although it is interesting to note that the sensitivity they displayed regarding press coverage of the drug issue was not unlike that exhibited by their American counterparts when journalists caught wind of the U.S. Army's morale woes.

CHAPTER SIX

The Legacy

LONG after the fall of Saigon in April 1975, the fragging phenomenon continued to haunt those it had affected. As the convicted fraggers served their sentences, their maimed victims faced challenges posed by their physical and psychological injuries while the families of the fallen were left to grieve over their loved ones.

Although many fraggers were sentenced to lengthy prison terms for their crimes, nearly all of them were paroled or released by the late 1970s. The last Vietnam fragger to leave prison, William E. Sutton, was briefly paroled but was rearrested after violating his conditional release and remained incarcerated until August 1999. One man never emerged from confinement: after exhausting all appeals, Reginald F. Smith was transferred to a federal prison to serve the balance of his forty-year sentence. Degenerating into mental illness, he was diagnosed as a paranoid schizophrenic and became increasingly violent, fighting with other inmates and allegedly slashing two of them in 1975. He was eventually dispatched to what was then known as the end of the line of America's prison system: the U.S. Penitentiary at Marion, Illinois, where he converted to Islam and assumed the name Ra'amahd Maulana Fadk Muhammad Suhuf.[1] On 25 July 1982, he was watching a cellblock television when another inmate crept up behind him and slit his throat. He bled to death while en route to a local hospital. Investigators were able to identify a suspect in the murder but no charges were preferred owing to a lack of evidence, and the crime remains unsolved.[2]

Smith's case, as it turned out, proved to be the exception among the incarcerated fraggers. Many of the others were able to achieve various successes while incarcerated and obtain early releases from confinement. Gary A. Hendrix was all of nineteen when he was convicted of murder and sentenced to life imprisonment. The man who in 1968 had volunteered to "go to Vietnam and kill some gooks" entered prison three years later as an angry, cynical individual harboring deep resentment toward authority figures. As his myriad legal appeals failed, he became involved with Quaker volunteers of the Prison Visitation Service, an interdenominational organization that provided ministry services to federal inmates. Slowly, the bitterness that dominated his youth subsided and he began to feel remorse for the murder he committed. "If any man deserve[d] to die," Hendrix said of his victim, "he did not. I have seen and heard about men being murdered because they, through stupidity or whatnot, caused other men to die in Vietnam. I don't even have that as a rationalization."[3] With the encouragement of several Friends, Hendrix wrote a searching autobiographical essay in which he attempted to explain himself and his crime:

I did kill Sergeant Tate in October 1970. During my court-martial no exact motive was ever established. In reality, there was no overwhelming reason for me to have murdered [him]. When I look back at it now, I see it as a matter of projection. The two nights preceding the murder I had been out on ambushes, which tend to leave a person physically and mentally tired because of lack of sleep. Sergeant Tate caught me sleeping on bunker watch and I wasn't angry with him for doing his job. In fact, my response was, what a stupid thing for me to have done on watch. But, because of that interaction with Sergeant Tate, he died.

That very small interaction with Sergeant Tate was a [catalyst] for me. During my childhood I had internalized a low self-image about myself, and my interaction with Sergeant Tate brought all of this to the surface for me. The self-doubts, fears, and sense of lack of personal value were all revolving around in my head. Another marine that I knew who happened to be with me at the bunker mentioned how screwed up some "lifers" were and the amount of fraggings that had occurred over in Nam. I think his intentions were to try to cheer me up because I must have appeared so gloomy to him and he was using the standard chatter of the enlisted personnel. Anyway, I then conceived of the idea of killing Sergeant Tate. From the time I first conceived the idea to actually doing it about a two-minute span of time had passed. I was convicted of premeditated murder, but it was only premeditated in a legal sense. I did not plan it or deliberate on the merits of it. . . .

I don't remember if I just picked up a grenade from the bunker I was at or on the way to Sergeant Tate's bunker. I remember that my thoughts locked into a pattern of seeing Sergeant Tate as trying to play God. I did not see the reality that I was the one who played God. I could not face myself so I blamed Sergeant Tate for all my troubles and killed him. . . . I did not kill Sergeant Tate because I was bitter towards him, I killed Sergeant Tate because I needed a scapegoat for my own emotions.

After the murder I went back to the bunker where I was on duty and told PFC Schmidt that I had just killed Tate. I then laid down and fell asleep almost instantly. Next morning I was arrested by C.I.D. [and] taken to the Da Nang stockade. . . . I was confused and disoriented. What the hell am I doing in this cage, was my reaction. I would not allow myself to look at what I had done. . . . [I]t was an escapist technique for me to avoid looking at the murder or at myself as a murderer.

It was only after many years that I could start breaking down that wall that I had built up inside of myself. It has only been within the last couple of years that I have known consciously that I killed Sergeant Tate. In recent months there has been a discovery about myself, an insight, that has unlocked most of my emotions and memories about 1970. Before the appeals process ended I could not respond to the issue of remorse because of the legal ramifications. Outside of that, I would not have been able to respond because I never even looked at the murder before. Remorse? I felt nothing at all. In line with my perceptions of what occurred, it was the same type of blockage in my head from the emotions. I am truly sorry that I took another man's life. Even now that I've begun to feel the emotions from the murder, there's an overwhelming feeling inside of me that asks, "Will God ever forgive me?"[4]

Hendrix maintained an exceptional disciplinary record in prison and even earned a college degree while incarcerated. Corrections officials rewarded his efforts by paroling him after he had served only ten years of his sentence. By the mid-1980s, he had gone on to earn a master's degree in criminal justice from the University of North Carolina and was eventually released from parole.

Irrespective of the amount of time they served behind bars, the convicted fraggers shall forever live with the stigma of their crimes. Despite a generous discharge-upgrade effort instituted by the Veterans Administration for Vietnam-era servicemen in the late 1970s, the fraggers were ineligible to partake in the program, as their punitive discharges were awarded owing to felonious conduct involving acts of violence that were subject to civilian criminal prosecution. Indeed, the men's criminal convictions proved to be a frequent impediment to their post-military endeavors. "I've found that if I lie on applications, that has been the only way I could become employed even in unskilled jobs," admitted one released murderer.[5] In many cases, readjustment to civil society proved to be a difficult process and a number of the men eventually wound up either homeless, dead, or, most commonly, back behind bars. Four are known to have committed homicides after leaving military confinement, while still others have been jailed for a multitude of lesser offenses. Following his release from the stockade, George M. Ercolin was convicted of crimes ranging from theft to cocaine and weapons possession and spent the next four decades rotating in and out of Florida prisons. Former marine Clyde W. Smith, Jr., served time in Georgia for drug dealing, forgery, burglary, and receiving stolen property. Nolberto Vasquez was convicted of bank robbery, jumping bail, and drug charges.[6] Robert Bell's prison sentence was reduced from thirty to seven years, and even then he was released early on parole. In 1976, he ran a traffic light while driving drunk and smashed his car into another vehicle, killing two of its occupants. He was returned to prison for several more years.[7] Richard A. McLeod, the prime suspect in the fragging death of Captain Richard J. Privitar, was murdered during a violent domestic dispute with his common-law wife in Philadelphia in 1978.[8] Vance D. Thompson died of a heroin overdose in Los Angeles. Isaac S. Bacon succumbed to chronic alcoholism in Rancho Cucamonga. Robert B. Rutledge battled alcohol and drug addiction and was arrested numerous times both before and after his military service. In 1987, he stabbed a local drug dealer to death in

Arizona after a dispute over a quarter gram of heroin. Rutledge was able to win parole after serving about half of his ten-year sentence but was arrested yet again on another drug charge and returned to prison.[9] Roy A. Clark was living a hand-to-mouth existence as a day laborer when he won $188,000 in a 1989 Florida lottery. He squandered the money within a year on alcohol, limousine rides, and other frivolities and was crushed to death after getting drunk and falling asleep inside a garbage dumpster at the Orange County Landfill. He was in possession of less than ten dollars when his body was found.[10] Marvin Baldwin abused alcohol and drugs for many years and was fired by numerous employers owing to his antisocial personality. After becoming indigent, he worked at odd jobs in order to obtain money for drugs, and was arrested for selling marijuana.[11] William E. Sutton, the longest-serving Vietnam fragger, was released for good in 1999 but hardly a month had passed before he was rearrested in Tennessee for burglary and theft. Bert S. Wait managed to stay out of trouble for years before being jailed for sexual assault.

Unlike many fraggers, Kenneth W. Chaky seemed to adjust well to the civilian world after completing his term of confinement. He married, fathered two children, and found a $29,000-a-year job as a computer programmer at the University of Florida. But as the family was about to move to a different city in 1991, he and his wife engaged in a series of heated arguments, several of which came to blows. Chaky eventually decided to kill her and collect nearly $200,000 from two life insurance policies he had taken out on her. He solicited a local auto mechanic to commit the murder, suggesting that the man follow him and his family when they went on vacation, and kill his wife after he had removed his children from their motel room. When the man refused, Chaky persisted, even offering to buy him a rifle he could use to commit the crime. In the end, Chaky did the job himself, bashing in the woman's skull with a blunt object. He buried her in a nearby trash mound but a passerby noticed her lifeless hand protruding from the heap and notified police. Several witnesses came forward, including the mechanic, and Chaky was arrested. He was eventually found guilty of first-degree murder as well as a solicitation charge. During the penalty phase of the trial, the prosecution cited Chaky's Vietnam fragging conviction as one of two aggravating circumstances and asked that the ex-infantryman be executed. The jury agreed, but an appellate court later reduced his death sentence to life imprisonment.[12]

While conducting research on this project, I was asked by several persons whether or not the military informed the families of fragging victims the truth regarding the nature of their loved ones' deaths. The answer is a complicated one. The next-of-kin of most if not all Vietnam fatalities were provided with an official death notification and letter of condolence from the man's unit commander, both of which contained terse summaries concerning the circumstances of death. Such brief explanations often raised more questions than answers; in one case, the officer escorting a murdered lieutenant's remains noted, "The family showed a great concern in obtaining casualty information. They wanted to know how their son died. I informed them that I did not have this information and if they desired further information they would have to write the Adjutant General." The parents of one victim contacted their senator, asking, "All we have been told is that an unknown person threw a grenade into his room and killed him. Is there any way we can find the particulars of his death? [We] also wonder what if anything is being or has been done with the person who threw the grenade. . . . Who could we contact about this?" In another instance, a casualty assistance officer warned:

> The deceased was killed by a friendly grenade under unusual circumstances. . . . The deceased's [family] expressed a determination to know the results of the investigation conducted into the circumstances surrounding [his] death. It is strongly recommended that the findings of the investigation be forwarded to this officer in order to preclude their pursuing other channels to obtain this information.[13]

Action was taken in this case and the family was eventually informed of the results, but family members sometimes had to go to great lengths to obtain information. "I nearly went crazy trying to deal with my children and my grief," remembered one widow.

When I was finally able to grasp what had actually happened, I started to inquire from the marine liaison, "What does 'friendly grenade' mean?" I started asking them for an explanation of [my husband's] death and of course they wouldn't tell me anything. Then I waged my own war against the Marine Corps and the government. I started writing letters and calling friends to let them know that information was kept from me. We [knew] an army colonel who . . . intervened for me along with a couple of congressmen and attorneys who gave their time and talent with no charge to try to help me.

I made weekly trips to the Judge Advocate General's Office trying to get help. One day I had a brilliant idea and had my brother go with me. I walked in and told them I had a reporter with me from the *Washington Post* and would expose the Navy and Marine Corps. Then things began to happen—in one week I got a visit with the Commandant and was offered a visit with the president. About two weeks later, I was called to Washington and sat down with a JAG officer and he told me what happened and gave me a copy of the court-martial conducted after [my husband's] death. The man went free, but I hope he burns in hell. They said it was the first time in the history of the military that a confidential investigation file was given to a civilian.

It took me nearly two years and weekly trips, but I finally got my answers. I sure found that the government tries to cover up mistakes. I won the battle but I lost the war! All I accomplished was that I let them know that they couldn't walk all over me.

In the case of Private First Class Yokoi, we have seen that tactical operations prevented authorities from conducting a formal criminal investigation and that the CID was never notified. The only probe that was ever made was an informal administrative investigation conducted several weeks after the incident occurred. But when Yokoi's mother contacted the Office of the Judge Advocate General seeking information regarding her son's death, the answers she received were at considerable variance from the facts. She was informed that the incident had been "thoroughly investigated" and that the grenade had been "brought" into Yokoi's tent, where it "accidentally exploded." In fact, the officer who conducted the administrative investigation concluded that "a person or persons outside of the tent" had detonated the grenade, and nowhere in his report does it state that the explosion was an accident.[14]

As America became aware of the fragging phenomenon, the families of several servicemen reported as having been killed accidentally by friendly ordnance began to fear the worst. A sergeant's widow informed authorities of letters her late husband had written to her shortly before his death in which he mentioned his fears that "attempts on his life might be made by . . . others in his organization who he thought to dislike him." Although the man's death had been found to be accidental in nature, the marines subsequently conducted a separate undercover investigation of the incident that confirmed their earlier conclusions.

In addition to the victims and their families, those personally involved with the cases still find themselves unable to shed their memories. Nearly thirty years after a change in witness testimony acquitted Walter Chambers, Jr., of murdering First Sergeant Furse, former marine prosecutor Edward F. Kelly admitted: "You are correct that I am if not bitter, somewhat chagrined at what occurred in [*United States v. Chambers*]. My feelings about this case remain as strong as they were some twenty-six plus years ago. I felt there had been a miscarriage of justice. . . . The problem is that we are bound by the federal rules of evidence and one could simply not impeach one's own witness at that time."[15]

Veterans remember their fallen comrades:

Tim [Rohweller] was a good man and I liked him. His death was a tremendous blow to me personally because it represented all that was bad about Vietnam. Tim was murdered because he was a good leader and insisted on marines being marines and not cowards.[16]

> Gordon M. Davis
> K Company, 9th Marines

Rick Arann was a good friend of mine. I flew right next to him. He was on his second tour. He survived a year of VC and NVA shooting at him, but not an American trying to kill another American.[17]

> Jim Schueckler
> 1st Aviation Brigade

First Sergeant Furse was like a father to most of us. He had time to lis-
ten to our problems and [offered] good advice in return. He was [obvi-
ously] a family man. He missed his family . . . and look[ed] forward to
going home. We told him we would miss him as he was loved by all in
the battery. When I found out what happened I was sick, and when I
found out that the man who did it was able to walk free, I was totally
shocked.[18]

> Jimmy F. Abbs
> D Battery, 11th Marines

Postwar Jurisdiction

The Vietnam War left behind hundreds of unsolved homicides. Most of
these crimes involved slayings of Vietnamese nationals but there were
also several dozen cases involving U.S. troops murdering their comrades. Once the offenders were discharged from the military, no legal
action could be taken against them, this due to a long-standing quirk in
the law. When the UCMJ was first instituted in the early 1950s, it permitted the armed forces to try ex-servicemen under military law for
serious offenses they had committed while in uniform.[19] The Supreme
Court, however, stripped military justice of this power with its 1955
Toth v. Quarles decision. In the majority opinion, Justice Hugo L. Black
argued that since veterans were no longer on active duty, they could not
be tried in military courts, as these venues offered defendants less due
process than their civil counterparts. Congress, Black pointed out, possessed the requisite authority to provide federal district court trials for
former servicemen,[20] but no action was taken toward this end, and the
legal loophole that emerged permitted scores of murderers, rapists, and
other offenders who had committed their crimes outside of U.S. territo-
rial jurisdiction to escape prosecution. By 1969, high-profile incidents
such as the My Lai massacre and the Green Beret case led the army to
consider several ways of trying culpable ex-soldiers but no suitable
remedy was found.[21] Suggestions offered over the years by a number of
legal scholars remained unexplored.

It was not until over forty years after the *Toth* decision that legislators were finally spurred to close the loophole. After a federal appeals

court cited a jurisdictional issue in overturning the conviction in a particularly disturbing child rape case, Congress passed the Military Extraterritorial Jurisdiction Act of 2000 (MEJA).[22] Among other things, the new law decreed that former service members accused of having committed serious offenses during military service overseas could now be tried in federal district courts, where they would receive the legal protections of civilian justice. But MEJA came too late for Vietnam-era murders, as the Constitution prohibits Congress from enacting ex post facto laws. This did not stop some from arguing that MEJA did not truly constitute an ex post facto law if applied to pre-2000 cases, as it merely established new venues to try serious offenses long proscribed by both civil and military jurisprudence. In the end, however, the government determined that the law could not be applied retroactively.[23] Even if substantial new evidence were to come to light in the Vietnam murder cases, the killers who managed to avoid detection by military authorities simply cannot be prosecuted. To be sure, the point was practically moot from a documentary standpoint in any case, as the air force and naval services have destroyed their Vietnam-era criminal investigation files in accordance with the twenty-five-year retention periods governed by the services' disposition schedules, and the surviving records maintained by the army are fragmentary at best.[24]

Fragging and Vietnam War Literature

The literature of the Vietnam War has afforded fragging a fair share of exposure. As with most history, several early studies examined the topic and forged the road that innumerable Johnny come-latelies followed. After Eugene Linden's *Saturday Review* article, the next important work to emerge appeared in the mid-1970s, when army psychiatrist Thomas C. Bond and psychologist David H. Gilooly published data compiled from their interviews with convicted fraggers imprisoned in the Leavenworth stockade. Antiwar GI David Cortright's *Soldiers in Revolt*, Guenter Lewy's *America in Vietnam*, and the above-cited *Crisis in Command* provided statistical data released by the Pentagon regarding the frequency of the incidents in the army, while the official Marine Corps history of the war covers fragging within its ranks. Charles

Levy's snooping in marine court-martial records, detailed in his book *Spoils of War*, also yielded some interesting results. To date, most other authors have simply copied their findings without adding additional data or analysis.

Several postwar historians lumped together fraggings with the other disciplinary problems that affected the military during the Vietnamization period. Their texts often portray grenade incidents as concomitants to the "talk it out" scenarios that sometimes took place between infantry officers and their men during combat operations during the later years of the war. Typical passages read (I paraphrase here), "And those leaders who persisted in issuing senseless orders and unnecessarily risking their men's lives could become the victims of fragging." This analysis simply does not provide a true picture of the fragging phenomenon. Most of the cases, as we have seen, took place in support units that did not engage in combat and during a period of time in which American casualties were greatly reduced. Moreover, the incidents usually involved personal disputes between the perpetrator and the victim rather than collective action on the part of any group.

Much of the coverage afforded to fragging in Vietnam literature assumes the form of oral history, a medium in which eyewitnesses provide first-person accounts of their experiences to historians. Unfortunately, interviewers are often too willing to take their veteran subjects at their word, and a number of these narratives, as we have seen in the Woods and Nell cases, are embellished or fabricated in their entirety. For this study, I investigated several fragging stories found in Vietnam War literature. These particular accounts were selected because they provided sufficient information for further research. My analyses regarding their veracity, recounted below, reveal a mixed bag of truth and fabrication.

Charles Levy's *Spoils of War* contains an account by Charles Ventura, alias Andrew Robert Pieszala, who claimed to have served as a medic in Vietnam: "That afternoon they placed a grenade under the front wheel of the jeep in front of the CO's room. And one guy ran out and threw a fucking grenade; fragging the fucking office. They got the fucking CO. He was only a first lieutenant. The second lieutenant comes flying out of the office and jumped into the jeep. He put it in clutch.

The concussion ripped the whole top of his body off. It just landed in the back seat."

Dr. Levy conceded that "it is probable that the accuracy of [Ventura's] Vietnam recollections was affected—as measured by an objective reality,"[25] and in this regard he is correct: both military records and Vietnam casualty statistics reveal this story to be fictitious. Ventura deserted the army several times and was later convicted of the 1971 double murder of his ex-girlfriend and her new husband in Cheektowaga, New York.[26] In 2008, I wrote to Ventura, who was incarcerated at New York's Attica Correctional Facility, and asked him about the account he provided for *Spoils of War*. "I wasn't a medic!" Ventura responded. "I was a 'sniper'! Since I was on trial for a double homicide, I thought it prudent to tell Dr. Levy and the court psychiatrists that I was a 'combat medic' while in Vietnam!"[27] Regarding the purported fragging, Ventura said that the incident "happened at Phuoc Vinh Base Camp, in early Oct. 1968, in the base S&T [Supply and Transportation] Unit, of the 101st Airborne." Military police files covering this time period contain no reference to any such incident. He then launched even further into fantasy, claiming that he had been "a sniper with a CIA 'spook' team assassination squad." "I got all my orders directly from Major General John Ware [sic]. My code name was 'The Fox,'" he wrote. After the fragging occurred, Ventura claimed, "MG Ware sent in his fox to find out who the chickens [were]! Did *my* job! Then the real CID MP's did their jobs!"[28] (General Keith Ware had been killed in September 1968 in a helicopter crash.)

In his book *Captain for Dark Mornings*, Floyd G. "Shad" Meshad tells of a fragging that supposedly occurred at Red Beach in 1970: "The medics had brought the casualty in. . . . 'They said it was a fragging, sir,' the chopper pilot told me. 'Someone rigged a Claymore in the man's hooch.' . . . The face wasn't recognizable, but the name tag finally registered—Major Max Plummer." This story is also fictitious. Only two commissioned officers died of fragging in 1970, neither of them was a major, nor were they anywhere near Red Beach. In fact, no army majors died of any cause in all of Quang Ngai Province in 1970.

Lieutenant Colonel Anthony B. Herbert's autobiography *Soldier* discusses fragging in the 173d Airborne Brigade during 1968–1969:

Fragging, the deliberate attack on a noncom or officer by an enlisted man or men, was not unknown in the 173d. One sergeant over in the signal section had made the mistake of raising hell with a trooper about the cleanliness of his area. The man wired a Claymore mine outside the sergeant's room, aimed it right through the wall at the switchboard, went to a phone and called his victim. The sergeant lost both legs. There was a fragging in the 2d Battalion, too, with seven wounded. They had tried to get [Lieutenant Colonel John W.] Nicholson with explosives and on another occasion they had tried to blow up his Tactical Operations Center. One of the men in the 2d Battalion had reportedly blown himself to bits with a Claymore mine, but my investigation failed to corroborate this. It had been in his hands, that was certain, but there were two men in a nearby bunker handling the controls to the mine when it went off. The victim had left the bunker to retrieve the mine at the request of the other two—and somehow, they said, the circuit had been completed. I wasn't a real detective, but even though two company commanders swore it was accidental, I did sign my report with a recommendation that the CID check into it. They never did.[29]

Colonel Herbert's charge that fragging was "not unknown in the 173d" in the 1968–1969 time frame is amply confirmed by military records.[30] The first case he cites is almost certainly a reference to an assault that occurred at An Loc on 24 December 1968 in which Staff Sergeant Joseph Brown was critically injured.[31] The second incident probably took place at LZ English and involved a grenade planted near a billet used by the 2/503d S-2 (intelligence) section.[32] However, neither the 18th Military Police Brigade's daily journal nor the CID Crime Records Center possesses any record of Colonel Nicholson ever being the victim of a fragging, and when asked about it, Nicholson vehemently denied the charge.[33] The army probed Herbert's story concerning the man in the "2d Battalion" (2/503d Infantry) killed by the Claymore mine and found that it was unable to identify any such incident,[34] though a review of the unit's casualty records from the time of Herbert's tenure as the brigade's acting inspector general reveals that one soldier, Specialist Four James M. Kelly, had indeed been killed by a Claymore he had been holding. But contrary to any claim of men "handling the controls of the mine," investigators found that the mine's firing device had been disconnected prior to its detonation. They determined that the blasting cap had not been removed from the mine, and as Kelly retrieved the firing wire, static electricity generated by his act of rolling the wire caused the mine to detonate. Two other soldiers were in fact occupying "a nearby bunker" at the time, but rather than causing the explosion, one of them, Specialist Four Michael T. Collins, was injured by the blast and had to be evacuated. Surviving documentation also indicates that the 173d's CID element did investigate the case.[35]

From Camelot to Kent State: The Sixties Experience in the Words of Those Who Lived It offers an account by ex-marine Clarence J. Fitch:

> I seen one fragging incident up close: a new lieutenant, fresh out of Quantico. He was an asshole, very gung-ho. . . . He would run patrols and set up ambushes, and he wasn't very careful. He took a lot of chances, and people didn't like it. They were trying to take him out, but they didn't get in the right kind of firefight that they could fire on him.
>
> One night we were stationed on this bridge. . . . About four or five in the morning, just before dawn, I seen this brother come out with this hand grenade and he said, 'Hey Fitch, don't say nothing, man.' The lieutenant's bunker was maybe ten yards from the bridge, and this guy went over, pulled the pin on the grenade, held it for a few seconds, and rolled it into the bunker. I said, 'Oh, shit, I don't want to see this.'
>
> Then I heard boom, and the lieutenant came staggering out of the bunker. They got a medevac helicopter and medevacked him out of there. He was hurt pretty bad, but he survived it. Went back to the States, I guess.[36]

Fitch served as a clerk in L Company of the 1st Marines.[37] The incident he recounted may have occurred in late 1968, when his company was tasked with security of the Ha Dong and Cau Do Bridges near Hill 55.[38] First Lieutenant Ernest H. Walrath, the company commander, recalled an instance in which a grenade was detonated, but insisted that no one was injured, let alone evacuated.[39] One ex–L Company enlisted man suggested that a platoon commander, First Lieutenant William M. Tucker, might have been the target of a fragger's grenade, but Tucker's personnel file does not mention him receiving any injuries during his time in Vietnam.[40] L Company's unit diaries indicate that another officer was wounded during Fitch's time in the company, but this incident predated the unit's assignment to the bridges.[41] Further research is difficult as both Fitch and Tucker are deceased.

In *A Matter of Conscience: GI Resistance During the Vietnam War*, army veteran Dave Blalock told the story of a fragging murder he claimed occurred in his unit: "So we went in morning formation with our new commanding officer. The former CO was blown away six weeks earlier—he was killed, fragged."[42] David Gerald Blalock's personnel file reveals that he served in Vietnam as a manual teletype operator and security guard with HHC, 210th Aviation Battalion (Combat).[43] No officers died in Blalock's company of any cause during the war. I also checked his battalion commanders and they too survived.[44]

In his book *Heroes*, Australian journalist John Pilger recounted his September 1970 visit to elements of the 1st Cavalry Division at Fire Support Base Snuffy: "At Snuffy I interviewed men who had 'fragged' two officers and shot another in the back. As we spoke, an officer ordered the men to report to him at the double. They ignored him; one man jerked a finger in the air. 'We'll get him later,' he said. The officer walked away."[45] There is no question that a number of young enlisted men offered Pilger commentary about officers being shot, as several clips of these interviews were included in the reporter's short film *The Quiet Mutiny*. But if such incidents did indeed occur, they do not seem to have taken place in units that were at the base during Pilger's visit, namely the 5/7th Cavalry, 1/9th Cavalry, or the 199th Light Infantry Brigade's 5/12th Infantry. No officers in any of these battalions were shot to death during 1970. I also checked the USARV fragging studies for 1969 and 1970 as well as the Serious Incident Reports for that time period and found no record of any officer fraggings in these units.

Another alleged officer shooting is described in Charley Trujillo's book *Soldados: Chicanos in Viet Nam*. According to veteran Mike M. Lemus, a large group of men who had recently returned from the field were smoking marijuana when a captain confronted them: "There wasn't any killing of each other than except this one time we came back from a hard mission, it was getting dark and this officer tried to be a hero—bust ninety guys. We were along the trenches and . . . they shot him. They threw him over a trench and shot him with a machine gun. No one said anything. Someone called on the radio and told them the captain had been shot by the gooks."[46] In his testimonial, Lemus claims to have served in a number of different units during his time in Vietnam. According to his personnel file, he was first assigned to C Company, 1/27th Infantry, 25th Infantry Division in late April 1968. Lemus remained with this unit for nearly two months before being transferred to D Troop, 3/17th Cavalry, where he spent the remainder of his tour until his return to the United States in April 1969.[47] Neither of these units sustained any officer fatalities during his time in their ranks.

During the above-mentioned Winter Soldier Investigation, several particular fragging cases were mentioned. Although some people have since criticized the motivation and veracity of these hearings, I found a Winter Soldier testimonial regarding fragging that is accurate, that of ex-serviceman Jim Umenhofer: "Black brothers were in the barracks. . . . Some, I cannot say they were white, however even if they were black, they must have had white thoughts, were throwing in grenades. They threw in two grenades from either door. Two of the brothers were killed and two of them were wounded." This incident occurred on 19 September 1970 at Phu Bai Combat Base. A grenade was thrown at the roof of Building 2–128, killing Private First Class Jesse L. Lenley and injuring three other men. Umenhofer believed that the murder was racially motivated, as did at least two blacks who were stationed at the base and took it upon themselves to threaten a white soldier on the following day. But the subsequent CID investigation of the crime failed to substantiate these claims, and the only individual ever cited as a possible principal to the murder was black.[48]

Another veteran who participated in the Winter Soldier hearings testified that any man under suspicion of committing a fragging "found himself on point, usually pretty fast," meaning that suspects in infantry units were forced to walk at the "point," or head of the formation during combat, an extremely dangerous assignment. During my own research, I was able to find an actual case of this practice. Shortly before his death in 1997, Louis W. Banks, the former commanding officer of A Company, 1/503d Infantry, 173d Airborne Brigade, told me that he placed Private First Class Frederick J. Osher, the suspect in the fragging murder of Staff Sergeant Paul E. Reed, on point for eight straight hours after the incident.[49]

Harry Maurer's *Strange Ground: Americans in Vietnam 1945–1975, an Oral History* provides an account by an army veteran, Sergeant Whitfield "Woody" Wanamaker, alleging a 1968 homicide of an NCO in the 269th Aviation Battalion. Wanamaker identifies the victim only as "Al," a senior NCO assigned to the battalion's intelligence section: "I was sitting next to the door. . . . Al was sitting on his bunk. . . . All of a sudden, out of the side of my eye I saw this shadow on the screen on the opposite side of the room. And I heard the spoon pop from a grenade. . . . They tossed it exactly on his bed. By the time he picked it up, he just doubled over on it. Where was he going to put it? You only have so many seconds before the grenade explodes. So I guess—I can only guess—that he was saving my life by taking the full blast. He wasn't actually blown to bits, but there wasn't too much left of a human being. I took some shrapnel. . . . He took 99 percent of everything that concussion grenade had. . . . The date was August 21, 1968."[50] Wanamaker goes on to tell a moving story of how he escorted the murdered sergeant's remains home to Vermont and met with the bereaved family. The only problem is that none of the voluminous records generated by the 269th Aviation Battalion, the USARV provost marshal, CID, and the army's casualty branch contain any reference to such an incident in any of the army's aviation units in South Vietnam. Colonel Delyle Redmond, the 269th's commander, bluntly stated that no such murder took place in the unit.

Conclusion

I T was no accident that the fragging phenomenon occurred during an unpopular war. Fighting for a cause that many came to care little about, it was inevitable that morale in the armed services would ebb during the war's later years. Compounded by such societal woes as drug abuse, racial tension, and the rebellion of America's youth, Vietnam brought all of these "warring factions" together in a violent environment where the military's traditional social control mechanisms had been greatly weakened. In their attempts to maintain order, leaders found themselves under attack not only from the enemy but also from their own men. While the motives for fraggings weren't always the same, the fact that the attacks were most often aimed at command figures reveals the two divergent viewpoints that developed within the military toward the conflict in Southeast Asia. Career officers and NCOs were serving in *the military* and sought to uphold their services' institutional customs and traditions, among them good order and discipline. Junior enlisted men, on the other hand, were serving in *Vietnam*, the war that the government was not making a real effort to win. When the men came to believe that their leaders' desire to attain organizational goals outweighed either their survival instincts (in the field) or their tolerance levels (in the rear), trouble resulted. The preponderance of assaults in rear areas is also indicative of the root cause: largely devoid of the dangers of war and often furnished with physical amenities unheard of in previous conflicts, the transcendence of fragging into this realm indicates that the cause lay with the larger picture.

Details such as the perpetrators' ages, backgrounds, or intelligence played only a limited role in the overall fragging phenomenon. Far more young Americans from broken homes fought in the Second World War, yet there was no epidemic of violence directed toward fellow servicemen. The same is true when speaking of racial tension and its effect on fragging. Blacks certainly faced more discrimination before the civil rights movement than they did during the Vietnam era, though it was not until the late 1960s that the military faced the problem of racial violence on such a large scale. One should also look to the larger social picture when seeking the root causes of the problem. A climate of hostility emerged among American troops in Vietnam that did not exist in other wars. This element, caused by factors unique to this historical period, is just as responsible for the fragging phenomenon as were single-parent households or limited educational opportunities. Where one should examine the fragger's personal factors, as Dr. Bond's study suggests, is in determining why some servicemen committed these crimes and others did not.[1]

In addition to the above-cited societal factors, historians who examine the Vietnam debacle must also consider the role played by the virtual destruction of the NCO corps in the decline of morale and discipline. Noncommissioned officers had served to offset potential turbulence during past periods of social change but the "war of attrition" designed to wear down the Viet Cong had the unintended consequence of eroding the ranks of American sergeants. By the time Vietnamization began, many of the NCOs who had manned the proud military of 1965 were either dead, wounded, or had left the service, and sufficient numbers of replacements were not forthcoming. The government's decision not to call up reserve forces or the National Guard deprived the services of older, more mature men who might have maintained more stability among the enlisted ranks. Instead, stopgap measures were adopted to produce replacement leaders, and these proved inadequate. As a result, the high standards of discipline maintained during the buildup years deteriorated, and social problems like drug abuse, racial tension, and the authority crisis assumed prominent positions within the ranks.

In an effort to explain the "why" of fragging, an army psychiatrist interviewed by Eugene Linden in 1971 declared that "virtually all officers who are fragged are partially at fault."[2] Did Sergeant Tate deserve to be murdered for reprimanding a sleeping sentry? Was Private Ercolin justified in fragging Lieutenant Hamilton over a haircut? Sergeant Neiswender was nearly killed over cigarettes. While it is true that some leaders struggled to exercise effective leadership within the peculiar scenario that existed in Vietnam, to insinuate that they were at fault for being fragged, even partially, justifies murder. Equally disturbing were the fictitious war stories involving fragging concocted by men such as Marine "Corporal" Nell. In an era of such books and films as *Friendly Fire*, in which the military was accused (with justification) of withholding information about casualties,[3] what were the families of the dead to believe when confronted with published accounts telling of "five or six" servicemen being murdered in one unit with the approval of "the entire company"?

When discussing the military's efforts to stop fragging, it can be said that regardless of tactics, there was simply no long-term solution to the problem. Although Operation Freeze and the other remedies did enjoy some success in identifying the perpetrators, they were ultimately doomed to failure because military leaders were not in a position to address the political and social causes of the fragging phenomenon. The only way to end fragging was to end the war, and this was clearly a political decision. In the end, it was President Nixon who was responsible for its demise when he withdrew the last U.S. ground units from Southeast Asia. The fact that the assaults continued into 1972, long after most American troops had been disengaged from the ground war, proves that this was the only solution.

Although fragging has occurred in other armies and during other wars, it was U.S. troops in Vietnam who coined the term and provided its conceptual basis. After the news media reported at length on the subject, the word became a permanent fixture within the parlance of war and was long associated with America's failed adventure in Southeast Asia.[4] When the Soviet army experienced problems of morale and discipline during the Afghan War in the 1980s, observers were quick to label the conflict "Russia's Vietnam" and likened the drug use and attacks on superiors that occurred to those that had taken place within the American ranks some two decades before.[5] The young GI who testified that fragging "couldn't happen anywhere but here in Vietnam" had spoken too soon: soldiers in any army who lose faith in their assigned mission and experience a crisis in morale might find themselves saying that "it couldn't happen anywhere but here in _____."

Popular attitudes regarding fragging underwent something of a change in the years after the war's end. Initially, the practice enjoyed a measure of acceptance among political radicals and understanding within certain intellectual circles. With the intense emotion and dramatic moral choices involved in the commission of such acts, it is not surprising that a number of plays and even a short television film appeared on the subject. These early productions tended to side with the grenade throwers, but in the years that followed, as American attitudes toward the war changed and several new books offered more nuanced treatment of the topic, a different picture emerged. Declassified military records revealed the physical particulars and motivations behind many grenade cases, and the view of fragging incidents as crimes rather than acts of survival or political resistance slowly found a voice within Vietnam War literature. Indeed, the early, more emotional portrayals of fragging were well suited for stage and screen; historians, however, found that the real story is far more complex.

The total number of fraggings that occurred in Vietnam will never be known. In the case of the marines, incomplete statistics rule out an exact count. In his study of Marine Corps justice during the war, Lieutenant Colonel Solis offered what he called a "necessarily rough" estimate of 100–150 incidents, basing his figure on "reported fragging cases, the number of marines in Vietnam, and the period during which fraggings are known to have occurred."[6] I have been able to confirm ninety-four incidents and agree with the colonel's overall estimate. Fifteen marines were killed and over one hundred more were injured. In addition, a grenade stolen in Vietnam was used in the 1967 murder of an enlisted marine at Camp Hansen, Okinawa.[7] The army, on the other hand, did prepare more complete fragging statistics, but as we have seen, many of the tallied cases were not felonious in nature while others that were intentional were omitted through administrative error. The total number of incidents ranges from 600 to 850 or possibly more. I researched each of the known cases in which fatalities were involved and found that forty-two soldiers were murdered in fragging incidents in Vietnam, and nearly a dozen others were killed by their own ordnance during apparent attempts to assault others.

There is also the matter of servicemen who may have been intentionally killed by their comrades during combat on the battlefield. Ru-

mors that circulated following the death of Lieutenant Elliott in the
173d Airborne Brigade were subsequently refuted by an exhaustive
CID investigation. My own research on similar talk concerning the
death of a particular officer in the 9th Infantry Division and the war
stories of "James D. Nell" about the 9th Engineer Battalion also met
with negative results. Nevertheless, there are other accounts, true and
false, that will no doubt persist. Without honest testimony from the men
who were there, the facts will simply never be known. During an April
1971 Senate discussion concerning the fragging phenomenon, this exchange between two legislators said it best:

> Mr. [Harold E.] Hughes: If I heard correctly, [it was] said that in the
>   past year, according to the Pentagon, there have been 209
>   [fragging] incidents.
> Mr. Mansfield: 209, for calendar year 1970.
> Mr. Hughes: And those that are recorded, I would presume, are
>   basically domiciliary type incidents, rather than on the battlefield.
> Mr. Mansfield: That is right.
> Mr. Hughes: So, in effect, we have no real knowledge, probably, of
>   what the total number of these so-called incidents of assassination
>   [is] if they did take place in battle.
> Mr. Mansfield: The Senator is correct.[8]

As for the perpetrators of the unsolved fragging homicides, they
may rest easy. Despite passage of the Military Extraterritorial Jurisdiction Act in 2000, the government is legally powerless to pursue them,
as the new law cannot be applied to decades-old Vietnam murders. The
lead suspects in several of the cases have since died and the surviving
offenders have nothing to fear. Each has succeeded in committing the
perfect crime.

Glossary of Terms, Abbreviations, and Acronyms

AFQT. Armed Forces Qualification Test; entrance examination administered
 to prospective members of the armed forces during the Vietnam era
AFVN. American Forces Vietnam Network; the U.S. military's radio and
 television network in South Vietnam
ARVN. Army of the Republic of Vietnam, the South Vietnamese army
ASU. American Servicemen's Union; an antiwar advocacy group intended for
 active-duty servicemen.
ATF. Australian Task Force
brig. naval confinement facility
CAP. Combined Action Program; a program in which small detachments of
 U.S. marines operated with local forces in Vietnamese villages
CID. the army's Criminal Investigation Division; renamed U.S. Army
 Criminal Investigation Agency in 1969 and U.S. Army Criminal
 Investigation Command (USACIDC) in 1971
C.O. commanding officer
COMUSMACV. Commander, United States Military Assistance Command
 Vietnam
CS. riot control agent (tear gas) used by the U.S. military in Vietnam
DA. Department of the Army
DEROS. date of estimated return from overseas
digger. slang term for an Australian or New Zealand soldier
DISCOM. Division Support Command
EOD. explosive ordnance disposal
frag (noun). soldier slang term for a fragmentation hand grenade
frag (verb). to employ a fragmentation hand grenade against a selected target
GI. government issue; long-time slang term for an American soldier
grunt. slang term for an infantryman
HHC. Headquarters and Headquarters Company
hooch. slang term for living quarters

lifer. derisive term for a career soldier

LMDC. Lawyers Military Defense Committee; a group of antiwar attorneys
    who provided legal assistance to military accused during the Vietnam-
    ization period

LTC. lieutenant colonel

LZ. landing zone

M79. single-shot grenade launcher used by U.S. troops in Vietnam

MACV. Military Assistance Command Vietnam; the senior U.S. military
    command in South Vietnam from 1962 to 1973

MAF. Marine Amphibious Force

MP. military police

NCO. noncommissioned officer

NVA. North Vietnamese Army

PFC. private first class

RAR. Royal Australian Regiment

REMF. rear-echelon motherfucker; derisive reference to rear-area support
    troops

RVN. Republic of Vietnam (South Vietnam)

SFC. sergeant first class

S.I.R. Serious Incident Report

S&T. Supply and Transportation

UCMJ. Uniform Code of Military Justice; system utilized by the armed forces
    during the Vietnam era and beyond

USA. United States Army

USARV. United States Army Vietnam; senior U.S. Army command in South
    Vietnam for much of the war

USMC. United States Marine Corps

USO. United Service Organizations

VC. Viet Cong

VMAC. Vietnam Major Army Commands

Known Vietnam Fragging Homicides by Organization

Organization	Deaths
U.S. Army	
1st Cavalry Division (Airmobile)	2
1st Infantry Division	0
4th Infantry Division	0
1st Brigade, 5th Infantry Division (Mechanized)	2
9th Infantry Division	1
23d Infantry Division (Americal)	3
25th Infantry Division	4
3d Brigade, 82nd Airborne Division	0
101st Airborne Division (Airmobile)	2
1st Logistical Command	4
1st Aviation Brigade	4
1st Signal Brigade	3
18th Engineer Brigade	2
18th Military Police Brigade	0
20th Engineer Brigade	1
44th Medical Brigade	0
173d Airborne Brigade (Separate)	5
199th Light Infantry Brigade	1
11th Armored Cavalry Regiment	0
I Field Force Vietnam	1
II Field Force Vietnam	1
USARV	6
MACV	0

U.S. Marine Corps

1st Marine Division	9
3d Marine Division	4
Force Logistic Command	1
1st Marine Air Wing	0
Combined Action Force	1

Ranks of Known Vietnam Fragging Fatalities

Rank	U.S. Army	U.S. Marine Corps
General	0	0
Lieutenant General	0	0
Major General	0	0
Brigadier General	0	0
Colonel	0	0
Lieutenant Colonel	0	0
Major	0	0
Captain	3	0
First Lieutenant	2	1
Second Lieutenant	1	0
Chief Warrant Officer 4	0	0
Chief Warrant Officer 3	0	0
Chief Warrant Officer 2	2	0
Warrant Officer WO1	0	0
Sergeant Major	0	0
First Sergeant, etc.	2	2
Sergeant First Class (USA)/Gunnery Sergeant (USMC)	7	0
Specialist Seven (USA)	0	—
Staff Sergeant	2	1
Specialist Six (USA)	0	—
Sergeant	3	1
Specialist Five (USA)	6	—
Corporal	0	2
Specialist Four (USA)	9	—
Private First Class (USA)/Lance Corporal (USMC)	4	5

Private E-2 (USA)/Private First Class (USMC)	1	2
Private	0	1
Totals:	42	15

Terms of Confinement
Served by Fraggers Convicted
of Murder in Vietnam

Name	Sentence	Release date	Time served
U.S. Army			
Baldwin, M.	1 year*	16 November 1967	10 months
Benoit, T. J.	Life	22 December 1972	3 years, 4 months
Hart, L. L.	Life**	1 February 1973	6 years
Locklin, D. K.	25 years	1 March 1979	8 years, 7 months
Sutton, W. E.	Life	6 August 1999	30 years***
Wheat, J. W.	20 years	21 June 1979	9 years, 3 months
U.S. Marine Corps			
Fowler, T. W.	Life	8 September 1977	7 years, 4 months
Hendrix, G. A.	Life	24 November 1980	9 years, 6 months
Smith, R. F.	40 years	(Murdered in prison, 25 July 1982)	12 years, 8 months
Thomas, J. W.	Life	15 September 1978	9 years, 2 months

*Baldwin was convicted of negligent homicide and not premeditated murder.

**Hart was sentenced to confinement at hard labor for life. A board of review later reduced the sentence to twenty years. This conviction was subsequently overturned and Hart was retried, reconvicted, and sentenced to nineteen years and seven months of confinement.

***Sutton's sentence was later reduced to thirty years. He was paroled several times but was invariably returned to federal custody until his sentence expired.

Notes

CHAPTER ONE

1. Letter to the author from the Federal Bureau of Prisons dated 24 June 2008.
2. *United States v. Chaky* (CM 426039).
3. Robert Presthus, *The Organizational Society* (New York: St. Martin's Press, 1978), 85.
4. "Other things being equal, or at least not tipped too far the disadvantageous way," the noted British historian M. R. D. Foot wrote, "superiority in battle goes to the forces with the highest morale." M.R.D. Foot, *Men in Uniform: Military Manpower in Modern Industrial Societies* (New York: Frederick A. Praeger, 1961), 28. See also Stanislav Andreski, *Military Organization and Society* (Berkeley: University of California Press, 1968), 162.
5. Samuel A. Stouffer et al., *The American Soldier: Combat and Its Aftermath* (Princeton: Princeton University Press, 1949), 77.
6. Jacques van Doorn, *The Soldier and Social Change* (Beverly Hills: Sage Publications, 1975), 5.
7. Robert Presthus, *The Organizational Society* (New York: St. Martin's Press, 1978), 4.
8. Jacques van Doorn, *The Soldier and Social Change* (Beverly Hills: Sage Publications, 1975), 16.
9. "Lovering Court Martial," *New York Times*, 22 December 1897, 7; Edward M. Coffman, *The Old Army: A Portrait of the American Army in Peacetime, 1784–1898* (New York: Oxford University Press, 1986), 196–98, 376.
10. Guardhouse conditions after the Civil War are described in ibid., 376. For a widely reported case involving the death of a military prisoner during the Philippine Insurrection, see "Mother Says Officer Tortured a Soldier," *New York Times*, 19 February 1903, 1. The courts-martial of several guards who served at an army confinement facility in France during the First World War are featured in "Gen. March Tells of Cruelty Found in Army Prisons," *New York Times*, 24 July 1919, 1.

Coverage of the Lichfield scandal that occurred during the Second World War can be found in Richard Suskind, "The 10th Replacement Depot at Lichfield," *After the Battle*, no. 27, 41. Similar abuses continued into the Vietnam era; for the case of a sadistic NCO who was convicted of beating military prisoners and forcing them to perform sexual acts upon each other, see *United States v. Tirado* (NCM 68–3284).

11. *United States v. Sinclair* (29816) (National Archives Records Group 153).

12. William T. Generous, Jr., *Swords and Scales: The Development of the Uniform Code of Military Justice* (Port Washington: Kennikat Press, 1973), 5.

13. Eliot A. Cohen, *Citizens and Soldiers: The Dilemma of Military Service* (Ithaca: Cornell University Press, 1985), 57–59.

14. Richard W. Stewart, ed. *American Military History Vol. II: The United States Army in a Global Era, 1917–2003* (Washington D.C.: Center of Military History, 2005), 118.

15. Stanislav Andreski, *Military Organization and Society* (Berkeley: University of California Press, 1968), 26, 29.

16. Samuel A. Stoufer et al., *The American Soldier: Adjustment during Army Life* (Princeton: Princeton University Press, 1949), 57.

17. Lawrence B. Radine, *The Taming of the Troops: Social Control in the United States Army* (Westport: Greenwood, 1977), 127.

18. U.S. House of Representatives, Subcommittee of the Committee on Appropriations, Department of Defense Appropriations for 1972, 92nd Cong., 1st sess., 1971, part 9, 598; Robert D. Heinl, Jr., "The Collapse of the Armed Forces," *Armed Forces Journal*, 7 June 1971, 30; General William C. Westmoreland, *A Soldier Reports* (Garden City: Doubleday, 1976), 192, 297, 410. See also Ronald H. Spector, "The Vietnam War and the Army's Self-Image," *Second Indochina Symposium*, ed. John Schlight (Washington D.C.: U.S. Army Center of Military History, 1986), 169.

19. Jack Shulimson, and Charles M. Johnson, *U.S. Marines in Vietnam: The Landing and the Buildup 1965* (Washington D.C.: History and Museums Division, Headquarters, U.S. Marine Corps, 1978), 69–83. The authors call Starlite "the first big battle" fought by the marines in South Vietnam.

20. John M. Carland, *Combat Operations: Stemming the Tide, May 1965 to*

October 1966 (Washington D.C.: Center of Military History, 2000), 73–84, 115–50.

21. MACV Command History, 1966, 183 (National Archives Records Group 472).

22. U.S. Army Criminal Investigation Command, Crime Records Directorate, "Survey of Narcotics Cases, 1 January 1961–30 April 1966" (American Soldier Files, U.S. Army Center for Military History).

23. Andrew F. Krepinevich, Jr., *The Army and Vietnam* (Baltimore: Johns Hopkins University Press, 1986), 192.

24. George L. MacGarrigle, *Combat Operations: Taking the Offensive, October 1966 to October 1967* (Washington D.C. Center of Military History, 1998), 237. For further praise of the army in Vietnam during the 1965–1966 time period, see Ronald H. Spector, "The Vietnam War and the Army's Self-Image," *Second Indochina Symposium*, ed. John Schlight (Washington D.C.: U.S. Army Center of Military History, 1986), 169.

25. MACV Command History, 1967, Volume II, 949 (National Archives Records Group 472); William T. Generous, Jr., *Swords and Scales: The Development of the Uniform Code of Military Justice* (Port Washington: Kennikat Press, 1973), 192–93.

26. Roger W. Little, "Buddy Relations and Combat Performance," in Morris Janowitz, ed., *The New Military: Changing Patterns of Organization* (New York: Russell Sage Foundation, 1964), 221.

27. Gary D. Solis, *Marines and Military Law in Vietnam: Trial by Fire* (Washington D.C.: History and Museums Division, Headquarters, U.S. Marine Corps, 1989), 124.

28. William C. Westmoreland, *A Soldier Reports* (Garden City: Doubleday, 1976), 295.

29. Samuel A. Stouffer et al., *The American Soldier: Combat and Its Aftermath* (Princeton: Princeton University Press, 1949), 109–10.

30. George L. MacGarrigle, *Combat Operations: Taking the Offensive, October 1966 to October 1967* (Washington D.C.: Center of Military History, 1998), 230–31.

31. Paul G. Savage and Richard A. Gabriel, *Crisis in Command: Mismanagement in the Army* (New York: Hill and Wang, 1978), 22–23.

32. Jack Shulimson, Leonard A. Blaisol, Charles R. Smith, and David A. Dawson, *U.S. Marines in Vietnam: The Defining Year, 1968* (Washington

D.C.: History and Museums Division, Headquarters, U.S. Marine Corps, 1997), 557.

33. Bruce Palmer, Jr., *The 25-Year War: America's Military Role in Vietnam* (Lexington: University Press of Kentucky, 1984), 170. See also Daniel J. Nelson, *A History of U.S. Military Forces in Germany* (Boulder: Westview Press, 1987), 103–10; "The Neglected and Troubled Seventh Army," *Newsweek*, 31 May 1971, 28; and Drew Middleton, "U.S. 7th Army in Germany Regains Combat Spirit after a Low in 1970," *New York Times*, 23 October 1976, 32.

34. Jack Shulimson, Leonard A. Blaisol, Charles R. Smith, and David A. Dawson, *U.S. Marines in Vietnam: The Defining Year, 1968* (Washington D.C.: History and Museums Division, Headquarters, U.S. Marine Corps, 1997), 227, 533–42, 572–74, 750; *United States v. Woodard* (NCM 70–2034).

35. In the case of the army, nearly sixty thousand soldiers were made to serve involuntary second or third tours in Vietnam by mid-1971. See Department of the Army, Public Information Division, News Branch, "Query–Personnel Statistics," 30 August 1971 (National Archives Records Group 319).

36. Jack Shulimson, Leonard A. Blaisol, Charles R. Smith, and David A. Dawson, *U.S. Marines in Vietnam: The Defining Year, 1968* (Washington D.C.: History and Museums Division, Headquarters, U.S. Marine Corps, 1997), 562–65.

37. CGUSARV, LBN, RVN to Army Commanders, "Mission Accomplishment, Drug Abuse and Military Discipline (U)," 19 July 1971 (National Archives Records Group 472); Ronald H. Spector, "The Vietnam War and the Army's Self-Image," *Second Indochina Symposium*, ed. John Schlight (Washington D.C.: U.S. Army Center of Military History, 1986), 173–79.

38. William H. Hammond, *Public Affairs: The Military and the Media, 1968–1973* (Washington D.C.: Center of Military History, 1996), 191–93.

39. John Patrick Finnegan, *Military Intelligence* (Washington D.C.: Center of Military History, 1998), 155.

40. CGUSARV, LBN, RVN to Army Commanders, "Mission Accomplishment, Drug Abuse and Military Discipline (U)," 19 July 1971 (National Archives Records Group 472).

41. This term was used by Leonard V. Smith in his book *Between Mutiny and Obedience* (Princeton: Princeton University Press, 1994), 11.

42. Robert Jay Lifton, *Home from the War: Vietnam Veterans—Neither Victims nor Executioners* (New York: Simon and Schuster, 1973), 178, 187. Lifton uses the term in several different contexts within his book; I am employing it here to describe the Vietnam environment of the Vietnamization period.

43. CGUSARV, LBN, RVN to Army Commanders, "Mission Accomplishment, Drug Abuse and Military Discipline (U)," 19 July 1971 (National Archives Records Group 472).

44. Headquarters, 3d Battalion, 8th Infantry, 4th Infantry Division, "Operational Report—Lessons Learned for 1–31 May 1970," 31 May 1970 (National Archives Records Group 472); CID Report of Investigation 70-CID258–40576 (U.S. Army Crime Records Center).

45. 101st Airborne Division (Airmobile), Provost Marshal. Military Police Desk Blotter, 17 May 1970 (National Archives Records Group 472).

46. Commanding General, 1st Marine Division (Rein), FMF, to Judge Advocate General of the Navy, "Investigation to Inquire into the Circumstances Connected with the Injuries and Death Sustained by Members of Company M, 3rd Battalion, 7th Marines, and One Vietnamese Female which Occurred at 1420 on 17 August 1970," 16 September 1970 (National Archives Records Group 125).

47. Graham Cosmas and Terrence P. Murray, *U.S. Marines in Vietnam: Vietnamization and Redeployment 1970–1971* (Washington D.C.: History and Museums Division, Headquarters, U.S. Marine Corps, 1986), 350–52.

48. Billy J. Biberstein, 13th Military History Detachment, "A Monograph of 2LT Nguyen Van Thong, Platoon Leader, Recon Co., 320th Regt., 1st NVA Div" (National Archives Records Group 550).

49. AVHGB to DCG, "Sapper Attacks in the 4th Infantry Division TAOR Resulting in No Enemy Losses," 19 November 1969 (National Archives Records Group 472).

50. *United States v. Miller* (CM 425335); AVCF-GO-H, ORLL, HQ, USA-SUPCOM, Qui Nhon, for Period Ending 31 July 1970 (National Archives Records Group 550).

51. Department of the Army, Headquarters, U.S. Army Support Command Cam Ranh Bay, Office of the Inspector General, "Report of Inquiry Concerning Attack on Hill 131," 19 January 1972 (National Archives Records Group 472).

52. Iver Peterson, "Enemy Saboteurs Invade U.S. Base and Blow Up

Fuel," *New York Times*, 25 May 1971, 1. Peterson called the attack "just one in a series of enemy breaches of American base security." See also "Abrams Cautions on Laxity by G.I.s," *New York Times*, 27 May 1971, 13.

53. Department of the Army, Office of the Adjutant General, "Senior Officer Debriefing Report: BG DeWitt C. Armstrong, CG, U.S. Army Forces, MR 2," 9 May 1972 (National Archives Records Group 550).

54. CGUSARV, LBN, RVN, to Army Commanders, "Mission Accomplishment, Drug Abuse and Military Discipline (U)," 19 July 1971 (National Archives Records Group 472).

55. Guenter Lewy, *America in Vietnam* (New York: Oxford University Press, 1978), 159.

56. Brigadier Edwin H. Simmons, ADC 1st Marine Division, Orientation Talk for Newly Joined Junior Officers, Vietnam, 10 January 1971, 13 [*Marines and Military Law in Vietnam* backup files (National Archives Records Group 127)].

57. Letter to the author from Joseph M. Kralich, 11 June 1995.

58. Ronald H. Spector, "The Vietnam War and the Army's Self-Image," *Second Indochina Symposium*, ed. John Schlight (Washington D.C.: U.S. Army Center of Military History, 1986), 173–74.

59. The term "fragging" was also used in reference to the employment of fragmentation grenades against the enemy, and possesses a completely different definition in the field of military aviation. For early use of this expression regarding crimes committed against fellow Americans or local nationals in Vietnam, see *United States v. Eicholtz* [*Marines and Military Law in Vietnam* backup files, Box 1 (National Archives Records Group 127)] and *United States v. Napier* (NCM 70–1453).

60. AVHDP to CofS and DCG, "Grenade Incidents," 14 March 1971 (National Archives Records Group 472).

61. 1st Marine Division/3d Marine Amphibious Brigade, Commanding General's Information Notebook, "Fragging Incidents, Calendar Years 1970/1971," 10 April 1971 [appended to the 3d Marine Amphibious Brigade Command Chronology, 14–30 April 1971, G-1–5h (U.S. Marine Corps History Division)].

CHAPTER TWO

1. Carl Van Doren, *Mutiny in January* (New York: Viking Press, 1943), 46–47. Other accounts give Captain Bettin's name as "Bitting."

2. Grady McWhiney, *Braxton Bragg and Confederate Defeat*, vol. 1 (New York: Columbia University Press, 1969), 97–98.

3. It should be noted, however, that several of these cases were the results of off-duty disputes between men of different units. See *United States v. Clark, United States v. Hodson, United States v. Hoyer*, and *United States v. Scott* (National Archives Records Group 153).

4. CID Report of Investigation 53–59051 (U.S. Army Crime Records Center).

5. *United States v. Taylor* (50836) (National Archives Records Group 153).

6. U.S. House of Representatives, Committee on Internal Security, *Investigation of Attempts to Subvert the United States Armed Services: Hearings Before the Committee on Internal Security*, 92nd Cong., 2nd sess., 1972, part 2, 6991–92. Marshall later amended his testimony, explaining, "When I said I had never run into fragging, I meant in a combat situation." Although a number of Marshall's assertions, including details of his military service and his claims regarding World War II fire ratios, have been refuted by historians, I have chosen to use his testimony here, as he did enjoy a unique vantage point to observe the U.S. Army during much of the twentieth century. See Russell W. Glenn's introduction to the 2000 reprint of Marshall's *Men Against Fire* (Oklahoma City: Oklahoma University Press, 2000), 1–8.

7. CID Report of Investigation 66–5509-HOMU-27 (U.S. Army Crime Records Center).

8. *United States v. Dolan* (NCM 67–1090). Dolan was released from confinement in 1968, after serving over a year of his sentence, and restored to duty. He was discharged from the Marine Corps in May 1969 [Stephen J. Dolan personnel record (National Personnel Records Center)].

9. First Lieutenant Wayne H. Brandon, USMCR, to Commanding Officer, 3d Battalion, 5th Marines, "Investigation Inquiring into the Circumstances Surrounding the Death of First Sergeant William R. Hunt, 652761, USMC," 19 April 1968 (Department of the Navy, Office of the Judge Advocate General).

10. MG Kerwin to GEN Abrams, 0402Z, 6 April 1968; GEN Abrams to LTG Palmer, et al., MAC 04599 6 April 1968 (Abrams Messages, U.S. Army Center of Military History).

11. Ibid.
12. USARV, Provost Marshal, Physical Security Branch, Serious Incident Reports, April 1968 (National Archives Records Group 472).
13. Ibid.
14. Department of the Army, Headquarters, 18th Military Police Brigade, "Report of Investigation Concerning USARV Installation Stockade," 13 September 1968 (National Archives Records Group 472). See also Cecil Barr Currey, *Long Binh Jail: An Oral History of Vietnam's Notorious U.S. Military Prison* (Washington D.C.: Brassey's, 1999), 103–39.
15. USACIDC, "Crimes Involving Grenade Incidents in Vietnam," 31 December 1970 (U.S. Army Crime Records Center); 18th Military Police Brigade, Assistant Chief of Staff for Operations (S-3), Daily Journal, January–December 1968 (National Archives Records Group 472).
16. Letter to the author from General William C. Westmoreland, USA (Ret.), 23 January 1995. The incident that Westmoreland referred to is almost certainly the murder of Staff Sergeant Ignacio E. Rios of the 604th Transportation Company at Camp Schmidt on 20 October 1968.
17. AVHDP-MMW to CofS and DCG, "Grenade Incidents," 14 March 1971 (National Archives Records Group 472).
18. Gary D. Solis, *Marines and Military Law in Vietnam: Trial By Fire* (Washington D.C.: History and Museums Division, Headquarters, U.S. Marine Corps, 1989), 111.
19. *United States v. Creek* (CM 426724).
20. *United States v. Beard* (CM 424167). For another case in the 170th involving a similar device, see *United States v. Pittman* (CM 422645).
21. See the *Beard* and *Pittman* cases cited above and 18th Military Police Brigade, Assistant Chief of Staff for Operations (S-3), Daily Journal, November 1971, Serious Incident Report 11–113, 6 November 1971 (National Archives Records Group 472). For a Marine Corps case that ended with similar results, see *United States v. Culver* (NCM 70–1681), *United States v. McNeil* (NCM 70–1665), *United States v. Smith* (NCM 70–1098), and *United States v. Vasquez* (NCM 70–1389).
22. USARV, Provost Marshal, Physical Security Branch, 1972 Serious Incident Reports (National Archives Records Group 472).

23. *United States v. Sutton* (CM 423094).

24. *United States v. Crampton* (CM 426570).

25. For the details, see Guenter Lewy, *America in Vietnam* (New York: Oxford University Press, 1978), 248–57.

26. James William Gibson, *The Perfect War: The War We Couldn't Lose and How We Did* (New York: Vintage Books, 1988), 212.

27. Jerome Kroll, "Racial Patterns of Military Crimes in Vietnam," *Psychiatry* 39 (February 1976), 55.

28. Second Lieutenant B. W. Smith, U.S. Marine Corps, to Commanding Officer, 1st Combined Action Group, "Investigation to Inquire into the Circumstances Connected with the Death of First Lieutenant Earl Kay Ziegler 099970/0130, U.S. Marine Corps, Which Occurred in the Vicinity of Quang Tin Province, Republic of Vietnam, on 22 January 1969," 12 April 1969 (National Archives Records Group 125); *United States v. Eason* (NCM 70–2612).

29. Mark Lane, *Conversations with Americans* (New York: Simon and Schuster, 1970), 46–47.

30. VA-163 Aircraft Accident Report 2–65A (U); VA-164 Aircraft Accident Report 6–66A; VF-111 Aircraft Accident Report 9–68A (Naval Historical Center).

31. Muster Rolls, USS *Oriskany* (CVA-34), 1965–1967 (National Archives Records Group 24).

32. 18th Military Police Brigade, Assistant Chief of Staff for Operations (S-3), Daily Journal, October 1969, Serious Incident Report 10–35, 3 October 1969; Daily Journal, March 1970, Serious Incident Report 3–298, 26 March 1970; Daily Journal, June 1970, Serious Incident Report 6–91, 10 June 1970 (National Archives Records Group 472).

33. 552d Military Police Station, II Field Force Vietnam, APO 96266, Military Police Desk Blotter, 18 October 1970 (National Archives Records Group 472).

34. *United States v. Martinson* (NCM 70–2988); Clinical Record, Martinson, George E., AN, USN, "Neuropsychiatric Consultation," 17 April 1970 (National Archives Records Group 125).

35. Co B, 502d MI Bn, EUSA MI Gp (Prov), "Possible Sabotage, Re: Mohawk OVI Bravo, 55th Aviation Company, K-16 Airfield, Seoul, Korea" (National Archives Records Group 550).

36. U.S. House of Representatives, Committee on Armed Services, *Alleged Drug Abuse in the Armed Services: Hearings by Special*

Subcommittee on Alleged Drug Abuse in the Armed Services, 91st Cong., 2nd sess., 1970–1971, 1692; U.S. Congress, *Congressional Record*, 92nd Cong., 1st sess., 1971, part 9: 10878.

37. 18th Military Police Brigade, Assistant Chief of Staff for Operations (S-3), Daily Journal, July 1969, Serious Incident Report 7–39, 4 July 1969 (National Archives Records Group 472).

38. Judge Advocate General to Commander, U.S. Naval Support Activity, Saigon, "Pending Court-Martial Case of SA Fredie Montanez, USN, B17 18 42"; Congressional Inquiry (National Archives Records Group 125).

39. Historical Data Record, 366 Munitions Maintenance Squadron, 1 October–31 December 1971 (Air Force Historical Research Agency, Maxwell AFB, Alabama).

40. USARV, Assistant Deputy Chief of Staff for Operations, Chief of Plans Division to XO, ADCSOPS, "Fraggings," 8 February 1971 (National Archives Records Group 472).

41. U.S. Congress, *Congressional Record*, 92nd Cong., 1st sess., 1971, part 9: 10877.

42. Letter to the author from Jack L. Harrington, 6 November 1997.

43. Maurice de Saxe, *Reveries on the Art of War* (Mineola, NY: Dover Publications, 2007), 91. This insightful passage was cited in Roy E. Appleman's *South to the Naktong, North to the Yalu*.

44. *United States v. Hernandez* (CM 423721).

45. *United States v. Hendrix* (NCM 71–2473); "South Viet Nam: The War Within the War," *Time*, 25 January 1971, 34.

46. See, for example, "To Really End the War," *Bond* 4, no. 9 (23 September 70), 2; Philip D. Beidler, *Late Thoughts on an Old War: The Legacy of Vietnam* (Athens: University of Georgia Press, 2004), 100; Michael Maclear, *Vietnam: The Ten Thousand Day War* (London: Thames Methuen, 1981), 272; John Pilger, *Heroes* (London: Jonathan Cape, 1986), 198; Al Santoli, *Everything We Had: An Oral History of the Vietnam War by Thirty-three American Soldiers Who Fought It* (New York: Random House, 1981), 95.

47. Mark Lane, *Conversations with Americans* (New York: Simon and Schuster, 1970), 242.

48. Unit personnel rosters of C Company, 9th Engineer Battalion, 1st Marine Division, FMF (National Archives Records Group 127); letter to the author from Headquarters, United States Marine

Corps, Administration and Resource Management, Freedom of Information and Privacy Act Division, 5 February 1997. The Marine Corps investigation revealed that Nell enlisted under the name Jimmie D. Nell, although several documents list him as Jimmy D. Nell. He was administratively discharged in February 1970 [Jimmie D. Nell military personnel record (National Personnel Records Center)].

49. 9th Engineer Battalion, Command Chronologies (National Archives Records Group 127); "9th Engineer Battalion, Fleet Marine Force, Vietnam" (Personal Papers Section File PC 2466, U.S. Marine Corps History Division, Quantico, VA).

50. Correspondence and interviews with Benjamin A. Barzousky, Herman L. Grantham, Raymond L. Grindle, Terry F. Harroun, Wilson S. Heltzel, David J. Knez, Harry D. Masters, Milton P. Kaup, John A. Rodermund, and Lyle W. Vick.

51. Correspondence and interviews with Paul M. Batty, Rocco J. Caldarella, Christian W. Dame, Harry T. Neill, James W. Nollenberger, John M. Pacyniak, Robert L. Pruett, Robert H. Railey, Charles H. Royer, Ralph W. Schenkel, Hugh B. "Barry" Speed, and Luis F. Urroz.

52. Unit personnel rosters of C Company, 9th Engineer Battalion, 1st Marine Division, FMF (National Archives Records Group 127); 9th Engineer Battalion, Command Chronologies (National Archives Records Group 127); letter to the author from Charles H. Royer, 5 May 1997; First Lieutenant Luis F. Urroz, USMCR, to Commanding Officer, 9th Engineer Battalion, FMF, "Investigation into the Circumstances Surrounding the Shooting and Subsequent Death of PFC James L. Wilks, USMC, which Occurred on 22 May 1969 at Company C, 9th Engineer Battalion, FMF," 30 May 1969 (Department of the Navy, Office of the Judge Advocate General).

53. Barry Lando, "The Herbert Affair," *Atlantic Monthly*, May 1973, 80.

54. MACV, Inspector General, "Report of Inquiry Concerning Allegations by LTC Anthony B. Herbert, Formerly of the 173d Airborne Brigade" (National Archives Records Group 472); Office of the Deputy Chief of Staff for Personnel (ODCSPER), Records of the Vietnam War Crimes Working Group, "Records Pertaining to the LTC Herbert Controversy, 1970–73," Boxes 1–4 (National Archives Records Group 319).

55. Anthony B. Herbert, with James T. Wooten, *Soldier* (New York: Holt, Rinehart, and Winston, 1973), 140–42, 385–87.

56. "Report of Anatomical Processing: Anatomical Chart," 9 September 1968, found in MACV, Inspector General, "Report of Inquiry Concerning Allegations by LTC Anthony B. Herbert, Formerly of the 173d Airborne Brigade" (National Archives Records Group 472); Office of the Deputy Chief of Staff for Personnel (ODCSPER), Records of the Vietnam War Crimes Working Group, "Records Pertaining to the LTC Herbert Controversy, 1970–73," Boxes 1–4 (National Archives Records Group 319).

57. MACV, Inspector General, "Report of Inquiry Concerning Allegations by LTC Anthony B. Herbert, Formerly of the 173d Airborne Brigade" (National Archives Records Group 472); and Office of the Deputy Chief of Staff for Personnel (ODCSPER), Records of the Vietnam War Crimes Working Group, "Records Pertaining to the LTC Herbert Controversy, 1970–73," Boxes 1–4 (National Archives Records Group 319).

58. Eugene Linden, "Fragging and Other Withdrawal Symptoms," *Saturday Review*, 8 January 1972, 12.

59. Comments of Robin B. Heath, 13 April 1995, personal communication with author.

60. The story of *GI Says* and the alleged bounty placed on Colonel Honeycutt was first recorded in Colonel Robert D. Heinl, Jr.'s article "The Collapse of the Armed Forces," *Armed Forces Journal*, 7 June 1971. However, no further information regarding *GI Says* has since come to light. In his thorough study of the underground GI press that emerged during the war, James Lewes was unable to find any copies of the sheet in the archival collections he consulted, and his activist interviewees who were involved with the antiwar press had no knowledge of it. See James Lewes, *Protest and Survive: Underground GI Newspapers during the Vietnam War* (Westport: Praeger, 2003), 64. A search of Colonel Heinl's papers, which are in the possession of the U.S. Marine Corps History Division, provided no further clues.

61. See Robert D. Heinl, Jr., "The Collapse of the Armed Forces," *Armed Forces Journal*, 7 June 1971, 30.

62. 101st Airborne Division (Airmobile), Provost Marshal, Military Police Desk Blotters, 1969; 18th Military Police Brigade, Assistant Chief of Staff for Operations (S-3), Daily Journal, 1969 (National Archives Records Group 472); letter to the author from the director, U.S. Army Crime Records Center, 20 July 1998.

63. Letter to the author from Brigadier General Weldon F. Honeycutt, USA (Ret.), 1 July 1998.

64. *United States v. Hurley* (NCM 67–2575).

65. USARV, Inspector General, Investigation and Complaint Division, Reports of Investigation Case Files, "Report of Investigation Concerning Alleged Fragging Incidents in the 1st Battalion, 7th Cavalry Rear Area," 28 February 1970 (National Archives Records Group 472).

66. Letter to the author from Samuel S. Vitucci, 11 August 1997.

67. 18th Military Police Brigade, Assistant Chief of Staff for Operations (S-3), Daily Journal, November 1971, Serious Incident Report 11–15, 1 November 1971 (National Archives Records Group 472); *United States v. Gallagher* (CM 426807).

68. Letter to the author from Samuel S. Vitucci, 11 August 1997.

69. USARV, Provost Marshal, Serious Incident Report 2–324, 28 February 1972 (National Archives Records Group 472).

70. Letter to the author from Samuel S. Vitucci, 11 August 1997.

71. "Summary of Proceedings" found in Glen A. Poe's military personnel record (National Personnel Records Center).

72. Letter to the author from Samuel S. Vitucci, 11 August 1997. Military personnel records on file at the National Personnel Records Center reveal that Dean, Gallagher, Hogans, Murphy, Poe, and Tattnall were discharged from the army by the end of May 1972. Collins and Parker were permitted to complete their enlistments and were released from active duty early the following year. Ancrum died in an automobile accident at Fort Hood in April 1973. The last of the group to leave the army was Baker, who was discharged in January 1974. See also CID Report of Investigation 73-CID034–33565–5H5 (U.S. Army Crime Records Center).

73. Thomas C. Bond, "The Why of Fragging," *American Journal of Psychiatry* 131 (11 November 1976), 1329.

74. Captain George P. Adams, USMC, to Commanding Officer, 2d Battalion, 11th Marines, 1st Marine Division (FMF), "Investigation to Inquire into the Circumstances Surrounding the Death of First Sergeant Warren R. Furse, 1187297, USMC, and Injury to Gunnery Sergeant Haywood W. Ballance, 1370320, USMC on or about 2400 27 February 1969," 11 March 1969 (Department of the Navy, Office of the Judge Advocate General).

75. *United States v. Chambers* (NCM 69–3501); letter to the author from

Edward F. Kelly, 4 December 1995. Following his acquittal, Chambers proved to be a chronic disciplinary problem, and he received an undesirable discharge from the Marine Corps in June 1970. He returned to his native Memphis, where, ironically, he became a corrections officer. In 1978, he attempted to have his discharge upgraded but was unsuccessful. He died of natural causes in 1994, aged forty-five [Walter Chambers, Jr., military personnel record (National Personnel Records Center)].

76. Charles R. Smith, *U.S. Marines in Vietnam: High Mobility and Standdown 1969* (Washington D.C.: History and Museums Division, Headquarters, U.S. Marine Corps, 1988), 116.

77. *United States v. Fowler* (NCM 70–3599).

78. CID Report of Investigation 71-CID648–49838 (U.S. Army Crime Records Center).

79. *United States v. Sutton* (CM 423094); CID Report of Investigation 69-CID458–41820 (U.S. Army Crime Records Center); letter to the author from Frederick A. Drew, 2 April 2002; CID Report of Investigation 70-CID648–39139 (U.S. Army Crime Records Center); *United States v. Wheat* (CM 425700); CID Report of Investigation 70-CID958–43687 (U.S. Army Crime Records Center); *United States v. Locklin* (CM 424813); Mansfield Papers, Collection 65, Series VII, Box 202, Folder 17 (Maureen and Mike Mansfield Library, University of Montana); CID Report of Investigation 71-CID448–45303 (U.S. Army Crime Records Center); CID Report of Investigation 71-CID648–49838 (U.S. Army Crime Records Center); John Saar, "The Outpost is a Shambles," *Life*, 31 March 1972, 32.

80. Charles J. Levy, *Spoils of War* (Boston: Houghton Mifflin, 1974), 44–45.

81. USARV Regulation 190–47 (National Archives Records Group 472).

82. CG, USARV, to Department of the Army, "Grenade Incidents in Vietnam," 17 February 1971 (National Archives Records Group 472). While testifying before a Congressional subcommittee, Lieutenant General Walter T. Kerwin, Jr., stated that 239 fraggings occurred in army units in Vietnam during 1969. This figure, of course, is incorrect, as it includes the "non-fragging" incidents. I believe that Kerwin arrived at this number by misreading the above-cited USARV document or, more likely, information copied from it. The latter theory is lent credibility by the discovery of a report generated by the Secretary of the Army's office, titled "Incidents Involving Explosives in Viet-

nam," in which the erroneous figure (239) is cited. Several postwar historians have copied this error [U.S. House of Representatives, Subcommittee of the Committee on Appropriations, *Department of Defense Appropriations for 1972*, 92nd Cong., 1st sess., 1971, part 3, 473; "Incidents Involving Explosives in Vietnam," undated (American Soldier Files, U.S. Army Center of Military History)].

83. 25th Infantry Division, Provost Marshal, Military Police Desk Blotters, 1969 (National Archives Records Group 472).

84. 1st Infantry Division, Provost Marshal, Military Police Desk Blotters, 1969, and 101st Airborne Division (Airmobile), Provost Marshal, Military Police Desk Blotters, 1969 (National Archives Records Group 472).

85. USARV, Information Office, News Media and Release Files, "Reply to AP," 31 December 1970 (National Archives Records Group 472).

86. USARV, Inspector General, Investigation and Complaint Division, Reports of Investigation Case Files, "Report of Investigation Concerning Alleged Fragging Incidents in the 1st Battalion, 7th Cavalry Rear Area," 28 February 1970 (National Archives Records Group 472).

87. USARV, Provost Marshal, "Fragging Incidents, 1969 and 1970," 1971 Study (U.S. Army Crime Records Center).

88. CG, USARV to Department of the Army, "Grenade Incidents in Vietnam," dated 17 February 1971 (National Archives Records Group 472). This report reveals that 386 S.I.R.s involving explosive devices were submitted in 1970. Upon review, 209 were categorized as actual incidents, 62 as possible incidents, and the rest as non-fragging incidents.

89. Several of the victims listed in the statistics as injured later died.

90. CID Report of Investigation 70-CID258–43305 (U.S. Army Crime Records Center).

91. *United States* v. *Wheat* (CM 425700).

92. *United States* v. *Addison* (NCM 70–2433); First Lieutenant Mark F. Tierney, USMCR, to Commanding Officer, 3d Battalion, 7th Marines, "Investigation to Inquire into the Circumstances Surrounding the Alleged Detonation of Two Fragmentation Grenades in the 3/7 Communications Message Center Resulting in the Death of One Marine and Injury to Two Others on or About 0700H, 18 April 1970," 9 May 1970 (Department of the Navy, Office of the Judge Advocate General); First CAG to CAF, "Serious Incident Report," 1 July 1970 (ibid.); *United States* v. *Hendrix* (NCM 71–2473).

93. Brigadier Edwin H. Simmons, ADC 1st Marine Division, Orientation Talk for Newly Joined Junior Officers, Vietnam, 10 January 1971, 24–27 [*Marines and Military Law in Vietnam* backup files (National Archives Records Group 127)].

94. "Tujunga Marine Blown Up in Viet Nam by Own Men," *Record-Ledger*, 4 September 1969, 1.

95. USMC Judge Advocate Division, Point Paper, "Testimony of Robert J. Parkinson, ex-USMC, Sgt, 2062846, on 18 August 1970 before Senator Dodd's Subcommittee on Juvenile Delinquency," 28 August 1970 [Robert J. Parkinson military personnel record (National Personnel Records Center)].

96. "Foe of Marijuana Says G.I. Threw Grenade at Him," *New York Times*, 19 August 1970, 16.

97. U.S. Marine Corps, Judge Advocate Division, Point Paper, "Testimony of Robert J. Parkinson, ex-USMC, Sgt, 2062846, on 18 August 1970 before Senator Dodd's Subcommittee on Juvenile Delinquency," 28 August 1970 [Robert J. Parkinson military personnel record (National Personnel Records Center)].

98. "Marines Suspected in Club Explosion," *New York Times*, 8 February 1970, 2; "Australian Recalls a Second Grenade in Danang Incident," *New York Times*, 9 February 1970, 12.

99. John Saar, "You Can't Just Hand Out Orders," *Life*, 23 October 1970, 32.

100. USARV, Information Office, "Reply to AP," 31 December 1970 (National Archives Records Group 472).

101. "Tense GIs Carry Vendettas to Explosive, Dramatic End," *Lima News*, 7 January 1971, 1. See also "'Fragging': When GIs Turn on Noncoms," *Fresno Bee*, 7 January 1971, 14-A; "GI Bomb Attacks on Officers Increase," *Philadelphia Inquirer*, 8 January 1971, 2; and "GIs Tossing Bombs at Noncoms, Officers," *Los Angeles Times*, 8 January 1971, 18.

102. LTG McCaffrey to GEN Abrams, confidential message, 7 January 1971 (National Archives Records Group 472).

103. See, for example, IO to DCS P&A, "News Query from U.S. News and World Report," 31 December 1971, and AVHDP-MMW to Chief, MPPD, "Press Query (Morale Indicators)," 16 April 1972 (National Archives Records Group 472).

104. William M. Hammond, *Public Affairs: The Military and the Media,*

1962–1968 (Washington D.C.: Center of Military History, 1988), 190.

105. "Army Makes Apology for Memo on TV Man," *New York Times*, 10 April 1971, 5.

106. Eugene Linden, "Fragging and Other Withdrawal Symptoms," *Saturday Review*, 8 January 1972, 12. Linden afforded Thompson the pseudonym Walt Ross in the article.

107. Routing Slip and Record of Action attached to AVHDP-MPD to DCS P&A, "Analysis of Fraggings," 10 February 1972 (National Archives Records Group 472). See also U.S. House of Representatives, Committee on Internal Security, *Investigation of Attempts to Subvert the United States Armed Services: Hearings Before the Committee on Internal Security*, 92nd Cong., 2nd sess., 1972, part 3, 7317–48, for a brief discussion of Linden's article.

108. For an objective analysis of military morale in Vietnam in early 1972, see Wendell S. Merick, "For GI's, It's a Different War—But Still Dangerous," *U.S. News & World Report*, 14 February 1972, 62.

109. AVHPM-PO to Department of the Army, "Assaults with Explosive Devices, CSGPA-1159," 15 June 1971 (National Archives Records Group 472).

110. CINCPAC to CINCUSARPAC, "Unauthorized Employment of Deadly Weapons (U)," 19 March 1971 (National Archives Records Group 472).

111. Michael R. Beschloss, ed., *Taking Charge: The Johnson White House Tapes, 1963–1964* (New York: Touchstone, 1997), 371.

112. For narrative treatment of Mansfield's role in Vietnam, see Gregory A. Olson, *Mansfield and Vietnam: A Study in Rhetorical Adaptation* (East Lansing: Michigan State University Press, 1995).

113. U.S. Congress, *Congressional Record*, 92nd Cong., 1st sess., 1971, part 9: 10871; "Mansfield Mourns 'Fragging' Death of Montana Lieutenant," *Los Angeles Times*, 21 April 1971, 1.

114. CID Report of Investigation 71-CID448–45303 (U.S. Army Crime Records Center).

115. "American Soldier Accused of Killing Officers," *London Times*, 8 September 1972, 8.

116. Ted Sell, "Blacks May Find New Cause in Trial of GI in 2 Viet Slayings," *Los Angeles Times*, 4 September 1972, A3; Wallace Turner,

"Draftee on Trial in Officer Deaths," *New York Times*, 7 September 1972, 17; "Activists to Picket GI's Vietnam Fragging Trial," *Independent Press-Telegram*, 4 September 1972, A-10; "Angela Davis Backs Pvt. Smith," *Manitowac Herald-Times*, 25 October 1972, 15.

117. Kate Buford, *Burt Lancaster: An American Life* (Cambridge: Da Capo Press, 2001), 266–67.

118. Ted Sell, "Blacks May Find New Cause in Trial of GI in 2 Viet Slayings," *Los Angeles Times*, 4 September 1972, A3.

119. *United States v. Smith* (CM 429555).

120. 1st Marine Division/3d Marine Amphibious Brigade, Commanding General's Information Notebook, "Fragging Incidents, Calendar Years 1970/1971," 10 April 1971 [appended to the 3d Marine Amphibious Brigade Command Chronology, 14–30 April 1971, G-1–5h (U.S. Marine Corps History Division)]; *United States v. Linkous* (NCM 71–1044).

121. U.S. House of Representatives, Subcommittee of the Committee on Appropriations, *Department of Defense Appropriations for 1972*, 92nd Cong., 1st sess., 1971, part 9, 583.

122. *United States v. Williams* (CM 428247).

123. 101st Airborne Division (Airmobile), Provost Marshal, Military Police Desk Blotter, 16 November 1969 and 17 December 1969 (National Archives Records Group 472).

124. *United States v. Johnson* (CM 429456). Johnson died in 2005, aged fifty-three.

125. CDR, USARV/MACV SUPCOM SGN to DA/DAPE-DDO, "Assault With Explosive Devices, RCS: GSGPA-1159," 8 January 1973 (National Archives Records Group 473).

126. USARV, Provost Marshal, Physical Security Branch, 1973 Serious Incident Reports (National Archives Records Group 472).

127. CID Reports of Investigation 71-CID448–45303, 71-CID558–51136, and 71-CID648–49838 (U.S. Army Crime Records Center).

CHAPTER THREE

1. Charles C. Moskos, Jr., *The American Enlisted Man: The Rank and File in Today's Military* (New York: Russell Sage Foundation, 1970), 64.

2. For classic studies of primary groups within the modern military context, see Samuel A. Stouffer et al., *The American Soldier: Combat and Its Aftermath* (Princeton: Princeton University Press, 1949),

130–43, and Edward A. Shils and Morris Janowitz, "Cohesion and Disintegration in the Wehrmacht," in James Burk, *On Social Organization and Social Control* (Chicago: University of Chicago Press, 1991), 160–74. For an interesting case study of primary group processes within an American infantry platoon during the Korean War, see Roger W. Little, "Buddy Relations and Combat Performance," in Morris Janowitz, ed., *The New Military: Changing Patterns of Organization* (New York: Russell Sage Foundation, 1964), 195–223.

3. U.S. Congress, *Congressional Record*, 92nd Cong., 1st sess., 1971, part 9: 10877.

4. Kurt Lang, "American Military Performance in Vietnam: Background and Analysis," *Journal of Political and Military Sociology* 8 (1980), 269–86.

5. Thomas G. Sticht et al., *Cast-off Youth: Policy and Training Methods From the Military Experience* (New York: Praeger, 1987), 41.

6. Gary D. Solis, *Marines and Military Law in Vietnam: Trial By Fire* (Washington D.C.: History and Museums Division, Headquarters, U.S. Marine Corps, 1989), 74, 203.

7. U.S. House of Representatives, Subcommittee of the Committee on Appropriations, *Department of Defense Appropriations for 1972*, 92nd Cong., 1st sess., 1971, part 9, 582; Jack Shulimson, Leonard A. Blaisol, Charles R. Smith, and David A. Dawson, *U.S. Marines in Vietnam: The Defining Year, 1968* (Washington D.C.: History and Museums Division, Headquarters, U.S. Marine Corps, 1997), 559–60.

8. U.S. House of Representatives, Subcommittee of the Committee on Appropriations, *Department of Defense Appropriations for 1972*, 92nd Cong., 1st sess., 1971, part 9, 582.

9. Raymond R. Crowe and Edward M. Colbach, "A Psychiatric Experience with Project 100,000," *Military Medicine*, March 1971, 271–73.

10. Gary D. Solis, *Marines and Military Law in Vietnam: Trial By Fire* (Washington D.C.: History and Museums Division, Headquarters, U.S. Marine Corps, 1989), 74.

11. Thomas C. Bond, "The Why of Fragging," *American Journal of Psychiatry* 131 (11 November 1976), 1330.

12. Eugene Linden, "Fragging and Other Withdrawal Symptoms," *Saturday Review*, 8 January 1972, 15–16.

13. *United States v. Hendrix* (NCM 71–2473).

14. *United States v. Garcia* (CM 426969).

15. *United States v. Barrios* (NCM 70–1408).

16. Thomas C. Bond, "The Why of Fragging," *American Journal of Psychiatry* 131 (11 November 1976), 1330.

17. This random sample was selected as part of a study on drug usage in Vietnam. See Lee N. Robbins et al., "Narcotic Use in Southeast Asia and Afterward: An Interview Study of 898 Vietnam Returnees," *Archives of General Psychiatry* 32 (August 1975), 956.

18. Austin H. MacCormick and Victor H. Evjen, "Statistical Study of 24,000 Military Prisoners," *Federal Probation*, April–June 1945, 7. This study found that the median age of general prisoners confined during and after the Second World War was one year younger than that of army enlisted men as a whole.

19. Lee N. Robbins et al., "Narcotic Use in Southeast Asia and Afterward: An Interview Study of 898 Vietnam Returnees," *Archives of General Psychiatry* 32 (August 1975), 956–57.

20. Thomas C. Bond, "The Why of Fragging, " *American Journal of Psychiatry* 131 (11 November 1976), 1329.

21. *United States v. Purifoy* (CM 428358).

22. *United States v. Locklin* (CM 424813).

23. *United States v. Shirley* (CM 422317).

24. *United States v. Ercolin* (CM 426967).

25. Lee N. Robbins et al., "Narcotic Use in Southeast Asia and Afterward: An Interview Study of 898 Vietnam Returnees," *Archives of General Psychiatry* 32 (August 1975), 957.

26. Austin H. MacCormick and Victor H. Evjen, "Statistical Study of 24,000 Military Prisoners," *Federal Probation*, April–June 1945, 10.

27. Thomas C. Bond et al., "Assaults with Explosive Devices on Superior Officers: Reports of Confined Offenders at the U.S. Disciplinary Barracks," 1972, Series B, Box 2, United States Disciplinary Barracks Collection (Combined Arms Research Library, U.S. Army Command & General Staff College, Fort Leavenworth, Kansas).

28. For a case in which an accused claimed to have entered the military under these circumstances, see *United States v. Locklin* (CM 424813).

29. *United States v. Wheat* (CM 425700).

30. *United States v. Baldwin* (CM 415536).

31. *United States v. Locklin* (CM 424813).

32. *United States v. Hendrix* (NCM 71–2473).

33. First Combined Action Group to Combined Action Force, "Serious Incident Report," 2 July 1970 (Department of the Navy, Office of the Judge Advocate General).

34. First Lieutenant Tibor R. Saddler, USMC, to Commanding Officer, 1st Combined Action Group, "Investigation to Inquire into the Circumstances Surrounding the Death of Lance Corporal Gilberto Garcia, 2585264/0341, U.S. Marine Corps, Which Occurred Between 1400 Hours and 1500 Hours, 1 September 1970, at Quang Nam Province, Republic of Vietnam," 6 September 1970 (Department of the Navy, Office of the Judge Advocate General).

35. CID Report of Investigation 69-CID258–40679 (U.S. Army Crime Records Center).

36. *United States v. Thomas* (NCM 69–4053).

37. Headquarters, 1st Marine Division (-) (Rein), FMF, "Standing Operating Procedures for Prevention of Crimes of Violence," 13 December 1970 (appended to the 1st Marine Division December 1970 Command Chronology) (U.S. Marine Corps History Division).

38. Thomas C. Bond, "The Why of Fragging," *American Journal of Psychiatry* 131 (11 November 1976), 1330.

39. *United States v. Locklin* (CM 424813).

40. *United States v. Hendrix* (NCM 71–2473).

41. *United States v. Aubert* (CM 427892).

42. *United States v. Crampton* (CM 426570).

43. Eugene Linden, "Fragging and Other Withdrawal Symptoms," *Saturday Review*, 8 January 1972, 12.

44. *United States v. Finch* (CM 422486).

45. *United States v. Schott* (CM 427113).

46. 18th Military Police Brigade, Installation Stockade, Individual Correction Record, PFC Roger L. Aubert (National Archives Records Group 472); *United States v. Bell* (CM 422276); *United States v. Chaky* (CM 426039).

47. Lee N. Robbins et al., "Narcotic Use in Southeast Asia and Afterward: An Interview Study of 898 Vietnam Returnees," *Archives of General Psychiatry* 32 (August 1975), 956.

48. See *United States v. Aubert* (CM 427892), *United States v. Pittman* (CM 422645), and *United States v. Sutton* (CM 423094).

49. Thomas C. Bond, "The Why of Fragging," *American Journal of Psychiatry* 131 (11 November 1976), 1329.

50. Eric Hoffer, *The True Believer: Thoughts on the Nature of Mass Movements* (New York: Harper & Brothers, 1951), 63–67.

51. Dr. Thomas C. Bond, "The Why of Fragging," *American Journal of Psychiatry* 131 (11 November 1976), 1329; David H. Gillooly and Thomas C. Bond, "Assaults with Explosive Devices on Superiors: A Synopsis of Reports from Confined Offenders at the U.S. Disciplinary Barracks," *Military Medicine*, October 1976, 700–702.

52. *United States v. Hendrix* (NCM 71–2473).

53. *United States v. Schott* (CM 427113).

54. *United States v. Spears* (CM 425344); USARV, Provost Marshal, Serious Incident Report 9–369, 25 September 1970 (National Archives Records Group 472).

55. Headquarters, 1st Marine Division (-) (Rein), FMF, "Standing Operating Procedures for Prevention of Crimes of Violence," 13 December 1970 (appended to the 1st Marine Division December 1970 Command Chronology) (U.S. Marine Corps History Division).

56. *United States v. Blaylock* (CM 425319).

57. *United States v. Hurley* (NCM 67–2575).

58. *United States v. Linkous* (NCM 71–1044).

59. *United States v. Hawkins* (CM 423687); Theodore L. Hawkins military personnel record (National Personnel Records Center).

60. *United States v. Schott* (CM 427113).

61. Letters to the author from John E. Gabel, 9 June 1997 and 22 July 1997.

62. *United States v. Thompson* (CM 427004).

63. *United States v. Benoit* (CM 422738).

64. Headquarters, 101st Airborne Division, General Orders, Number 7498, 22 June 1969 (National Archives Records Group 472). Records reveal that Hernandez also received the Bronze Star for meritorious service. See Headquarters, 101st Airborne Division, General Orders, Number 10695, 18 August 1969.

65. U.S. House of Representatives, Committee on Armed Forces, *Alleged Drug Abuse in the Armed Services: Hearings by Special Subcommittee on Alleged Drug Abuse in the Armed Services of the Committee on Armed Services*, 91st Cong., 2nd sess., 1970–1971, 1928.

66. MG Bowers, DCS (P&A), USARV, to BG Greene, ACOFS, MACV J1, undated message (National Archives Records Group 472).

67. *United States v. Locklin* (CM 424813).

68. *United States v. Smith* (NCM 70–0500).

69. Letter from Gary A. Hendrix to Reverend Robert Horton, 15 July 1978 [Swarthmore College Peace Collection, Records of Prison Visitation and Support (DG 223), Box 38].

70. *United States v. Wynn* (CM 424277).

71. *United States v. Bumgarner* (CM 427113), *United States v. Schott* (CM 427113).

72. Thomas C. Bond et al., "Assaults with Explosive Devices on Superior Officers: Reports of Confined Offenders at the U.S. Disciplinary Barracks," 1972, Series B, Box 2, United States Disciplinary Barracks Collection (Combined Arms Research Library, U.S. Army Command & General Staff College, Fort Leavenworth, Kansas).

73. Lee N. Robbins et al., "Narcotic Use in Southeast Asia and Afterward: An Interview Study of 898 Vietnam Returnees," *Archives of General Psychiatry* 32 (August 1975), 957.

74. U.S. House of Representatives, Committee on Armed Services, *Alleged Drug Abuse in the Armed Services: Hearings by Special Subcommittee on Alleged Drug Abuse in the Armed Services*, 91st Cong., 2nd sess., 1970–1971, 1894.

75. U.S. Congress, *Congressional Record*, 92nd Cong., 1st sess., 1971, part 9: 10876.

76. U.S. House of Representatives, Committee on Armed Forces, *Alleged Drug Abuse in the Armed Services: Hearings by Special Subcommittee on Alleged Drug Abuse in the Armed Services*, 91st Cong., 2nd sess., 1970–1971, 1928.

77. U.S. House of Representatives, Committee on Armed Services, *Inquiry into Alleged Drug Abuse in the Armed Services: Report of a Special Subcommittee of the Committee on Armed Services*, 91st Cong., 2nd sess., 23 April 1971, 2182.

78. U.S. Congress, *Congressional Record*, 92nd Cong., 1st sess., 1971, part 9: 10876.

79. U.S. House of Representatives, Committee on Armed Services, *Inquiry into Alleged Drug Abuse in the Armed Services: Report of a Special Subcommittee of the Committee on Armed Services*, 91st Cong., 2nd sess., 23 April 1971, 2171.

80. Thomas C. Bond, "The Why of Fragging," *American Journal of Psychiatry* 131 (11 November 1976), 1330.

81. *United States v. Hendrix* (NCM 71–2374).

82. *United States v. Benoit* (CM 422738).

83. John R. Lilly military personnel record (National Personnel Records Center).

84. *United States v. Shirley* (CM 422317); Headquarters, 101st Airborne Division, General Orders, Number 9377, 23 July 1969 (National Archives Records Group 472).

85. *United States v. Cornett* (CM 429339); Alan G. Cornett, Jr., military personnel record (National Personnel Records Center).

86. CG, USARV, to Department of the Army, "Grenade Incidents in Vietnam," 17 February 1971 (National Archives Records Group 472).

87. 1st Marine Division/3d Marine Amphibious Brigade, Commanding General's Information Notebook, "Fragging Incidents, Calendar Years 1970/1971," 10 April 1971 [appended to the 3d Marine Amphibious Brigade Command Chronology, 14–30 April 1971, G-1–5h (U.S. Marine Corps History Division)].

88. Charles C. Moskos, Jr., *The American Enlisted Man: The Rank and File in Today's Military* (New York: Russell Sage Foundation, 1970), 71.

89. Howard Brotz and Everett Wilson, "Characteristics of Military Society," *American Journal of Sociology* 51, no. 5 (March 1946), 373; Clifton D. Bryant, *Khaki-Collar Crime: Deviant Behavior in the Military Context* (New York: Free Press, 1979), 110–11.

90. Charles R. Anderson, *The Grunts* (Novato: Presidio Press, 1983), 187–88.

91. Roger W. Little, "Buddy Relations and Combat Performance," in Morris Janowitz, ed., *The New Military: Changing Patterns of Organization* (New York: Russell Sage Foundation, 1964), 209.

92. Author's telephone interview with Robin Heath, 9 March 1995.

93. Charles R. Anderson, *The Grunts* (Novato: Presidio Press, 1983), 190.

94. For the company commander's explanation of his innovation, see Robert T. Rohweller Oral History Interview (U.S. Marine Corps History Division). For a senior officer's positive evaluation of it, see Robert T. Rohweller's military personnel record (National Personnel Records Center).

95. The negative enlisted view was typified by criticism of the company commander's "tactics out in the bush with the company," and remarks such as "I did not like serving out in the field with Lieutenant Rohweller" [*United States v. Napier* (NCM 70-1453)].

96. ACTIV to ADCOPS, 6 February 1972 (National Archives Records Group 472).

97. *United States v. Napier* (NCM 70–1453).

98. Reginald F. Smith military personnel record (National Personnel Records Center).

99. *United States v. Napier* (NCM 70–1453).

100. Robert T. Rohweller military personnel record (National Personnel Records Center). For a published account of one of these operations, see J. C. Sternberg, "8 Swim Into—and Out of—Trouble on Patrol," *Pacific Stars and Stripes*, 4 October 1965, 7.

101. Robert T. Rohweller military personnel record (National Personnel Records Center). In his memoirs, General Raymond C. Davis, commander of the 3d Marine Division, called Rohweller "a fine young lieutenant" [Raymond C. Davis, *The Story of Ray Davis, General of Marines* (Fuquay-Varina, N.C.: Research Triangle Publishing, 1995), 232].

102. Letter to the author from Jack L. Harrington, 6 November 1997.

103. Letter to the author from Gordon M. Davis, 15 December 1995.

104. *United States v. Napier* (NCM 70–1453).

105. This is Smith's version of the incident. See *United States v. Napier* (NCM 70–1453) and *United States v. Greenwood* (NCM 70–3843).

106. *United States v. Napier* (NCM 70–1453).

107. Author's telephone interview with Stanley L. Smith, 23 January 1996.

108. Gary D. Solis, *Marines and Military Law in Vietnam: Trial By Fire* (Washington D.C.: History and Museums Division, Headquarters, U.S. Marine Corps, 1989), 134–38.

109. *United States v. Napier* (NCM 70–1453).

110. Correspondence and interviews with Bailey E. Billups, Charles E. Bores, Richard F. Cullen, Gordon M. Davis, Stephen G. Fairman, John E. Gabel, Jack L. Harrington, Kenneth W. Jackson, Joseph L. Leffelman, Adam W. Mackow, Thomas M. Tigue, Victor J. Tyynismaa, and Dennis C. Wilson.

111. Letter to the author from Gordon M. Davis, 15 December 1995.

112. Letters to the author from Stephen G. Fairman, 1 April 1997 and 30 June 1997.

113. Letter to the author from Adam W. Mackow, 8 January 1997.

114. Federal Inmate Record, Reginald F. Smith, Reg. No. 28530–138 (U.S. Department of Justice, Federal Bureau of Prisons).

115. *United States v. Smith* (NCM 70–0500).

116. *United States v. Greenwood* (NCM 70–3843); *United States v. Napier* (NCM 70–1453).

117. Charles R. Smith, *U.S. Marines in Vietnam: High Mobility and Stand-down 1969* (Washington D.C.: History and Museums Division, Headquarters, U.S. Marine Corps, 1988), 170.

118. *United States v. Elliot* (CM 426967).

119. Letter to the author from Courtney L. Frobenius, 6 March 1995, with additional comments made by John Sperry during a telephone interview on 2 March 1995.

120. CID Report of Investigation 67–3346-HOMU-MIO-27 (U.S. Army Crime Records Center).

121. Morning reports, A Battery, 1/8 Artillery, October 1966 to January 1967 (National Personnel Records Center); S-3 Journal, 1st Battalion, 8th Artillery (National Archives Records Group 472). Beasley's personnel record reveals that he served in HH&S Battery, 1/8th Artillery for several days in October 1966. I checked this battery's morning reports and found that it did not engage in combat against the enemy or sustain any casualties during that period [Merrill V. Beasley military personnel record and morning reports, HH&S Battery, 1/8th Artillery (National Personnel Records Center)].

122. Paul G. Savage and Richard A. Gabriel, *Crisis in Command: Mismanagement in the Army* (New York: Hill and Wang, 1978), 171.

123. See Paul E. Reed, Robert T. Rohweller, and Richard L. Tate military personnel records (National Personnel Records Center).

124. *United States v. Shirley* (CM 422317).

125. Emanuel Tanay, "The Dear John Syndrome during the Vietnam War," *Diseases of the Nervous System* 37, no. 3 (1976), 167.

126. *United States v. McCracken* (CM 423370).

127. CID Report of Investigation 70-CID958–43687 (U.S. Army Crime Records Center); *United States v. Locklin* (CM 424813).

128. *United States v. Wheat* (CM 425700).

129. *United States v. Ercolin* (CM 426967).

130. *United States v. Bost* (CM 427767).

131. Morris J. MacGregor, Jr., *Integration of the Armed Forces* (Washington D.C.: U.S. Army Center of Military History, 1981), 291.

132. Joan Morrison and Robert K. Morrison, *From Camelot to Kent State: The Sixties Experience in the Words of Those Who Lived It* (New York: Times Books, 1987), 76.

133. Charles C. Moskos, Jr., *The American Enlisted Man: The Rank and File in Today's Military* (New York: Russell Sage Foundation, 1970), 116.

134. Headquarters, 3d Marine Division, "Rights and Obligations of Marines," 19 June 1969 [*Marines and Military Law in Vietnam* backup files (National Archives Records Group 127)].

135. For an interesting overview of this social construction by a former army officer, see William Stuart Gould, "Racial Conflict in the U.S. Army," *Race* 15 (1 July 1973), 8–13.

136. CG USARV, to Department of the Army, "Grenade Incidents in Vietnam," 17 February 1971 (National Archives Records Group 472).

137. III MAF Fact Sheet, "I Corps Tactical Zone Watch Committee, Recapitulation of Race-Related Incidents: Oct 68–Jun 69," 7 August 1969 [*Marines and Military Law in Vietnam* backup files (National Archives Records Group 127)].

138. Brigadier Edwin H. Simmons, ADC 1st Marine Division, Orientation Talk for Newly Joined Junior Officers, Vietnam, 10 January 1971, 10 [*Marines and Military Law in Vietnam* backup files (National Archives Records Group 127)].

139. Gary D. Solis, *Marines and Military Law in Vietnam: Trial By Fire* (Washington D.C.: History and Museums Division, Headquarters, U.S. Marine Corps, 1989), 193–96.

140. Author's telephone interview with Fred C. Johnson, 20 January 1996.

141. *United States v. McDonald* (NCM 70–2256).

142. Report of unknown provenance, "Detailed Breakout of Disturbances" (undated) (National Archives Records Group 472); CID Report of Investigation 69 CID858–42502 (U.S. Army Crime Records Center). Weeks after this incident, army CID learned that a Vietnamese "Kit Carson" scout may have detonated the grenades, but no further information regarding this lead was ever developed. See 18th Military Police Brigade, Assistant Chief of Staff for Operations (S-3), Daily Journal, December 1969, Serious Incident Report 9–16 (Supplemental #3), 5 December 1969 (National Archives Records Group 472).

143. 18th Military Police Brigade, Assistant Chief of Staff for Operations (S-3), Daily Journal, January 1971, Serious Incident Report 1–129, 10 January 1971 (National Archives Records Group 472).

144. *United States v. Prince* (CM 427290).

145. 18th Military Police Brigade, Assistant Chief of Staff for Operations (S-3), Daily Journal, August 1971 (National Archives Records Group 472).

146. *United States v. Perry* (CM 424936).

147. 23d Infantry Division, Provost Marshal, Military Police Desk Blotter, 2 March 1971 (National Archives Records Group 472); *United States v. Chaky* (CM 426039).

148. MG George L. Mabry, Jr., to various commanders, "Black Panther Party" dated 28 April 1970 (National Archives Records Group 472).

149. MG Brown to GEN Abrams and LTG McCaffrey, "Current Situation 1/10 Cav–Camp Radcliff" dated 29 January 1971; BG Kendall to COL Read dated 31 January 1971 (National Archives Records Group 472).

150. *United States v. Moyler* (CM 427398).

151. MACV, Inspector General, "Report of Investigation into the State of Discipline in the 1st Squadron, 10th Cavalry," dated 7–13 February 1971 (National Archives Records Group 472). Despite General McCaffrey's efforts, Mason remained in the army and was later promoted to full colonel. He retired in 1977 after twenty-one years of service [John Mason military personnel record (National Personnel Records Center)].

152. *United States v. Paul* (CM 425399).

153. 18th Military Police Brigade, Assistant Chief of Staff for Operations (S-3), Daily Journal, January 1971, Serious Incident Report 1–109, 8 January 1971 (National Archives Records Group 472); "South Viet Nam: The War Within a War." *Time*, 25 January 1971, 34.

154. 18th Military Police Brigade, Assistant Chief of Staff for Operations (S-3), Daily Journal, May 1970, Serious Incident Report 5–362, 31 May 1970 (National Archives Records Group 472).

155. *United States v. Robinson* (CM 425317).

156. CG, USARV, to DA, Blue Bell Report dated 1 January 1971 (National Archives Records Group 472).

157. CID Report of Investigation 71-CID348–41229 (U.S. Army Crime Records Center).

158. William Stuart Gould, "Racial Conflict in the U.S. Army" in *Race* XV (1 July 1973), 11.

159. MG George L. Mabry, Jr. to various commanders, "Black Panther Party," 28 April 1970 (National Archives Records Group 472).

160. 18th Military Police Brigade, Installation Stockade, Individual Correction Record, SP4 Arthur L. Caruthers (National Archives Records Group 472).

161. Letter to the author from Joseph M. Kralich, 11 June 1995.

162. MACV Command History, 1966, 191 (National Archives Records Group 472).

163. MACV Command History, 1967, Volume II, 957 (National Archives Records Group 472).

164. MACV Command History, 1968, Volume III, xiv–4 (National Archives Records Group 472).

165. Report of unknown provenance, "Deaths Due to Heroin and Other Drugs in RVN" (National Archives Records Group 319).

166. MACV Command History, 1970, Volume II, xiv–4 (U.S. Army Center of Military History); Guenter Lewy, *America in Vietnam* (New York: Oxford University Press, 1978), 147; MACV Command History, 1971, Volume II, x–16 (National Archives Records Group 472).

167. For official statistics, see U.S. House of Representatives, Committee on Armed Services, *Alleged Drug Abuse in the Armed Services: Hearings by Special Subcommittee on Alleged Drug Abuse in the Armed Services*, 91st Cong., 2nd sess., 1970–1971, 1307–8 and 1781–4 (U.S. Navy) and 1496–8 and 1799–1806 (U.S. Air Force).

168. Charles R. Smith, *U.S. Marines in Vietnam: High Mobility and Standdown 1969* (Washington D.C.: History and Museums Division, Headquarters, U.S. Marine Corps, 1988), 157.

169. *United States v. Garcia* (CM 426050).

170. CID Report of Investigation 70-CID058–40242 (U.S. Army Crime Records Center); 18th Military Police Brigade, Assistant Chief of Staff for Operations (S-3), Daily Journal, May 1970, Serious Incident Report 2–86 (Terminal), 16 May 1970 (National Archives Records Group 472).

171. 1st MP Battalion, Command Chronology, January 1971 (U.S. Marine Corps History Division).

172. 18th Military Police Brigade, Assistant Chief of Staff for Operations (S-3), Daily Journal, January 1971, Serious Incident Report 1–172, 13 January 1971 (National Archives Records Group 472).

173. U.S. House of Representatives, Committee on Internal Security, *Investigation of Attempts to Subvert the United States Armed Services: Hearings Before the Committee on Internal Security*, 92nd Cong., 2nd sess., 1972, part 3, 7348.

174. Thomas C. Bond, "The Why of Fragging," *American Journal of Psychiatry* 131 (11 November 1976), 1329.

175. Larry H. Ingraham, "'The Nam' and 'The World': Heroin Use by U.S. Army Enlisted Men Serving in Vietnam," *Psychiatry* 37 (2 May 1974), 123.

176. *United States v. Boyd* (CM 424834).

177. *United States v. Harris* (SPCM 6674).

178. See, for example, *United States v. Lilly* (CM 428548) and *United States v. Pickrum* (CM 424228).

179. CID Report of Investigation 70-CID658–43561–5H1 (U.S. Army Crime Records Center).

180. 18th Military Police Brigade, Installation Stockade, Individual Correction Records, PFC Richard W. Buckingham and SP4 Richard O. Strain (National Archives Records Group 472).

181. U.S. Army Provost Marshal, Long Binh/Bien Hoa, Military Police Desk Blotter, 12 April 1971 (National Archives Records Group 472). Army records indicate that there were actually *two* assaults on Sergeant Vega: the first took place on 8 April, the second on 11 April.

182. *United States v. Buckingham* (CM 423495).

183. Ruben Castaneda, "Judge Orders Killer's Release," *Washington Post*, 27 October 1999, B1.

184. David Binder, "Army Court Told of Racial Tension," *New York Times*, 28 October 1970, 15.

185. *United States v. Breckenridge* (CM 427003).

186. Lieutenant Commander Vernon J. Vawter, U.S. Navy, and Captain Larry C. Tasby, USMCR, to Commanding Officer, U.S. Naval Ammunition Depot, Hawthorne, Nevada, "Investigation to Inquire into the Circumstances Connected with the Incident Which Occurred in the Vicinity of Building 64, Industrial Area Garage, on Thursday, 6 May 1971" (Department of Veterans Affairs); Charles H. Henderson and Charles E. Bauer, Jr., military personnel records (National Personnel Records Center); Department of Justice, Federal Bureau of Investigation, Las Vegas File 100–1161, "Charles Henry Henderson" (Las Vegas, Nevada, Field Office).

187. Co B, 502d MI Bn, EUSA MI Gp (Prov), "Investigation of Incident Involving Damage to CH-47 Helicopter #66–118 at Camp Humphreys, Korea, 23 May 1971," 9 June 1971 (National Archives Records Group 550).

188. U.S. House of Representatives, Committee on Armed Services, *Inquiry into Alleged Drug Abuse in the Armed Services: Report of a Special Subcommittee of the Committee on Armed Services*, 91st Cong., 2nd sess., 23 April 1971, 2184.

189. "GI Justice in Vietnam: An Interview with the Lawyers Military Defense Committee," *Yale Review of Law and Social Action* 2, no. 1 (Fall 1971), 36.

190. CINCUSARPAC to USARV and other commands, "GI International Strike, 15 April 1970" (U), 11 April 1970 (National Archives Records Group 472); David Cortright, *Soldiers in Revolt: The American Military Today* (Garden City: Anchor Press/Doubleday, 1975), 66.

191. U.S. House of Representatives, Committee on Internal Security, *Investigation of Attempts to Subvert the United States Armed Services: Hearings Before the Committee on Internal Security*, 92nd Cong., 2nd sess., 1972, part 3, 7500.

192. "Another Lifer Dropped from the Rolls," *Bond* 4, no. 12 (16 December 1970), 5.

193. Mark Allen, "The Case of Billy Dean Smith," *Black Scholar*, October 1972, 15.

194. U.S. House of Representatives, Committee on Internal Security, *Investigation of Attempts to Subvert the United States Armed Services: Hearings Before the Committee on Internal Security*, 92nd Cong., 2nd sess., 1972), part 3, 7374.

195. BG J. R. Burton, ADC-A, 1st Cavalry Division, to LTG Michael Davison, CG, IIFFV, 11 November 1970 (American Soldier Files, U.S. Army Center of Military History).

196. CID Report of Investigation 70-CID158–53927 (U.S. Army Crime Records Center).

197. 18th Military Police Brigade, Assistant Chief of Staff for Operations (S-3), Daily Journal, November 1970, Serious Incident Report 11–175, 12 November 1970 (National Archives Records Group 472).

198. BG J. R. Burton, ADC-A, 1st Cavalry Division, to LTG Michael Davison, CG, IIFFV, 11 November 1970 (American Soldier Files, U.S. Army Center of Military History).

199. William H. Brown, Jr., Jeffery J. Fryer, Garen P. Thibodeaux, and Michael S. Vanderberg military personnel records (National Personnel Records Center); 18th Military Police Brigade, Installation Stockade, Individual Correction Record, SP4 Jeffery J. Fryer (National Archives Records Group 472); *United States v. Brown* (CM 425575).

200. *United States v. Ridgway* (CM 423533).

201. *United States v. Blaylock* (CM 425319).

202. CID Report of Investigation 66–20292-HOMU/ASAG-27 (U.S. Army Crime Records Center); *United States v. Baldwin* (CM 415536).

203. 25th Infantry Division, Provost Marshal, Military Police Desk Blotter, 24 February 1967 (National Archives Records Group 472).

204. Frank Contreras military personnel record (National Personnel Records Center).

205. CID Report of Investigation GP-(USARV-87th)-66–129 (U.S. Army Crime Records Center).

206. "South Viet Nam: Rising Resentment of the U.S.," *Time*, 24 October 1969, 28; Larry H. Ingraham, "'The Nam' and 'The World': Heroin Use by U.S. Army Enlisted Men Serving in Vietnam," *Psychiatry* 37 (2 May 1974), 120.

207. Charles C. Moskos, Jr., *The American Enlisted Man: The Rank and File in Today's Military* (New York: Russell Sage Foundation, 1970), 151.

208. Guenter Lewy, *America in Vietnam* (New York: Oxford University Press, 1978), 95–107.

209. Headquarters, 18th Military Police Brigade, "Police Information Report August 1971," 12 November 1971 (National Archives Records Group 472); Brigadier Edwin H. Simmons, ADC 1st Marine Division, Orientation Talk for Newly Joined Junior Officers, Vietnam, 10 January 1971, 38–39 [*Marines and Military Law in Vietnam* backup files (National Archives Records Group 127)]; "Vietnam Riot: Anti-G.I. Feelings Boil Over," *New York Times*, 14 December 1970, 1. For numerous reports regarding these incidents, see the records of USARV, Deputy Chief of Staff, Operations, Plans, and Security, Civil-Military Operations Division and 18th Military Police Brigade, Assistant Chief of Staff for Operations (S-3), Daily Journal (National Archives Records Group 472).

210. MACV Command History, 1968, Volume 2, 836 (National Archives Records Group 472).

211. 18th Military Police Brigade, Assistant Chief of Staff for Operations (S-3), Daily Journal, March 1969 (National Archives Records Group 472). See also David H. Hackworth, *About Face: The Odyssey of an American Warrior* (New York: Touchstone, 1989), 693.

212. Captain George A. Kiesel, USMC, to Commanding Officer, 3d Combined Action Group, III Marine Amphibious Force, "Investigation: Death of PFC Thomas J. Mead, 2494145, USMC, and the Wounding of CPL Gregory M. Witt, 2355440, USMC, on 3 June 1969," 8 June 1969 (Department of the Navy, Office of the Judge Advocate General).

213. CID Report of Investigation ROI 69-CID548–38261 (U.S. Army Crime Records Center). The three ARVN officers, Lieutenant Colonel Can and Captains Do Ngoc Nuoi and Pham Van Bach, were eventually charged with killing the Americans, and appeared before a South Vietnamese court in December 1969. After hearing the case, the five-man panel of judges declined to issue a verdict and ordered that a new investigation of the incident be made, but no further action was ever taken. Colonel Can was subsequently killed in action during the Battle of An Loc in June 1972. "3 S. Viet Officers on Trial in Saigon Slaying of 2 GIs," *Stars and Stripes*, 18 December 1969, 4; Richard Pyle, "Saigon Unit Leapfrogged to Positions," *Sheboygan Press*, 30 June 1972, 12.

214. 18th Military Police Brigade, Assistant Chief of Staff for Operations (S-3), Daily Journal, April 1970, Serious Incident Report 4–198 (Supplemental #1), 24 April 1970 (National Archives Records Group 472).

215. USARV, Provost Marshal, "Fragging Incidents, 1969 and 1970," 1971 Study (U.S. Army Crime Records Center).

216. See, for example, D. Bruce Bell and Thomas J. Houston, *The Vietnam Era Deserter: Characteristics of Unconvicted Army Deserters Participating in the Presidential Clemency Program* (Alexandria, Va.: Army Research Institute for the Behavioral Sciences, 1976), 29. The authors of this study wrote, "For most participants (87%), desertion was a means to an end, personal rather than political." Academic G. David Curry reached a similar conclusion: "Outspoken, ideologically astute resistors of American imperialism are as common to the evening news as they are uncommon to the population of Vietnam offenders." See G. David Curry, *Sunshine Patriots:*

Punishment and the Vietnam Offender (Notre Dame: University of Notre Dame Press, 1985), 24.

CHAPTER FOUR

1. Headquarters, Department of the Army, *Field Manual 22–100: Military Leadership* (Washington D.C.: Department of the Army, 1965), 11.

2. Letter to the author from General William C. Westmoreland, USA (Ret.), 23 January 1995.

3. For a list of the fragging incidents that occurred in the 3d Marine Division's area of operations between January and August 1969, see *United States v. Smith* (NCM 70–0500).

4. Headquarters, 3d Marine Division (Rein), Division Order 5370.4, "Standing Operating Procedures for Apprehension of Individuals Involved in Acts of Violence Towards Members of this Command," 4 July 1969 [*Marines and Military Law in Vietnam* backup files (National Archives Records Group 127)].

5. Brigadier Edwin H. Simmons, ADC 1st Marine Division, Orientation Talk for Newly Joined Junior Officers, Vietnam, 10 January 1971, 25 [*Marines and Military Law in Vietnam* backup files (National Archives Records Group 127)].

6. Graham Cosmas and Terrence P. Murray, *U.S. Marines in Vietnam: Vietnamization and Redeployment 1970–1971* (Washington D.C.: History and Museums Division, Headquarters, U.S. Marine Corps, 1986), 364; III Marine Amphibious Force, Command Chronology, July 1970 (U.S. Marine Corps History Division).

7. 1st Marine Division/3d Marine Amphibious Brigade, Commanding General's Information Notebook, "Fragging Incidents, Calendar Years 1970/1971," 10 April 1971 [appended to the 3d Marine Amphibious Brigade Command Chronology, 14–30 April 1971, G-1–5h (U.S. Marine Corps History Division)].

8. U.S. House of Representatives, Committee on Armed Services, *Alleged Drug Abuse in the Armed Services: Hearings by Special Subcommittee on Alleged Drug Abuse in the Armed Services*, 91st Cong., 2nd sess., 1970–1971, 1918–19.

9. USARV, Inspector General, Investigation and Complaint Division, Reports of Investigation Case Files, "Report of Investigation Concerning Alleged Fragging Incidents in the 1st Battalion, 7th Cavalry Rear Area," 28 February 1970 (National Archives Records Group 472).

10. Ibid.

11. AVII-JA to Deputy Commanding General, USARV, "Pretrial Confinement," 19 August 1971 (National Archives Records Group 472).

12. USARV, Inspector General, Investigation and Complaint Division, Reports of Investigation Case Files, "Report of Investigation Concerning Racial and Other Incidents Within the 1st Battalion, 7th Cavalry, 1st Cavalry Division (AM)," 19 July 1970 (National Archives Records Group 472); *United States v. Stevenson* (CM 424913).

13. Department of the Army, Headquarters, USARV, "Reduction of Noncombat Grenade and Firearm Incidents," 2 September 1970 (National Archives Records Group 472).

14. *United States v. Boyd* (CM 424834).

15. Commanding General, XXIV Corps, to Commanding General, 23d Infantry Division, "Crimes of Violence," 18 December 1970 (National Archives Records Group 472).

16. Entries in the division's military police desk blotter alternately refer to the group as "the interrogation team," "the interview team," "the investigation team," "S.H.I.T.," etc.

17. Letter to the author from Verner N. Pike, 8 July 1995.

18. MG James L. Baldwin to Deputy Commanding General, USARV, "Shooting and Grenade Incidents," 20 April 1971 (National Archives Records Group 472). See also John Durham, "Crackdown on 'Fragging' Started," *Pacific Stars and Stripes*, 14 January 1971, 7.

19. Commanding General, 173d Airborne Brigade, to Commanding General, USARV, "Draft USARV Circular Number 190–3, 'Control Over Firearms and Dangerous Weapons,'" 30 April 1971 (National Archives Records Group 472).

20. Commanding General, 173d Airborne Brigade to Commanding General, USARV, "Issue and Control of Fragmentation Grenades," 6 May 1971 (National Archives Records Group 472).

21. U.S. House of Representatives, Committee on Armed Services, *Alleged Drug Abuse in the Armed Services: Hearings by Special Subcommittee on Alleged Drug Abuse in the Armed Services*, 91st Cong., 2nd sess., 1970–1971, 1928.

22. Department of the Army to CINCUSARPAC, "Grenade Incidents in Vietnam," 29 January 1971 (National Archives Records Group 472).

23. AVHDP to CofS, "Reduction of 'Fragging' Incidents," 5 February 1971 (National Archives Records Group 472).

24. Vietnam Interview Tape 873: Interview with COL Walter H. Root, Jr., ADCSP&A, USARV (U.S. Army Center of Military History).

25. AVHDP to CofS, "Reduction of 'Fragging' Incidents," 5 February 1971 (National Archives Records Group 472).

26. AVHCS, Memorandum for the Chief of Staff, "'Fragging' Incidents," 5 February 1971 (National Archives Records Group 472).

27. Chief, Intelligence and Security Division, to ADCSOPS, "Fragging," 10 February 1971 (National Archives Records Group 472).

28. AVHDP to CofS and DCG, "Reduction of 'Fragging' Incidents," Tab B (DCSOPS Comments), 5 February 1971 (National Archives Records Group 472).

29. AVHDP-MMW to CofS and DCG, "USARV Cir 190–30 (Shooting and Grenade Incidents)," 11 May 1971 (National Archives Records Group 472).

30. Routing Slip and Record of Action, "USARV Cir 190–3 (Shooting and Grenade Incidents)," 9 May 1971 (National Archives Records Group 472).

31. Commanding General, 173d Airborne Brigade, to Commanding General, USARV, "Draft USARV Circular Number 190–3, 'Control Over Firearms and Dangerous Weapons,'" 30 April 1971 (National Archives Records Group 472).

32. For two examples, see CG, 23d Inf Div, to CG, USARV, "Draft USARV Cir 190–3," 30 April 1971, and AVFA-CS to CG, USARV, "USARV Draft Circular 190–3, Control Over Firearms and Dangerous Weapons," undated (National Archives Records Group 472).

33. COMUSMACV to VMAC, "Use of the Term 'Fragging,'" 6 May 1971 (National Archives Records Group 472).

34. 18th Military Police Brigade, Assistant Chief of Staff for Operations (S-3), Daily Journal, June 1971, Serious Incident Report 6–380, 18 June 1971 (National Archives Records Group 472).

35. 18th Military Police Brigade, Assistant Chief of Staff for Operations (S-3), Daily Journal, June 1971, Serious Incident Report 6–410, 19 June 1971 (National Archives Records Group 472).

36. Transcript of USARV Commanders' Conference, 8 July 1971 [Vietnam Interview Tape 942 (U.S. Army Center of Military History)].

37. Report of unknown provenance, "Assaults/Possible Assaults w/ Explosive Devices, CY 71" (National Archives Records Group 472).

38. LTG William J. McCaffrey to General Creighton W. Abrams, 9 No-

vember 1971 (National Archives Records Group 472). See also Headquarters, 18th Military Police Brigade, "Police Information Report August 1971," 12 November 1971 (National Archives Records Group 472).

39. 18th Military Police Brigade, Assistant Chief of Staff for Operations (S-3), Daily Journal, June–December 1971 (National Archives Records Group 472); USARV, Provost Marshal, to various offices, "Demographic Analysis of Fragging Incidents," 1 April 1972 (National Archives Records Group 472).

40. Letter to the author from Samuel S. Vitucci, 11 August 1997.

41. CID Report of Investigation ROI 71-CID648–49838 (U.S. Army Crime Records Center).

42. CID Report of Investigation ROI 72-CID448–50865 (U.S. Army Crime Records Center).

43. AVHDP-MMW to PM, "Control Over Firearms and Dangerous Weapons," 12 June 1971 (National Archives Records Group 472).

44. AVHDP-MMW to DCS P&A, "CBS Request for USARV Circular 190–30," undated (National Archives Records Group 472).

45. Routing and Transmittal Slip attached to AVHDP-MMW to DCS P&A, "CBS Request for USARV Circular 190–30," 27 June 1971 (National Archives Records Group 472).

46. AVHDP-MMW to CofS and DCG, "Analysis of 'Fraggings,'" 16 February 1972, AVHDP-MPD to DCS P&A, "Analysis of Fraggings," 6 July 1972 (National Archives Records Group 472). These documents and General Westmoreland's trip itinerary indicate that the fragging discussion took place at USARV Headquarters on 27 January [Westmoreland Papers at the Center of Military History, 1962–1972, Folder 497 (National Archives Records Group 319)].

47. USARV Chief of Staff to USARV Deputy Commanding General, 22 February 1972 (National Archives Records Group 472).

48. BG Gard, DAPE-HR, DCSPER, to COL Von Der Bruegge, USARV, DCSP&A, "Assaults with Explosive Devices Study," 30 August 1972 (National Archives Records Group 472).

49. James S. White, "Race Relations in the Army," *Military Review* 50, no. 7 (July 1970), 4–12.

50. MACV Command History, 1971, Volume II, pages X-11–X-15 (National Archives Records Group 472).

51. Gary D. Solis, *Marines and Military Law in Vietnam: Trial By Fire*

(Washington D.C.: History and Museums Division, Headquarters, U.S. Marine Corps, 1989), 171.

52. Lieutenant Colonel James S. White, "Briefing for Seminars on Racial Tension and Equal Opportunity" (National Archives Records Group 472).

53. U.S. House of Representatives, Committee on Armed Services, *Inquiry into the Disturbances at Marine Corps Base, Camp Lejeune, N.C., on July 20, 1969: Report of the Special Subcommittee to Probe Disturbances on Military Bases*, 91st Cong., 1st sess., December 15, 1969, 5051.

54. Charles R. Smith, *U.S. Marines in Vietnam: High Mobility and Stand-down 1969* (Washington D.C.: History and Museums Division, Headquarters, U.S. Marine Corps, 1988), 156–57.

55. MACV Command History, 1968, Volume II, page 839 (National Archives Records Group 472).

56. Courtney L. Frobenius, "Ewell's Killing Machine: Part II," unpublished monograph, undated.

57. MACV Command History, 1969, Volume III, xiv–6 (National Archives Records Group 472).

58. MACV Command History, 1970, Volume II, pages xii–6 (U.S. Army Center of Military History).

59. U.S. House of Representatives, Committee on Armed Forces, *Alleged Drug Abuse in the Armed Services: Hearings by Special Subcommittee on Alleged Drug Abuse in the Armed Services*, 91st Cong., 2nd sess., 1970–1971, 1928–29; Alvin M. Shuster, "G.I. Heroin Addiction Epidemic in Vietnam," *New York Times*, 16 May 1971, 1; Craig R. Whitney, "Pleiku Center for Addicts Source of Dispute," *New York Times*, 19 May 1971, 6.

60. Department of the Army, Public Information Division, News Branch, "Query—Drugs," 8 June 1971 (National Archives Records Group 319).

61. MACV Command History, 1971, Volume II, pages X-16–X-21 (National Archives Records Group 472); C. L. Sulzberger, "General Abrams Says Addiction in Vietnam is Down and Morale Up," *New York Times*, 26 February 1972, 1–2.

62. U.S. House of Representatives, Committee on Armed Services, *Inquiry into Alleged Drug Abuse in the Armed Services: Report of a Special Subcommittee of the Committee on Armed Services*, 91st Cong., 2nd sess., 23 April 1971, 2226.

63. Ibid., 2161; Gary D. Solis, *Marines and Military Law in Vietnam: Trial By Fire* (Washington D.C.: History and Museums Division, Headquarters, U.S. Marine Corps, 1989), 171.

64. Henry Kamm, "Drive Fails to Halt Drug Sale in Vietnam," *New York Times*, 30 August 1971, 1.

65. U.S. House of Representatives, Committee on Armed Services, *Inquiry into Alleged Drug Abuse in the Armed Services: Report of a Special Subcommittee of the Committee on Armed Services*, 91st Cong., 2nd sess., 23 April 1971, 2226.

66. Gary D. Solis, *Marines and Military Law in Vietnam: Trial By Fire* (Washington D.C.: History and Museums Division, Headquarters, U.S. Marine Corps, 1989), 171.

67. Brigadier Edwin H. Simmons, ADC 1st Marine Division, Orientation Talk for Newly Joined Junior Officers, Vietnam, 10 January 1971, 25–28 [*Marines and Military Law in Vietnam* backup files (National Archives Records Group 127)].

68. Graham A. Cosmas and Terrence P. Murray, *U.S. Marines in Vietnam: Vietnamization and Redeployment 1970–1971* (Washington D.C.: History and Museums Division, Headquarters, U.S. Marine Corps, 1986), 363.

69. Department of the Army, Public Information Division, News Branch, "Query—Personnel," 12 July 1971 (National Archives Records Group 319).

70. Army CID was reorganized twice during the war. Originally known as the U.S. Army Criminal Investigation Division, it became the U.S. Army Criminal Investigation Agency in 1969 and finally the U.S. Army Criminal Investigation Command (USACIDC) in September 1971. Despite these changes, the investigators and their parent organization were (and are) universally known as simply CID and I have followed suit in the text. Department of the Army, Office of the Chief of Public Information, News Release, "Formation of the U.S. Army Criminal Investigation Command," 17 September 1971 (National Archives Records Group 319).

71. Letter to the author from Robert F. Coucoules, 7 April 1995. See also CID Reports of Investigation 68-CID448–60470 and 69-CID448–36777 (U.S. Army Crime Records Center).

72. Letter to the author from Robert F. Coucoules, 7 April 1995.

73. Letter to the author from John Fay, 8 May 1995.

74. See, for example, CID Reports of Investigation 69-CID958–41529, 70-CID348–36264, and 70-CID258–43305 (U.S. Army Crime Records Center); Major Dale D. Dorman, USMC, Headquarters and Service Company, 2d Battalion, 1st Marines, to Commanding Officer, "Investigation into the Circumstances Surrounding the Deaths of Private First Class G.E. Butler, USMC, Corporal W.M. Stevenson, USMC, Corporal G.C. Shuey, USMC, and Injuries to Private First Class L.D. Florang, USMC, and Lance Corporal J.N. Buchanon, USMC, all of Company F, 2d Battalion, 1st Marines," 29 December 1969 (Department of the Navy, Office of the Judge Advocate General). The incidents examined in these reports alone account for twelve deaths.

75. U.S. House of Representatives, Subcommittee of the Committee on Appropriations, *Department of Defense Appropriations for 1972*, 92nd Cong., 1st sess., 1971, part 9, 583.

76. See, for example, *United States v. Chambers* (NCM 69–3501).

77. CID Report of Investigation 68-CID348–60148 (U.S. Army Crime Records Center).

78. First Lieutenant Wayne H. Brandon, USMCR, to Commanding Officer, 3d Battalion, 5th Marines, "Investigation Inquiring into the Circumstances Surrounding the Death of First Sergeant William R. Hunt, 652761, USMC," 19 April 1968 (Department of the Navy, Office of the Judge Advocate General).

79. CID Report of Investigation 71-CID958–52279 (U.S. Army Crime Records Center).

80. *United States v. Hanley* (CM 424091).

81. CID Report of Investigation 70-CID658–43561–5H1 (U.S. Army Crime Records Center). For another case in which inclement weather hampered a murder investigation, see CID Report of Investigation 70-CID648–54222 (U.S. Army Crime Records Center).

82. Graham A. Cosmas and Terrence P. Murray, *U.S. Marines in Vietnam: Vietnamization and Redeployment 1970–1971* (Washington D.C.: History and Museums Division, Headquarters, U.S. Marine Corps, 1986), 364.

83. Letter to the author from John Fay, 8 May 1995.

84. Morris Janowitz, "Cohesion and Disintegration in the Wehrmacht," in James Burk, *On Social Organization and Social Control* (Chicago: University of Chicago Press, 1991), 165.

85. Letter to the author from Stephen G. Fairman, 1 April 1997.

86. Letter to the author from William Marrow-El, 11 August 1997.

87. USARV Regulation 633–1 governed army pretrial confinement in Vietnam. It recommended that the practice was to be reserved for "exceptional cases": (1) for perpetrators of serious acts of violence, such as murder, rape, robbery, or aggravated assault; (2) to prevent further acts of violence committed either by or against the suspect; (3) to ensure the presence of an individual who had violated moral restraining measures before an investigation or trial. While these guidelines seem to include fraggers, this was not always the case. "The mere communication of a threat does not justify confinement," commanders were told (USARV, Inspector General, Investigation and Complaint Division, Reports of Investigation Case Files, "Report of Investigation Concerning Alleged Fragging Incidents in the 1st Battalion, 7th Cavalry Rear Area," 28 February 1970 (National Archives Records Group 472). See also Ronald H. Spector, "The Vietnam War and the Army's Self-Image," *Second Indochina Symposium*, ed. John Schlight (Washington D.C.: U.S. Army Center of Military History, 1986), 173–74.

88. *United States v. Boyd* (CM 424834).

89. *United States v. Aubert* (CM 427892).

90. *United States v. Barrios* (NCM 70–1408).

91. Commanding General, III Marine Amphibious Force, Force Order 3120.4, "Standard Operating Procedure for Investigation of Acts of Violence Towards Members of this Command When Such Acts Occur in Camp or Cantonment," 14 August 1970; 1st Marine Division/3d Marine Amphibious Brigade, Commanding General's Information Notebook, "Fragging Incidents, Calendar Years 1970/1971," 10 April 1971 [appended to the 3d Marine Amphibious Brigade Command Chronology, 14–30 April 1971, G-1–5h (U.S. Marine Corps History Division)].

92. Charles J. Levy, *Spoils of War* (Boston: Houghton Mifflin, 1974), 45.

93. U.S. House of Representatives, Committee on Armed Forces, *Alleged Drug Abuse in the Armed Services: Hearings by Special Subcommittee on Alleged Drug Abuse in the Armed Services*, 91st Cong., 2nd sess., 1970–1971, 1928.

94. USARV, Provost Marshal, Physical Security Branch, 1972 Serious Incident Reports (National Archives Records Group 472).

95. *United States v. Crampton* (CM 426570).

96. *United States v. Elliot* (CM 426967).

97. *United States v. Fitzgerald* (CM 426222).

98. *United States v. Hurley* (NCM 67–2575).

99. CID Report of Investigation 70-CID958–43687 (U.S. Army Crime Records Center).

100. *United States v. McCracken* (CM 423370).

101. *United States v. Peterson* (CM 425057).

102. *United States v. Shirley* (CM 422317).

103. *United States v. Spears* (CM 425344).

104. *United States v. Strate* (CM 427295).

105. *United States v. Thompson* (CM 427004).

106. Letter to the author from Joseph M. Kralich, 13 June 1995.

107. See, for example, *United States v. Fowler* (NCM 70–3599).

108. *United States v. Crampton* (CM 421207).

109. *United States v. Napier* (NCM 70–1453).

110. *United States v. Smith* (CM 429555).

111. Letter to the author from Gary L. Noller, 19 February 1996.

112. *United States v. Perry* (CM 424936).

113. Letter to the author from Richard M. Magner, 5 September 1995.

114. Walter Chambers, Jr., military personnel record (National Personnel Records Center).

115. CID Report of Investigation 70-CID658–43561–5H1 (U.S. Army Crime Records Center).

116. CID Report of Investigation 68-CID348–60141 (U.S. Army Crime Records Center).

117. CID Report of Investigation 70-CID648–54222 (U.S. Army Crime Records Center).

118. 101st Airborne Division (Airmobile), Provost Marshal, Military Police Desk Blotter, 15 March 1969 and 3 April 1969 (National Archives Records Group 472).

119. Headquarters, 101st Airborne Division, General Orders, Number 5864, 27 May 1969 (National Archives Records Group 472).

120. Letter to the author from John Fay, 8 May 1995.

121. CID Report of Investigation 70-CID958–43687 (U.S. Army Crime Records Center).

122. 23d Infantry Division (Americal), Provost Marshal, Military Police Reports of Investigation, 1971 (National Archives Records Group 472).

123. Papers of John J. Pershing, Entry NM1023, Box 1: List of Officers, Soldiers, and Others Convicted by General Court-martial in the American Expeditionary Forces (AEF), June 8, 1917–August 20, 1919 (National Archives Records Group 200).

124. "Inmate Unrest," Topical File, Series B, Box 2, United States Disciplinary Barracks Collection (Combined Arms Research Library, U.S. Army Command and General Staff College, Fort Leavenworth, Kansas).

125. "Communist Infiltration of the U.S. Armed Forces, 1920–1950" (National Archives Records Group 319).

126. DD Form 98.

127. AVHGA-P for DCSPER, "Assignment of PV2 Mark Yoffe Liberman," 25 June 1970 (National Archives Records Group 472); Mark Y. Liberman military personnel record (National Personnel Records Center).

128. U.S. House of Representatives, Committee on Internal Security, *Investigation of Attempts to Subvert the United States Armed Services: Hearings Before the Committee on Internal Security*, 92nd Cong., 2nd sess., 1972, part 3, 7222; John D. Fink military personnel record (National Personnel Records Center).

129. U.S. House of Representatives, Committee on Internal Security, *Investigation of Attempts to Subvert the United States Armed Services: Hearings Before the Committee on Internal Security*, 92nd Cong., 2nd sess., 1972, part 3, 7320.

130. CG 25th Inf Div to CG USARV, "Dissidence in the Army," 30 July 1970 (National Archives Records Group 472).

131. U.S. House of Representatives, Committee on Internal Security, *Investigation of Attempts to Subvert the United States Armed Services: Hearings Before the Committee on Internal Security*, 92nd Cong., 2nd sess., 1972, part 3, 7045.

132. AVHGB-C to USARPAC and MACV, "Dissidents in the Army," 4 April 1970 (National Archives Records Group 472).

133. CGUSASIX to RUEADWD/ACSI DA, "Dissidents in the Army— Spot Report No. AMINT-J2-3-70," 9 March 1970 (National Archives Records Group 472). For an account of the Isla Vista violence, see Winthrop Griffith, "The Isla Vista War—Campus Violence in a Class by Itself," *New York Times Magazine*, 31 August 1970, 10.

134. MG George L. Mabry, Jr., to various commanders, "Black Panther Party," 28 April 1970 (National Archives Records Group 472).

135. CG 25th Inf Div. to USARV, "Dean, Howard M., Jr.," 23 September 1970 (National Archives Records Group 472); Howard M. Dean, Jr., military personnel record (National Personnel Records Center). Following his discharge, Dean returned to his native Los Angeles and was shot to death in December 1973.

136. William C. Westmoreland and George S. Prugh, "Judges in Command: The Judicialized Uniform Code of Military Justice in Combat," *Harvard Journal of Law and Public Policy* 3, no. 1 (1980), 8–15.

137. George S. Prugh, *Vietnam Studies, Law at War: Vietnam 1964–1973* (Washington D.C.: Department of the Army, 1975), 98, 100.

138. "GI Justice in Vietnam: An Interview with the Lawyers Military Defense Committee," *Yale Review of Law and Social Action* 2, no.1 (Fall 1971), 32.

139. *United States v. Oaks* (CM 427752).

140. *United States v. Mycko* (CM 428325).

141. For one notable example, see *United States v. Harris* (NCM 70–2331).

142. "GI Justice in Vietnam: An Interview with the Lawyers Military Defense Committee," *Yale Review of Law and Social Action* 2, no.1 (Fall 1971), 31.

143. Correspondence between several naval officials and Representatives Herman Badillo and John Conyers, Jr. (National Archives Records Group 125); Walter Chambers, Jr., military personnel record (National Personnel Records Center).

144. *United States v. Boyd* (CM 424834).

145. John Jay Douglass, "The Judicialization of Military Courts," *Hastings Law Journal* 22 (January 1971), 222.

146. See *United States v. Hendrix* (NCM 71–2473) and *United States v. Smith* (NCM 70–0500).

147. *United States v. Smith* (CM 429555).

148. Gary D. Solis, *Marines and Military Law in Vietnam: Trial By Fire* (Washington D.C.: History and Museums Division, Headquarters, U.S. Marine Corps, 1989), 125.

149. John Jay Douglass, "The Judicialization of Military Courts," *Hastings Law Journal* 22 (January 1971), 220–23.

150. "The Young Peers of Long Binh," *Time*, 8 November 1971, 81, 83; Joseph Remcho, "Military Juries: Constitutional Analysis and the Need for Reform," *Indiana Law Journal* 47, no. 2 (Winter 1972).

151. *United States v. Woodmancy* (CM 425594); author's interview with Joseph Remcho, 20 September 2002.

152. Letter from W. Hays Parks to LtCol Gary D. Solis, USMC, 22 December 1988 [*Marines and Military Law in Vietnam* backup files, Box 1 (National Archives Records Group 127)].

153. Reginald F. Smith federal inmate record (U.S. Department of Justice, Federal Bureau of Prisons, Kansas City, Kansas); letter to the author from the Federal Bureau of Prisons, 18 June 2008; *United States v. Hendrix* (NCM 71–2374); *United States v. Sutton* (CM 423094).

154. Gary D. Solis, *Marines and Military Law in Vietnam: Trial By Fire* (Washington D.C.: History and Museums Division, Headquarters, U.S. Marine Corps, 1989), 240.

155. *United States v. Johnson* (CM 429456). For other fragging convictions that were subsequently overturned at the appellate level, see *United States v. Benoit* (CM 422738), *United States v. Culver* (NCM 70–1681), *United States v. Dolan* (NCM 67–1090), *United States v. Fitzgerald* (CM 426222), *United States v. Hart* (CM 416145), *United States v. Paro* (NCM 70–1774), *United States v. Smith* (NCM 70–1098), and *United States v. Thomas* (NCM 69–4053). Of these reversals, only Benoit, Culver, Hart, and Thomas were retried. Benoit, Hart, and Thomas were reconvicted and returned to confinement. Culver too was reconvicted but this second guilty verdict was also overturned on appeal and the charge dismissed. Culver, Dolan, Fitzgerald, Paro, and Smith were all subsequently restored to duty in their respective services.

156. *United States v. Creek* (CM 426724).

157. *United States v. Fowler* (NCM 70–3599); letter to the author from the Federal Bureau of Prisons, 18 June 2008.

158. Robert S. Rivkin, *GI Rights and Army Justice: The Draftee's Guide to Military Life and Law* (New York: Grove Press, 1970), 331.

159. 555 F. 2d 785 (1977).

160. *United States v. Garcia* (CM 426969); Ignacio Garcia, Jr., military personnel record (National Personnel Records Center).

161. *United States v. Benoit* (CM 422738).

162. *United States v. Sutton* (CM 423094); letter to the author from the Federal Bureau of Prisons, 24 June 2008.

163. William C. Westmoreland and George S. Prugh, "Judges in Command: The Judicialized Uniform Code of Military Justice in Combat," *Harvard Journal of Law and Public Policy* 3, no. 1 (1980), 67.

164. CINCPAC to CJCS, "Mission Accomplishment and Military Discipline," 19 July 1971 [Melvin R. Laird Papers (Washington National Records Center)].

165. For several critical views, see Gary D. Solis, *Marines and Military Law in Vietnam: Trial By Fire* (Washington D.C.: History and Museums Division, Headquarters, U.S. Marine Corps, 1989), 241–43.

166. William C. Westmoreland and George S. Prugh, "Judges in Command: The Judicialized Uniform Code of Military Justice in Combat," *Harvard Journal of Law and Public Policy* 3, no. 1 (1980), 4 and 53, as cited in Gary D. Solis, *Marines and Military Law in Vietnam: Trial By Fire* (Washington D.C.: History and Museums Division, Headquarters, U.S. Marine Corps, 1989), 242.

167. Roger K. Griffith, *The U.S. Army's Transition to the All Volunteer Force, 1968–1974* (Washington D.C.: Center of Military History, 1997), 40–41.

168. "Army Relaxes Hair Rules but Only by a Whisker," *New York Times*, 11 May 1971, 35.

169. U.S. House of Representatives, Subcommittee of the Committee on Appropriations, *Department of Defense Appropriations for 1972*, 92nd Cong., 1st sess., 1971, part 9, 587; Chief, FD Division to ADCSOPS, "Fragging," 8 February 1971 (National Archives Records Group 472).

170. Roger K. Griffith, *The U.S. Army's Transition to the All Volunteer Force, 1968–1974* (Washington D.C.: Center of Military History, 1997), 166, 194.

171. Eugene Linden, "Fragging and Other Withdrawal Symptoms," *Saturday Review*, 8 January 1972, 12.

172. "GI Justice in Vietnam: An Interview with the Lawyers Military Defense Committee," *Yale Review of Law and Social Action* 2, no.1 (Fall 1971), 35.

173. USARV, Inspector General, Investigation and Complaint Division, Reports of Investigation Case Files, "Report of Investigation Concerning Alleged Fragging Incidents in the 1st Battalion, 7th Cavalry Rear Area," 28 February 1970 (National Archives Records Group 472).

174. MG Gettys to MG Cushman, undated message (National Archives Records Group 472).

175. Letter to the author from John "Dutch" DeGroot, 16 June 1995.

176. U.S. House of Representatives, Committee on Armed Forces, *Alleged Drug Abuse in the Armed Services: Hearings by Special Subcommittee on Alleged Drug Abuse in the Armed Services*, 91st Cong., 2nd sess., 1970–1971, 1939.

177. Letter to the author from Theodore C. Mataxis, 6 May 1998.

178. *United States v. Rosine* (SPCM 7887).

179. USARV, Provost Marshal, Physical Security Branch, CID Final Reports of Investigation, 1973, 72-CID448–50865/5H1H (National Archives Records Group 472).

180. LtGen Victor H. Krulak, USMC (Ret.), interview 1973 (Oral History Collection, U.S. Marine Corps History Division).

181. Richard Boyle, *The Flower of the Dragon: The Breakdown of the U.S. Army in Vietnam* (San Francisco: Ramparts Press, 1972), 187.

182. William Shawcross, *Sideshow: Kissinger, Nixon, and the Destruction of Cambodia* (New York: Simon and Schuster, 1979), 191.

183. Letter to the author from Theodore C. Mataxis, 6 May 1998.

184. 18th Military Police Brigade, Assistant Chief of Staff for Operations (S-3), Daily Journal, March 1970, Serious Incident Report 3–234, 17 March 1970 (National Archives Records Group 472); *United States v. Goings* (CM 426050).

185. 18th Military Police Brigade, Assistant Chief of Staff for Operations (S-3), Daily Journal, January 1970, Serious Incident Report 1–137, 12 January 1970 (National Archives Records Group 472); CID Report of Investigation 70-CID448–37047 (U.S. Army Crime Records Center); Thomas J. Vernor military personnel record (National Personnel Records Center). After the shooting, Sergeant Vernor served yet another tour in Vietnam and retired from the army in 1972. In his later years, he was active in several veterans' organizations. He died in 2007.

186. USARV, Inspector General, Investigation and Complaint Division, Reports of Investigation Case Files, "Report of Investigation Concerning the Actions of 1SG McNerney, Co B, 2d Battalion, 8th Cavalry," 28 October 1969 (National Archives Records Group 472).

187. Letter to the author from Frederick A. Drew, 2 April 2002.

188. 25th Infantry Division, Provost Marshal, Military Police Desk Blotter, 10 November 1969 (National Archives Records Group 472); CID Report of Investigation 69-CID458–41820 (U.S. Army Crime Records Center).

189. First Lieutenant John F. Higgins, USMCR, to Commanding Officer, 1st Battalion, 4th Marines, "An Investigation into the Facts and Circumstances Surrounding the Explosion of an M-26 Fragmentation Grenade Resulting in the Death of PFC Yokoi and the Injuries Sustained by LCpl Scruggs, PFC Duncan, Cpl Bowes, PFC Martin, PFC Roberts, LCpl Sykiw, and PFC Staggs which Occurred at Cua Viet R&R Center, Quang Tri Province, RVN on or about 11 July 1969," 20 August 1969 (Department of the Navy, Office of the Judge Advocate General).

190. Several well-known combat refusals were reported in the press. See William H. Hammond, *Public Affairs: The Military and the Media, 1968–1973* (Washington D.C.: Center of Military History, 1996), 193–200. For combat refusals in the Marine Corps, see *United States v. Crout* (NCM 68–1762), *United States v. Davis* (NCM 68–1366), *United States v. Fee* (NCM 68–2656), and *United States v. Krebs* (NCM 68–1594).

191. USARV, Inspector General, Investigation and Complaint Division, Records of Investigations, "Report of Inquiry," 21 November 1968 (National Archives Records Group 472).

192. Robert Eugene Edwards military personnel record (National Personnel Records Center).

193. Charles Hatcher, Clarence L. Jackson, and Ledridge Taylor, Jr., military personnel records (National Personnel Records Center).

194. USARV, Inspector General, Investigation and Complaint Division, Records of Investigations, "Report of Inquiry," 21 November 1968 (National Archives Records Group 472). For a similar incident that occurred in the 9th Infantry Division, in which an NCO shot and wounded a grenade-wielding enlisted man, see 18th Military Police Brigade, Assistant Chief of Staff for Operations (S-3), Daily Journal, September 1968, Serious Incident Report 9–23, 3 September 1969 (National Archives Records Group 472).

195. Roger W. Little, "Buddy Relations and Combat Performance," in Morris Janowitz, ed., *The New Military: Changing Patterns of Organization* (New York: Russell Sage Foundation, 1964), 208.

196. *United States v. Haracivet* (CM 425305). The second case is summarized in David Cortright's book *Soldiers in Revolt: The American Military Today*. The officer in that instance received a suspended sentence.

197. William T. Generous, Jr., *Swords and Scales: The Development of the Uniform Code of Military Justice* (Port Washington: Kennikat Press, 1973), 34.

198. USARV, Inspector General, Investigation and Complaint Division, Reports of Investigation Case Files, "Report of Investigation Concerning Alleged Fragging Incidents in the 1st Battalion, 7th Cavalry Rear Area," 28 February 1970 (National Archives Records Group 472).

199. AVHDP-SPA, "Stockade Interview," 18 February 1971 (National Archives Records Group 472).

200. U.S. House of Representatives, Subcommittee of the Committee on Appropriations, *Department of Defense Appropriations for 1972*, 92nd Cong., 1st sess., 1971, part 3, 473.

201. Jacques van Doorn, *The Soldier and Social Change* (Beverly Hills: Sage Publications, 1975), 99.

202. "Tense GIs Carry Vendettas to Explosive, Dramatic End," *Lima News*, 7 January 1971, 4.

CHAPTER FIVE

1. Peter G. Bourne, *Men, Stress, and Vietnam* (Boston: Little, Brown, 1970), 175–81. Bourne, a psychiatrist, interviewed a large number of Australian officers and men in Vietnam.

2. Ian McNeill, *To Long Tan: The Australian Army and the Vietnam War* (Sydney: Allen & Unwin, 1993), 78.

3. P. G. Edwards, *A Nation at War: Australian Politics, Society and Diplomacy during the Vietnam War 1965–1975* (Sydney: Allen & Unwin, 1997), 49, 75, 158.

4. Ian McNeill and Ashley Ekins, *On the Offensive: The Australian Army in the Vietnam War, January 1967–July 1968* (Sydney: Allen & Unwin, 2003), 303–4.

5. P. G. Edwards, *A Nation at War: Australian Politics, Society and Diplomacy during the Vietnam War 1965–1975* (Sydney: Allen & Unwin, 1997), 369.

6. Ian McNeill and Ashley Ekins, *On the Offensive: The Australian Army in the Vietnam War, January 1967–July 1968* (Sydney: Allen & Unwin, 2003), 497, note 148.

7. P. G. Edwards, *A Nation at War: Australian Politics, Society and Diplomacy during the Vietnam War 1965–1975* (Sydney: Allen & Unwin, 1997), 79, 366.

8. 1 ATF to AUSTFORCE VIETNAM, "Press Report on Drug Usage in SVN" (Australian War Memorial, AWM 103, R271/1/86/1).

9. "Diggers in Vietnam Using Marihuana, Court Told," *Australian*, 3 March 1970, 3.

10. Australian Force Vietnam, "Possession and Use of Drugs," 13 April 1971; HQ 1 ATF, Nui Dat, "Possession and Use of Drugs," 16 May 1971 (Australian War Memorial, AWM 103, R271/1/86/1).

11. Ian McNeill and Ashley Ekins, *On the Offensive: The Australian Army in the Vietnam War, January 1967–July 1968* (Sydney: Allen & Unwin, 2003), 268.

12. Re Feriday's Appeal (21 FLR 86).

13. Trial of Gnr Newman–Re Lt Birse (National Archives of Australia, A471, 94258, Folder 4); Ian McNeill and Ashley Ekins, *On the Offensive: The Australian Army in the Vietnam War, January 1967–July 1968* (Sydney: Allen & Unwin, 2003), 266–67.

14. Det AFV Pro Unit, 1 ATF, Nui Dat to OC SIB, Vung Tau, "Unlawful Explosion Causing Damage to Military and Civilian Property in 1 Fd Sqn, RAE," 24 January 69 (Australian War Memorial, AWM 98, R723/1/129).

15. HQ, AFV, "Report on Unlawful Explosions" dated 10 September 1969 (Australian War Memorial, AWM 103, R478/1/77).

16. Det AFV Pro Unit, 1 ATF, Nui Dat to OC SIB, Vung Tau, "Unlawful Explosion Causing Damage to Military and Civilian Property in 1 Fd Sqn, RAE dated 24 Jan 69" (Australian War Memorial, AWM 98, R723/1/129).

17. HQ, AFV, "Report on Unlawful Explosions," 10 September 1969 (Australian War Memorial, AWM 103, R478/1/77).

18. Department of Defense, Personal Documents Dossier, 38627 R.T. Convery (National Archives of Australia, Series B2458); HQ 1 ATF, Summary of Evidence, 61905 Private Peter Denzil Allen (Australian War Memorial, AWM 103, Control Symbol 629).

19. Department of Defense, Personal Documents Dossier, 61905 P. D. Allen (National Archives of Australia, Series B2458); Transcript of Court-Martial Proceedings Against 61905 Pte P. D. Allen (Australian War Memorial, AWM 103, Control Symbol 631).

20. HQ AFV, DADLS, "Investigation Report into the Death of Lieutenant R.T. Convery—B Coy 9 RAR (Australian War Memorial, AWM 98, Control Symbol 25); Transcript of Court-Martial Proceedings Against

61905 Pte P. D. Allen (Australian War Memorial, AWM 103, Control Symbol 631).

21. Transcript of Court-Martial Proceedings Against 61905 Pte P. D. Allen (Australian War Memorial, AWM 103, Control Symbol 631).

22. Ian McNeill and Ashley Ekins, *On the Offensive: The Australian Army in the Vietnam War, January 1967–July 1968* (Sydney: Allen & Unwin, 2003), 160.

23. Transcript of Court-Martial Proceedings Against 61905 Pte P. D. Allen (Australian War Memorial, AWM 103, Control Symbol 631).

24. Investigation, General, "Unlawful Explosion—Spr F. Denley—1 Fd. Sqn," 19 July 1970 (Australian War Memorial, AWM 103, R478/1/231).

25. Investigation, General, "Unlawful Use of Explosives by Persons Unknown Admin Coy 8 RAR," 22 November 1970 (Australian War Memorial, AWM 103, R478/1/281).

26. For the details of these three incidents, see Australian War Memorial, AWM 98, R723/271/9, AWM 98, R723/271/42, and AWM 103, R478/1/355.

27. Robert A. Hall, *Combat Battalion: The Eighth Battalion in Vietnam* (Sydney: Allen & Unwin, 2000), 228–32.

CHAPTER SIX

1. Reginald F. Smith federal inmate record (U.S. Department of Justice, Federal Bureau of Prisons, Kansas City, Kansas).

2. Federal Bureau of Investigation, SI 70A-1899 (U.S. Department of Justice, Federal Bureau of Investigation Field Office, Springfield, Illinois).

3. Letters from Gary A. Hendrix to Fay Honey Knopp, 28 December 1977, and to Reverend Robert Horton, 15 July 1978 [Swarthmore College Peace Collection, Records of Prison Visitation and Support (DG 223), Box 38].

4. Letter from Gary A. Hendrix to CPT Paul S. Embert, USAF, 30 December 1977 [Swarthmore College Peace Collection, Records of Prison Visitation and Support (DG 223), Box 38].

5. Letter from Gary A. Hendrix to Fay Honey Knopp, 8 October 1984 [Swarthmore College Peace Collection, Records of Prison Visitation and Support (DG 223), Box 38].

6. 66 F.3d 337; letter to the author from the Federal Bureau of Prisons, 6 January 2009.

7. *United States v. Bell* (CM 422276); *The People of the State of New York v. Robert Bell, a.k.a. Robert Woodhull*, Indictment Nos. 45387–76 and 45449–76 (County Court, Nassau County, New York).

8. Philadelphia, Pennsylvania, Police Department, Homicide Record, Case No. H78–369.

9. *The State of Arizona v. Robert Burton Rutledge*, Cause No. CR8707743.

10. "Fantasy 5 Winner Found Dead at Dump, Had Only $10," *Miami Herald*, 6 September 1990, 6B.

11. 349 F.3d 549.

12. *State of Florida v. Kenneth Wayne Chaky*, Case No. 81,325.

13. Robert T. Rohweller military personnel record (National Personnel Records Center).

14. Correspondence between various offices of the Department of the Navy's Office of the Judge Advocate General and Mrs. Vicenta S. Yokoi, 1970 (National Archives Records Group 125).

15. Letter to the author from Edward F. Kelley, 4 December 1995.

16. Letter to the author from G. Miles Davis, 15 December 1995.

17. Letter to the author from Jim Schueckler, 30 May 1996.

18. Letter to the author from Jimmy F. Abbs, 23 September 1996.

19. William R. Willis, Jr., "*Toth v. Quarles*: For Better or for Worse?," *Vanderbilt Law Review* 9 (1956), 534. The old Articles of War did not wield this authority. See "U.S. Arrests Lo Dolce for Italy in '44 Death of O.S.S. Major," *New York Times*, 29 March 1952, 1.

20. 350 U.S. 21; Fred P. Graham, "Army Lawyers Seek Way to Bring Ex-G.I.'s to Trial," *New York Times*, 26 November 1969, 10.

21. Department of the Army, Public Information Division, News Branch, "Query—Green Beret," April 1971 (National Archives Records Group 319).

22. Michael J. Apol, "Getting Away with Murder: The Forty Year Jurisdictional Gap over DoD Civilians Stationed Overseas and the Military Extraterritorial Jurisdiction Act of 2000," master's thesis, George Washington University, 2001.

23. Letter to the author from Rodney P. Frelinghuysen, 5 February 2008.

24. Letter to the author from HQ AFOSI/XILI, 20 May 2005.

25. Charles J. Levy, *Spoils of War* (Boston: Houghton Mifflin, 1974), 145–47.

26. Peter Lovenheim, "Police on Trial," *Syracuse Herald-American*, 29 October 1978, 4. Ventura's male victim, William A. Deyo, Jr., was an honorably discharged veteran who had served in Vietnam with the 101st Airborne Division [William A. Deyo, Jr., military personnel record (National Personnel Records Center)].

27. Letter to the author from Charles Ventura, 23 April 2008.

28. Letters to the author from Charles Ventura, 5 and 18 May 2008.

29. Anthony B. Herbert with James T. Wooten, *Soldier* (New York: Holt, Rinehart, and Winston, 1973), 153.

30. 18th Military Police Brigade, Assistant Chief of Staff for Operations (S-3), Daily Journal, January 1968–December 1969 (National Archives Records Group 472).

31. 18th Military Police Brigade, Assistant Chief of Staff for Operations (S-3), Daily Journal, December 1968, Serious Incident Report 232, 24 December 1970 (National Archives Records Group 472).

32. 18th Military Police Brigade, Assistant Chief of Staff for Operations (S-3), Daily Journal, November 1968, Serious Incident Report 10–206, 19 November 1970 (National Archives Records Group 472).

33. Letter to the author from Brigadier General John W. Nicholson, USA (Ret.), 13 May 1999.

34. Records of the Vietnam War Crimes Working Group, Records Pertaining to the LTC Herbert Controversy, MACV, Office of the Inspector General, "Report of Inquiry Concerning Allegations by LTC Anthony B. Herbert, formerly of the 173d Airborne Brigade" (National Archives Records Group 319).

35. 18th Military Police Brigade, Assistant Chief of Staff for Operations (S-3), Daily Journal, January 1969, Serious Incident Report 110, 14 January 1969 (National Archives Records Group 472). For similar cases involving accidental Claymore detonations, see Commanding Officer, Combined Action Company 2–4, Second Combined Action Group, to Commanding Officer, Second Combined Action Group, "Investigation to Inquire into the Circumstances Connected with the Detonation of a Friendly Explosive Device from Undetermined Cause, Which Resulted in the Death of Private First Class Robert J. Twist, 2390745/0311, USMC, Which Occurred Outside the Combined

Action Platoon 2–4-3 Compound on 26 August 1968," 9 October 1968 (Department of the Navy, Office of the Judge Advocate General), and 18th Military Police Brigade, Assistant Chief of Staff for Operations (S-3), Daily Journal, January 1971, Serious Incident Report 1–178, 14 January 1971 (National Archives Records Group 472).

36. Joan Morrison and Robert K. Morrison, *From Camelot to Kent State: The Sixties Experience in the Words of Those Who Lived It* (New York: Times Books, 1987), 79.

37. Clarence J. Fitch military personnel record (National Personnel Records Center).

38. Third Battalion, First Marines Command Chronologies, July 1968–January 1969 (Marine Corps Historical Center).

39. Author's interview with Ernest H. Walrath, 9 May 1998.

40. William M. Tucker military personnel record (National Personnel Records Center).

41. L Company, 3d Battalion, 1st Marines, Unit Diaries, 1968–1969 (National Archives Records Group 127).

42. Willa Seidenberg and William Short, *A Matter of Conscience: GI Resistance during the Vietnam War* (Andover: Addison Gallery of American Art, 1992), 30.

43. David G. Blalock military personnel record (National Personnel Records Center).

44. HHC, 210th Aviation Battalion (Combat), "Annual Historical Summary of the Headquarters and Headquarters Company, 210th Combat Aviation Battalion, 12th Combat Aviation Group, 1st Aviation Brigade," 1968–1970 (U.S. National Archives Records Group 472). I also checked battalion-level histories prepared by the 210th, and these documents confirmed the company-level reports.

45. John Pilger, *Heroes* (London: Jonathan Cape, 1986), 198.

46. Charley Trujillo, ed., *Soldados: Chicanos in Viet Nam* (San Jose: Chusma House Publications, 1990), 35.

47. Mike M. Lemus military personnel record (National Personnel Records Center).

48. CID Report of Investigation 70-CID648–49830 (U.S. Army Crime Records Center); telephone interview with Jim Umenhofer.

49. Author's interview with Louis W. Banks, January 1997.

50. Harry Maurer, *Strange Ground: Americans in Vietnam 1945–1975 An Oral History* (New York: Henry Holt, 1989), 243–44.

CONCLUSION

1. Thomas C. Bond, "The Why of Fragging," *American Journal of Psychiatry* 131 (11 November 1976), 1330.

2. Eugene Linden, "Fragging and Other Withdrawal Symptoms," *Saturday Review*, 8 January 1972, 13.

3. In his memoir *It Doesn't Take a Hero*, General H. Norman Schwarzkopf provided an account of the tragedy that provided the basis for *Friendly Fire*. In it, he called the army casualty reporting system "clumsy and evasive." This assessment holds true for many fragging deaths as well. H. Norman Schwarzkopf, *It Doesn't Take a Hero* (New York: Bantam Books, 1992), 183.

4. "Grunts, Fraggings Yield a New Roget's," *Los Angeles Times*, 29 March 1978, 8.

5. Alexander Alexiev, *Inside the Soviet Army in Afghanistan* (Santa Monica: Rand Corporation, 1988), 37–38; Artyom Borovik, *The Hidden War: A Russian Journalist's Account of the Soviet War in Afghanistan* (New York: Atlantic Monthly Press, 1990), 121–22; Kevin Klose, "Defectors Say Morale is Low in Afghan War," *Washington Post*, 2 August 1984, A28; U.S. Senate, Committee on Governmental Affairs, *Federal Government's Handling of Soviet and Communist Bloc Defectors: Hearings before the Permanent Subcommittee on Investigations* 100th Cong., 1st sess. 8, 9, 21 October 1987, 142.

6. Gary D. Solis, *Marines and Military Law in Vietnam: Trial By Fire* (Washington D.C.: History and Museums Division, Headquarters, U.S. Marine Corps, 1989), 110–11.

7. First Lieutenant V. II. Faries, USMC, to Commanding Officer, Maintenance Battalion, 3d Force Service Regiment, "Investigation to Inquire into the Circumstances Connected with the Death of Lance Corporal B.G. Barnhill, 2240533, USMC, and Injuries to Lance Corporal D.J. Epping, 2240105, USMC, as a Result of an Explosion Which Occurred at Barracks 2339, Camp Hansen, Okinawa, on or about 0845, 25 December 1967," 9 February 1968 (Department of the Navy, Office of the Judge Advocate General).

8. U.S. Congress, *Congressional Record*, 92nd Cong., 1st sess. Part 9: 10872.

Works Consulted

PRIMARY SOURCES

I. U.S. National Archives, Washington D.C.

Records Group 153: Records of the Office of the Judge Advocate General (Army)
Courts-Martial:
United States v. Sinclair (29816)
United States v. Taylor (50836)

II. U.S. National Archives II, College Park, Maryland

Records Group 24: Records of the Bureau of Naval Personnel
Muster Rolls:
USS Oriskany (CVA-34)
Records Group 125: Office of the Judge Advocate General (Navy)
Administrative Branch, Law and Legal Records, 1967–1968, Box 5
Administrative Branch, Law & Legal Records, 1969–1970, Boxes 1–19
Military Justice Division, Law and Legal Records, Box 3
Records Group 127: Records of the United States Marine Corps
Unit Diaries (various)
Marines and Military Law in Vietnam backup files, boxes 1–4
Records Group 200: National Archives Gift Collection
Papers of John J. Pershing, Entry NM1023, Box 1: List of Officers, Soldiers, and Others Convicted by General Court-martial in the American Expeditionary Forces (AEF), June 8, 1917–August 20, 1919
Records Group 319: Records of the Army Staff
Internal Medicine
Drug Abuse, Boxes 1–7
Investigative Records Repository (IRR), Impersonal Records
Communist Infiltration of the U.S. Armed Forces, 1920–1950, 3 vols.
Media Relations, 1971, various
Records of the Vietnam War Crimes Working Group

Records Pertaining to the LTC Herbert Controversy, MACV, Office of the Inspector General, "Report of Inquiry Concerning Allegations by LTC Anthony B. Herbert, formerly of the 173d Airborne Brigade"

Westmoreland Papers at CMH, various

Records Group 472: U.S. Army in Southeast Asia, 1964–1975

Military Assistance Command Vietnam (MACV)

MACV Command Histories, 1965–1971

Inspector General

Investigations Division

Miscellaneous Reports of Investigation, various

Provost Marshal, Security and Investigation Division

General Records, various

Staff Judge Advocate, International Law & Military Justice Division

General & Special Courts-Martial

United States v. Creek (CM 426724)

United States v. Crook (SPCM 8416)

United States v. Garcia (CM 426969)

United States v. Goings (CM 426050)

United States v. Hibbard (CM 428455)

United States v. Jones (CM 424051)

United States v. Ridgway (CM 423533)

United States v. Spears (CM 425344)

United States v. Sutton (CM 423094)

United States v. Sydnor (CM 428729)

United States v. Wheat (CM 425700)

United States v. Williams (CM 428247)

United States Army, Vietnam

Deputy Chief of Staff for Personnel and Administration

Human Relations Branch, various

Military Personnel Policy Division, various

Plans & Programs Division, various

Special Actions Division, various

Information Office

News Media and Release Files

Inspector General, Investigation and Complaint Division

Records of Investigation

"Report of Investigation Concerning Alleged Fragging Incidents in the 1st Battalion, 7th Cavalry Rear Area," 28 February 1970

"Report of Investigation, Shooting Incident, 54th Ordnance Company (Ammunition)," undated

Provost Marshal

    Administrative Office, Physical Security Branch

        CID Serious Incident Reports, 1968

        CID Blue Bell Reports, 1970

        CID Serious Incident Reports, 1972–1973

        CID Final Reports of Investigation, 1973

    Plans & Operations Division

Staff Judge Advocate, Military Justice Division

    Appellate Courts-Martial:

        United States v. Aubert (CM 427892)

        United States v. Benoit (CM 422738)

        United States v. Blaylock (CM 425319)

        United States v. Bost (CM 427767)

        United States v. Boyd (CM 424834)

        United States v. Buck (SPCM 423893)

        United States v. Bumgarner (CM 427113)

        United States v. Chaky (CM 426039)

        United States v. Crampton (CM 426570)

        United States v. Dingle (SPCM 8416)

        United States v. Dunn (CM 427880)

        United States v. Edmeade (CM 427486)

        United States v. Elliot (CM 423470)

        United States v. Ercolin (CM 426967)

        United States v. Ervin (CM 426423)

        United States v. Fay (CM 427224)

        United States v. Finch (CM 422486)

        United States v. Fitzgerald (CM 426222)

        United States v. Harris (CM SPCM 6674)

        United States v. Hawkins (CM 423687)

        United States v. Held (SPCM 6183)

        United States v. Kaufman (CM 427301)

        United States v. Lilly (CM 428548)

        United States v. Locklin (CM 424813)

United States v. Mays (SPCM 7313)
United States v. McCracken (CM 423370)
United States v. Montoya (SPCM 7156)
United States v. Morris (CM 425565)
United States v. Mycko (CM 428325)
United States v. Peebles (CM 423670)
United States v. Peterson (CM 425057)
United States v. Pickrum (CM 424228)
United States v. Pittman (CM 422645)
United States v. Prince (CM 427290)
United States v. Rakestraw (SPCM 7964)
United States v. Randolph (SPCM 6257)
United States v. Robinson (CM 428205)
United States v. Rosas (CM 426736)
United States v. Rosine (SPCM 7887)
United States v. Schott (CM 427113)
United States v. Simpson (CM 425769)
United States v. Spears (CM 425344)
United States v. Strate (CM 427295)
United States v. Thompson (CM 427004)
United States v. Velarde (CM 427893)
United States v. Wait (CM 428359)
United States v. Williams (SPCM 428247)
United States v. Wynn (CM 424277)

I Field Force, Vietnam
   Inspector General
      Reports of Investigation, 1968–1971
1st Infantry Division
   Provost Marshal, Military Police Desk Blotters, 1967–1970
23d Infantry Division (Americal)
   Provost Marshal, Military Police Desk Blotters, 1971
25th Infantry Division
   Provost Marshal, Military Police Desk Blotters, 1966–67,
      1969
101st Airborne Division (Airmobile)
   General Orders, 1969
   Provost Marshal, Military Police Desk Blotters, 1966–67,
      1969–70

18th Military Police Brigade
>> Assistant Chief of Staff for Operations, Daily Journals, 1967–1972
>> Installation Stockade, Individual Correction Files, various
196th Light Infantry Brigade
>> Military Police Investigation Reports, 1971
Records Group 550: U.S. Army, Pacific
>> Military Historian's Office, Command Reporting Files, various

III. U.S. Army Crime Records Center, Fort Belvoir, VA

CID Reports of Investigation, various

USACIDC study, "Crimes Involving Grenade Incidents in Vietnam" (31 December 1970)

USARV Provost Marshal's Office study, "Fragging Incidents, 1969–1970" (1971)

IV. U.S. Army Judiciary, Arlington, Virginia

Courts-Martial:
> *United States v. Baldwin* (CM 415536)
> *United States v. Beard* (CM 424167)
> *United States v. Bell* (CM 422276)
> *United States v. Breckenridge* (CM 427003)
> *United States v. Brown* (CM 425575)
> *United States v. Clark* (CM 426029)
> *United States v. Cornett* (CM 429339)
> *United States v. Dukes* (CM 429234)
> *United States v. Franks* (CM 421876)
> *United States v. Gallagher* (CM 426807)
> *United States v. Hanley* (CM 424091)
> *United States v. Haracivet* (CM 425305)
> *United States v. Hernandez* (CM 423721)
> *United States v. Hober* (SPCM 8177)
> *United States v. Hugg* (CM 422286)
> *United States v. Johnson* (CM 429456)
> *United States v. Jordan* (CM 428674)
> *United States v. Newsome* (CM 421878)
> *United States v. Oaks* (CM 427752)
> *United States v. Perry* (CM 424936)
> *United States v. Phronebarger* (CM 422003)
> *United States v. Purifoy* (CM 428358)

United States v. Robinson (CM 425317)
United States v. San Nicolas (CM 420950)
United States v. Shirley (CM 422317)
United States v. Smith (CM 429555)
United States v. Troche-Perez (CM 429354)
United States v. Walentiny (CM 428347)
United States v. Woodmancy (CM 425594)

V. Combined Arms Research Library, U.S. Army Command and General Staff College, Fort Leavenworth, Kansas

United States Disciplinary Barracks Collection, Box 2, Series B: Topical Files

"Inmate Unrest"

"Fraggers" (1972 Study)

VI. U.S. Army Center of Military History, Washington D.C.

MACV Command History, 1970

Vietnam Interview Tapes (VNITs), various

"American Soldier" files, various

VII. U.S. Army Military History Institute, Carlisle, Pennsylvania

George L. Mabry, Jr., Papers, "Analysis of Fraggings," 1972

VIII. University of Montana, Maureen and Mike Mansfield Library, Missoula, Montana

Mansfield Papers, Collection 65, Series VII, Box 202, Folder 17

IX. U.S. Marine Corps History Division, Quantico, Virginia

Marine Corps casualty reports, various

Oral History Interviews, various

Personal Papers Section, various

X. Navy & Marine Corps Appellate Review Activity, Washington D.C.

Naval Courts-Martial:
    United States v. Addison (NCM 70–2433)
    United States v. Barrios (NCM 70–1408)
    United States v. Bretzke (NCM 68–0341)
    United States v. Carroll (NCM 68–2038)
    United States v. Chambers (NCM 69–3501)
    United States v. Culver (NCM 70–1681)
    United States v. Dolan (NCM 67–1090)
    United States v. Eason (NCM 69–2612)
    United States v. Evans (NCM 71–0624)

United States v. Fowler (NCM 70–3599)

United States v. Greenwood (NCM 70–3843)

United States v. Harris (NCM 70–2331)

United States v. Hendrix (NCM 71–2473)

United States v. Hurley (NCM 67–2575)

United States v. Kimbrough (NCM 71–0183)

United States v. Linkous (NCM 71–1044)

United States v. Martinson (NCM 70–2988)

United States v. McDonald (NCM 70–2256)

United States v. McNeil (NCM 70–1665)

United States v. Napier (NCM 70–1453)

United States v. Paro (NCM 70–1774)

United States v. Pierre (NCM 68–2440)

United States v. Rutledge (NCM 71–1037)

United States v. Smith (NCM 70–0500)

United States v. Smith (NCM 70–1098)

United States v. Smith (NCM 70–3511)

United States v. Smith (NCM 71–1182)

United States v. Thomas (NCM 69–4053)

United States v. Vaiksnis (NCM 70–3454)

United States v. Vasquez (NCM 70–1389)

United States v. Wall (NCM 70–0494)

United States v. Wolfe (NCM 68–1872)

United States v. Woodard (NCM 70–2034)

XI. Department of the Navy, Office of the Judge Advocate General, Washington D.C.

Reports of Investigation:

First Lieutenant Wayne H. Brandon, USMCR, to Commanding Officer, 3d Battalion, 5th Marines, "Investigation Inquiring into the Circumstances Surrounding the Death of First Sergeant William R. Hunt, 652761, USMC," 19 April 1968.

Captain George P. Adams, USMC, to Commanding Officer, 2d Battalion, 11th Marines, 1st Marine Division (FMF), "Investigation to Inquire into the Circumstances Surrounding the Death of First Sergeant Warren R. Furse, 1187297, USMC, and Injury to Gunnery Sergeant Haywood W. Ballance, 1370320, USMC on or about 2400, 27 February 1969," 11 March 1969.

First Lieutenant Luis F. Urroz, USMCR, to Commanding Officer,

9th Engineer Battalion, FMF, "Investigation into the Circumstances Surrounding the Shooting and Subsequent Death of Private First Class James L. Wilks, USMC, Which Occurred on 22 May 1969 at Company C, 9th Engineer Battalion, FMF," 30 May 1969.

Captain George A. Kiesel, USMC to Commanding Officer, 3d Combined Action Group, III Marine Amphibious Force, "Investigation: Death of PFC Thomas J. Mead, 2494145, USMC and the Wounding of Cpl Gregory M. Witt, 2355440, USMC, on 3 June 1969," 8 June 1969.

First Lieutenant John F. Higgins, USMCR, to Commanding Officer, 1st Battalion, 4th Marines, "An Investigation into the Facts and Circumstances Surrounding the Explosion of an M-26 Fragmentation Grenade Resulting in the Death of PFC Yokoi and the Injuries Sustained by LCpl Scruggs, PFC Duncan, Cpl Bowes, PFC Martin, PFC Roberts, LCpl Sykiw, and PFC Staggs which Occurred at Cua Viet R&R Center, Quang Tri Province, RVN on or about 11 July 1969," 20 August 1969.

First Lieutenant Mark F. Tierney, USMCR, to Commanding Officer, 3d Battalion, 7th Marines, "Investigation to Inquire into the Circumstances Surrounding the Alleged Detonation of Two Fragmentation Grenades in the 3/7 Communications Message Center Resulting in the Death of One Marine and Injury to Two Others on or About 0700H, 18 April 1970," 19 May 1970.

First Lieutenant Tibor R. Saddler, USMC, to Commanding Officer, 1st Combined Action Group, "Investigation to Inquire into the Circumstances Surrounding the Death of Lance Corporal Gilberto Garcia, 2585264/0341, U.S. Marine Corps, which Occurred Between 1400 Hours and 1500 Hours, 1 September 1970, at Quang Nam Province, Republic of Vietnam," 6 September 1970.

First Lieutenant V. H. Faries, USMC, to Commanding Officer, Maintenance Battalion, 3d Force Service Regiment, "Investigation to Inquire into the Circumstances Connected with the Death of Lance Corporal B.G. Barnhill, 2240533, USMC, and the Injuries to Lance Corporal D.J. Epping, 2240105, USMC, as a Result of an Explosion Which Occurred at Barracks 2339, Camp Hansen, Okinawa, on or about 0845, 25 December 1967," 9 February 1968.

XII. Naval Historical Center, Washington Navy Yard
Aircraft accident reports, various

XIII. Air Force Historical Research Agency, Maxwell AFB, Alabama
Historical Data Record, 366 Munitions Maintenance Squadron, 1 October–31 December 1971

XIV. U.S. Department of Justice
Federal Bureau of Investigation
Springfield, Illinois, Field Office
SI 70A-1899 (Murder of Reginald F. Smith, U.S. Penitentiary, Marion, Illinois)
Las Vegas, Nevada, Field Office
File 100–1161: Charles Henry Henderson
Federal Bureau of Prisons
North Central Regional Office, Kansas City, Kansas
Federal Inmate Record: Reginald F. Smith, Reg. No. 28530–138

XV. National Personnel Records Center, St. Louis, Missouri
Military personnel records, various
Morning reports, various organizations

XVI. Washington National Records Center, Suitland, Maryland
Melvin R. Laird Papers

XVII. Philadelphia, Pennsylvania, Police Department
Homicide Record, Case No. H78–369 (Murder of Richard A. McLeod)

XVIII. County Court, Nassau County, New York
The People of the State of New York v. Robert Bell, a.k.a. Robert Woodhull, Indictment Nos. 45387–76 and 45449–76

XIX. Maricopa County Superior Court, Maricopa County, Arizona
State of Arizona v. Robert Burton Rutledge, Cause No. CR8707743

XX. Swarthmore College Peace Collection, Swarthmore, Pennsylvania
Collection DD-223: Records of Prison Visitation and Support, Box 38 (Gary Hendrix)

XXI. National Archives of Australia, Melbourne
Department of Defense, Personal Documents Dossiers, Series B2458
61905 P. D. Allen
38627 R. T. Convery

XXII. National Archives of Australia, Canberra
Series A471/6, 94258, Folder 4: Trial of 1731829 Gunner Leonard Edward NEWMAN —Re 215349 Lieutenant Robert Graham BIRSE

XXIII. Australian War Memorial, Canberra

Official Records Collection

AWM 98, 25: Investigation Report into the Death of Lieutenant R T Convery—B Coy 9 RAR

AWM 98, R723/1/129: Reports, General, Explosion in Living Quarters, SSgt Land.

AWM 98, R723/271/9: Reports, Mil. Pers. 1971, Investigation into Attempted Bombing 1 Fd Sqn 1 Feb 71

AWM 98, R723/271/42: Unusual Incident—Grenade Explosion—1 May 71

AWM 103, 631: Transcript of Court-Martial Proceedings Against 61905 Pte P. D. Allen

AWM 103, R271/1/86/1: Discipline—General—Illegal Use of Drugs

AWM 103, R478/1/77: Investigations—General. Unlawful Explosion, B Squadron, 3 Cavalry Regiment, 23 August 1969

AWM 103, R478/1/78: Investigations, General. Unlawful Discharge—M26 Grenade, A Coy 6 RAR 26 August 69

AWM 103, R478/1/231: Investigation, General. Unlawful Explosion—Spr F. Denly [sic]—1 Fd Sqn

AWM 103, R478/1/281: Investigation, General. Unlawful Use of Explosives 8 RAR

AWM 103, R478/1/355: Investigations, General. Grenade Incident—Brooks—2 April 71

XXIV. Correspondence and Interviews

U.S. Army

Allen, Herman. 47th Infantry Platoon (Scout Dog), 101st Airborne Division (Airmobile)

Berry, John Stevens. Judge Advocate, IIFFV

Braden, Joseph. B Company, 25th S&T Battalion, 25th Infantry Division

Canaday, Stephen S. HHC, 1/7th Cavalry, 1st Cavalry Division (Airmobile)

Casimano, Charles. 47th Infantry Platoon (Scout Dog), 101st Airborne Division (Airmobile)

Coucoules, Robert. Det C, 8th Military Police Group (CI)

DeGroot, John D. 23d Military Police Battalion, 23d Infantry Division (American)

Drew, Frederick A. B Company, 4/23d Infantry, 25th Infantry Division

Duren, Francis S. HHC, 1/6th Infantry, 23d Infantry Division (Americal)

Epperson, Allen. C Company, 326th Medical Battalion, 101st Airborne Division (Airmobile)

Fay, John. HHC, 173d Airborne Brigade (Separate)

Frobenius, Courtney L. B Company, 3/60th Infantry, 9th Infantry Division

Gollie, Joseph S. HHC, 63d Signal Battalion

Hines, Les. A Co., 23d Aviation Battalion, 23d Infantry Division (Americal)

Honeycutt, Weldon F. 3/187th Parachute Infantry, 101st Airborne Division (Airmobile)

Janousek, Dick. 178th Aviation Company, 1st Aviation Brigade

Kralich, Joseph M. C Company, 326th Medical Battalion, 101st Airborne Division (Airmobile)

Mataxis, Theodore C. HHC, 23d Infantry Division (Americal)

McCumber, Kenneth, Jr. C Company, 2/22nd Infantry, 25th Infantry Division

Nicholson, John W. 2/503d Infantry, 173d Airborne Brigade (Separate)

Noller, Gary L. E Company, 1/46th Infantry, 23d Infantry Division (Americal)

Perrin, Everitt I., Jr. Provost Marshal, 23d Infantry Division (Americal)

Pike, Verner N. Provost Marshal, 23d Infantry Division (Americal)

Rooney, Neal E. L Company (Ranger), 75th Infantry, 101st Airborne Division (Airmobile)

Sperry, John. B Company, 3/60th Infantry, 9th Infantry Division

Steinhebel, Frank J. 47th Infantry Platoon (Scout Dog), 101st Airborne Division (Airmobile)

Thompson, Craig E. B Company, 2/503d Infantry, 173d Airborne Brigade (Separate)

Umenhofer, Jim. 2/501st Infantry, 101st Airborne Division (Airmobile)

Vitucci, Sam S. HHC, 2/8th Cavalry, 1st Cavalry Division (Airmobile)

Westmoreland, William C. COMUSAMACV, later Chief of Staff, U.S. Army

U.S. Marine Corps

Abbs, Jimmie F. D Battery, 11th Marines, 1st Marine Division

Barzousky, Benjamin A. C Company, 9th Engineer Battalion, 1st Marine Division

Batty, Paul M. C Company, 9th Engineer Battalion, 1st Marine Division

Billups, Bailey E. K Company, 9th Marines, 3d Marine Division

Bores, Charles E. K Company, 9th Marines, 3d Marine Division

Caldarella, Rocco J. C Company, 9th Engineer Battalion, 1st Marine Division

Cullen, Richard F. K Company, 9th Marines, 3d Marine Division

Cummings, Patrick T. 3d 8-inch Howitzer Battery, 1st Marine Division

Dame, Christian W. C Company, 9th Engineer Battalion, 1st Marine Division

Davis, Gordon M. K Company, 9th Marines, 3d Marine Division

Fairman, Stephen G. K Company, 9th Marines, 3d Marine Division

Gabel, John E. K Company, 9th Marines, 3d Marine Division

Grantham, Herman L. C Company, 9th Engineer Battalion, 1st Marine Division

Grindle, Raymond L. C Company, 9th Engineer Battalion, 1st Marine Division

Harrington, Jack L. K Company, 9th Marines, 3d Marine Division

Harroun, Terry F. C Company, 9th Engineer Battalion, 1st Marine Division

Heltzel, Wilson S. C Company, 9th Engineer Battalion, 1st Marine Division

Hynes, Thomas. L Company, 5th Marines, 1st Marine Division

Jackson, Kenneth W. K Company, 9th Marines, 3d Marine Division

Johnson, Fred C. Supply Battalion, Force Logistic Command

Kaup, Milton O. C Company, 9th Engineer Battalion, 1st Marine Division

Kelley, Edward F. Judge Advocate, 1st Marine Division

Knez, David J. C Company, 9th Engineer Battalion, 1st Marine Division

Krulak, Victor H. Commanding General, Fleet Marine Force, Pacific

Leffelman, Joseph L. K Company, 9th Marines, 3d Marine Division

Mackow, Adam W. K Company, 9th Marines, 3d Marine Division

Magner, Richard M. D Battery, 11th Marines, 1st Marine Division

Masters, Harry D. C Company, 9th Engineer Battalion, 1st Marine Division

McGinty, Brian. D Battery, 11th Marines, 1st Marine Division

Neill, Harry T. C Company, 9th Engineer Battalion, 1st Marine Division

Newton, Harvey. K Company, 5th Marines, 1st Marine Division

Nollenberger, James W. C Company, 9th Engineer Battalion, 1st Marine Division

Pacyniak, John M. C Company, 9th Engineer Battalion, 1st Marine Division

Provine, Jack. Judge Advocate, Force Logistic Command

Pruett, Robert L. C Company, 9th Engineer Battalion, 1st Marine Division

Railey, Robert H. C Company, 9th Engineer Battalion, 1st Marine Division

Rodermund, John A. C Company, 9th Engineer Battalion, 1st Marine Division

Royer, Charles H. C Company, 9th Engineer Battalion, 1st Marine Division

Schenkel, Ralph W. C Company, 9th Engineer Battalion, 1st Marine Division

Smith, Stanley L. Judge Advocate, 3d Marine Division

Speed, Hugh B. C Company, 9th Engineer Battalion, 1st Marine Division

Tigue, Thomas M. K Company, 9th Marines, 3d Marine Division

Tyynismaa, Victor J. K Company, 9th Marines, 3d Marine Division

Urroz, Luis F. C Company, 9th Engineer Battalion, 1st Marine Division

Vick, Lyle W. C Company, 9th Engineer Battalion, 1st Marine Division

Wilson, Dennis C. K Company, 9th Marines, 3d Marine Division

Civilians:

Addlestone, David F. Lawyers' Military Defense Committee

Remcho, Joseph. Lawyers' Military Defense Committee

ARTICLES AND BOOKS

Alexiev, Alexander. *Inside the Soviet Army in Afghanistan*. Santa Monica: Rand Corporation, 1988.

Anderson, Charles R. *The Grunts*. San Rafael: Presidio Press, 1976. This book is not only one of the best Vietnam memoirs written to date but it also contains trenchant analyses regarding the Vietnam generation and the war it fought in Southeast Asia.

Andreski, Stanislav. *Military Organization and Society*. Berkeley: University of California Press, 1968. An analysis of what the author calls the "military participation ratio," cohesion, subordination, and their effects on civil society.

Apol, Capt. Michael J. "Getting Away with Murder: The Forty Year Jurisdictional Gap over DoD Civilians Stationed Overseas and the Military Extraterritorial Jurisdiction Act of 2000," master's thesis, George Washington University, 2001.

Bond, Thomas C. "The Why of Fragging," *American Journal of Psychiatry*, November 1976, 1328–31. A fascinating survey of over twenty convicted fraggers, conducted by the author while he was chief of psychiatry at the Leavenworth stockade.

Borovik, Artyom. *The Hidden War: A Russian Journalist's Account of the Soviet War in Afghanistan*. New York: Atlantic Monthly Press, 1990.

Bourne, Peter G. *Men, Stress, and Vietnam*. Boston: Little, Brown, 1970. Bourne, a British-born psychiatrist, spent a year in Vietnam studying combat stress among soldiers and compiling the material for this volume. He visited several units in the field, including an extended stay at a remote Special Forces camp. His book has not received the attention it deserves in the Vietnam War literature.

Boyle, Richard. *The Flower of the Dragon: The Breakdown of the U.S. Army in Vietnam*. San Francisco: Ramparts Press, 1972. A radical journalist's monochromatic view of the war.

Brotz, Howard, and Everett Wilson. "Characteristics of Military Society," *American Journal of Sociology*, March 1946, 371–75.

Bryant, Clifton D. *Khaki-Collar Crime: Deviant Behavior in the Military Context*. New York: Free Press, 1979.

Buford, Kate. *Burt Lancaster: An American Life*. Cambridge: Da Capo Press, 2001.

Carland, John M. *Combat Operations: Stemming the Tide*, May 1965 to October 1966. Washington D.C.: Center of Military History, 2000.

Coffman, Edward M. *The Old Army: A Portrait of the American Army in Peace-time, 1794–1898.* New York: Oxford University Press, 1986. A wonderful history of the army's first century.

Cohen, Eliot A. *Citizens and Soldiers: The Dilemmas of Military Service.* Ithaca: Cornell University Press, 1985.

Conroy, Michael R. *Don't Tell America!* Red Bluff, Calif.: Eagle Publishing, 1992. A day-by-day account of Operation Dewey Canyon, told by a veteran of the 9th Marines.

Cortright, David. *Soldiers in Revolt: The American Military Today.* New York: Anchor Press/Doubleday, 1975. This work boasts an impressive collection of data on the rise of the GI movement but its seeming insistence that every act of Vietnam era indiscipline amounted to political resistance is overstated.

Cosmas, Graham A., and Terrence P. Murray. *U.S. Marines in Vietnam: Vietnamization and Redeployment 1970–71.* Washington D.C.: History and Museums Division, Headquarters, U.S. Marine Corps, 1986. This fifth volume of the official U.S. Marines in Vietnam series is both interesting and informative. The marines are remarkably candid when discussing the morale problems that plagued them in Vietnam, though they never seem to tire of slinging mud at the army in this (or any other) respect.

Davis, Raymond C. *The Story of Ray Davis, General of Marines.* Fuquay Varina, N.C.: Research Triangle Publishing, 1995. The late general's memoir of his distinguished service in three wars.

Douglass, John Jay. "The Judicialization of Military Courts," *Hastings Law Journal* 22 (1971), 213–35. A well-informed appraisal of the Military Justice Act of 1968, authored by the commandant of the U.S. Army Judge Advocate General's School.

Edwards, P. G. *A Nation at War: Australian Politics, Society and Diplomacy during the Vietnam War 1965–1975.* Sydney: Allen & Unwin, 1997. This award-winning volume examines the political aspects of Australia's war in Vietnam. Sue Langford's appendix provides exhaustive treatment of the national service scheme.

Finnegan, John Patrick. *Military Intelligence.* Washington D.C.: Center of Military History, 1998.

Foot, M. R. D. *Men in Uniform: Military Manpower in Modern Industrial Societies.* New York: Frederick A. Praeger, 1961.

Generous, William T., Jr. *Swords and Scales: The Development of the Uniform Code of Military Justice.* Port Washington: Kennikat Press, 1973. A

first-rate analysis of the origins and early years of the UCMJ in general
and the Court of Military Appeals in particular.

George, Alexander L., and Andrew Bennett. *Case Studies and Theory Development in the Social Sciences*. Cambridge: MIT Press, 2005.

Gibson, James William. *The Perfect War: The War We Couldn't Lose and How We Did*. New York: Vintage Books, 1988.

Gillooly, David H., and Thomas C. Bond. "Assaults with Explosive Devices on Superiors: A Synopsis of Reports from Confined Prisoners at the U.S. Disciplinary Barracks," *Military Medicine*, October 1976, 700–702.

Griffith, Roger K., Jr. *The U.S. Army's Transition to the All-Volunteer Force, 1968–1974*. Washington D.C.: Center of Military History, 1997. Definitive treatment of the role of army staff in the creation of the all-volunteer military.

Hall, Robert A. *Combat Battalion: The Eighth Battalion in Vietnam*. Sydney: Allen & Unwin, 2000.

Hammond, William M. *Public Affairs: The Military and the Media, 1962–1968*. Washington D.C.: Center of Military History, 1988. Hammond's excellent two-volume set approaches a controversial subject with something that MACV and the press frequently accused each other of lacking during the war: objectivity.

———. *Public Affairs: The Military and the Media, 1968–1973*. Washington D.C.: Center of Military History, 1996.

Headquarters, Department of the Army. *Field Manual FM 22–100: Military Leadership*. Washington D.C.: Department of the Army, 1965.

Heinl, Robert D., Jr. "The Collapse of the Armed Forces," *Armed Forces Journal*, 7 June 1971. Many antiwar authors have pointed to this article, and its opening statements in particular, as evidence that the stress of Vietnam nearly destroyed the U.S. military. Senior officials disagreed, dismissing what they believed were the author's "sweeping conclusions" on the subject.

Herbert, Anthony B. *Soldier*. New York: Holt, Rinehart, and Winston, 1973. Colonel Herbert's general statements regarding conditions in Vietnam, such as his revelation that drastically under-strength infantry companies operated in the field while thousands of support troops occupied secure rear areas and never engaged the enemy, are accurate and valuable to historians. However, the enormous ax he had to grind with his superiors and several personalities within his unit mars his account. The army subsequently investigated many of his accusations and judged a number of them to be unfounded.

Hoffer, Eric. *The True Believer: Thoughts on the Nature of Mass Movements.* New York: Harper & Brothers, 1951. I used this classic study only as background reading but it is highly recommended.

Hubbard, Douglass H., Jr. *Special Agent, Vietnam: A Naval Intelligence Memoir.* Washington D.C.: Potomac Books, 2006.

Ingraham, Larry H. "'The Nam' and 'The World': Heroin Use by U.S. Army Enlisted Men Serving in Vietnam," *Psychiatry*, May 1974, 114–28.

Janowitz, Morris, ed. *The New Military: Changing Patterns of Organization.* New York: Russell Sage Foundation, 1964.

Janowitz, Morris. *On Social Organization and Social Control.* Edited by James Burk. Chicago: University of Chicago Press, 1991. An excellent collection of essays by the father of military sociology, thoughtfully assembled by one of his former students.

Keniston, Kenneth. *Youth and Dissent: The Rise of a New Opposition.* New York: Harcourt Brace Jovanovich, 1971.

Krepinevich, Andrew F., Jr. *The Army and Vietnam.* Baltimore: Johns Hopkins University Press, 1986. A devastating critique of the army's "big unit" approach to counterinsurgency warfare in Vietnam.

Kroll, Jerome. "Racial Patterns of Military Crimes in Vietnam," *Psychiatry* 39 (February 1976), 51–64.

Lando, Barry. "The Herbert Affair," *Atlantic Monthly*, May 1973, 73–81. A CBS News producer tells the story of his loss of faith in Lieutenant Colonel Herbert.

Lane, Mark. *Conversations with Americans.* New York: Simon and Schuster, 1970. Critics panned this volume of Vietnam oral history upon its publication, showing that many of its interviewees either did not serve in Vietnam or were unreliable. I generally agree.

Lang, Kurt. "American Military Performance in Vietnam: Background and Analysis," *Journal of Political and Military Sociology* 8 (1980), 269–86.

Levy, Charles J. *Spoils of War.* Boston: Houghton Mifflin, 1974. Although the author makes little effort to conceal his antimilitary bias, his analyses are thought-provoking, particularly in regard to the frequency of fragging incidents.

Lewes, James. *Protest and Survive: Underground GI Newspapers During the Vietnam War.* Westport: Praeger, 2003.

Lewy, Guenter. *America in Vietnam.* New York: Oxford University Press, 1978. Professor Lewy is critical of many of the decisions made by U.S.

officials in Vietnam but takes a conservative view when discussing the war's moral issues.

Lifton, Robert Jay. *Home from the War: Vietnam Veterans—Neither Victims nor Executioners*. New York: Simon and Schuster, 1973.

Linden, Eugene. "Fragging and Other Withdrawal Symptoms," *Saturday Review*, January 1972, 12–55. Linden's article was the first to describe the fragging phenomenon at length, and countless postwar authors have relied on his study when discussing the topic.

Lowry, Thomas P. *Don't Shoot that Boy! Abraham Lincoln and Military Justice*. Mason City, Ia.: Savas Publishing Company, 1999.

MacGarrigle, George L. *Combat Operations: Taking the Offensive, October 1966 to October 1967*. Washington D.C.: Center of Military History, 1998.

MacGregor, Morris J., Jr. *Integration of the Armed Forces*. Washington D.C.: U.S. Army Center of Military History, 1981. Excellent.

Maurer, Harry. *Strange Ground: An Oral History of Americans in Vietnam, 1945–1975*. New York: Henry Holt, 1989.

McNeill, Ian. *To Long Tan: The Australian Army and the Vietnam War*. Sydney: Allen & Unwin, 1993.

McNeill, Ian, and Ashley Ekins. *On the Offensive: The Australian Army in the Vietnam War*, January 1967–July 1968. Sydney: Allen & Unwin, 2003.

Morrison, Joan, and Robert K. Morrison. *From Camelot to Kent State: The Sixties Experience in the Words of Those Who Lived It*. New York: Times Books, 1987.

Moskos, Charles C., Jr. *The American Enlisted Man: The Rank and File in Today's Military*. New York: Russell Sage Foundation, 1970. This is an outstanding sociological portrait of the Vietnam-era American soldier by the leading expert on the subject. Anyone interested in studying the sociology of the U.S. military will find this invaluable.

———. *Soldiers and Sociology*. Alexandria: United States Army Research Institute for the Behavioral and Social Sciences, 1988.

Olson, Gregory A. *Mansfield and Vietnam: A Study in Historical Adaptation*. East Lansing: Michigan State University Press, 1995.

Palmer, Bruce, Jr. *The 25-Year War: America's Military Role in Vietnam*. Lexington: University Press of Kentucky, 1984.

Presthus, Robert. *The Organizational Society*. New York: St. Martin's Press, 1978. A classic examination of the personality types found within the modern bureaucracy.

Prugh, George S. *Vietnam Studies, Law at War: Vietnam 1964–1973*. Washington D.C.: Department of the Army, 1975.

Radine, Lawrence B. *Taming the Troops: Social Control in the United States Army*. Westport: Greenwood Press, 1977. The author concedes to being no friend of the military but gives the services a fair shake in his book. Of particular note are his analyses regarding the changes in leadership styles and the role of military psychologists.

Remcho, Joseph. "Military Juries: Constitutional Analysis and the Need for Reform," *Indiana Law Journal* 47, no. 2 (Winter 1972), 197–231. Remcho, an LMDC attorney, critiques the military's court selection process and argues in favor of a random selection system that would include junior enlisted men.

Rivkin, Robert S. *GI Rights and Army Justice: The Draftee's Guide to Military Life and Law*. New York: Grove Press, 1970.

Robins, Lee N. et al. "Narcotic Use in Southeast Asia and Afterward: An Interview Study of 898 Vietnam Returnees," *Archives of General Psychiatry* 32 (August 1975): 955–61. This study, which identified Vietnam drug users and followed their progress after their return to civilian life, is perhaps the finest single contribution to the study of drug use by U.S. troops in Southeast Asia.

Saar, John. "The Outpost is a Shambles," *Life*, 31 March 1972, 28–37. The sad story of the army's Vung Chua Signal Site.

Savage, Paul G., and Richard A. Gabriel. *Crisis in Command: Mismanagement in the Army*. New York: Hill and Wang, 1978. An indictment of the army's officer corps for its decision to replace traditional military leadership techniques with those more closely associated with entrepreneurial-type management. While the authors shed needed light on the problem of careerism among the brass, they overstate their case when applying it to what went wrong in Vietnam.

Saxe, Maurice de. *Reveries on the Art of War*. Mineola, N.Y.: Dover Publications, 2007.

Schwarzkopf, H. Norman. *It Doesn't Take a Hero*. New York: Bantam Books, 1992.

Seidenberg, Willa, and William Short. *A Matter of Conscience: GI Resistance During the Vietnam War*. Andover, Mass.: Addison Gallery of American Art, 1992. Vietnam oral history from antiwar veterans.

Shawcross, William. *Sideshow: Kissinger, Nixon, and the Destruction of Cambodia*. New York: Simon and Schuster, 1979.

Shulimson, Jack, and Charles M. Johnson. *U.S. Marines in Vietnam: The Landing and the Buildup, 1965*. Washington D.C.: History and Museums Division, Headquarters, U.S. Marine Corps, 1978.

Shulimson, Jack, Leonard A. Blaisol, Charles R. Smith, and David A. Dawson. *U.S. Marines in Vietnam: The Defining Year, 1968*. Washington D.C.: History and Museums Division, Headquarters, U.S. Marine Corps, 1997.

Smith, Charles R. *U.S. Marines in Vietnam: High Mobility and Standdown 1969*. Washington D.C.: History and Museums Division, Headquarters, U.S. Marine Corps, 1988.

Solis, Gary D. *Marines and Military Law in Vietnam: Trial By Fire*. Washington D.C.: History and Museums Division, Headquarters, U.S. Marine Corps, 1989.

Stewart, Richard W., ed. *American Military History Vol. II: The United States Army in a Global Era, 1917–2003*. Washington D.C.: Center of Military History, 2005.

Sticht, Thomas G., William B. Armstrong, Daniel T. Hickey, and John S. Caylor. *Cast-Off Youth: Policy and Training Methods from the Military Experience*. New York: Praeger, 1987. This defense of the Project 100,000 manpower program effectively argues its merits but fails to appreciate the deleterious effects it had upon the Vietnam-era military at a time when the services could ill afford them.

Stoufer, Samuel A., et al. *The American Soldier: Adjustment during Army Life*. Princeton: Princeton University Press, 1949. The first volume of the classic set that helped to establish military sociology.

———. *The American Soldier: Combat and Its Aftermath*. Princeton: Princeton University Press, 1949.

Tanay, Emanuel. "The Dear John Syndrome during the Vietnam War," *Diseases of the Nervous System* 37, no. 3 (1976), 165–67.

U.S. Congress. *Congressional Record*. 92nd Cong., 1st sess., 1971, part 9.

U.S. House of Representatives, Committee on Armed Services. *Inquiry into the Disturbances at Marine Corps Base, Camp Lejeune, N.C., on July 20, 1969: Report of the Special Subcommittee to Probe Disturbances on Military Bases*. 91st Cong., 1st sess., December 15, 1969.

U.S. House of Representatives, Committee on Armed Services. *Alleged Drug Abuse in the Armed Services: Hearings by Special Subcommittee on Alleged Drug Abuse in the Armed Services*. 91st Cong., 2nd sess., 1970–1971.

U.S. House of Representatives, Committee on Armed Services. *Inquiry into Alleged Drug Abuse in the Armed Services: Report of a Special Subcommittee of the Committee on Armed Services*. 92nd Cong., 1st sess., 23 April 1971.

U.S. House of Representatives, Committee on Internal Security. *Black Panther Party: Hearings Before the Committee on Internal Security*, 91st Cong., 2nd sess., 1970.

U.S. House of Representatives, Committee on Internal Security. *Investigation of Attempts to Subvert the United States Armed Forces: Hearings before the Committee on Internal Security*. 92nd Cong., 2nd sess., 1971–1972.

U.S. Senate, Committee on Veterans' Affairs. *Eligibility for Veterans' Benefits Pursuant to Discharge Upgrades: Hearing before the Committee on Veterans' Affairs*. 95th Cong., 1st sess., 23 June 1977.

Van Doorn, Jacques. *The Soldier and Social Change*. Beverly Hills: Sage Publications, 1975. A classic of military sociology.

Van Doren, Carl. *Mutiny in January*. New York: Viking Press, 1943.

Westmoreland, General William C. and Major General George S. Prugh. "Judges in Command: The Judicialized Uniform of Military Justice in Combat," *Harvard Journal of Law and Public Policy* 3 (1980).

White, James S. "Race Relations in the Army," *Military Review* 50, no. 7 (July 1970), 3–12.

Willis, William R., Jr. "*Toth v. Quarles*—For Better or for Worse?" *Vanderbilt Law Review* 9 (1956), 534–41.

Wyatt, Walter. *United States Reports, Volume 350: Cases Adjudged by the Supreme Court at October Term, 1955*. Washington D.C.: Government Printing Office, 1956.

Index

The word *insert* refers to images in the photo insert.

About the Author

After several years in the U.S. Army, George Lepre is currently pursuing a graduate degree at the New School for Social Research. His first book, *Himmler's Bosnian Division*, was the recipient of the Sydney Zebel History Award from Rutgers University.